William Charteris Macpherson

The Baronage and the Senate

Or the House of Lords in the Past, the Present, and the Future

William Charteris Macpherson

The Baronage and the Senate
Or the House of Lords in the Past, the Present, and the Future

ISBN/EAN: 9783337154516

Printed in Europe, USA, Canada, Australia, Japan

Cover: Foto ©Suzi / pixelio.de

More available books at **www.hansebooks.com**

THE
BARONAGE AND THE SENATE

OR

THE HOUSE OF LORDS IN THE PAST,
THE PRESENT, AND THE FUTURE.

BY

WILLIAM CHARTERIS MACPHERSON

LONDON:
JOHN MURRAY, ALBEMARLE STREET.
1893.

LONDON:
PRINTED BY WILLIAM CLOWES AND SONS, LIMITED,
STAMFORD STREET AND CHARING CROSS.

PREFACE.

FOR many years past, the House of Lords has been the object of persistent and unmerited attack on the part of a certain section of the Radical press and the advocates of the new democracy, who have shown a singular ignorance of the real status and composition of our hereditary Peerage, and have even ignored the essential distinction that exists between a Baronage and a Senate. Although these attacks have been usually passed over in dignified silence, the time seems to have come when something in the way of a detailed reply and defence is both natural and justifiable. An attempt, therefore, has been made in these pages to trace the growth and constitution of our existing Peerage; to explain the true position and *raison d'être* of a Second Chamber; to review and contravene, as dispassionately as possible, the various charges and accusations which have been from time to time so freely brought both against the Peers as a class, and against the Peerage itself as an institution; and, finally, to offer certain practical suggestions for the reform and expansion of the Upper House, which it is hoped may commend themselves in part, if not in their entirety, to the unprejudiced politician, whether Liberal or Conservative; even though in the latter case he may not altogether acquiesce in the somewhat drastic scheme of reform advocated by Mr. Macpherson, for which, it may be added, he alone is responsible.

All existing materials and authorities have been freely made use of in these pages, and frequent references are made to standard works on the subject, such as those of Professor Freeman and the Bishop of Oxford, as well as to such foreign writers as have made a study of the English Constitution; while in the Appendices (which it is hoped may prove not the least useful portion of the volume to a political student) will be found a *résumé* of the historical aspect and conditions of the Peerage, drawn mainly from the compilations of Sir Harris Nicolas, Sir Bernard Burke, and Mr. James Doyle.

It remains to be said that, as Mr. Macpherson is residing in Australia, it has been necessary to pass the sheets of this volume through the press without his personal revision. Every effort, however, has been made to detect and eliminate any errors; and if any such have been overlooked, it is hoped that the reader will show some indulgence on this score, in consideration of the unavoidable absence of the author.

CONTENTS.

PART I.
INTRODUCTORY.

CHAPTER I.

WHAT THE HOUSE OF LORDS IS NOT.

                                                                             PAGE

Union with Scotland—Scottish Peerage—Scottish Peerage after the Union—Irish Peerages—Bishops of the Church of England —True meaning of a "nobility"—What the House of Lords is not 3

CHAPTER II.

THE ORIGIN AND CONSTITUTION OF THE HOUSE OF LORDS.

Origin of the House of Lords—The various grades of Peerage— Lords Spiritual—Life Peers—Baronies by writ—Scottish Earldoms—Constitutional changes 24

CHAPTER III.

THE COMPOSITION OF THE HOUSE OF LORDS.

"Hereditary legislators"—Composition of the House of Lords— Effects of the Reformation—Reformation in Scotland—The Church after the Restoration—The great Whig families— Composition of the House of Lords 39

PART II.

THE RADICAL CASE AGAINST THE HOUSE OF LORDS.

CHAPTER I.

THE RADICAL CASE AGAINST THE LORDS TEMPORAL AS A NOBILITY.

Creation of Peerages since 1837—Bishops in the House of Lords—Lord Beaconsfield's criticisms—Mr. Millbank in "Coningsby"—Ancient English titles—Ancient Scotch titles—Ancient pedigrees—Noble families—Rise of families—Ancient titles—Charles II. and the Dukes—Legitimate and illegitimate descent—Aristocracy and plutocracy—Birth and wealth—Middle-class Puritanism—Peerage a reward for service—The Peerage and plutocracy—Examination of Dr. Bryce's criticisms—The Lords Temporal as a nobility—Pitt and the Irish Peerage—Napoleonic nobility—The Lords Temporal as a nobility—Extension of family names—The Peerage is representative—Real value of honours 59

CHAPTER II.

THE RADICAL CASE AGAINST THE HOUSE OF LORDS AS A SECOND CHAMBER.

Theories of the equality of men—Elective monarchies—Elective hereditary rulers—Hereditary legislators—Duties of landed proprietors—Charges against the House of Lords—The nobility in foreign States—The unity of France—Loss of the American colonies—Whig policy in eighteenth century—The Peers as statesmen—The Peers and Reform—Fox and the French Revolution—Pitt and the Tory party—England and her Colonies—The Manchester school—The Liberal party and the Colonies—Concessions to the Colonies—Colonial interests—The Peers and religious disabilities—Henry VIII. and the Church—The Puritan tyranny—Nonconformist disabilities—The Nonconformist conscience—Position of Church of England—Disabilities of Roman Catholics—Roman Catholic Emancipation—The Irish Church—Anglo-Irish aristocracy—Home Rule in Ireland—Vindication of the Tory Peers—Duties of a Second Chamber—Defects of representative system—Use of the Royal Veto—Real importance of House of Lords—The Bishops in the House of Lords ... 113

CONTENTS. ix

PART III.
RADICAL REMEDIES.

CHAPTER I.
THE ABOLITION OF THE HOUSE OF LORDS.

PAGE

Sir Charles Dilke's scheme — Theory of British colonization — Colonial view of the House of Lords—Sir Charles Dilke's scheme—Prevalence of bicameral system—Constitutional safeguards—The House of Lords in 1649—Monarchy and a single Chamber—The consequences of abolition—A political forecast —The Peerage and the House of Lords—Difficulties of abolition—Means of abolition 191

CHAPTER II.
A UNITED STATES SENATE.

Elective Second Chambers—Senates in foreign States—Senate of Victoria—Australian Senates—Continental analogies—Italian and Spanish Senates — Italian characteristics — Continental nobility—The French Senate—Continental analogues—German and American Senates—Colonial schemes of representation—Agents-General—United States Senate — The United Kingdom—Union of States—The American Senate—American system of representation—Function of American Senate— Foreign affairs : England and America—Conversion of House of Lords—Insular Home Rule—Present position of House of Lords—Policy of the Liberal party 222

PART IV.
CONSERVATIVE REFORMS.

CHAPTER I.
THE NEED FOR REFORM.

True spirit of Toryism—Progress and reform—Changes in House of Lords—Decay of territorial influence—Expansion of the Peerage—Qualifications for a Peerage—Defects of the House of Lords — Colonial representation — Colonial aristocracy — Colonial Peers—Development of the House of Lords—Reforms in the House of Lords—House of Lords should reform itself 273

CHAPTER II.

LIFE PEERS.

Creation of Life Peers—Qualifications of Life Peers—Colonial Life Peerages—Limitations of the Peerage—Colonial Life Peers—Representation of literature—University representation—Summary of proposed reform—True meaning of a Life Peerage ... 300

CHAPTER III.

HEREDITARY PEERS.

Scottish and English Peerages—The Irish Peerage—Amalgamation of the Peerages—Senatorial system—Defects in the hereditary system—Superfine morality—A new Imperial Peerage—Peers by creation and inheritance—Modes of election to the Peerage—Electoral colleges—Peers in the House of Commons—Summary of suggested reforms 320

CHAPTER IV.

LORDS SPIRITUAL.

Bishops in the House of Lords—Expansion of the episcopate—Additional spiritual Peers—Nonconformist representation—Roman Catholic representation—Position of national Churches—Nonconformist Life Peers—Advantages of such extension ... 344

CHAPTER V.

CONCLUSION.

Summary of previous arguments—The reformed House of Lords—Reasonableness of proposed reforms—Practicable and necessary reforms 362

APPENDIX A.

PEERS OF IRELAND NOT HEREDITARY LEGISLATORS (JAN., 1892) IN THE ORDER OF THEIR ADMISSION INTO THE PEERAGE.

Irish Peerages ... 371

CONTENTS. xi

APPENDIX B.

PEERAGES OF THE UNITED KINGDOM, CREATED BETWEEN THE ACCESSION OF QUEEN VICTORIA AND AUGUST, 1886, EXCLUDING THOSE OF LIFE PEERS, PEERESSES (UNLESS TRANSMITTED TO DESCENDANTS), AND THE PRINCE OF WALES.

Peers created during present reign 375

APPENDIX C.

COMPOSITION OF THE HOUSE OF LORDS (1892).

Composition of House of Lords 380

APPENDIX D.

LIST OF PEERS, WHOSE ANCIENT TITLES HAVE BEEN MERGED IN THOSE OF HIGHER BUT MORE RECENT CREATION.

Ancient titles merged in modern creations 386

APPENDIX E.

LIST OF PEERS HOLDING BARONETCIES OR TITLES OF OLDER CREATION THAN THEIR PRESENT PEERAGES.

Peers holding ancient baronetcies—Ennobled branches of titled families—Ancient descent of modern Peers—Revived or restored Peerages—Revived and restored Peerages 389

APPENDIX F.

LIST OF PEERS WHOSE ANCESTORS HAVE DISTINGUISHED THEMSELVES IN THE PUBLIC SERVICE.

Peers with distinguished ancestors 403

INDEX ... 409

PART I.
INTRODUCTORY.

THE BARONAGE AND THE SENATE.

CHAPTER I.

WHAT THE HOUSE OF LORDS IS NOT.

THE House of Lords is divided into two Estates—Lords Temporal and Lords Spiritual.

All members of the House of Lords are Lords of Parliament; but all Lords of Parliament are not Peers, nor are all Peers Lords of Parliament. Consequently it follows that the House of Lords is not identical with the Peerage, since it excludes some men who are Peers, while it includes some men who are not Peers.

Nor again is the House of Lords identical with the nobility, since it includes some men who are not of necessity noble in blood, and it excludes a great number of men who are noble.

It is necessary to understand what the House of Lords is not, in order to understand clearly what it is.

Of the two Estates into which it is divided, one, the Lords Spiritual, is composed of men who are not Peers; the other, the Lords Temporal, includes no one who is not a Peer, but excludes some who are Peers.

The Lords Temporal may be divided into two classes: Peers who sit in the House of Lords as representing themselves, and Peers who sit in the House of Lords as representing other Peers. To the former class belong all Peers of England, of the United Kingdom of Great Britain, or of the

United Kingdom of Great Britain and Ireland. To the latter class belong sixteen Representative Peers of Scotland, and twenty-eight Representative Peers of Ireland.

The Representative Peers of Scotland are elected for each Parliament by the whole body of Scottish Peers. The Representative Peers of Ireland are elected for life, as vacancies occur in their number, by the whole body of Irish Peers.

All Peers of England, all Peers of the United Kingdom of Great Britain (who may be conveniently distinguished as Peers of Great Britain), and all Peers of the United Kingdom of Great Britain and Ireland (who may be conveniently distinguished as Peers of the United Kingdom), not being disqualified by age, crime, sex, or mental incapacity, nor undischarged bankrupts, are entitled to receive a writ of summons to the House of Lords. No Peer of England, Great Britain, or the United Kingdom, can sit in the House of Commons, nor can any Peer of Scotland sit in that assembly. Nor can any Peer abandon or relinquish his peerage, or otherwise free himself from this legal disability. But a Peer of Ireland, without losing or relinquishing his peerage, can sit in the House of Commons for any constituency not in Ireland, if he has not been chosen to represent his fellow Peers of Ireland in the House of Lords. Lord Palmerston himself, being a Peer of Ireland, sat in this way during the whole of his Parliamentary career in the House of Commons; and in the Parliament, originally elected in July, 1886, three Irish Peers—the Earl of Cavan, Lord Dunsany, and Lord Muncaster —represented constituencies in Great Britain.

A Peer of Scotland, not belonging to any other branch of the Peerage, unless elected to represent the other Peers of Scotland in the House of Lords, is incapable of sitting in Parliament at all. A Peer of England, Great Britain, or the United Kingdom, sits in the House of Lords, and cannot sit in the House of Commons. A Peer of Ireland may sit in either of the Houses, or in neither.

The origin of all these differences and distinctions is to be found in the history of the British Empire.

Before the year 1707 England and Scotland were mutually independent Kingdoms, united only by their allegiance to a common Sovereign, while Ireland, though styled a Kingdom since the time of Henry VIII., was subordinate to, and dependent upon, England. The Personal Union of the Scottish and Anglo-Irish Monarchies in 1603, by the accession of the House of Stuart to the Anglo-Irish throne, had not affected the position of either England or Scotland in international law. A judgment of the English Courts of Law, and an Act of the Parliament of Scotland, soon after the succession of King James to Queen Elizabeth, had extended the rights of citizenship in each country to those born after the Personal Union in the other; and under the later Stuarts a close naval and military alliance had replaced the former hostility between the two Powers. But further than this, the union had not gone. The well-meant efforts of King James the First and Sixth to achieve a fuller union were premature and completely failed, while that amalgamation of the British Isles which existed for a few years under Cromwell had united the three nations only in a common hatred of his name. But now, under the last *de facto* Monarch of the House of Stuart, that Parliamentary Union of Great Britain took place for which the way had been prepared by the Personal Union a hundred years earlier, and which itself prepared the way for the Parliamentary Union of the British Isles nearly a century later.

A Parliamentary Union may be of two kinds, Federal or Corporate; and it is the former that the people of Scotland would have preferred. Fortunately for the Scottish nation, though unjustly as it seemed to them at the time, their wishes were overruled. Fortunately, we repeat: for while on the one hand the Scottish members by acting together as one body in the common Parliament on all Scottish questions retained for their country in most respects a practical Home Rule, on the other hand, without the erection of one sole and single sovereign authority for the whole Empire the creation and maintenance of the Colonies and India would have been impossible. As a Parliamentary Union may be either

Federal or Corporate, so a Federal Parliamentary Union may be of two kinds. It may establish a really supreme and national Government with powers indefinite, as in the case of the Dominion of Canada. Or it may merely delegate certain strictly defined and limited powers to the central Government, while the contracting parties retain their sovereign and otherwise independent character, as in the case of the United States. Now, since it is certain that a Federal Parliamentary Union of Great Britain would at that time have been of the latter kind, not of the former—of the American type, not the Canadian,—there can be no hesitation in rejoicing that a Corporate Union was effected, as by far the less of two indubitable evils. The changes recently wrought in the character of the joint Monarchy by the Revolution of 1689 had rendered a Parliamentary Union a necessity. Those powers of the Crown which before had sufficed for the principal purposes of union had been so far abridged that, as events convincingly proved in the reign of Queen Anne, under the new constitutional practice a union only through the Crown was in effect no real union at all. Without this concentration of Imperial authority in the British Isles, there never could have taken place that marvellous expansion of England, Scotland, and Ireland, by colonization, commerce, and conquest, which has produced the existing British Empire. And as the sovereign authority, vested, under the new Constitution, not in the King alone, nor in the King in Council, but, in the King in Parliament, necessitated the creation of one supreme Parliament, so the very fact of its absolute and unquestioned supremacy has enabled, enables, and will continue to enable it, to establish, out of the plenitude of its own powers, whatever local legislatures have been or yet may be required, from a County Council to a Dominion Parliament.

But while the Parliamentary Union was Corporate, not Federal, it was sought at the same time to secure to each country all the protection and benefits which Federalism affords, free from its attendant disadvantages. By the Acts of each Parliament, which alone gave and give the Treaty of

Union legal validity, it was sought to place the Church Establishments in England and Scotland, and various other local matters, beyond the reach of legislative interference for ever.

The Union being Corporate, not Federal, no new legislative body was created either for Great Britain, or for England and Scotland respectively. The two Parliaments coalesced, and were blended into one. The Parliament of Great Britain, as regards historic continuity, was not the Parliament of England only, but the Parliament of Scotland also. But in the details of its internal arrangement, the Parliament of Great Britain followed the example of the English Parliament, not of the Scottish.

In the Scottish Parliament, which consisted of one Chamber, but could not with any degree of propriety or justice be described as democratic, the Peers had necessarily sat in the same House, since there was no other, with the Commissioners of Shires and Burghs, the greater barons with the representatives of the minor barons and of the towns. A body known as the Lords of the Articles, though this had been abolished at the Revolution, had marked it off in other important particulars from the Parliament of England.

Now, however, following the English model, the bicameral system was adopted throughout. The representatives of the Commons of Scotland found their place with the representatives of the Commons of England, and in due course the Peers of Scotland should have found their place as a body in the Upper Chamber. But here an initial difficulty presented itself. The Scottish Peers were proportionately far more numerous than the Peers of England. On the Union Roll of the Peerage of Scotland there were ten Dukes, three Marquesses, seventy-five Earls, seventeen Viscounts, forty-nine Barons,—in all, a hundred and fifty-four. In England, on the other hand, though beyond all comparison the more populous and wealthy country, the Peers numbered some hundred and fifty in 1688, and had latterly risen to between a hundred and sixty and a hundred and seventy. The English Peers themselves were, as a rule, far more opulent than the Peers of

Scotland, whose power and influence, for the most part, lay rather in the number of armed men they could bring into the field than in the extent of their rent-roll. Like a certain corps or regiment of the British army, the Scottish Peers were "poor and proud," though not, it may be feared, in every instance "pious." The English Peers were eminently plutocratic. In defiance of the great masses of the English people, but in intimate alliance with the Dissenting commercial class, then, as now, an unpopular, but active and vigilant minority, and with the reluctant and temporary acquiescence of the English Church and landed gentry, they had but lately achieved that great triumph of oligarchical ascendency, the English Revolution. Fresh from and fired with this triumph, the prime movers in which based the political and social fortunes of their families on the vast estates which Henry VIII. had denationalized at the dissolution of the monasteries, and filched from the community to bestow on individuals, the English Whig Peers were full of an unbridled insolence which has rarely or never found its equal. Only twelve years after the Union a daring attempt was made by their leaders to change and subvert the whole character of the Constitution by the conversion of the House of Lords into a close corporation, "independent of the Crown, and irresponsible to the people."* By the Peerage Bill brought into the House of Lords in 1719 by the Duke of Somerset, which the great Whig historian, Macaulay, describes as a "most pernicious measure," "the Crown was to be restrained from the creation of more than six beyond the existing number of one hundred and seventy-eight peerages, the power being still reserved of creating a new peerage whenever a peerage should become extinct." "The Peerage Bill of 1719," writes that staunch Liberal, the late Professor Freeman, "would have altogether changed the character of the Peerage as a political body. It is plain that the Peers would have become an oligarchy, a close body cut off from the Crown and from the mass of the people." It is easy to imagine how a body putting forward such pretensions, and flushed with a victory at which none

* Erskine May, "Constitutional History," vol. i. ch. 5.

can have been more astonished than those who had achieved it, would view a proposal to incorporate the whole Scottish Peerage in the House of Lords. The House of Lords, it must be remembered, was at that time a far more important member of the body politic than it has been since the reforms effected in its composition by King George the Third, and that gradual reformation of the House of Commons in the present century, which, beginning with the first Reform Bill, now awaits completion (as some of us believe) by the admission of the representatives of Australasia and Canada.

In the arrogance of its claims, and the powers exercised by its members, the English House of Lords closely resembled the existing United States Senate. If the sinister project for the dismemberment of the Empire by the annexation of Canada to the United States were ever to approach practical discussion, it is not easy to imagine the American Senate contemplating its own fusion or union on equal terms with the Upper House of the Dominion Parliament. This comparison will enable us to understand the attitude of the English Whig Peers, and to see that they were not altogether without some show of reason. To have admitted the Scottish Peers in a body would have been not less unjust than to exclude them altogether, but unjust to the people of England, and to the new Great British nation, not to the English Peers, who, if they far surpassed the Scottish Peers in wealth, could, as a whole, scarcely claim to be their equals either in long descent or the inherited repute of famous deeds and other like elements of aristocracy. The admission of the Scottish Peers *en masse* would have given Scotland a preponderance to which she could not in fairness be said to be entitled in the Upper Chamber of the common Parliament. Moreover, the comparative poverty of many of the Scottish Peers, coupled with their large number, must have tended, with a Corporate Union of both Peerages, to diminish the regard and the esteem in which the Peers of England were held by their own fellow-countrymen.

In Scotland less was popularly thought of wealth than blood, though wealth, of course, was not wholly disregarded.

But in England antiquity or purity of race, dissociated from the possession of large, or at the least considerable, landed property, has never commanded popular enthusiasm. A Highland chief, robbed of his estates for participation in a Jacobite rising, could raise a regiment by merely appearing among his people and claiming their devotion as clansmen. But in England the "strong common sense of a Teutonic people" has always rejected such idle and unprofitable sentiment. The English Peerage, always associated with property, but in the Middle Ages also with the discharge of duty, had steadily gained in materialism and lost in spirituality from the accession of the House of York. In 1477 George Neville, Duke of Bedford, had been degraded from the Peerage by Act of Parliament on the score of poverty, an occurrence to which it would be impossible to find a parallel in the history of Scotland or France. Nor had the rising flood of a somewhat vulgar, if practical, materialism in any way been lessened by the enrichment of some families with the spoils, and the foundation of others on the ruin, of the monasteries. It was the day of oligarchy, and oligarchy is before everything materialistic. Those who had taken so large a share in the most gigantic act of public plunder ever perpetrated, who had as it were robbed all the hospitals, all the almshouses, all the orphanages and benevolent asylums in the land, and had since succeeded in placing under eclipse the very Monarchy itself, were unlikely to regard with any tender or superstitious reverence a claim to equality of rank, of political rights, of public position, unsupported by a full equality of wealth and fortune. Nor can it be denied that the Peers of Scotland, as was natural and unavoidable in the social and political leaders of a country so much poorer, and a people so far less numerous, were less amply endowed than their English fellows with that which always and everywhere commands a large measure of the world's respect. The homage which may be withheld from genius, ancestry, and virtue all combined, in union with poverty, is seldom refused to the scantiest modicum of any of these qualities accompanied by the possession of the universal object of desire. Nor does this in right or reason call for so much censure as too ethereal philosophers pretend. For where genius may be disputed, virtue questioned or hidden, and ancestry unknown, wealth is a thing tangible and definite, and, since it gives power in the community, must and should also give position. And in wealth the Scottish Peers were conspicuously deficient by comparison with their southern neighbours.

Scotland at that time was a far poorer country by comparison with England than she is to-day, and will appear still more so if we exclude modern London from the comparison as being, not merely the capital of England, but also, and in virtue of the Union, the centre of that Empire which without the Union never had existed. The early prosperity of Scotland under her Celtic Kings had been destroyed in the Wars of Independence and those constant English inroads which were retaliated and revenged, but not easily repaired ; and the latter prosperity of Scotland had not yet arisen. The words of Lord St. Albans in his Essay "Of Nobility" will apply only too well to the Scottish Peers at the time of the Union:—" A numerous nobility causeth poverty and inconvenience in a State ; for it is a surcharge of expense ; and besides, it being of necessity that many of the nobility fall in time to be weak in fortune, maketh a kind of disproportion between honour and means." This "disproportion between honour and means," always a patent fact to an English mind, was not, it may be conceived, the less vividly realized for the memory of ancient conflicts and of recently threatened hostilities.

By the Treaty of Union, therefore, it was settled that the Peers of Scotland should be represented in the House of Lords by sixteen of their number elected for each Parliament; that no more Peers of Scotland should be created ; and that the Peerage of England should for the future be replaced by a Peerage of Great Britain, having the same rights and privileges as the pre-Union English Peerage. At the same time, it was enacted that Peers of Scotland not returned to the House of Lords should enjoy all the other rights and privileges of Peerage, and that no Scottish Peer should be eligible to the House of Commons. This latter provision was not inserted to place them at a disadvantage, but, together with the provision that no more Scottish peerages should be created, was adopted at the instance of the Peers of Scotland, anxious to place their status as Peers in both countries beyond cavil or dispute, and, it may be conjectured, to avert the possibility of any future degradation of their order.

Before the Union some Scotsmen, especially Scottish Peers, had been created Peers of England, and some Englishmen had been created Peers of Scotland. The second Marquis of Hamilton had been created Earl of Cambridge in 1619, and the first and last Duke of Lauderdale had been created Earl of Guilford in 1674, though these peerages had since become extinct. The Scottish Dukes of Lennox, a branch of the royal house of Stuart, had been created Dukes of Richmond, and both peerages had been revived in combination for a son of King Charles the Second. The ill-fated Monmouth, on marrying the heiress of the Scotts, had with his bride been created Duke and Duchess of Buccleuch. The Lord Fairfax of the Great Rebellion had inherited a Scottish peerage from his father. The first Viscount Falkland, Henry Cary, was an English Viceroy of Ireland. The second Lord Falkland, the illustrious Cavalier, had sat in the English House of Commons, and at a latter date Lord Preston had followed his example.

A Scottish Peer, before the Union, unless also an English Peer, was a Commoner in England. The Scottish Peers therefore at the Union, fearing the continuance of such a practice as that of Lord Falkland and Lord Preston as a disparagement and infringement of their Peerage, procured that it should be forbidden; and to prevent the Scottish Peerage from being degraded into an inferior order, a sort of stepping-stone or lobby to the Peerage of Great Britain, as the Peerage of Ireland afterwards came to be regarded, they caused it to be enacted that no more Scottish Peerages should be created, and thus enhanced the value of their own.

But, although the number of Scottish Representative Peers was fixed at sixteen at the Union and has never been increased, there are many other Scottish Peers who now sit in the House of Lords, not as Scottish Peers, but as Peers of England, Great Britain, or the United Kingdom. The majority of these sit in virtue of Great British or United Kingdom peerages bestowed upon themselves, or upon their ancestors, as Scottish Peers. This practice of creating Peers of Scotland Great British or United Kingdom Peers began early, though for a time it was suspended through the violent opposition of the English Whig Peers.

"In 1711, when the English [*i.e.* Great British] Dukedom of Brandon was conferred on the Duke of Hamilton, the Whig majority, including Somers and Cowper, passed a resolution declaring that, although the Sovereign had an undoubted right to confer English [*i.e.* Great British] peerages on Scottish Peers, these peerages did not carry with them the right of sitting or voting in the House of Lords, or of taking part in the trial of Peers. This decision was dictated mainly by party and national feeling. . . . It was not rescinded till the unanimous opinion of the judges was given against its legality in 1782."*

From 1786, when this opinion was acted upon by the creation of the Earl of Abercorn to be Viscount Hamilton, and the Duke of Athole, heir to the English Barony of Strange, to be Earl Strange, a steady flow of such creations has gone on till the present time, and thirty-seven Peers of Scotland have in this way been absorbed into the House of Lords.

But in the meantime, before this decision, "dictated mainly by party and national feeling," had been rescinded, the ingenuity of lawyers or politicians had discovered a way of meeting the difficulty. It could not in reason be contended that the inheritance of a Scottish peerage by a Peer of England or Great Britain could deprive him of his previous right of sitting and voting in the House of Lords. Accordingly the eldest son of a Scottish Peer would be created a Peer of Great Britain, and he, succeeding in due course to his father's honours, would thus promote the absorption of the Scottish Peerage. Thus the Earldom of Kinnoull obtained representation in the House of Lords in 1714 through union with a

* Lecky, "History of England," vol. ii. ch. v.

Barony of Hay created in 1711; the Dukedom of Montrose in 1742 through an Earldom of Graham created in 1722; the Dukedom of Argyll in 1770 through a Barony of Sundridge created in 1766; the Earldom of Bute (since united with the Earldom of Dumfries) in 1792 through a Barony of Cardiff created in 1766.

Besides this, Scottish peerages have been inherited by Peers of Great Britain or the United Kingdom, such as the Barony of Forrester of Corstorphine by Lord Verulam in 1808, the Barony of Dingwall by Earl Cowper in 1871, and the Earldom of Sutherland by the third Marquis of Stafford and second Duke of Sutherland in 1839. The first Viscount Dunblane succeeded as Duke of Leeds in 1712; the English Baronies of Hastings, Hungerford, Botreaux, and Molines have been united since 1871 with the Scottish Earldom of Loudoun; and the Great British Earldoms of Mansfield and Mansfield of Caen Wood, founded in 1776 and 1792 by the fourth son of the fifth Viscount Stormont, have been united with that Scottish peerage since 1843 and 1793 respectively.

The number of Scottish Peers on the Union Roll has been diminished by the inheritance of Scottish peerages by Peers of Scotland, some of them at the time or since Peers of the United Kingdom or Great Britain. Nineteen Scottish peerages have become extinct. Others have become dormant, or, their bearers having been attainted in 1716 or .1746, are still under an attainder which has not been reversed. On the other hand, one Dukedom, two Marquisates, three Earldoms, and six Baronies have been subsequently added to the Union Roll. Of these, however, the Dukedom, that of Rothesay, being inseparably united with the English Dukedom of Cornwall, may be omitted from consideration.

On the whole the number of actually current Scottish peerages have been considerably reduced. On January the first, 1892, there were forty-nine Peers of Scotland, not counting the Duke of Rothesay, with seats in the House of Lords, independently of the Representative Peers system, and thirty-seven Peers of Scotland without such seats, of whom, however, three were Peeresses.

These are the peerages now extant, but the twenty-eight dormant peerages of Scotland must not be forgotten, for any of these is liable to be revived at any time on any person establishing a clear title to it. Nor must the twelve Scottish peerages still under attainder be left out of account, for such peerages also are commonly revived, when a clear title has been established, by the process of reversing the attainder. But since the Earldom of Winton, attainted in 1716, is represented in the United Kingdom Peerage by the Earldom of Winton bestowed in 1851 on the Scottish Earl of Eglinton, the Earldom of Kilmarnock, attainted in 1746, by the Barony of Kilmarnock conferred in 1831 on the Scottish Earl of Erroll, and the Earldom of Cromarty, attainted in 1746, by the Earldom of Cromarty created in 1861 for the first wife of the third Duke of Sutherland, the number of peerages, dormant or attainted, that are liable to be revived, may be reduced to thirty-seven.

It must be borne in mind that the Great British or United Kingdom peerages held by Scottish Peers, being acquired since the creation of their Scottish peerages, are not in the majority of cases inseparably united with the latter. Thus the second Duke of Queensberry was created Duke of Dover in 1708, but this Great British peerage expired on the death of the second Duke of Dover in 1778. The second Duke of Roxburghe was created Earl Ker in 1722 before succeeding to the Dukedom, which he did in 1742, but the Earldom became extinct on the death of the third Duke in 1804. The fourth Earl of Breadalbane was created a Baron of the United Kingdom in 1806, and a Marquis in 1831, but both peerages expired with the second Marquis in 1862. The first Duke of Buckingham and Chandos was also Scottish Lord Kinloss, but this connection ceased on the death of the third and last Duke in 1889. Many Scottish peerages descend to and through females, and coming into a family in this way pass out of it again in the same manner. Peerages of Great Britain or the United Kingdom usually pass only to the descendants in the male line of the first, or, sometimes, of the second Peer. Consequently the Peerages of Scotland with seats in the House of Lords virtually attached to them, apart from the Representative Peers system, change, and fluctuate in number from time to time. A peerage that has obtained such representation in the House of Lords loses it, and then perhaps after an interval obtains it again.

Enough has been said to show that as regards Scotland the House of Lords is not identical with the Peerage.

Into the history of the Union of Ireland with Great Britain it is unnecessary to enter at any length, since it closely followed the lines of the Union of Great Britain. The Irish Parliament having in 1782 asserted or regained its independence, which was formally and explicitly recognized in the Act of Renunciation passed by the Parliament of Great Britain in the year following, Ireland was a Kingdom no longer dependent upon and in subordination to Great Britain, but independent and co-ordinate. The same person was King of Ireland and King of Great Britain, but beyond this all bonds of constitutional and legal union had vanished.

The Parliament of Ireland, unlike the Scottish Parliament, was a body framed on the exact model of the Parliament of England, with the bicameral system fully developed. Ireland had always been in far closer connection with England than had North Britain. Her Peerage, like her Parliament, her law, and so many other of her institutions, had been directly introduced and reproduced from England. Nothing in her political constitution was of spontaneous native growth. Regarded and treated for many generations as an English colony, even in the realization of her distinct Irish nationality she had preserved the monuments of English rule. Irish peerages had always been freely bestowed not only on English, and at a later date on Scottish, settlers in Ireland, but on Englishmen, and in the eighteenth century on Scotsmen, without even the connection with Ireland of absentee landlords of alien origin. Of the eighty-seven Irish peerages now united with peerages of England, Great Britain, or the United Kingdom, twenty-nine had been incorporated in the Peerage of England or the Peerage of

Great Britain previously to the Irish Union. All through the eighteenth century the Peerage of Ireland was looked upon as a cheap substitute for the Peerage of Great Britain, and as such was bestowed on all manner of persons whose services or influence were insufficient to obtain for them the higher order. It was treated in practice as an honorary rather than substantial distinction, bridging the gulf between the order of baronets and the Peerage of Great Britain. The Irish Peerage was no such national institution as the Peerage of Scotland. Putting aside the fact that many genuine Irish landlords were the lineal descendants of sixteenth century Puritan adventurers, there were many Peers of Ireland who were not Irishmen at all, who were without a drop of either Irish or Anglo-Irish blood in their veins, who even might never have so much as set foot on Irish soil. The great mass of the native aristocracy, and many Anglo-Norman or Norman-Irish families with them, had perished in the Elizabethan, Cromwellian, and later confiscations, dispossessed of their land, beggared, butchered, or driven into exile; and strangers ruled in their stead, comparative strangers for the most part as Irish landlords, total strangers in many cases in the Irish House of Lords. The long political subjection of Ireland to England had set a stamp of social inferiority on the later Irish Peerage.

In numbers it bore no such disproportion to the population as had the Peerage of Scotland, and at the date of the last Union Ireland was both absolutely and relatively a more populous portion of the British Isles than at the present day. In 1891 the population of Ireland was 4,700,000 to the 33,000,000 of Great Britain. In 1801 the population of Ireland was 5,216,000 to 10,685,000 in Great Britain; nearly one-third of the whole.

Following the precedent of the Anglo-Scottish Union, the Peers of Ireland were not admitted as a body into the House of Lords of the United Parliament; but in consideration of the greater political importance of Ireland at this period, they were to be represented by a larger portion of their number. By a nearer approach to the tenure of their seats by English and Great British Peers, Irish Representative Peers once elected were to hold their seats for life, not the duration of a single Parliament. Instead of prohibiting future additions to the Peerage of Ireland, it was ordained that the number of Irish Peers should always be kept up to a hundred, exclusive of those entitled to sit in their own right in the House of Lords. This rule, however, has apparently fallen into desuetude, since the number of Peers of Ireland not sitting to represent themselves in the Upper Chamber is now eighty-nine. It was also enacted that one new Irish peerage might be created for every three in existence at the time of the Union that should become extinct, or so often as an Irish Peer might become entitled by creation or descent to a peerage conveying the right of sitting in person in the House of Lords.

Few additions to the Peerage of Ireland have been made since the Union, and none of recent years, the latest new creation in the Irish Peerage having been that of Lord Rathdonnell, in 1868, and the last promotion that of Viscount Strabane, Scottish Earl and Great British Marquis of Abercorn, to the Dukedom of Abercorn. One Irish Peer has since the Union inherited a peerage of Great Britain, and another a peerage of the United Kingdom, while three Peers of the United Kingdom have inherited Irish peerages, and fifty-three Irish Peers have been created Peers of the United Kingdom. In all there are eighty-seven Peers of Ireland entitled, apart from election, to sit in person in the House of Lords.

But in their case, as in that of the Scottish Peers so entitled, the connection between the two Peerages is of somewhat uncertain and precarious duration. The third Lord Sherard was created Baron Sherard in 1714, Viscount Sherard in 1718, and Earl of Harborough in 1719, in the Peerage of Great Britain; but all these peerages became extinct on the death of the sixth Earl in 1859, and the Irish Barony of Sherard is no longer directly associated with the House of Lords. The second Earl of Cork was created Lord Clifford of Lanesborough in the Peerage of England in 1644, and Earl of Burlington in 1664. Both Earldom and Barony became extinct on the death of the third Earl in 1753 ; but the Earldom of Cork passed to the Earls of Orrery, the first Earl of Orrery having been third son of the first Earl of Cork. The fourth Earl of Orrery had been created Lord Boyle in 1711 in the Peerage of Great Britain, and thus the Earldom of Cork regained its representation in the Great British House of Lords.

From a review of these facts, then, it appears that the House of Lords is not identical with the Peerage ; that even the single Estate of the Lords Temporal, were full advantage taken of the Representative Peers system, would still exclude more than eighty actually current peerages, to say nothing of those at present in abeyance ; and, further, that, in the absence of special legislation there is no prospect of the Lords Temporal becoming at any near date identical with the Peerage.

The other Estate in the House of Lords, the Lords Spiritual, consists of the two Archbishops and twenty-four of the Bishops of the Church of England. Of these the Archbishops of Canterbury and York, and the Bishops of London, Durham, and Winchester receive a writ of summons to the House of Lords, whatever the date of their consecration or translation to those sees. The remaining twenty-one Bishops are the senior in appointment, whether by consecration or translation, out of all the diocesans of the Church of England other than those already specified ; that is to say in 1892, the senior among the Bishops of Bangor, Bath and Wells, Carlisle, Chester, Chichester, Ely, Exeter, Gloucester and Bristol, Hereford, Lichfield, Lincoln, Liverpool, Llandaff, Manchester, Newcastle, Norwich, Oxford, Peterborough, Ripon, Rochester, St. Albans, St. Asaph, St. David, Salisbury, Southwell, Truro, Wakefield, and Worcester. Thus seven Bishops are at present excluded. Besides these there is the Bishop of Sodor and Man, whose diocese forms part of the ecclesiastical Province of York, and who is himself permitted to sit in the House of Lords, but has not and has never had a voice or vote in the proceedings.

The House of Lords excludes more than eighty Peers, who are not *in esse*, though they are *in posse*, Lords of Parliament. It includes twenty-six Lords of Parliament who are not Peers.

Once again it must be repeated that the House of Lords is not identical with the Peerage, though it includes the greater portion of it. Neither is the House of Lords, nor are the Lords Temporal taken by themselves, identical with the nobility. The Peers are not the nobility, but a Baronage. The Peers are noble as a result of their Peerage, if not on other grounds; they are not Peers as a consequence of their nobility. As the Lords Temporal embrace only a portion, though the greater portion, of the Peerage, so the Peerage embraces only a portion, but a far smaller portion, of the nobility. The Peers are not the nobility, but the heads of the families of a certain class of the nobility. There are nobles who are Peers, and there are other, and many more, nobles who are Commoners. "If the word nobility has any real meaning," declares Professor Freeman, "it must take in all who bear coat armour by good right." The distinction popularly drawn between the nobility and gentry is one which does not exist. The nobility are the gentry, and every gentleman is noble. "The class in England," writes the same historian, "which answer to the noblesse of other lands is the class that bears coat armour, the gentry strictly so called." There are families out of the Peerage as ancient, if not as illustrious, as any in it. The people who petitioned for the release of the notorious Tichborne claimant incurred much ridicule by describing him as "the unfortunate nobleman now languishing in Dartmoor prison." But, had he been that which he claimed to be, this description would have been strictly accurate. Nobility of blood, unrecognized in English or Scottish law, rests on descent and social opinion. "English law," says Bishop Stubbs,[*] "recognizes simply the right of Peerage, not the privilege of nobility as properly understood; it recognizes office, dignity, estate, and class,

[*] "Constitutional History," ch. xv.

but not caste. Social opinion and the rules of heraldry, which had perhaps their chief use in determining an international standard of blood, alone recognize the distinction. . . . In our system the theory of nobility of blood as conveying political privilege has no legal recognition."

The confusion existing in the minds of some men on this subject is due to the fact that, whereas nobility rests only on descent and social opinion, peerages and other public honours are conferred by the King. The popular mind searching for a nobility in Great Britain and Ireland naturally fastens on the Peerage, and on those cadets and junior members of Peerage families who bear what are known as courtesy titles, the children of Peers, and sometimes of Peers' eldest sons. And these, whatever their descent, are noble by royal creation, the Crown being the fountain of honour. But this nobility existing in, and proceeding from, the Peerage, does not preclude the existence of other nobles whose nobility consists in the antiquity and purity of their descent. "Kings have everywhere nowadays, and in many countries have had for centuries, the power of ennobling. This road to nobility has been so long trodden that men have forgotten that there ever was another route."* As the Peerage of the British Isles always remained an order, not a caste, so there has always existed a nobility unrecognized in law and independent of royal grant. There is nothing derogatory in the name of Commoners. All younger sons of Peers are Commoners, the eldest son of a Peer is a Commoner till he succeeds to his father's peerage, the younger sons of the Sovereign are Commoners unless and until they are created Peers. It is a curious and characteristic fact that the most ancient and wealthy of our English families, if they happen to be unconnected with the Peerage, are not considered "noble" in the ordinary sense of the term.†

Once again, the House of Lords is not identical with the Peerage, and still less is it identical with the nobility. Both Peers and nobles may be members of the House of Commons.

* Sir Henry Maine, "Early History of Institutions," lecture v.
† Freeman, "Essay on the Peerage."

Lord Randolph Churchill, for example, is a noble, but neither a Peer nor a member of the House of Lords, sitting as a fact in the House of Commons. The Earl of Cavan, though noble and a Peer, sits as has been seen in the House of Commons. A Bishop, again, though neither a Peer nor noble, unless in virtue of his holy office, may be a member of the House of Lords.

This nobility as distinguished from, though in part dependent on, the Peerage, is both titled and untitled, hereditary and non-hereditary. Amongst those with titles the baronets, whose baronetcies descend chiefly to males in the order of primogeniture, must be considered a lower order of nobility by royal creation. These are strictly hereditary. The members of the various orders of Knighthood, and the Knights bachelors, must be ranked as life members of the same class. The younger sons of Peers, and in some cases their grandchildren, enjoy courtesy titles, but as these die with them and are not transmitted to their descendants, the latter must be placed in the class of untitled nobility. To this class, of which the majority of the nobility, apart from the Peers and their immediate families, is composed, belong many long-descended country gentlemen in the three kingdoms and the chiefs of Highland clans. Members of this class, though with no hereditary right to rank or precedence recognized by law, are often of more ancient and illustrious descent than a number of the families which in modern times have found place in the Peerage, and in some cases they enjoy an equal or greater amount of social consideration. In this class are such families as the MacMurrough Kavanaghs and Herberts of Muckross in Ireland, the Welds and Towneleys and Howards of Corby in England, the Macleods of Macleod and Camerons of Lochiel in Scotland, to mention a few only of the most distinguished. Some families which would otherwise be placed in this class invest the order of baronets with a distinction in which, as a whole, it would be without them somewhat wanting. Such are the Wynns of Wynnstay, the Tichbornes, Swinburnes, and Trelawneys in England, the Fitzgeralds, Knights of Kerry, in Ireland, the

Colquhouns of Luss, and numerous Campbell and Mackenzie chieftains in Scotland. The heads of such families, being noble already, were created baronets as in some sort a recognition of their nobility.

The House of Lords is not identical with the nobility, nor is the Peerage. Either the House of Lords or the Peerage or both might be abolished by Act of Parliament, but no Act of Parliament can abolish the nobility. Even supposing the Peerage, and the Baronetage also, were to be swept away to-morrow, and it were made an offence punishable with fine and punishment to assume, or to address any other person by, a title, as in France during the revolution, the nobility itself would still be unaffected. The most ingeniously destructive legislation cannot abolish the nobility, for nothing can take away a man's family or make him the child of any parents but his own. The abolition of the Peerage could only increase the power of the nobility by setting it entirely free from all State regulation and control. So far is such a change from being a measure conceived in the interest of democracy, that it might consistently be advocated by an unscrupulous and far-sighted fanatic of aristocracy.

It is clear, therefore, that the Peerage is not the nobility, but a Peerage, and that the House of Lords was never intended to comprehend the aristocracy, but to represent it.

CHAPTER II.

THE ORIGIN AND CONSTITUTION OF THE HOUSE OF LORDS.

WE have seen what the House of Lords is not, that it is neither the Peerage nor the nobility. It now remains to see what the House of Lords is, and this is to be discovered from an examination of its history.

Professor Freeman, who in party politics, it is well to remember, was a Liberal, was accustomed to declare that the House of Lords was lineally descended from the Anglo-Saxon National Assembly known as the Witenagemôt. "Whatever view," he wrote in his essay on the Peerage, "may be taken of the ancient Witenagemôt, we may safely assume that that assembly, with whatever changes in its constitution, is personally continued in the House of Lords." This he evidently considered the greatest compliment that could be paid the Upper Chamber. It is difficult to say how far this fact, if fact it be, and it comes to us on this very high authority, would be likely to carry weight with "the People's League for the Abolition of the House of Lords;" but it is not one which it is necessary, or would be wise, to rely upon for the defence. The history of a State begins with the history of its foreign policy, as of a man with his relations to the world around him, not with the courtship of his parents; and the history of England begins with that Norman Conquest which made England a nation. For all practical purposes, the Witenagemôt is a matter of antiquarian lore, not of political history. It has less practical bearing on the House of Lords than the Roman Senate, for the latter was the governing body of a great and civilized people presenting many points of curious resemblance to ourselves.

If, then, we strike the Witenagemôt out of the pleadings, we shall find on investigation that the House of Lords had its ultimate source in the system of land tenure prevailing under the Norman Kings. The House of Lords, as regards the Estate of the Lords Temporal, is a Baronage, and what was a Baron? We cannot do better than take Bishop Stubbs's definition :—

"The title of Baron, unlike that of Earl, is a creation of the Conquest. The word, in its origin equivalent to *homo*, receives under feudal institutions, like *homo* itself, the meaning of vassal. Homage (*hominium*) is the ceremony by which the vassal becomes the man of his lord, and the *homines* of the King are Barons. . . . It is probable that the title or dignity of Baron, or King's Baron, involves, from its first entrance into English history, nothing more than the idea of royal vassal or tenant-in-chief. Of these there were many grades, besides the great distinction of *majores* and *minores* which appears in Magna Charta. . . . Some were summoned to the host, to court and council, were summoned 'propriis nominibus;' others not. . . . The Baronage was ultimately and essentially defined as an Estate of the Realm by the royal action in summons, writ, and patent. It was by special summons that Henry I., Henry II., and the Barons of Runnymede, separated the greater from the smaller vassals of the Crown; and the constitutional change which at last determined the character of Peerage was the making the status of the Peer depend on the reception of the writ, rather than on the tenure which had been the original qualification for summons. The determination of the persons who could be summoned rested finally with the Crown, limited only on one side by the rule of hereditary right." *

First we have as Barons by tenure all the King's lay tenants-in-chief. Out of these the greater tenants gradually emerge as Barons by writ of summons, a system fully established by the time of Edward I., the occasional summons growing into the perpetual, and the perpetual into the hereditary, while the minor barons losing their baronial character come as freeholders to be represented in Parliament by the Knights of the shire. One portion of the original Baronage sinks while the other rises in the scale of power and dignity. Finally we have the system of creation by patent introduced, at first existing side by side with the

* "Constitutional History of England," chs. ii., xv.

system of creation by writ of summons, but tending gradually to supersede it, till in the end the latter disappears. The greater Barons secured the rights of being summoned in person by the King by Magna Charta, which "parts them off from other tenants-in-chief," and "puts them alongside of the prelates and Earls. . . . Two classes of men who have, with a certain interval in the seventeenth century, sat continuously in the councils of the nation from the earliest times." *

The Earl previous to the Norman Conquest, as successor of the more ancient Ealdorman, had been rather an executive officer, in rank next to the King, than anything that is now understood by the title. Under the Norman Kings, by whom this dignity was at first very sparingly bestowed, Earls with few exceptions were simply the greatest of the Barons, with or without some fragments of the former territorial jurisdiction of the Ealdorman, as to which point historians are in doubt. The exceptions are of three or four Palatine Earldoms, which, however, scarcely require further consideration, as they disappeared early, or were annexed in one way or another by the Crown, and have altogether failed to affect the character of the modern Peerage. The principal of these Counts Palatine was the Earl of Chester, who, says Bishop Stubbs, "was in fact a feudal Sovereign in Cheshire as the King was in Normandy." The Earldom was settled by Edward I. as a provision for the successive heirs apparent, and since the accession of Henry IV. has been annexed to the Principality of Wales. The only other County Palatine of much historical importance was that of Durham, attached to the Bishopric, which was not represented in the House of Commons till the time of Charles II., and retained many features of its semi-independent existence down to the reign of William IV.

Out of the system of special and personal investiture, by which the dignity of an Earldom was conferred, grew the system of creation by patent, at first applied to Earls, but afterwards extended to Barons. From the year 1295 the system of Barony by writ is fully established. In 1387 the

* Freeman.

first Baron by patent is created; and from 1444 this method of creating them becomes the general rule.

To the original orders of Earl and Baron were afterwards added three new grades of Peerage, Duke, Marquis, and Viscount. The first Dukedom was that of Cornwall, and was created by Edward III. in 1337, as the perpetual dignity of the heir apparent to the throne. The first Marquis was created by Richard II. in 1384. The first Viscount was created by Henry VI. in 1440. The members of all these different grades of Peerage have always been equal in political rights and power, the difference between them being merely one of rank and precedence. These titles were in each case of foreign origin, and it is the merest chance that some other foreign titles were not introduced as well or in their place—Prince instead of Duke or Marquis, Châtelain or Vavasseur instead of Viscount. The title of Prince as a territorial dignity has never been used in England except in connection with Wales. The title of Prince of Wales was introduced by Edward I. in 1301, after the death of the last Welsh Prince of Wales, and by long established usage it is never borne except by the heir apparent to the Throne.

Thus, as regards one Estate in the House of Lords, we see that the Peerage is a Baronage, that the greater Barons by tenure, and those greatest Barons distinguished as Earls, form its original structure to which new ornamental orders of Peerage were subsequently added.

As regards the Lords Spiritual we have seen that Bishops were from the earliest time summoned, and they were summoned, not as Peers or Barons, but as Bishops. "The two Archbishops and the eighteen Bishops formed the most permanent element in the House of Lords: when a see was vacant, the guardian of the spiritualities was summoned in place of the Bishop; and showed by his compliance with the writ that the seat of the Bishop did not depend on the possession of a temporal Barony, as was the case with that of an Abbot or Prior." * The Abbots and Priors formed a very considerable proportion of the House in some centuries of

---

* Stubbs, "Constitutional History."

the Middle Ages. The number of them summoned varied almost incredibly. In 1301, for example, eighty were summoned, but in the following year only forty-four. Under Edward III. the average was twenty-seven, which was the number summoned to the last Parliament of Henry VI. But, as a rule, between the reigns of Henry IV. and Edward IV. the number of Temporal Peers varied between forty and fifty; while the number of Spiritual Peers steadily increased during the same period.

"Before the dissolution of the monasteries by Henry VIII. in 1539, when the Abbots and Priors sat with the Bishops, the Lords Spiritual actually exceeded the Lords Temporal in number. First in rank and precedence, superior in attainments, exercising high and extended influence, they were certainly not inferior in political weight to the great nobles with whom they were associated. Even when the Abbots and Priors had been removed, the Bishops alone formed about one-third of the House of Lords. But while the Temporal Lords have been multiplied since that period about eight-fold, the English Bishops sitting in Parliament have only been increased from twenty-one to twenty-six, to whom were added for a time the four Irish Bishops. The ecclesiastical element in our legislature has become relatively inconsiderable and subordinate. Instead of being a third of the House of Lords as in former times, it now forms less than a fifteenth part of that assembly," [and in 1892 less than a twentieth]. *

It should be observed before leaving this subject that the mitre worn by permission of the Pope by some heads of religious houses had nothing to do with their seat in Parliament. The Pope never possessed the right of creating Lords Spiritual. "Mitred and Parliamentary Abbots were not identical:" some Priors who sat in Parliament were not mitred, and some mitred Abbots were not Lords of Parliament. And it should further be observed that all of them, though Lords Spiritual, sat, not like the Bishops in virtue of their office, but as landlords, in virtue of the large landed property of their communities.

Henry VIII., who secularized so much of the soil of England, in doing so by necessary consequence largely secularized the House of Lords. But as some set off to the number of Lords Spiritual displaced by him, he added five

* Sir T. Erskine May, "History of the Constitution."

Bishops—of Oxford, Peterborough, Chester, Gloucester, and Bristol,—of which sees the two last have since been united.

In 1642 the movement against the Church and the Monarchy of the Puritans and those who afterwards became the Whigs, resulted in the exclusion of the Bishops from the House of Lords by an Act of Parliament, which in 1661 was repealed. The House of Lords itself was "abolished" in 1649, by a vote of the House of Commons, though the Peers kept their titles and precedence, and were eligible to the Lower Chamber; but this vote was treated as null in 1660.

At the time of the Irish Union the Churches of England and Ireland were "united," in the hope of giving security to the latter, and the preservation of each was made an "essential and fundamental part of the Union." Out of the twenty Archbishops and Bishops, then existing, of the Church of Ireland, four were to sit by rotation of sessions in the House of Lords as Lords Spiritual, of whom one was always to be an Archbishop. This arrangement, however, was swept away by the Irish Church Act, 1869.

At the Anglo-Scottish Union there had, of course, been no question of Scottish Bishops sitting in the Great British House of Lords, for the Revolution of 1689 had disestablished the Church of Scotland, and handed over its endowments to the Presbyterians.

No further addition was made, after the time of Henry VIII., to the number of the Lords Spiritual sitting in Parliament, till the creation of the diocese of Ripon in 1836 brought it up to twenty-six, at which it has ever since remained. For by the Act which created the See of Manchester in 1847 it was specially provided that the number of Lords Spiritual sitting in Parliament should not thereby be increased, but that the junior Bishop of any see other than Canterbury, York, London, Durham, or Winchester, should not be entitled to receive a writ of summons till a vacancy occurred among the Bishops of the new class thus defined. By the operation of this Act, and the subsequent extension of the Episcopate by the establishment of the new dioceses of St. Albans, Southwell, and Truro in the Province of Canterbury, and Liverpool, Newcastle, and Wakefield in the Province of York, two distinct classes of Lords Spiritual have been instituted—those who are Lords of Parliament *in esse*, and those who, like Scottish or Irish Peers, without seats in the Upper Chamber, are only Lords of Parliament *in posse*. Again, a distinction is established between the two Archbishops and three of the Bishops on the one hand, and the remaining Bishops on the other. The former sit by a right hereditary in their sees: the sees of the latter have only an hereditary possibility of being represented in the Upper Chamber. As Peers are not all Lords of Parliament, so now Bishops, even of dioceses, are not all Lords of Parliament. Those Bishops who are not Lords of Parliament are represented by their senior colleagues.

Bishops are not Peers: they take no part in the trial of Peers; and if put upon their trial are themselves tried by a jury of Commoners, as in the famous case of "the Trial of the Seven Bishops."

Besides the Bishops another body of public officers were summoned to attend early Parliaments, and might conceivably have succeeded in establishing an hereditary right of summons for their office, though not for their family. These were the Judges. But although summoned to give Parliament the benefit of their advice in the House of Lords, they were summoned with irregularity, they never obtained the right of voting, and were never looked upon as Peers nor exercised any of the distinctive rights of Peers. "It would have been not unreasonable," contends Professor Freeman, "if in the many shiftings which took place before the constitution of the two Houses finally settled itself, the Judges had come to hold official seats in the House of Lords in the same way as the Bishops." But, as a matter of fact, they never did so: they never even obtained the position held by Lords of Appeal in Ordinary at the present day as Life Peers.

There were no Life Peers in the original institution of the Baronage; and although Life Peers have occasionally been created, none such ever sat in the House of Lords before the present century. An attempt was made in the present reign to introduce, or, as its authors asserted, to revive, a system of Life Peers, by the creation of Lord Wensleydale as a Peer for life only. But the House of Lords decided that he was unable to take a seat in that assembly. Professor Freeman insists that "the Wensleydale decision was in the teeth of history," that " powers exercised by Edward I. could be exercised by the Queen unless specifically surrendered or withdrawn by Act of Parliament." But Bishop Stubbs and Sir Harris Nicolas negative this view of the question.

"Although instances occur," says the former, "in which a person qualified to receive a summons as a judge or councillor has been summoned to Parliament, and has yet not transmitted an hereditary peerage to his descendants, it is not probable that the Crown ever contemplated the creation by such single summons of a Barony for life only. The higher ranks of the Peerage were occasionally granted for life only. No Baron, however, was ever created for life only without a provision as to the remainder or right of succession after his death. . . . In two cases, the Barony of Hay in 1606, and of Reede in 1644, the creation was for life, but it was provided that the bearers of the title should not sit in Parliament."

In the debate on the Wensleydale case (1856), the great legal authorities of the time, such as Lords Lyndhurst, Campbell, and St. Leonards, all declared life peerages giving a seat in the House of Lords to be illegal and opposed to the *consuetudo parliamenti;* and there can be no doubt that the House of Lords was thoroughly justified in its decision that although the Crown could create Life Peers, such creation did not entitle them to sit in Parliament.* In face of the facts adduced by two such writers, of authority in these matters at least equal to his own, " the manifest right " claimed by Professor Freeman for the Crown "to name no successor at all, that is to say to create a life peerage," must be held, if it ever existed, to have been long lost by disuse.

But although Life Peers never before sat in the House of Lords, by the Appellate Jurisdiction Act, 1876, the Lords of

* Lord Campbell's Life, ii. 338.

Appeal in Ordinary under that statute were to be created Peers for life with the rights exercised by ordinary United Kingdom Peers during their continuance in office. And on the retirement of Lord Blackburn, who had been created a Life Peer under this Act, the statute was revised and further extended to allow Peers so created to retain their right of sitting and voting in Parliament after retiring from the Bench. Thus, for the first time in the history of the House of Lords, it now includes a class, though a small one, of Life Peers. Bishops also, regarded as individuals, may be said to be life members of the House, but they are not Life Peers.

A Peer, being a member of the House of Lords, is not only a counsellor of the Sovereign, but a legislator and a judge. But the Appellate Jurisdiction formerly exercised by the House of Lords has been practically handed over to the new tribunal bearing that name and consisting of the four Lords of Appeal in Ordinary with such other Peers as are holding or have held high judicial office.

A Peer cannot divest himself of his Peerage and become a Commoner. Resolutions passed by the House of Lords in 1648 and 1672 lay down that a Peer is unable to relinquish his Peerage, and a Peerage can be forfeited only by attainder or by Act of Parliament. An attainder for high treason extinguishes a peerage of any kind. An attainder for felony extinguishes a peerage by writ, but not a peerage by patent. A Peer while bankrupt is incapable of sitting or voting in the House of Lords.

A peerage can be created with any remainder; that is to say, it can pass in any line of succession, however apparently eccentric or capricious, that may be named in the patent. Instances are given by Sir Harris Nicolas where the remainder has been to the second son and his issue male; to such second son and his issue male with remainder to an eldest son in like manner; to the issue male of the body of the grantee by a particular woman; to the heirs general of the body of the grantee; to the issue male of the father or grandfather of the grantee failing the heirs male of his body;

to natural brothers of the grantee; to sons-in-law of the grantee; to the issue of a wife whom the grantee might afterwards marry (thus excluding previous issue): and so forth.* But as a general rule, peerages by patent since their first creation have been limited to the heirs of the body male of the grantee, or to the younger son, brother, nephew, or other near kinsman of the grantee, and the heirs of the body male of such a person.

Baronies by writ descend to heiresses.

"When the Baron by writ dies leaving only female heirs, the dignity, being indivisible, reverts to the Crown as the fountain of honour, to be conferred on such one of the coheirs as the Sovereign should think fit to name, or in default to remain in the Crown until there is a sole heir in whom it can legally vest. During this period of suspense the Barony is said to be in abeyance. The representation of the Barony by writ is always vested in the heirs of the person first created, the females of each generation being preferred to the males of the preceding generation."

Where there is one daughter only, and no sons, the Barony descends to her; but if there is more than one daughter it goes for the time into abeyance, but is liable to be revived.

"In the early centuries of the Peerage, the same happened to an Earldom as to a Barony when it fell among coheirs. No one coheir more than another could enjoy the dignity, and it became the King's, to dispose of at his pleasure. But when (as in the instances of Chester, Gloucester, Huntingdon, Essex, Albemarle) the whole of the lands of an Earldom passed to one of several daughters and coheirs, and were in no degree divided, the dignity passed with them to the husband and issue of such coheir. Salisbury, Warwick, Norfolk, Surrey, Devon, Oxford, Pembroke, were all instances where the Earldom descended through heirs of the body, whether male or female. Subsequently to 1387 the grant to heirs male of the body of the grantee became the rule of limitation."†

No English peerages of higher rank than Baron are now in existence that descend, perpetually, through females. Nor are any Earldoms or Baronies by tenure now in existence, the Earldom of Arundel which came to Philip Howard, son and heir of Thomas, fourth Duke of Norfolk, by the marriage

* Sir Harris Nicolas. " Historic Peerage."   † Ibid.

of the latter with Mary, daughter and eventually sole heir of Henry Fitzalan, seventeenth Earl, having been resettled by Act of Parliament in 1627, and the claim for a Barony of Berkeley, held by tenure of Berkeley Castle, having been rejected by the House of Lords.

It is worthy of note, as showing how far more rigid and uniform the Peerage system has become than it was in mediæval times, that the husband of an heiress was summoned to represent her in the House of Lords. "Of the countless examples of this practice," says Bishop Stubbs, "which applied anciently to the Earldoms also, it may be enough to mention Sir John Oldcastle, who was summoned as the husband of the heiress of Cobham, and in common parlance bore the title of Lord Cobham; Ralph of Monthermer, husband of the widowed Johanna of Acre, Countess of Gloucester, sat as Earl of Gloucester during the minority of his stepson; Richard Neville gained the [Montacute] Earldom of Salisbury, and his son that [the Beauchamp Earldom] of Warwick, as the husbands of heiresses. The usage was not materially broken down till the system of creation with limitation to heirs male was established."

In Ireland, where the Peerage was a direct offshoot from that of England, it does not differ in any respect from the Peerage of the latter country.

But though many Scottish Peerages descend to and through females, they never go into abeyance among coheiresses, like the English baronies by writ, but pass to the elder or eldest of the daughters, sisters, or other female relatives of the last Peer, on the same principle as that which governs the descent of the British Crown.

The feudal system was first introduced into Scotland by David I. (1124-1153), and extended, as opportunity offered, by his successors. The first Earls in Scotland were the Celtic Mormaers, who were gradually transformed into feudal magnates. In the eighth century the Kingdom of the Picts was divided into seven provinces, each with a Ri or Regulus under the Ardri, and each consisting of two districts with a sub-Ri to each. In the tenth century the Kingdom of Alban, which had replaced that of the Picts, was also divided into seven, though not the same seven, provinces.

"But instead of a subordinate sub-King, each district (except Argyll) has now a Mormaer, or great Maer or Steward, while the Mormaer of Moray appears occasionally under the title of Ri or King. These Mormaers held a position in the scale of power and dignity only inferior to that of the Ardri or supreme King. . . . The office of Mormaer was hereditary in a family. . . . The next rank under the Mormaers of Buchan was held by persons named Toisechs, who possessed a similar relation, in a subordinate capacity, to the land and the people. . . . In the Kingdom of Alexander I. [1107–1124], we find the Celtic Mormaer appearing as Comes or Earl, while the name of Thanus or Thane was applied to the Toisech. . . . The old Celtic earldoms were rather official and personal, than territorial dignities, and the territory of the earldom which afterwards formed its demesne, was more of the nature of mensal land appropriated to the support of the dignity. . . . The relation of these old Celtic Earls or Mormaers to the Crown on the one hand had hitherto been purely official, and that towards their districts was not a purely territorial one. It was a relation more towards the tribes who peopled it than towards the land. David's desire would be to place them in the position of holding the land they were officially connected with as an Earldom of the Crown-in-chief." Accordingly he introduced feudal charters of earldoms. "Each of the seven provinces of Scotland consisted of two districts, a Mormaer ruling over each; but when they appear in the reign of Alexander I., under the name of Comes or Earl, we find the number reduced to six: and, with the exception of the two districts of Mar and Buchan, each of which is represented by an Earl, with one of its districts possessing an Earl, and the other without one. . . . The new policy was to appoint new Earls to the vacant districts who were feudally invested with their Earldoms, while the others would be gradually feudalized as opportunity offered. An Earldom was converted into a purely feudal holding which, like all such holdings created at this time, was descendible to heirs female."

Those Earldoms which had not been feudalized were looked upon as subject to Celtic, and not to feudal law. In such cases not only the dignity, but all the land attaching to it, went to the elder or the eldest sister. But

"those [Earldoms] which had been either feudalized or created by the districts being erected into Earldoms by the Crown, were in no different position from an ordinary Barony, and were regulated by the feudal law, the land being parted between coheirs; but the dignity and chief messuage belonging to the eldest coheir." *

The custom of peerages descending through females seems

* Skene, "Celtic Scotland," bk. iii. ch. ii.

to have thoroughly impressed itself on Scotland, for many peerages created at a later date descend in the same manner. Amongst those Scottish peerages of early and of late creation which descend through females, may be mentioned the Earldoms of Dumfries, Dysart, Erroll, Loudoun, Mar, Newburgh, Orkney, Rothes, Seafield, and Sutherland; the Baronies of Dingwall, Forrester, Gray, Herries, Kinloss, Napier, Nairne, Ruthven, Saltoun, and Sempill.

Among English Baronies by writ not in abeyance are those of Le Despencer (held by Viscount Falmouth), Dacre (held by Viscount Hampden), de Ros, de Clifford, Hastings, Mowbray, Botetourt, Botreaux, Segrave, Stafford, Beaumont, Norreys, North, Zouche, Vaux, Windsor, Wentworth, Berkeley, Berners, Brayl, Clinton, Grey de Ruthyn, Howard de Walden, Willoughby de Eresby, and Willoughby de Broke.

The principal constitutional changes, then, that the House of Lords has undergone in modern times, looking upon the English House of Lords as having grown into the House of Lords of Great Britain, and from that into the House of Lords of the United Kingdom of Great Britain and Ireland, have been those wrought by the Unions with Scotland and Ireland, and by the Appellate Jurisdiction Act, 1876, with its subsequent modifications, as regards the Lords Temporal; and by the dissolution of the monasteries and the nineteenth century growth of the episcopate, as regards the Lords Spiritual.

From the Scottish and Irish Unions comes the fact that the House of Lords no longer includes the Peerage; that there are Peers who are not Lords of Parliament, who are not hereditary members of the House of Lords, but only possessed of an hereditary right of electing, and an hereditary chance of being elected to that body.

To the statutes dealing with the Lords of Appeal we owe it that there is now for the first time in the history of the Empire a class of Life Peers, not merely life members of the House of Lords, but Peers, though unable to transmit their seats and dignities to their descendants. The Bishops were life members of the House of Lords, but not Peers. And the Irish Representative Peers were life members of the House of Lords, and also Peers, but not Life Peers : since on the one hand their peerages were not for life only, but capable of descending to their heirs, while on the other hand their seats did not directly depend upon their peerages, but on their election by, and from among, other Peers. The acting and retired Lords of Appeal are the first Life Peers. By this important innovation a principle of far-reaching consequence has been newly imbedded in the constitution of the Upper Chamber.

From the dissolution of the monasteries, and the attendant expulsion of Abbots and Priors from the House of Lords, comes the contrast between the present and former position of the Lords Spiritual. And from the recent growth of the English episcopate comes the division of the sees of the Church of England into two classes, one with an hereditary right of being represented in the House of Lords by their Bishops, the other with only an hereditary chance of being directly represented in the Upper Chamber at any given moment. The case of the Isle of Man, ecclesiastically, but not politically, part of England, stands, and has always stood, by itself.

From the example of the Scottish and Irish Peers it becomes evident that a seat in the House of Lords is no necessary or inseparable feature of a peerage ; that it is just as feasible for Peers to be represented by their elected members in the Upper Chamber, as for Commoners to be so represented in the Lower Chamber of the Imperial Legislature.

From the example of the Lords of Appeal it becomes evident that it is possible to vary the nature of Lords Temporal by the explicit substitution of a senatorial for a baronial qualification, and a senatorial for a baronial tenure without in any way destroying or impairing their historic continuity and character. From the one we get the principle of the representation of heredity by further selection, from the other the principle of qualification by office.

And from the changes wrought in the Lords Spiritual we may draw the conclusion that a seat in the House of Lords is not of the essence of a Christian bishop; that it is even possible, though not perhaps advisable, to conceive of a House of Lords without any bishops at all. And we may draw the further and more important conclusion that all bishops are not of equal value as regards seats in a Legislative Chamber, and that the local position of the Anglican Church in the Kingdom of England, its spiritual rights and temporal endowments, would nowise be injuriously affected by a second readjustment of the ecclesiastical elements represented by the Lords Spiritual to the altered conditions of our time.

CHAPTER III.

THE COMPOSITION OF THE HOUSE OF LORDS.

FROM an inquiry into the origin, and an examination of the various constituent elements of the House of Lords, we may pass by a natural transition to the consideration of those who actually compose it.

Following the line of the great division into Lords Temporal and Lords Spiritual, we may put the latter for the time aside with the reminder that, while personally life members of the House, not Life Peers, there is an hereditary right of representation attaching to five sees, and an hereditary possibility of representation attaching to the rest.

Having done so, we shall next be struck with the shallowness and the injustice of those who describe the House of Lords as an assembly exclusively composed of "hereditary legislators." For in the first place we are confronted with the forty-four Scottish and Irish Representative Peers, and the Lords and ex-Lords of Appeal, who have neither inherited their seats nor can transmit them to their descendants. The Scottish and Irish Representative Peers are hereditary Peers, and as such hereditary counsellors of their Sovereign. But they are not hereditary legislators. They owe their seats to election by their fellows. It is true that without their peerages they could not be elected. But hereditary eligibility to an Assembly is not the same thing as an hereditary seat in it. Every Commoner has an hereditary eligibility to the House of Commons, but to say that a member of that body owed his seat to hereditary right, or to describe him as an hereditary legislator, would be justly resented as pedantic trifling. The Scottish and Irish Representative Peers are not hereditary legislators, but hereditary Peers and elected legislators. Far from being hereditary legislators, the Scottish Representative Peers are not even legislators for life.

An "hereditary legislator" may mean one of two things. It may mean, as it is vulgarly employed to mean, a legislator whose right of legislation may hereafter be inherited. Or it may mean, and properly ought to mean, a legislator who has inherited his right of legislation. Now it is obvious that the Lords and ex-Lords of Appeal are in neither sense "hereditary legislators." They owe their seats to appointment by the Sovereign consequent on an official qualification, and their peerages and seats die with them. If, then, we add to their number that of the Scottish and Irish Representative Peers, we get at once forty-nine Lords Temporal, out of an actual total in January, 1892, of some five hundred and fifteen, who are not hereditary legislators, or nearly one in ten; and while thirty-three of these non-hereditary legislators are members of the House of Lords for life, or for so much of that as remains to them after their creation or election, sixteen are members for the still shorter term of the duration of a single Parliament.

But among those normal Peers of England, Great Britain, or the United Kingdom, who are entitled to sit and vote in their own person, not all Peers of the United Kingdom are hereditary legislators. To call a man an hereditary legislator who has not inherited his right of legislation, and who is without heirs to inherit it, is to abuse the English language. Every new Peer, every Peer who has not inherited his peerage, is in the true sense of the term a non-hereditary legislator. Every new Peer who is without heirs to inherit his peerage, although not in constitutional law a Life Peer, is in fact a Peer for life only. The son of a new Peer of the United Kingdom becomes an hereditary legislator on succeeding to his father's peerage, but the new Peer himself is not an hereditary, but a new legislator. And what is true of Commoners created Peers of the United Kingdom is true also of Scottish and Irish Peers incorporated in the Union Peerage. They are hereditary Peers, but they are new members of the House of Lords, and the peerages which give them and their heirs a seat in the House of Lords are not and do not become "hereditary" till they have actually been inherited. Every new Peer of the United Kingdom is a non-hereditary legislator; and every such Peer without heirs is in effect a Life Peer. The Lords Temporal are not all, or nearly all, hereditary legislators; they are not all even legislators for life.

As we have seen, a peerage of the United Kingdom without a remainder, except in the case of the Lords of Appeal, cannot have existence, or at least cannot convey the right of sitting or voting in the House of Lords, and therefore, except in the case of Peeresses, never is created. But a United Kingdom peerage bestowed on a man advanced in life who has never married, or who if married has no children, though with a nominal remainder to the heirs of his body inserted as a necessary matter of form in the patent of creation, is to all intents and purposes a life peerage. A Peer without heirs, whether his own children or other near kinsmen, is a Peer whose peerage cannot be inherited. And a Scottish or Irish Peer newly created a Peer of the United Kingdom, with heirs to his Scottish or Irish peerage, but without heirs to his peerage of the United Kingdom, is a Peer whose personal right of legislation in the Upper Chamber will not be inherited.

In January, 1892, there were, including the Prince of Wales, but excluding the Life Peers of the United Kingdom, four hundred and eighty-eight Peers and Peeresses of England, Great Britain, and the United Kingdom. Of this number six were Peeresses: the Viscountess Hambledon, and the Baronesses Berkeley, Berners, Burdett-Coutts, Bolsover, and Macdonald of Earnscliffe.

Thirteen Peers were minors: the Duke of Albany, the Marquis of Camden, Earl Beauchamp, the Earl of Cottenham, Earl Granville, the Earl of Guilford, the Earl of Hillsborough (Irish Marquis of Downshire), Viscount Torrington, Lord Granard (Irish Earl of Granard), Lord Lovat, Lord O'Hagan, Lord Ramsay (Scottish Earl of Dalhousie), and Lord Strathspey (Scottish Earl of Seafield).

Deducting the Peeresses and minors we get four hundred and sixty-nine Peers, exclusive of the Lords of Appeal, entitled to sit in person in the House of Lords.

Of these four hundred and sixty-nine Peers two held their seats by a peculiar tenure.

The Prince of Wales, Duke of Cornwall by birth, sat by an hereditary right as the eldest son of the Sovereign and heir apparent to the throne. Since the bitterest opponent of hereditary legislators would scarcely object to the presence in the House of Lords of the eldest son of the Sovereign, while there is a Sovereign and a House of Lords, the Prince of Wales may be left out of the discussion.

The other extraordinary Peer is Lord Lovaine (Earl Percy), who has been summoned to the House in a Barony belonging to his father, the Duke of Northumberland. The practical effect is as though he had been created a Peer for his father's lifetime. "But the case of a son," it is laid down by Bishop Stubbs, "summoned to the House of Lords in his father's lifetime [in a Barony held by his father], is not to be understood as the creation of a new peerage; the first recorded instance of this practice occurs in 1482, when the heir of the Earl of Arundel was summoned in his father's Barony of Maltravers." Eldest sons so summoned must be considered to sit by an anticipated hereditary right.

Classing Lord Percy with ordinary Peers, but omitting the Prince of Wales, whose presence rests on the existence of the Monarchy, not of the House of Lords, we get a reduced total of four hundred and sixty-eight. Three of these might further be dismissed, since Lord Bowes (Scottish Earl of Strathmore) is also a Representative Peer of Scotland, and the Earl de Montalt (Irish Viscount Hawarden) and Lord (Irish Viscount) Powerscourt are Representative Peers of Ireland. But retaining them we get four hundred and sixty-eight ordinary Peers of the United Kingdom to five Life

Peers, fifteen Representative Peers of Scotland, twenty-six Representative Peers of Ireland, and the twenty-six Bishops: four hundred and sixty-eight to seventy-two.

These figures, however, give a wholly incorrect idea of the real proportion of hereditary legislators to non-hereditary in the House of Lords.

Taking the same date of January, 1892, there were then one Viscount (Lord Sherbrooke), and seventeen Barons (Lords Alcester, Ardilaun, Armstrong, Bramwell, Burton, Castletown, Connemara, Field, Hobhouse, Lingen, Mount Stephen, Penzance, Rowton, Sandford, Thring, Wantage, and Winmarleigh), who were first Peers of the United Kingdom, having previously been Commoners, and who were without heirs to inherit their titles. That is to say, in everything but law they were Life Peers.

There were two first Peers of the United Kingdom, Peers of Scotland, Lord Herries and Lord Reay, who, being without heirs to their United Kingdom peerages, were legislators and members of the House of Lords for life.

There were three first Peers of the United Kingdom, the Irish Viscounts Hawarden and De Vesci and the Irish Earl of Howth, who, sitting as Earl de Montalt and the Barons De Vesci and Howth, were in the same position as Lord Herries and Lord Reay.

Thus there were eighteen commonly styled "hereditary legislators" who were in everything but name Life Peers. There were twenty-three "hereditary legislators" who were only life members of the House of Lords.

To these there might have been added the since lamented Duke of Clarence and Avondale, but inasmuch as his peerage in the ordinary course of nature would have some day become merged in the Crown, a juster view would place him on one side with the Prince of Wales.

No such reasoning, however, will apply to the Duke of Edinburgh and the Duke of Connaught and Strathearn. It is true, doubtless, that they owe their seats to the fact that they are the sons of the Sovereign, but they were not born Peers like the Duke of Cornwall and Rothesay. Either the whole class of Peers descended in the male line from a British Sovereign must be put on one side as appertaining to the Monarchy, not the House of Lords; or, with the previous exceptions, they must be ranked in the same way as all other subjects. If the Duke of Cambridge and the Duke of Cumberland are to be accounted "hereditary legislators," the Duke of Connaught and the Duke of Edinburgh must be placed among those legislators who have not inherited a right of sitting in the House of Lords.

To the Dukes of Edinburgh and Connaught must be added those other first Peers of the United Kingdom, who have heirs to inherit their seats: forty-three previously Commoners —one Earl (Selborne), four Viscounts (Cranbrook, Cross, Hampden, Wolseley), thirty-eight Barons (Aberdare, Acton, Alington, Ashbourne, Basing, Brabourne, Brassey, Coleridge, Derwent, Donington, Ebury, Emly, Esher, Grimthorpe, Halsbury, Hamilton of Dalzell, Herschell, Hillingdon, Hothfield, Iveagh, Knutsford, Masham, Moncreiff, Monk Bretton, Montagu of Beaulieu, Northbourne, Norton, Revelstoke, Rothschild, St. Levan, St. Oswald, Savile, Stalbridge, Stanley of Preston, Tennyson, Trevor, Tweedmouth, and Wimborne): seven Barons, Peers of Scotland—the Marquis of Tweeddale (Lord Tweeddale), the Earl of Southesk (Lord Balinhard), the Earl of Strathmore (Lord Bowes), Lord Rollo (Lord Dunning), Lord Napier (Lord Ettrick), and the Lords Elphinstone and Colville of Culross, whose style in both Peerages is the same: one Marquis (Dufferin and Ava), one Viscount (Bridport), and nine Barons, Peers of Ireland—the Earls of Listowel (Lord Hare), Normanton (Lord Somerton), and Arran (Sudley), Viscounts Galway (Lord Monckton), Monck (Lord Monck), and Powerscourt (Lord Powerscourt), and Lords Clermont (Lord Carlingford), Henley (Lord Northington), and Kensington (Lord Kensington): making a grand total of sixty-three legislators, not themselves hereditary, but whose right to legislate will be inherited.

Adding the twenty-three first Peers of the United Kingdom without heirs to the sixty-three with heirs, we get eighty-six Peers of the United Kingdom who had not inherited their

CHAP. III.] COMPOSITION OF THE HOUSE OF LORDS. 45

seats in the House of Lords. Deducting these, with the Duke of Clarence and the Prince of Wales, from the remaining Peers of England, Great Britain, and the United Kingdom, we find that the total number of hereditary legislators, properly so called, was three hundred and eighty-one in a House of five hundred and forty-one members, with, on the other side, one hundred and thirty-two of the Lords Temporal who have not inherited their seats, or, if the Bishops be included, one hundred and fifty-eight members of the House.

We may then classify the House of Lords as follows:—

I. Lords Temporal.
   A. Extraordinary—
      Prince of Wales ⎫
      Duke of Clarence ⎭ 2
   B. Ordinary—
      (I.). Hereditary legislators—
         i. Who have inherited a peerage of England, Great Britain, or the United Kingdom ... 380 ⎫ 381
         ii. Summoned in a father's Barony 1 ⎭
      (II.). New legislators—
         i. New Peers of the United Kingdom—
            a. with heirs ... ... 63 ⎫ 86
            b. without heirs ... 23 ⎭
         ii. Lords and ex-Lords of Appeal 5   132
         iii. Representative Peers of
            a. Scotland ... ... 15 ⎫ 41
            b. Ireland ... ... 26 ⎭

II. Lords Spiritual.
   i. Sitting by right hereditary in the see ... 5 ⎫ 26
   ii. Sitting by seniority ... ... 21 ⎭

Thus in this "House of hereditary legislators," there were one hundred and fifty-eight members who, considered as persons, had not inherited their seats: there were one hundred and fifty-six, for here we must exclude the Dukes of Edinburgh and Connaught, who did not owe their seats to "the accident of birth," less than a third but more than a fourth of the whole assembly : there were seventy who, whether or not in name, were in effect members for life only : and there were fifteen who were not even members for life.

If indeed the Peerage Bill of 1719 had been passed ; if the Whig party of the eighteenth century, the lineal ancestor of the Liberal party of the nineteenth, had succeeded in still further degrading the Monarchy, in opposing fresh and more formidable obstacles to the free exercise of a beneficent prerogative, the House of Lords would long ago have come to consist of "hereditary legislators," and of nothing else. Ceasing to gather up into itself from age to age all the various elements of aristocracy that rise to the surface of our public life, it would have passed into a close corporation, and would, like all such bodies, have been righteously and justly swept away. The attempt of the Whig Peers in the measure of 1719 to convert themselves into a Venetian oligarchy has been deservedly denounced for its double assault, upon the liberty of the people, and upon that power of the Crown, which is the best, the surest, the one certain safeguard of the nation's freedom. But fatal as it must have proved, if carried out, alike to public liberty and to the consecrated symbol and centre of the national existence, the Peerage Bill would in the end have been found out to be still more disastrous to the few great families that had been rash and insane enough to project it. Deprived of every buttress of support, cut off by an impassable moat from the people, and itself the standing memorial of the downfall of the Throne, the House of Lords would have come down with a mighty crash and involved the whole nobility in its ruin.

The Peerage Bill marks the crest of that great wave of resuscitated feudalism and oligarchical ascendency which had achieved its superb and insolent triumph in sweeping away the national dynasty of Stuart. Feudalism, in the strict sense of the word, may be said to have died in England with "the last of the Barons." Perjured more deeply than any man of his faithless generation, a rebel of rebels, a liar of liars, and a traitor of traitors, the false Warwick was a fitting representative of all those arrogant pretensions of the mediæval Baronage which with him happily expired. Though it never carried with it so gigantic and hideous a menace to King and Kingdom as in Germany or France, the power of the great feudal nobles had, even in England, worked a sufficiency of ill. But struck down as it had been by the newly arisen Monarchy under the Houses of York and Tudor, the very King under whom that Monarchy culminated sowed the seeds of the future resurrection of the Baronage. The lavish grants of Church lands bestowed by Henry VIII. at the dissolution of the monasteries on the founders of the future Whig houses, prepared the way for the rise of the plutocratic oligarchy which, allying itself with a Puritan *bourgeoisie*, opened attack on the two great democratic forces of the English Constitution, the Crown and the Church. In sweeping away what he doubtless regarded as the Roman garrison in England, Henry unwittingly created for his successors a far more serious danger than any that lay in the antiquarian pretensions of Emperor or Pope.

"The Reformation," says its Calvinist historian, Merle d'Aubigné—and by "the Reformation" he means, not the Anglican, but the widely different Continental movement bearing that name—"the Reformation was a great middle-class movement." And Professor Thorold Rogers almost echoes his words. "The Puritan movement," he writes of the English analogue to the Continental Reformation, "was essentially and originally one of the middle classes."[*] Everywhere, in Scotland as in England, in Germany and France as in Great Britain, the great nobles allied themselves with Puritanism or with its Continental counterpart, and with a Protestant middle class, in a desperate endeavour to win back, or to increase and perpetuate, their power.

In France feudalism, struck down by Louis XI., revived once more, and cloaking itself in the Geneva gown, rallied to a last effort to achieve the disintegration of the kingdom. "The nobles," as Dean Kitchin puts it, much too euphemisti-

[*] "Economic Interpretation of History," ch. iv.

cally, in his "History of France, "whether from their higher culture, or from their German blood, or from the spirit of independence still strong in them, generally and warmly accepted the Reformation." We may take it that it was, at all events, not "their higher culture" that influenced the French nobles in their desire to bring back and preserve mediæval barbarism and disintegration. The Huguenots, establishing their *imperium in imperio*, soon taught France the true meaning of the ominous alliance. But the great nobles found more than their match in the iron Minister, who paved the way for the civilized and scientific government which, under the Great Monarch, made France the model and admiration of all Europe. Richelieu knew well how to deal with recalcitrant nobles, and brought them to the scaffold by the dozen. In 1642, just before the death of the great Cardinal, the historian notices "twenty-one exiles, all of them the noblest names in France: sixty-five banished: seventy-three prisoners of state: and beheaded or dead in prison forty-three."

In Germany the common cause of Protestantism and feudalism triumphed, nor was it any fortuitous connection that had united them against the Emperor and Pope. Protestantism in Germany, unlike the anti-Papal movement in England, was no outcome of the Renaissance, but its direct antithesis. It was the last word of Teutonic mediævalism against the new birth of the human spirit. What had revolted Luther in Rome was not its superstition, but its enlightenment. The German Reformation was a protest against the Italian Renaissance.

The Peace of Westphalia in 1648, as the outcome of the Thirty Years' War, secured the practical independence of the States ruled by Protestant princes, assigned to them, "originally mere vassals, no greater than a Count of Champagne in France, or an Earl of Chester in England," the rights and powers of Sovereign potentates, and "marks the last stage in the decline of the Empire." The Protestants secured a liberal share of Church lands, the establishment in some States of their religion.

"But," says Professor Bryce, "the substantial advantage remained with the German princes, for they gained the formal recognition of their territorial independence. . . . Germany was forced to drink to its very dregs the cup of feudalism, feudalism from which the feelings that once ennobled it had departed. Properly, indeed, it was no longer an Empire at all, but a Confederation, and that of the loosest sort. For it had no common treasury, no efficient common tribunals, no means of coercing a refractory member; its States were of different religions, were governed according to different forms, were administered judicially and financially without any regard to each other. The representatives of those who had been fief-holders of the first and second rank before the Great Interregnum were now independent potentates: and what had been once a monarchy was now an aristocratic federation."*

In Scotland, the same growth of a vigorous civilization which had proved fatal to the Nevilles in England, destroyed that house of Douglas which, ever since the death of the last Bruce, had been the curse of the Kingdom. The days were over for a time when, as in 1462, an Earl of Douglas and an Earl of Ross could conspire with an English King for the partition of Scotland. But Protestantism soon brought such days back. The "Gospel light" which "shone in Boleyn's eyes" shone for the Scottish Peers and nobles in the Church lands. This was the bribe with which their adhesion was secured to the cause of "pure religion." Henry VIII. had urged his nephew, James V., to follow his example; but the King, whose misplaced chivalry led to the defeat at Flodden, had returned an indignant refusal. His bastard, "the Lord James," afterwards the Regent Moray, entertained no such scruples with regard to this or any other matter, and in conjunction with John Knox the deed was done. The Calvinist clergy secured the Church lands to the great nobles, and in return the great nobles gave the Calvinist clergy a free hand—allowed them to tyrannize over the commonalty, betray the Queen, and place the country at the feet of Elizabeth.

"The resources of the Church were enormous: it has been estimated, though the estimate is probably much exaggerated, that the clergy drew in one form or another half of the annual income of the land. . . . If the title of the aristocracy to the

---

* Bryce, "Holy Roman Empire."

patrimony of the Church of Rome [Scotland?] had not been identified with Protestantism, it is probable that the Church of Knox would have been short-lived."* Thus in Scotland as in England a party was created, at first calling itself Protestant and afterwards Whig, whose opposition to historic Christianity, and to the Crown as the ally of the Church, was based on the most solid of all reasons. Quickly as the zeal of the great nobles cooled for "the religion," its maintenance had now become identified with their own interests.

In England, as in Scotland, the feudal spirit revived through the plunder of the Church. The great nobles allied themselves with the Continental Reformation, and with those who sought to reproduce it in England, against the Crown, the Church, the lesser nobility or "gentry," and the masses of the people. "The politics of the first Revolution and the politics of the second were equally aristocratic," as the late Mr. Thorold Rogers, himself a vehement Radical member of Parliament, expressed it. And this judgment is strikingly confirmed from an opposite quarter. "The first Reform Bill," wrote Lord Beaconsfield, "sounded the knell of 'the cause for which Hampden died on the field, and Sidney on the scaffold.'" The names and number of the Peers, and Peers' eldest sons, who sided with the Parliament in the Great Rebellion are sufficient evidence of these assertions. Amongst them were the Earls of Pembroke, Leicester, Lincoln, Rutland, Northumberland, Essex, Warwick, Stamford, Bedford, Salisbury, Manchester, Musgrave, and Bolingbroke, Lord Wharton, Lord Saye and Sele, Lord Brooke, Lord Delawarr, Lord Fairfax, Lord Robartes, Lord Howard, Lord Willoughby, Lord St. John, and Lord Fielding.

What these lords had in view was the work successfully accomplished half a century later by their Whig successors. But they reckoned without their host. Behind them was that power which sooner or later mounts to the top in every Revolution. When the Crown went, the House of Lords went with it; when the Bishops had been expelled, the Peers soon followed them, to be followed in their turn at no distant

* Skelton, "Scotland under Mary Stuart."

date by the House of Commons which had by vote abolished them. One by one the institutions of the country disappeared, till there was no power left but the army, nor in that army any power but Cromwell. The ambitious and incompetent aristocrats who had aspired to direct the Great Rebellion to their own advantage, were thrust aside by the stern Puritan soldier with as little ceremony, if not as much contempt, as was shown later by Napoleon in sweeping from his path the sanguinary imbeciles of the French Revolution.

After the Restoration their vigour to some extent revived, and showed itself in the furious assaults upon the Monarchy, led by the astute Earl of Shaftesbury. Beaten at every point by Charles II., their leaders beheaded or driven into exile ere his death, the impatience and want of address of James II. and VII., coupled with his religious monomania, at last gave them the opportunity of which they were in search. Though the danger threatened by that Monarch to the position of the Church of England was as nothing to the menace since constantly held out to her by the party who dragged him from the throne, nor the changes attempted by him in the English Universities to be compared for a moment in point of gravity with those carried out in our own day by the University Commissioners, skilfully exaggerated and misrepresented they served to alienate the Anglican clergy and laity from the House of Stuart at this most critical period of its fortunes. The Church, for the first and last time since the break with Rome, deserted the Monarchy, and has suffered the penalty of ill-doing ever since. Triumphant for an hour under Anne, partly in consequence of too precipitate Whig persecution, she tasted to the full in the ensuing reigns of the sweet cup of Revolution settlement. Her Convocation silenced, her episcopal bench flooded with Deist and Socinian bishops, the nominees of the Duchess of Kendal or Sir Robert Walpole, the sycophants of some foreign mistress of an alien king, she has never to this day succeeded in recovering the constitutional liberty assured to her by the Great Charter of English freedom, the free self-government which is not refused to the humblest Dissenting sect in the land. The people, deceived at the moment by the lying fable, deliberately concocted to seduce them, that the Prince of Wales was no true son of the King, discovered too late how they had been tricked and gulled. The Tory section of the titled and untitled aristocracy, excluded by degrees from power, paid the penalty of their error in political ostracism from the accession of the House of Hanover to that of George the Third.

Under the Prince of Orange, whose one thought was of his native Holland, and who used England merely as a convenient weapon against Louis XIV., the insolence of the Whig oligarchy was to some extent restrained by the knowledge that William had only to go to put their necks in the utmost peril. "The reign of William the Third, as Mr. Hallam happily says, was the Nadir of the national prosperity. It was also the Nadir of the national character." * Such is the deliberate judgment of the two great Whig historians on this age of degradation, in which virtue was the only thing that seemed unnatural. William, who never condescended to dissimulate his deep contempt for the twofold traitors who surrounded him, refused to put himself wholly into the hands of the Whigs, and treated their grandees with an open scorn which was only too well merited. A contemplation of this reign and the debased beings who crowd it will reveal, what must otherwise remain a mystery, whence it was that Swift derived the dreadful inspiration of "Gulliver's Travels." His own Yahoos never equalled in the utter vileness of their degradation the courtiers of Kensington and Hampton Court.

Under Anne, too, the Whigs had not yet reached the fullness of their triumph. Herself a Stuart, she buoyed up the people with hopes of the succession of her brother, and leaned for support on the great democratic force of the Church. "We hope your Majesty is for High Church and Doctor Sacheverell," was the cry that met her in the streets, and the hopes of the people were in this respect fulfilled. Had the voice of the people been able to assert itself then as

* Macaulay, "Essay on Hallam's Constitutional History."

it can now, not even the honourable but unfortunate adhesion to the Church of Rome of him who was of right King James the Third and Eighth could have prevented a second and happier Restoration.

But though the hearts of the people were with their exiled princes, the power of the country on the death of Anne had come through a bold *coup d'état* into the hands of the Whig houses. Then they introduced their dummy Sovereigns, and for the best part of two reigns misgoverned the three Kingdoms in their name. As we have seen, they attempted to turn the House of Lords into a close corporation, " independent of the Crown, irresponsible to the people." A House of Commons elected under their influence, by a fraudulent malversation of the public confidence, extended the term of its own existence from three years to seven. Never had the power of the Crown and the people sunk so low. Britain was then, what she never has been since, "a disguised Republic," and a Republic whose scanty and suggestive veil served but to emphasize its true indecency and shamelessness.

The substitution of a foreign line for the native royal family was for the Whigs a masterstroke of policy, for a Monarchy in ceasing to be national loses the one sole reason of its existence. And now in the noontide of their triumph they anticipated the sordid maxim of the American demagogue, that the spoils of victory are to the conquerors. They rewarded themselves, and sought to consolidate their power, with a gigantic system of corruption, bribery, and public robbery such as no modern wirepuller in the United States themselves has as yet succeeded in outdoing. But the political philosophy of Henry St. John, the true founder of modern Toryism, at length yielded its first fruits. A patriot statesman who had taken a leading part in the overthrow of Sir Robert Walpole prepared the way for a patriot King. On the accession of the Monarch who gloried in the name of Briton, the House of Hanover received that tardy moral assent of the three nations of the British Isles which was necessary to make good the original defect of its title in strict legal and constitutional validity. Now, once again, the people rejoiced in a national and truly legitimate King, and before the revived Monarchy the power of the Whig houses melted away like the mists of night before the morning sun.

George the Third restored the Monarchy, and saved the House of Lords. From a Whig oligarchy he changed the House of Lords into a Tory aristocracy; from a small and exclusive body, almost the private property of a limited number of great families, he converted it into a living representation of the principal elements of aristocracy then existing in the Britannic State. He saved the House of Lords from the unfailing ruin that the Whig families would have brought upon it, and he saved the Whig families from themselves. He threw the doors of the Imperial Senate wide open to enterprise and genius. He so broadened, and deepened, and strengthened its foundations that the House has emerged with success and unabated vitality from all the party conflicts and democratic changes of the nineteenth century. But for George the Third, the House of Lords would never have survived the first Reform Bill. But for George the Third, the Whig families would to-day sulk powerless and forgotten in a Faubourg St. Germain. As in his own person he had restored the national character of the Monarchy, so he proceeded to restore the national character of the House of Lords: to win for it the respect and attachment of the people instead of that hatred which of late years they had justly extended to it, to reform it from the mausoleum of a dead feudalism into a Pantheon of demigods and heroes, a Westminster Abbey of immortal names, the appointed shrine and resting-place of genius and eminence in every branch of the public service, in every department of the nation's life, where the people might on all sides feast their eyes with the living monuments of noble action.

It was for this beneficent and patriotic achievement, well-worthy of one who all his lifetime was "the people's King," that George the Third has been stigmatized as a dullard and unscrupulous by men who as regards intelligence and honesty would have been unfit to clean the royal stables. The nauseous cant of the professional apologists engaged by the Whig families to defend the misdeeds of their ancestors has been erected into a sort of stereotyped formula to be glibly repeated by every tenth-hand thinker who seeks to pass for an authority. That the Radicals may, from a partisan point of view, have just grounds of complaint against a Sovereign but for whom the House of Lords would not now be in existence, may readily be granted them. But that the Whig families, and their champions, should revile the memory of the Monarch but for whom they and all their absurd, impossible pretensions would be as utterly extinct as the dodo, is the blackest and basest of ingratitude.

Oligarchy, which is the vicious excess of aristocracy, is inconsistent and incompatible with monarchy and with democracy, but aristocracy in its just mean is the support and the defence of both. Aristocracy is an element of stability in a State. A dynasty may be destroyed, or a people fall under the rule of a military tyrant; but an aristocracy is too numerous to be easily exterminated, and too pertinacious to be easily subdued. But an oligarchy, such as that of ancient Venice, almost precludes the existence of an even nominal Monarch, and absolutely precludes any true or real participation of the people in the government.

Bearing in mind that the late Professor Freeman used the word "aristocracy," not in its generally accepted modern sense, but as synonymous with oligarchy, his weighty declaration on the subject is worth quoting.

" It is only in a republic that a real aristocracy [oligarchy] can exist. Corinth and Rome, Venice and Geneva, Bern and Nürrberg bear out what I am saying. Aristocracy in its true sense [oligarchy] is something essentially republican, something to which the monarchic state can present only a faint approach. So far as a monarchic state is aristocratic [oligarchic], as our own country has been at some times [e.g. under the first two Georges], it can only be in proportion to the degree that, through the lessening of the powers both of the Crown and of the people, it approaches to a commonwealth in the hands of certain ruling families." *

George the Third changed the House of Lords from the vicious and intriguing oligarchy into which it had degenerated,

* " Comparative Politics."

into a loyal and useful aristocracy. It is to him especially that we must refer the beginning of the gradual transformation, still proceeding, in substance and character, though not in outward form, of the Lords Temporal, from a feudal and mediæval Baronage into a modern and Imperial Senate. Under him the Peerage began to be less exclusively connected with the possession of great estates, and to pass into the customary reward of definite services to the nation, and the recognized receiving-house of those who have held high civil or military office.

PART II.

THE RADICAL CASE AGAINST THE HOUSE OF LORDS.

CHAPTER I.

THE RADICAL CASE AGAINST THE LORDS TEMPORAL AS A NOBILITY.

IT has been seen in the foregoing chapters that that portion of the House of Lords known as the Lords Temporal was by King George the Third reformed from a Whig oligarchy into a Tory aristocracy. "On the accession of George III.," writes Erskine May, "when the domination of the great Whig families had lasted for nearly half a century, the House of Lords was mainly Whig. Hence it was that, on the accession of William IV., when the Tory rule commenced under Lord Bute, strengthened by Lord North, and consolidated by Mr. Pitt, had enjoyed ascendency for an even longer period, the House of Lords was mainly Tory." And Tory in the main the House of Lords has continued to be down to the present day. Notwithstanding the fact that Whig or Liberal Administrations have held office during the greater part of the Queen's reign, the politics of the Lords Temporal are a standing grievance with the Liberal party.

In the space of time that elapsed between the accession of Her Majesty in June, 1837, and the formation of the second Salisbury Ministry in August, 1886, the Liberal or Whig party had held office for more than thirty-two years, and the Tories or Conservatives for less than seventeen. On the first of January, 1892, one hundred and six peerages of the United Kingdom—one hundred and four, subtracting those of Albany and Edinburgh—were in existence which had been created on the advice of Liberal Ministers during this period, and only fifty-seven, or subtracting Connaught fifty-six, which had been created on the advice of Tory Ministers or of Sir Robert Peel. If we take into account only those United Kingdom peerages which were in existence on the date specified, we find that Lord Melbourne, whose Administration, formed under King William, lasted into the present reign for four years after the Queen's accession, advised in those four years the creation of twenty new United Kingdom peerages—fourteen for Commoners, three for Scottish Peers, and three for Peers of Ireland. Lord John Russell in his Ministry of July, 1846, became responsible for six new United Kingdom peerages—three bestowed on Commoners, one on a Scottish Peer, and two on Peers of Ireland; and, as Earl Russell, in his Ministry of November, 1865, became responsible for six more—four bestowed on Commoners, and two on Peers of Ireland. During the Administration of Lord Palmerston, formed in February, 1855, four United Kingdom peerages were created for Commoners, and three for Irish Peers; and under his ministry of June, 1859, eight were created for Commoners, and one for a Peer of Scotland. Mr. Gladstone, in his first Administration of December, 1868, advised the creation of twenty-three new peerages—seventeen for Commoners, four for Scottish, two for Irish Peers; in his second Administration of April, 1880, he advised the creation of twenty-eight new peerages—nineteen for Commoners, four for Scottish, and five for Irish Peers; and in his third Administration, lasting a hundred and seventy-eight days, of February, 1886, he advised the creation of seven new peerages —six for Commoners, and one for an Irish Peer.

Now, if we turn to the other side, we shall find that Sir Robert Peel, in his Ministry of September, 1841, was responsible for three new peerages, all bestowed on Commoners. Lord Derby, in his ministry of February, 1852, advised the creation of two new peerages, both for Commoners; in his Ministry of February, 1858, he advised the creation of five new peerages, all for Commoners; and in his Ministry of July, 1866, the creation of six new peerages —three for Commoners, and three for Irish Peers. Under the Disraeli Administration of February, 1868, seven new peerages were created—five for Commoners, and two for Irish Peers. Under the Disraeli Administration of February, 1874, twenty-one new peerages were created—seventeen for Commoners, two for Scottish, and two for Irish Peers. Under the Salisbury Administration of June, 1885, thirteen new peerages were created—eleven for Commoners, and two for Peers of Scotland.

This enumeration, it is proper to observe, does not include the Lords and ex-Lords of Appeal, who, as regards both the origin and the tenure of their peerages, form a distinct class of Peers. Nor have the peerages of ladies created Peeresses in their own right been taken into account unless, as in the case of the Earldom of Cromarty, they now seat a Peer in the House of Lords.

Studying these figures, we see at once that the Conservatives have shown far greater moderation in advising the creation of new peerages than their political opponents, and that, if during the last decade or two they display a tendency to vie with the Liberals, this may be reasonably accounted for by their previous long exclusion from power, and the increasing number of Liberal creations. We see further that it needed only eight more Liberal creations to make them outnumber the Conservative by two to one; that out of the hundred and six Liberal creations no less than fifty-eight, or nearly three in five, were made on the advice of Mr. Gladstone; and that these Gladstonian peerages, taken by themselves, were more numerous than all the Tory peerages created in the present reign up to the year 1886.

It should be noted, too, that the number of Liberal creations might have been augmented by counting the Barony of Campbell created in 1839 on the advice of Lord Melbourne, and the Barony of Eddisbury created in 1848 on the advice of Lord John Russell; but, insomuch as these peerages have since been united respectively with the Barony of Stratheden created in 1836, and that of Stanley of Alderley created in 1839, it seemed scarcely fair to include them. On the same principle, the 1847 Barony of Acheson, the 1861 Barony of Herbert of Lea, and the 1864 Barony of Buckhurst, created on the advice of Liberal Ministers, have been excluded, as since united with English, Great British, or United Kingdom peerages of earlier creation. But the inheritance of the old English Barony of Dacre, descendible through females, by the first Viscount Hampden, has not been held to affect the creation of the latter peerage descending to heirs male, nor, in like manner has the inheritance of the Barony of Willoughby d'Eresby by the present Lord Ancaster been held to affect this United Kingdom Barony of 1856. No notice has been taken of promotions in rank, for a Baron being the Peer of a Duke has no more power and no less; nor did the United Kingdom Dukedom of Gordon conferred in 1876 on the Duke of Richmond in any way affect his English peerage.

Notwithstanding the vast preponderance of Liberal over Conservative creations in the last fifty or sixty years, the Tory party possesses on most questions a great, on some questions an overwhelming, majority in the House of Lords. An excess of forty-nine creations over those of their opponents has not only failed to give the Liberals a majority in the Upper Chamber, but has not even enabled them to hold their own. There has been, and is, a great growing divergence of opinion on all questions of policy, foreign or domestic, Imperial or insular, between the House of Lords and the Liberal party in Great Britain. One or the other of them, either the Liberal party in Great Britain or else the House of Lords, must, it is clear, be in the wrong, and greatly in the wrong. It is perhaps not unnatural in the circumstances that the Liberal party in Great Britain, unable otherwise to account satisfactorily for the phenomenon, has arrived at the conclusion that there is something seriously amiss with the House of Lords. Seeing that not even Gladstonian creations can appreciably affect their permanent minority, the Radicals have discovered that the fault lies in the constitution of the Upper Chamber. Angry dissatisfaction, concisely expressed in the demand that the House of Lords shall be "ended or mended," in other words abolished or reformed, finds vent in multitudinous complaints based on various and often inconsistent grounds. Sometimes it is the presence of the Bishops in the House of Lords that is objected to, although the episcopal bench takes but a small part, perhaps too small a part, in current politics, and although it would be difficult to adduce a measure in the last thirty years bearing even remotely upon current politics, the fortune of which has been materially affected by their opposition, with the single exception of the Deceased Wife's Sister Bill. Sometimes it is "the hereditary principle" that is arraigned with pompous incoherence, and we are told that the House of Lords ought to be abolished because every eldest son of a great man does not as a matter of course inherit the paternal genius. Sometimes it is alleged vaguely that the House of Lords "oppresses the people," and it cannot be denied that the House of Lords has prevented a good many cherished projects of the English Liberal party from passing into law, and has seriously retarded the passage into law of many others. Sometimes, again,—and this, in the mouth of Radicals, is perhaps the strangest objection of all, the House of Lords, with which they identify the Peerage and confound the nobility, is charged with being a parvenu imposture, with putting forward claims which would be tenable enough if advanced, say, by the German Granddukes or the French Dukes and Peers before the Revolution, but can only be laughed at in the case of such a modern, mushroom growth as the Peerage of the British Empire.

Now, the bishops, as we have already seen, in 1892 constituted not a twentieth part of the Upper Chamber, and until the recent innovation of Life Peers they were the only life members of that assembly who were not also Hereditary Peers. They form, and always have formed, considered as individuals, a democratic element in the House of Lords, though from another and not inconsistent point of view, regarded as officials, they may be said to represent the aristocracy of beneficence and virtue. The Radicals, however, would scarcely, it is to be presumed, allege the presence of the Bishops as a sufficient reason for its abolition were the House of Lords in other respects fortunate enough to meet with their approval.

Nor, again, would "the hereditary principle" stand in any danger of being called in question if its practical working were now, as it was once, to give a standing Liberal majority in the Upper Chamber. The proof of a pudding is in the eating, and to the Radical mind the disproof of this pudding lies in its disagreement with the Radical digestion. The real offence of the House of Lords is that the majority of its members are Tory, or at least anti-Radical. The supposed absurdity and mischief of "the hereditary principle" is only an after thought, and, as we shall see later, far from a happy one.

We come next to the charge that the House of Lords " oppresses the people," and if this charge were true, it would be a sufficient reason for its abolition. So sufficient would it be, indeed, that to the mere stupid Tory all the other reasons suggested would appear superfluous. But for our Radical friends, conscious perhaps of their inability to establish this charge, which we shall presently examine, this is not enough. No, they say, not only does the aristocracy oppress the people but it is not aristocratic : it commits murder, and it drops its *h*'s. If the House of Lords really oppressed the people, it would, surely, be no defence that each member of it, to quote Mr. Andrew Lang, was "a direct descendant of the Dukes of Edom mentioned in Holy Writ." But this is not enough for the Radicals. Choosing to confound the House of Lords with the Peerage, and the nobility with both, they declare that this nobility is not noble, that this aristocracy is not aristocratic.

It has been seen already that the Peerage is not identical with the House of Lords, nor even with the Lords Temporal, and that neither the House of Lords, nor the Lords Temporal, nor the Peerage, nor all three together, are identical with the nobility. The Peerage is a Baronage, and the Lords Temporal embrace only a portion, though the greater portion of the Peerage ; and the House of Lords was never intended to comprehend the aristocracy but to represent it. The fact that there are thousands of men outside the House of better family than some of those who sit inside it, is a necessary feature of its constitution, a necessary, unavoidable, and most desirable outcome of that great law of primogeniture which has made the Peerage an order, not a caste. The Lords Temporal are no foreign noblesse, but a body of legislators, counsellors, and judges; and in some cases hereditary legislators and judges, in other cases legislators and judges for a term of life or less, in nearly all cases hereditary counsellors.

The House of Lords, say the Radicals, and by the House of Lords they mean the Peerage, which they also confound with the nobility, is not aristocratic. They allege against the House of Lords a lack of antiquity and a lack of distinction. Nothing is more common than to meet the assertion that Lord Beaconsfield "exposed" or "refuted" or "disproved" the House of Lords, in his early novel of "Coningsby." They might as well claim that he "refuted" the Aurora Borealis, that he "disproved" the Gulf Stream, or that he "exposed" the Equator. The antiquity of the Peerage is no question of the opinion of any individual, however illustrious or eminent, but of hard facts and legal evidence. It is easy to understand that minds emasculated by the habitual attribution of divine infallibility to every chance utterance of a political Grand Lama should seek to quote Mr. Disraeli against the Earl of Beaconsfield; but "the stupid party" has no Pope. The Liberal party may, if it will, bind itself to Mr. Gladstone's discovery of the Athanasian Creed in Homer, but the Tory party is not pledged to every chapter of Lord Beaconsfield's novels. It is possible, one may hope, to admire Lord Chatham, and yet reject his well-known description of the Church of England as having "a Popish liturgy, a Calvinistic creed, and an Arminian clergy." And it is possible to admire Lord Beaconsfield, and reject his baseless sneer of "the Mass in masquerade" levelled at that which, as a sober fact of history, is nothing else than the mass itself, done into English from the Sarum Mass Book, in parts amplified and in parts condensed. If Lord Beaconsfield, or rather Mr. Disraeli, had attempted to "disprove" the House of Lords, that would have been unfortunate—for Mr. Disraeli. But as a matter of fact he attempted nothing of the sort. His earlier novels were directed to show how a Whig oligarchy had usurped the name of the people of England, and endeavoured to reduce the Sovereign to a Venetian Doge. And he pointed out, with force and truth, that the families most active in that assault upon the Monarchy in the seventeenth century which is known as the Revolution of 1688, were the same families who had been most active in that assault upon the Church in the sixteenth century which is known as the dissolution of the monasteries, and who had founded their fortunes on that episode of sacrilegious spoliation. It was not his design, nor, had it been his design, would it have been in his power, or in that of any other man, to establish what is not the case, namely, that the Lords Temporal or the Peers are as a whole deficient either in antiquity or nobility of origin. Lord Beaconsfield had a magnificent disregard for minute accuracy in matters of detail, and chance expressions might, no doubt, be culled from his works reflecting on the Peerage, as there might also be culled from the Bible expressions reflecting on the Deity. And in this very novel of "Coningsby" there are some harsh remarks upon the Peerage which, had Lord Beaconsfield put them forward in a speech, would go far to explain the Radical assertion. But these remarks are not made by Coningsby nor by any other personage in the book who might even conceivably pass for Lord Beaconsfield himself. They are put into the mouth of a Radical manufacturer, one Millbank; and we have no more right to identify the artist with his creation in this case than to identify Shakespeare with Bottom or Christopher Sly. "Collier," says Lord Macaulay in his "Essay on the Dramatists of the Restoration," —" Collier blames Vanbrugh for putting into Lord Foppington's mouth some contemptuous expressions respecting the Church service; though it is obvious than Vanbrugh could not better express reverence than by making Lord Foppington express contempt."

But since this passage in Coningsby is frequently misapplied and misunderstood by persons who unfortunately fail to devote any attention to the study of Lord Beaconsfield's works as a whole, it may be as well perhaps to give it in full.

"'An ancient lineage!' said Mr. Millbank, 'I never heard of a peer with an ancient lineage. . . . I can point you out Saxon families in this country who can trace their pedigree beyond the Conquest; I know of some Norman gentlemen whose families undoubtedly came over with the Conqueror. But a peer with an ancient lineage is to me quite a novelty. No, no; the thirty years of the Wars of the Roses freed us from those gentlemen. I take it after the battle of Tewkesbury a Norman baron was almost as rare a being in England as a wolf is now.'

"'I have always understood,' said Coningsby, 'that our peerage was the finest in Europe.'

"'From themselves,' said Millbank, 'and the heralds they pay to paint their carriages. But I go to facts. When Henry VII. called his first Parliament there were only twenty-nine temporal peers to be found, and even some of them took their seats illegally, for they had been attainted. Of these twenty-five not five remain; and they, as the Howards for instance, are not Norman nobility. We owe the English peerage to three sources: the spoliation of the Church, the open and flagrant sale of honours by the elder Stuarts, and the boroughmongering of our own times. These are the three main sources of the existing peerage of England, and in my opinion disgraceful ones.'"

Would it be possible to draw a more striking picture of the latter-day, unreasonable Radical, the superfine gentleman for whom the system which contents the Talbots and Courtenays, the Butlers and Fitzgeralds, the Douglases and Gordons, is too *bourgeois* or too democratic? Lord Beaconsfield appears to have divined by anticipation the criticisms of Mr. Labouchere and Professor Bryce. No one is ever quite such a terrible and exacting aristocrat as the man who seeks to abolish the House of Lords. In his strictures on the Peerage he is wont to remind one of the German Chapter which rejected the candidature of Louis XIV. on account of his Medici grandmother, the spouse in second nuptials of le Roi Galant.

But let us "go to facts," and we shall see that Lord Beaconsfield with fine dramatic feeling, not perhaps obvious to a political Dissenter, endowed Mr. Millbank with just so much light as to make his darkness the more visible. So far from there not being five of the Lords Temporal of date anterior to the reign of Henry VII., there were in January,

1892, no less than forty-one actual members of the House of Lords in their own right, and potential members only debarred from sitting by reason of their age or sex, with English, Scottish, or Irish Peerages of date anterior to 1485; and of these a score were English.

A subsequent creation does not cancel or annul an earlier peerage. Thus the third Baron Barnard was created Earl of Darlington, and the third Earl of Darlington was created Marquis and Duke of Cleveland. The Dukedom, Marquisate, and Earldom became extinct with the fourth Duke a short time since, and there is again a Lord Barnard sitting under that title in the House of Lords. In considering the aristocratic character of the Peerage, if stress is to be laid upon antiquity, we must go to the first peerage of a Lord Temporal, not the last; and in the case of Scottish and Irish Peers we must go, not to the Great British or United Kingdom Peerage which gives them a seat in the House of Lords, but to their first creation in the Scottish or Irish Peerage.

Sometimes Peers after gaining or inheriting a peerage have succeeded to the representation of a peerage of more ancient date originally in another family, and in such case they are entitled to the full benefit, whatever that may be, of its antiquity. But in considering the origin of their seat in the House of Lords, they are entitled to put forward whichever peerage may give them the best moral claim to sit there.

There are thirteen English Peers and Peeresses of date anterior to 1485 whose rank and title have remained the same as at the creation of their peerage:—Lords de Ros, de Clifford, Hastings, and Mowbray, of thirteenth century creation; Lords Beaumont, Zouche, Willoughby de Eresby, Grey de Ruthyn, Clinton, and Camoys, dating from the fourteenth century; the Earl of Shrewsbury, the Baroness Berners, and the Baroness Berkeley, dating from 1442, 1455, and 1421.

But, besides these, there are others, whose antiquity in the Baronage is obscured by the comparative modernness of their higher titles—such as the Dukes of Norfolk, Beaufort, Leinster, and others. If this list be examined, it will be found that there are no less than thirty-eight actual members of the House of Lords with peerages anterior to 1485, and three more who are only debarred from sitting in it by reason of their age or sex; and these are just as "Norman" as they ever were. If they are not more "Norman" it is because Baronies by writ did not exist in Norman days, and because the now-prevailing system of the descent of peerages to heirs male was not invented by the lawyers till generations after the Conquest. Out of these forty-one Peers and Peeresses the Fitzgeralds, the Butlers, the Fitzmaurices, the Lindsays, the Frazers, the Gordons, the Talbots, the Montgomeries, are undoubtedly "Norman;" the Somersets being Plantagenets are Angevin or Breton; the Nevilles are Saxon; the Campbells and Kennedys are better than "Norman," being Gaelic.

The House of Normandy, even including Stephen, did not reign for a hundred years all told, and most of the great Norman houses that came in with the Conqueror soon perished in subsequent rebellions. But a vast number of French and other Continental families settled in England under the Plantagenets; and a large proportion of the men who "came over with the Conqueror" were not Normans at all, but Flemings, Bretons, and other foreign adventurers, attracted by the hope of plunder and high pay from all parts of France, if not of the Continent. National vanity has sought to disguise from the English people by the use of the word "Norman," and pedantic flourishes and phantasies concerning the Teutonic race, that it was in fact a French Conquest. But contemporaries express this latter view. The victors of Hastings are called French on the Bayeux Tapestry as in the Irish Annals of Ulster and Innisfallen, and their descendants who settled in Scotland were described as French in the Charters of those Gaelic Kings who so greatly favoured them. It is not a little amusing that the same ill-mannered and illiberal school of Teutomaniacs who persist in calling all the English-speaking peoples Englishmen in spite of Scottish, Irish, Canadian, Afrikander, and Australasian repudiations of "English" nationality, refuse to call the French-speaking "Normans" Frenchmen in spite of the fact that a large proportion of them had nothing to do with Normandy at all.

If we turn to the Irish Peerage, in and out of the House of Lords, we find no less than twenty-four Peers either descended from those "Norman" settlers who became more Irish than the Irish, or, being of Celtic or Danish family, from those who were there before the arrival of the "Normans;" and all these are actual or potential members of the House of Lords. The Marquis of Ormonde, the Earls of Carrick and Lanesborough, Lord Mountgarret, and Lord Dunboyne are Butlers; the Duke of Leinster is a Fitzgerald; the Earl of Kerry and Shelburne (Marquis of Lansdowne) is a Fitzmaurice; the Marquis of Clanricarde and the Earl of Mayo are De Burghs or Burkes; Lord Kinsale is a De Courcy; the Earl of Howth is a St. Lawrence; while such a name as Lord Talbot de Malahide speaks for itself. The Earl of Fingall, Lord Dunsany, and Lord Louth are Plunkets; while the native Irish element is represented by Lord Dunraven, Lord Clanwilliam, Lord Inchiquin, Lord Guillamore, Lord Lismore, and Lord Dunsandle. To these must be added the later English settlers in Ireland of "Norman" origin, such as the Lords Carew and the Brabazons, Earls of Meath; settlers of Scoto-Norman family, like the Lords Castle-Stewart; and Peers of Scoto-Gaelic, that is to say pure Scottish, race, like the Lords Macdonald.

The "Wars of the Roses" did not affect "the Norman barons" of Scotland, nor what Mr. Skene delights in calling her "old Celtic earldoms." The Scottish Peerage has a fair proportion of Peers of Norman family in the Duke of Lennox, the Marquises of Huntly and Tweeddale, the Earls of Aberdeen, Caithness, Crawford, Dalhousie, Bute, Elgin, Galloway, Kinnoull, Melville, Moray, Lindsay, and Orkney, Viscount Falkland, Lord Balfour of Burleigh, Lord Colville of Culross, Lord Lovat, Lord Saltoun, and Lord Blantyre, to give those only whose Norman descent is a matter of absolute and proven certainty. But the Scottish Peers not of Norman origin are as a rule of much older native families. In England and Ireland the native landlords were largely dispossessed or swept away by successive waves of foreign invasion and conquest. But in Scotland, which was never a conquered country, which has nothing in its history resembling or even distantly approaching either the Roman, or the Saxon, or the Danish, or the Norman Conquest, the landowners up to the beginning of the present century represented, for the most part, either by direct male descent or through the marriage of heiresses, the old Celtic landed proprietary dating from time immemorial. Their ethnic origin was concealed from view by the territorial surnames which they assumed under feudal influence in the twelfth century, just as the Highland lairds at a later date came to be commonly addressed and mentioned by the names of their estates. The "Norman," Flemish, and other foreign families who settled in Scotland, came not as conquerors, but as fortune-hunters, or, as the apostles of the French culture then fashionable throughout western Europe, on the invitation of the Scottish Kings, full of that hunger and thirst after civilization and good government which they transmitted to their Stuart descendants.

"Before the death of William the Lion [1214] one of the old Celtic earldoms had passed by succession into the hands of a foreign baron. William Comyn, the head of the Norman house of that name, became possessed of the Earldom of Buchan by his marriage with Marjory, daughter of Fergus, the last Celtic earl." *

With these Norman, or rather French, families came a far smaller number of Saxon origin, refugees from the Conquest, or in the household of Queen St. Margaret, who were settled in Scotland by the enlightened policy of her Celtic princes to further their own just pretensions to the English throne. The supposed foreign descent of many Scottish families which fatally misled the historian Palgrave has been effectively disproved by the researches and learning of Mr. W. F. Skene and the late Mr. E. W. Robertson. The old mania

* Skene.

for deriving every distinguished clan or family from elsewhere or some one else, the Clan Chattan, for example, from the Catti, and so forth, was only another form of the old mania for deriving every long word in the English vocabulary "through Latin from the Greek, and so from the Hebrew." The groundless fictions which passed muster in a former day with a pre-scientific generation have been disposed of by the patient investigation and laborious research of Dr. Skene, who is an historian, not a "herald," and who, in exploding the mythical foreign descent of the Grants, Campbells, Camerons, Macleans, Mackenzies, and others, has done more to sweep away spurious pedigrees than the most hostile critic of the Peerage.

Again, what can be more preposterous than Mr. Millbank's protest against the Howards as not being of Norman descent in the male line? We have already seen that the limitation of peerages to heirs male was not so much as introduced for several centuries after the Conquest, that it is in fact a modern innovation on the older system of descent. Even after the later system was introduced the Crown never abandoned its right of naming any line of descent in the patent of creation. There is no especial sanctity about heirs male; the descent of a peerage through males exclusively is *primâ facie* evidence of a modern, rather than an ancient origin. It is no more ridiculous for the Percys of Northumberland to be represented by a Smithson than for the Braganzas of Portugal to be represented by a Coburg. The Crowns of Britain, Spain, and Russia all pass through and to females. Formerly the Crowns of many other countries did so; that they do not pass in this way now has been due to the spread of absurd and pernicious German ideas of aristocracy, and to the success of German princes, of not more distinguished origin at best than a Duke of Leinster or a Duke of Argyll, in giving themselves out for Royalties. The original fraud of German Kings pretending to be Roman Emperors has been outdone by the less antique imposture of German Dukes pretending to be Kings. They, like the Sovereigns of the Court of Pumpernickel, have succeeded in persuading the world to accept them at their own high and mighty valuation. But aristocracy, like monarchy, and like democracy, requires to be handled with tact and reason: like them it is no mathematical formula, but a free outcome of the human spirit. Birth has always been reverenced among all Aryan nations, but there is always a danger of poetry freezing into etiquette. The Peerage, as it now exists, is an attempt of the nation to give expression to its natural reverence for its great men, and to embalm and preserve their memory. The House of Lords is an unconscious hero-worship. There is no more reason to reject aristocracy on account of the German and Hindu caste systems than to reject monarchy on account of Russia, or democracy on account of Hayti. There is nothing that cannot be burlesqued.

But if some of the Radicals base their attack upon the House of Lords on a misunderstanding of Lord Beaconsfield, there are others whose less-guarded strictures are conceived rather in the vein of the romantic lady novelist. "His earldom," writes Ouida, in her novel "Syrlin," of Lord Avilion and Pontefract, a wicked nobleman who resents the consolation proffered to his wife by a virtuous French actor— "his earldom had its existence in the days of Ethelred ; and such ancientness of date is extremely rare in England, where the aristocracy as a rule is as modern as the railway stations which they attach to their park gates." "Such ancientness of date" is indeed "rare in England," so rare as to be unknown; nor does Ouida's exception at all assist in establishing her rule. Without wishing to lay stress on the charming feminine exaggeration of a writer who is always delightful, never dull, the latter part of Ouida's sentence provides such a capital summary of the Radical position—or, to put it in another way, the Radicals, in their attack upon the Peerage, are so extremely Ouidaesque, though not always delightful, and sometimes, it must be owned, a trifle dull—that it would be impossible to do better than take it for a text.

It is difficult for the low Tory order of intellect to understand this new Radical craze for mere antiquity. The point, surely, with regard to any given peerage, is not its antiquity, but what it represents.

> "But by your fathers' worth if yours you rate,
> Count me those only who were good and great.
> Go! if your ancient but ignoble blood
> Has crept through scoundrels ever since the Flood.
> Go! and pretend your family is young,
> Nor own your fathers have been fools so long.
> What can ennoble sots, or slaves, or cowards?
> Alas! not all the blood of all the Howards."

So was this ethical truth, which ought to be a truism, expressed long ago in the sublime verse of that "Essay on Man," which the great Tory poet dedicated to the great Tory statesman, Bolingbroke. It is remarkable, certainly, that one of the oldest of our institutions should be attacked by the party "of progress," on the ground that for the members of that party it is too new. This bitter cry of the Liberation Society that the House of Lords is insufficiently mediæval is, to the Tory ear, not a little bewildering. The morbid craving for mere antiquity reminds one of the parvenu's wife in "New Men and Old Acres" determining to have her grounds "laid out in ruins." It is as possible to be too old as to be too new. For a descendant of Sesostris the proper place would be the British Museum. The partly modern character of the Peerage is proof of living growth and unexhausted vitality, that it is not a mere curious survival. The House of Lords is like a portrait gallery, to which additions are constantly being made, not a museum of extinct antiquities. It brings to mind the saying attributed to a foreign Sovereign with regard to Oxford, that there was nothing new in it that did not seem old, nor anything old that did not seem new.

One reason for the preponderance of comparatively modern peerages is that many of the old ones have died out or gone into abeyance: those old peerages which still exist represent "the survival of the fittest." Another reason is that in former times there were far fewer Peers, a natural consequence of the far smaller population. Greatly as the Peerage has expanded it has not kept pace with the expansion of the British people in the British Isles alone, to say nothing of the British Colonies. Absolutely it has increased in numbers, but relatively it has diminished. Some more of the old English baronies might be called out of abeyance to satisfy the Radicals, but in the meantime it should console them to remember that many Peers of Scotland are now incorporated in the Union Peerage, and that, inasmuch as all Scottish peerages date of necessity from before 1708, the newest of them is nearly two hundred years old.

The Radical objection is not to the rank of a Peer in the Peerage, but to his seat in the House of Lords. Hence the date of the first peerage held by a Peer must be considered, not the date of the last; and in the case of Union Peers also Peers of Ireland or Scotland we must go back to the first creation in the Scottish or Irish Peerage. The antiquity of many families is obscured by the novelty of their titles. There are families which have been noble for centuries, but in the Peerage only for a few generations. Much of the delusion with regard to the supposed lack of antiquity in the Lords Temporal is due to mistaking the founder of the peerage for the founder of the family. Such has sometimes been the case, but very rarely. A Lord Eldon or a Lord St. Leonards is the exception, not the rule. It is not easy to comprehend the Liberal prejudice against men who have risen from the ranks, unless it is a Whig survival; but, as a matter of fact, such men have in the Peerage been comparatively few. A peerage, in nineteen cases out of twenty, is the culminating point, not the starting point, of a family. The reasonable presumption is in every case that the family is much older than its peerage. New Peers are often of extremely old family, as the Lambtons with their nineteenth-century Earldom of Durham, or the Knightleys of Fawsley raised to the peerage in the present year, but with a pedigree that goes back to the Conquest.

The Peerage, it cannot be too often repeated, is not the nobility, but only contains a few of its selected representatives, singled out for one reason or another from age to age.

Many knightly families grew by degrees into baronial ones. This was the almost invariable rule till recent times. There are more than a hundred Peers in the House of Lords whose families passed through the Baronetage before attaining to the Peerage. The great majority of the founders of peerages have been either the sons of knights and baronets, or cadets of families already in the Peerage. Sometimes a cadet branch of a peerage family wins a peerage for itself, and afterwards succeeds to the honours of the elder line, as in the case of Shrewsbury and Talbot. Until of late years the chief sources from which the Peerage has been recruited in modern times have been politics, the Services, and the Bar; and Peers obtained from such sources were nearly always gentlemen at starting. Until the present century, except at the dissolution of the monasteries, and in the case of the Indian "Nabobs," there were few suddenly acquired great fortunes to win for their fortunate possessors enrolment in the Peerage.

"In the olden times," wrote Mr. Abraham Hayward, in the *Quarterly Review*, " a forensic career afforded no presumption whatever of plebeian origin. So exclusive was the Bar, that there exists an ordinance countersigned by Bacon, closing its portals, the Inns of Court, against all but gentlemen entitled to coat armour. It must not therefore be hastily inferred that every family sprung from law or commerce had a mean beginning."

In Scotland, an essentially aristocratic country, the Faculty of Advocates constituted a sort of *noblesse de robe*. Many peerages of modern date represent extinct or attained peerages of far older creation. There can be no greater mistake than to suppose that George the Third, in breaking down the Whig oligarchy, impaired the aristocracy of the Peerage. The great families whom he brought to book, and punished for their own good, were many of them, like the Cavendishes and Seymours and Russells, by no means more aristocratic than the great body of country gentlemen whom they despised. The Revolution Houses were not, as a rule, remarkable for blood, but only for their arrogance and wealth. " The country Knight," says Bishop Stubbs, " was always regarded as a member of the noble class," and he explains how, by slow degrees, many county families worked themselves up into the Peerage. "A Bourchier is Chancellor to Edward III.; his descendant becomes a Viscount under Henry VI., partly by prowess, mainly by a lucky marriage. . . . But the promotion to the rank of peerage is very slow; and most of the families which have furnished sheriffs and county members in the Middle Ages have to wait for baronies and earldoms until the reigns of the Tudors and Stuarts."

The Peers, in considering their aristocracy, have a right to be judged by their best descent. To inherit the representation of an English barony or Scottish earldom through an heiress is not the same thing as a mere collateral descent through females. In a peerage created by patent any special remainder is possible. Thus the first Duke of Somerset had the children of his second wife preferred to those of his first in the succession to that peerage. The line of the first wife did not succeed to the Dukedom till 1750, on the death of the seventh and last Duke of the younger branch. Readers of Macaulay will remember the proud reply of Sir Edward Seymour to the Prince of Orange: "I think, Sir Edward," said "the little Dutchman," "you are of the family of the Duke of Somerset." "No, sir," was the rejoinder, "the Duke of Somerset is of my family."

It does not necessarily follow that one family which acquires a peerage from another is inferior to it in point of blood. Thus the Kers of Roxburghe are represented by the ancient house of Innes of that ilk, the Macdonalds of Antrim by the Kerrs of Lothian. Sometimes, again, peerages have been in families and passed away from them through females, while the same family has retained a subsequently acquired peerage of later date; while, as a matter of fact, in the vast majority of cases neither the date of the first Peerage held by a family, nor the date of its last promotion in the Peerage, gives any true measure of the antiquity or nobility of the family.

The instances given in Appendix E, of peers holding baronetcies or titles of older creation than their present peerages, though far from exhausting the list, will suffice to show that the actual date of the present creation of a peerage is by no means to be relied upon as affording in every case the true measure of its antiquity. Nor even when the first and present creations of a peerage are identical, do they go far to determine the antiquity of the family which holds it. The Scottish Viscounty of Arbuthnot dates from 1641, but, says Mr. Skene,* " Duncan de Aberbuthnot, thane of Aberbuthnot in 1202, was the ancestor of the noble family of Arbuthnot, who afterwards held the thanage as a barony." From thanes they became minor Barons, from minor Barons the greater Barons known as Peers.

That a peerage was in a family at a given date is evidence that at the date given that family was noble, but it is no evidence that the family was not noble previous to its peerage. On the contrary, it affords a strong presumption in favour of long previous nobility.

Some Peers represent Peers of creation whose peerages have or had become extinct, though they have not since been revived in any form for their representatives. The Dukedom of Portland dates from 1716, and the Earldom of Portland from 1689, but through the marriage of the second Duke with Lady Margaret Harley, daughter of the second Harley Earl of Oxford by Lady Henrietta Holles, daughter of John Holles, first Duke of Newcastle (1692) by Lady Margaret Cavendish, daughter and heiress of Henry, second and last Duke of Newcastle, the Dukes of Portland represent William Cavendish, Duke of Newcastle in 1665. In the same way the Earls Fitzwilliam represent the first and great Earl of Strafford. The first Earl Fitzwilliam in the Peerage of Great Britain, and third in that of Ireland, married in 1744 Lady Anne Wentworth, sister and coheiress of Charles, second Marquis of Rockingham, who died in 1782. The first Marquis of Rockingham, Thomas Watson Wentworth, was sixth Baron Rockingham of 1645, and grandson of the second Baron. The second Lord Rockingham, Edward Watson, married in 1654 Lady Anne Wentworth, eldest daughter of the Great Earl. Her brother, the second Earl, died childless

---

* " Celtic Scotland," bk. iii. ch. vii. 1.

in 1695. The first Earl of Strafford of the present 1847 creation, John Byng, was a great-grandson of the third Earl of Strafford of the 1640 creation, who was a cousin, not a descendant, of the Great Earl.

Peerages to which it is impossible to assign a definite origin, judicial, naval or military, or in the civil administration, may nevertheless commemorate those who have played a great part in our history. Thus the first Lord Barnard was the son and heir of Sir Harry Vane. The first Lord Eliot, founder of the Earldom of St. Germans, represented the Sir John Eliot who played a conspicuous part in the Parliamentary opposition to King Charles the First.

The lack of distinction alleged against the Peerage is a charge not less unfounded and absurd than the charge of a lack of antiquity. But before leaving the latter it may be as well to quote some words of Mr. Abraham Hayward with regard to the silly and unpatriotic exaltation of foreign nobles at the expense of our own that is affected by some writers. "The alleged superiority of the continental aristocracies vanishes or diminishes apace when we apply to them the critical tests to which we habitually subject our own. . . . Many of the more obscure Teutonic families produce better pedigrees than the Metternichs or Schwarzenburgs. But when we reject presumption and require proof, we find the best of them lost about the same time, in the same mists of uncertainty, with our Nevilles, Stanleys, Berkeleys, Courtenays, Herberts, and Howards." No error can be greater than that of supposing that because the Peerage is not a noblesse, it therefore is not noble.

Peerages have not only been founded by men of genius or of public distinction, but subsequently illustrated by men of eminence; and where the founder of a peerage is comparatively unknown, some brilliant descendant has often invested the title with lustre and fame. Who pauses to think of the Cavalier Lord Byron when he remembers the poet? What antiquity is needed by the name, ancient though it is, for ever glorified by the Great Marquis of Montrose? Who cares to recall an English Viceroy of Ireland when the name of Falkland summons up before him the patriot and loyalist, the lover of liberty, and the chivalrous soldier of his King?

And in a sphere less exalted but still high the names of the tenth Earl of Dundonald, better known to fame as Lord Cochrane the naval commander, of Indian Viceroys like the Marquis of Dalhousie or the Marquis of Dufferin, of statesmen like Lord Palmerston and Lord Melbourne, the fourteenth Earl of Derby and the present Marquis of Salisbury, have either augmented a celebrity already existent or created one where it did not exist.

The second Lord Fairfax was the Parliamentary General. The second Lord Amherst was Governor-General of Bengal. The second Lord Bathurst, and first Lord Apsley, became Lord High Chancellor of Great Britain before his father was advanced in rank from a Baron to an Earl. The fourth Earl of Chesterfield, one of the most successful of Irish Viceroys, was an Ambassador, a Secretary of State, a Foreign Member of the French Academy, and, higher distinction than all, the author of "Chesterfield's Letters." The fourth Earl of Carnarvon, the second and third Earls Grey, all amply justified the peerages they had inherited. The second Lord Lytton, like the first, won double honours as a statesman and as a man of letters.

It is equally curious and characteristic that the enemies of the House of Lords posing as democrats should demand its abolition on the ground that the Peerage is not aristocratic. Thus we have certain public men austerely resenting the peerages bestowed in former times upon the illegitimate scions of Royalty, and likening the House of Lords in this respect to a Common Council in which "the illegitimate descendants of former Lord Mayors" should hold hereditary seats. And this, no doubt, is very clever and amusing, only unfortunately the likeness does not exist. What possible resemblance is there between the hereditary chief of the nation, and an elected municipal officer, between the Lord Mayor of London and the Sovereign of the British Empire? If it is meant to imply that the British Sovereign is a mere figure head, such is notoriously not the case ; it never has been the case except in the instances of George the First and George the Second. It is impossible to compare two personages so completely dissimilar, and the attempt to do so is as poor in logic as it is in taste. But it aptly illustrates the sort of mud with which the Radicals discolour and darken the clear waters of discussion. By dint of persistent Radical assertions an impression has grown up that Charles the Second flooded the House of Peers with his numerous family not born in lawful wedlock. Now, to vindicate the House of Lords it is not necessary to justify the *liaisons* of Charles the Second, and still less the manner in which he blazoned them forth to the whole world. "Autres temps, autres mœurs :" we have grown more decent or more hypocritical : though it is only justice to remember that the great tidal wave of shamelessness, which lasted from the time of Charles the Second to that of George the Third, was the natural and national reaction from the Puritan tyranny of the Commonwealth. It is also fair to bear in mind that the state of public feeling did not in former times require the private character of a King to be not merely no worse than that of the generality of his subjects, but a great deal better. If then we "go to facts," we shall find that there are only seven Peers to whom the sneer could possibly apply, the Dukes of Beaufort, Richmond, Grafton, and St. Albans, the Duke of Buccleuch sitting as Earl of Doncaster, the Earl of Munster, and the Earl of Moray sitting as Lord Stuart of Castle-Stuart. And we find, further, that in nearly every case the sneer is wholly out of place. Every Duke of St. Albans since the first has represented the ancient line of the de Veres, Earls of Oxford from 1155 : every Duke of St. Albans would hold that Earldom, had it descended in the same way as countless others descended in the Middle Ages : every Duke of St. Albans since the fifth has also sat as Lord Vere of Hanworth. The Duke of Grafton represents the celebrated Restoration statesman Arlington, and holds his Barony and Earldom in virtue of the marriage of the first Duke to his daughter and heiress. The Duke of Buccleuch holds Monmouth's Earldom of

Doncaster, though the attainted Dukedom has never been restored, but if the heiress of Buccleuch had not bestowed her hand and fortune on an illegitimate son of Charles the Second, born before his marriage, the handsomest man of his time, and the object of the passionate devotion of his wife, it is safe to say that she would have married some one else, and that the descendants of the marriage would now be sitting in the Upper Chamber. Each Duke of Buccleuch since 1810 has also held the Douglas Dukedom of Queensberry. Whatever may have been the origin of the Dukedom of Richmond, the Duke of Richmond is now Duke of Gordon, and represents the former Dukes of Gordon of from 1684 to 1836. The Earls of Moray get their Earldom from the bastard brother of Queen Mary, but as Barons Doune they are the descendants in the male line of another Regent of Scotland, the Duke of Albany, younger son of Robert the Second, and, barring the attainder of the second Duke, legitimate princes of the royal House of Stuart. And even to the Regent Moray an objection comes with sorry grace from the party which once canonized him as a saint.

Again, the first Earl of Worcester, ancestor of the Dukes of Beaufort, entered the Peerage as Lord Herbert, not in virtue of his descent from John of Gaunt, but as the husband of the heiress of the earlier line of Herberts, Earls of Pembroke. The second Earl inherited his mother's Barony of Herbert created in 1461, and the Dukes of Beaufort are now also Lords Bottetourt of 1305. The first Earl of Munster and his brothers were illegitimate sons of William the Fourth, but a natural child born of unwedded parents is a very different thing from the offspring of adultery. According to the Canon Law, the law of Scotland, and the law of many Continental countries, the former could be legitimated by the subsequent marriage of the parents. That this is not so south of the Tweed is not in the natural order of things, but is simply due to a harsh, inhuman, and antimoral peculiarity of the law of England. It was impossible, for reasons of State, that the Duke of Clarence and St. Andrews should marry Mrs. Jordan, but his sacrifice of private feeling to the public interest is not to be held as casting a slur upon his children. But all objections on the score of bastardy are inadmissible in those who seek to pass for democrats, and ludicrous in the party which caused the enactment of the English Divorce Act. The morality of the Roman Catholic Church is consistent and logical, but the morality, which condemns illegitimacy and sanctions the remarriage of women divorced by their husbands, is purely capricious. Each of these "illegitimate descendants of former Lord Mayors," with the exception of the Earl of Munster, is a legitimate descendant of an older and more honourable line. But were this not so, the illegitimate descendant even of a British King need not be so abject and ignominious a creature as the sneer supposes. Such a man as the first Duke of Berwick, the son of James the Second, and the nephew of Marlborough, whose military genius won for him the batons of a Spanish Captain-General and a Marshal of France, might well claim to be his own ancestor. Founder of the Dukedoms of Liria and Xerica in Spain, and of that of Fitzjames in France, the English peerage, which he forfeited by his honourable fidelity to the cause of his House, ought, as a matter of historical justice, to be restored to his descendants.

Again, when we are told that George the First and George the Second bestowed peerages on the Duchess of Kendal and the Countess of Yarmouth and the like, their "fat German mistresses," as Radicals coarsely, if not inappropriately, express it, there is the obvious rejoinder that all such peerages have died out. These poor ladies, whose homely and ungraceful naughtiness outraged our national passion for the picturesque, were only created Peeresses for life, a practice common enough in the case of those incapable by nature of sitting in the House of Lords, and, so far as is known, they left no descendants.

But when we pass from the light raillery of Mr. Labouchere to the ponderous onslaught of Professor Bryce, we find that in the latter we have also left for the time the philosophic historian, and have only to encounter a party politician of the Liberal party in Great Britain. "They [the Americans] remark, with truth," declares Professor Bryce, "that since Pitt in England and Napoleon in France prostituted hereditary titles, these have ceased to be either respectable or useful. 'They do not,' say the Americans, 'suggest antiquity, for the English families that enjoy them are mostly new; they are not associated, like the ancient titles, with the history of the nation; they are merely a prize offered to wealth, the expression of a desire for gilding that plutocracy which has replaced the ancient aristocracy of your country.'"*

This is just the sort of absurd and impertinent remark that a certain class of underbred Americans might be supposed to make. As the Realists say of anything abnormal, "it pants with actuality." The tone of patronage finely blended with crude reasoning from defective knowledge and superficial observation is entirely true to life. But, however great its subjective truth as a manifestation of intellect and character, as a statement of fact it is an absolute falsehood. Whatever may be the date of any given peerages, "the families that enjoy them," English, Scottish, or Irish, are not "mostly new," in any sense which a citizen of the United States is entitled to attribute to the word "new." The newer a peerage the more active the part taken, as a rule, by its first possessor, in shaping the history of the nation. No "plutocracy" has "replaced the ancient aristocracy" of Britain, though the aristocracy, titled and untitled, like all other classes have had their share in that general nineteenth-century material prosperity which they had also a share, and the principal share, in making possible, and though some rich men have from time to time been adopted into that titled and untitled aristocracy, as rich men always have been from the earliest times.

Let us deal with the last accusation first. That the partly plutocratic character of the English Peerage is nothing new, we saw from the degradation of the Duke of Bedford by an Act of Parliament in 1477, which expressly assigns the poverty of the Duke as the reason of this shameful proceeding. The Peerage at the present time, it may be affirmed with confidence,

* "American Commonwealth," part vi. ch. cvi.

is far more spiritual than it ever was before, far more so certainly than when it was almost exclusively bound up with property representation as it was in the Middle Ages. The Baronage had its origin in the system of land tenure under the Norman and early Plantagenet Kings, and in those days land was the principal, and almost the only form of wealth. The House of Lords was a House of landlords. The Statute of Mortmain, passed to restrain the alienation of land to the Church, was needed to prevent the Church from acquiring a monopoly of the principal and most tangible form of wealth then in existence. The Peerage was always associated with the possession of wealth. At first the connection was indissoluble. Gradually, as the Baronage grew into its present shape, the connection grew less and less intimate, a process facilitated by parallel changes in the law of Real Property, till at last there came to be no necessary connection at all.

As members of the Knightly class passed by easy steps of transition into Barons, so, according to Bishop Stubbs,—

"it is probable that there was no period in English history at which the barrier between the knightly and mercantile class was regarded as insuperable, since the days of Athelstan, when the merchant who had made his three voyages over the sea, and made his fortune, became worthy of thegn right: even the higher grades of chivalry were not beyond his reach, for in 1439 we find William Estfield, a mercer of London, made Knight of the Bath. . . . The leading men in the towns, like the De la Poles, formed an urban aristocracy that had not to wait more than one generation for ample recognition. The younger sons of the country Knight sought wife, occupation, and estate, in the towns." *

The de la Poles became the Dukes of Suffolk familiar to readers of Henry VI. This double process of emigration from the town to the country and from the country to the town, was early in operation. The political power attendant on the possession of land under the old Constitution, and the social prestige which accompanied the political power, and still survives it, naturally attracted the man who had realized a fortune in commerce, just as commerce held out tempting prizes to the younger and poorer members of the classes connected with land. The healthy and beneficent system of

* "Constitutional History," chs. xv., xxi.

primogeniture, perhaps the greatest cause of national prosperity, sent forth a host of younger sons for whom war or the liberal profession could not always provide a sufficient opening.

"Any line of life," says Mr. Abraham Hayward, "which leads to wealth and honours, will always attract recruits of promise from all ranks ; and indications are not wanting that long before the profession of arms had ceased to arrogate precedence, youths of gentle birth were occasionally bred up to trade. Thus (in 'The Fortunes of Nigel') Scott describes Tunstall, one of George Heriot's apprentices, as the last hope of an ancient race ; and 'Rashleigh Osbaldistone (in 'Rob Roy'), with all his pride of birth, was willing to take his cousin's place in the counting-house. Sir Dudley North, the Turkey merchant, was a Peer's son. Sir William Capel, founder of the Essex earldom, was the younger son of a son of a Knight."

It would require some temerity to challenge the accuracy of Sir Walter Scott in matters relating to the social life of the eighteenth century, but if additional evidence is called for we have the testimony of Pope in Epistle I. of the "Moral Essays."

> "Boastful and rough, your first son is a squire ;
> The next a tradesman, meek and much a liar ;
> Tom struts a soldier, open, bold, and brave ;
> Will sneaks a scrivener, an exceeding knave."

We should say now, in our milder modern fashion, that "the next" was "in tea" or "on the Stock Exchange," or, more vaguely, that he was "something in the City."

That the Americans should complain of that want of hard and fast lines, of caste divisions, which has always existed in the British nation, must be regarded as the extremity of revolt from their own conditions. That a land where all men are, in theory, not only free, but equal, should look askance at the career open to talent existing in an effete Old World country, is perhaps too natural to be surprising. It is not to be expected that in a new Continent resolutely rebelling against the influence of European civilization and of the great seats of Old World culture, a continent where after a period of chaos society is beginning to reconstruct itself on the familiar and inevitable lines, the leaders in such a transformation should be able to regard those a generation or two behind themselves in the social struggle with the calm and easy tolerance and liberality of an old-established, and, except in books, an undisputed, aristocracy. It is from the United States, by an easily comprehensible reaction, that the world has received Mr. Henry George and the author of the dazzling and too delightful Utopia described in "Looking Backwards;" but the distressing materialism which they see on all sides around them should not mislead the philosophers of Boston into drawing a fanciful picture of the mediæval Baronage, nor betray them into sentimental regrets for its supposed corruption by base modern money. In Britain, in spite of the pardonable exaggerations to the contrary effect made by poets and aldermen, wealth has never been deified and never disregarded.

"The opposition commonly set up," writes Sir Henry Maine in the "Early History of Institutions," "between birth and wealth, and particularly wealth other than landed property, is entirely modern. In French literature, so far as my knowledge extends, it first appears when the riches of the provincial officers of the French monarchy—the Superintendents and Farmers-General—began to attract attention. With us it seems to be exclusively the result of the great extension and productiveness of industrial undertakings on the largest scale. But the heroes of the Homeric poems are not only valiant but wealthy : * the warriors of the Niebelungen Lied are not only noble but rich. In the later Greek literature we find pride of birth identified with pride in seven wealthy ancestors in succession, ἕπτα πάπποι πλόυσιοι; and you are well aware how rapidly and completely the aristocracy of wealth assimilated itself in the Roman state to the aristocracy of blood."

The whole idea, which Professor Bryce attributes to the Americans, of an aristocracy as an exclusive caste from which all new elements are to be rigidly excluded, is entirely foreign to the institution of the British Peerage, and to all the conceptions of nobility ever held by the peoples of the British Isles. Such an idea, promulgated by an aristocracy, is a symptom that cannot be mistaken of its incipient stagnation and decay; put forward by those with no pretension to nobility, it can in them only be regarded as an empty and somewhat vulgar affectation.

* "Odyssey," xiv. 96.

"The old English laws," we are assured by Professor Freeman, "point out ways by which the churl might rise to thegn's rank, and we find mention, both in England and elsewhere, of the rise of new men to posts of authority. The story that Earl Godwine himself was of churlish birth, whether true or false, marks the possibility of such a rise. A still wilder tale is told of Hugh Capet, as the son of a butcher of Paris. Stories like this prove more than the real rise of Hagano or Eadric."

The Old Irish Laws, according to Sir Henry Maine, are on this point in agreement with the Old English or Anglo-Saxon :—

"The Brehon tracts point out in several places, with legal minuteness, the mode in which a peasant freeman in ancient Ireland could become a chief. There are few personages of greater interest spoken of in the laws than the Bo-Aire, literally the 'cow-nobleman.' He is, to begin with, simply a peasant who has grown rich in cattle, probably through obtaining the use of large portions of tribe land. The true nobles, or Aires, are divided into seven grades. Each grade is distinguished from the others by the amount of wealth possessed by the Chief belonging to it, by the weight attached to his evidence, by his power of binding his tribe by contracts, by the dues which he receives in kind from his vassals, and by his Honour Price, or special damages incurred by injuring him. At the bottom of the scale is the chief or noble called the Aire-desa ; and the Brehon law provides that when the Bo-Aire has acquired twice the wealth of an Aire-desa, and has held it for a certain number of generations, he becomes an Aire-desa himself. The advantage secured to wealth does not exclude respect for birth, but works into it. 'He is an inferior chief,' says the 'Senchus Mor,' 'whose father was not a chief,' and there are many other strong assertions of the reverence due to inherited rank. The primary view of chieftainship is evidently that it springs from purity or dignity of blood ; but noble birth is regarded as naturally associated with wealth, and he who becomes rich gradually climbs up to a position indistinguishable from that which he would have occupied if he had been nobly born." *

It would be impossible to give a better description of the system now existing in the British Isles. "The advantage secured to wealth does not exclude respect for birth, but works into it." The Irish, a civilized people when "the Anglo-Saxon race" were illiterate barbarians, had developed a system which must always and everywhere commend itself to rational minds, and this system is with but small differences literally reproduced in the modern Peerage.

* "Early History of Institutions."

Wealth is a form of power, and for the State wilfully to ignore and alienate the possessors of any form of power is contrary to all sound policy. The old Irish and modern British systems hit the happy mean between the exclusion of new wealth altogether practised by decaying castes, and that adoption of wealth as the sole standard of merit which prevails in a greater or less degree in all countries without a recognized class of hereditary nobles, and in particular in the United States.

The extravagant panegyrics on wealth indulged in by the Liberals of a past generation have been replaced by its equally extravagant disparagement on the part of their successors. Cobdenism has in due course given birth to Socialism, just as the sordid materialism of the United States has drawn forth the protests of the Anarchist outrages at Chicago and the quaint dreams of shoddy bliss enounced at Boston. But the alternative to serving Mammon is not the serving Mr. Hyndman, and the crude denunciation of capital as capital, by those who once hailed Mr. Bright and Mr. Cobden as inspired with fire from heaven, is not more wide of the mark, though possibly less sordid, than the glowing encomiums of the Free-trade prophets on "our marvellous industrial prosperity." It is written that "man shall not live by bread alone," but neither shall he live by News from Nowhere. To attack the Peerage on the score of its including many rich men appears as foolish as to decry individual Peers on account of the modernness of their titles. The point, surely, with regard to any given peerage is not its antiquity, but what it represents : and equally so, the point, with regard to wealth, is the use that its possessors make of it. Like every other form of power, its virtue or its vice lies, not in the mere fact of its possession, but in its employment for noble or ignoble ends. If it is not, as the Liberals formerly pretended, any merit in a man to make his own fortune, still less is it, as some of them would now apparently imply, any crime in a man to do so. Nor does the fact of a man inheriting or acquiring a large fortune destroy any previous claims he may have had to be a man of family.

The existence of Belgravia does not constitute the Duke of Westminster a parvenu : and it is possible even for a man who has created his own wealth to be a gentleman in that original sense of the word which Doctor Johnson would alone admit.

There seems to be no little unreality and affectation in the fashionable modern outcry against money. Why should the sudden acquisition of wealth be regarded as infamous and degrading? Who would not like to become suddenly beautiful, to go to bed a Satyr and awake Hyperion, except for possible difficulties as to subsequent identification? Every one would like to be rich, except a few rich people who have never known and are unable to imagine what it is to be poor. The "Arabian Nights" and the fairy stories popular with childhood testify equally to the universality of the desire—Fortunatus with his daily replenished purse, Aladdin with his wonder-working lamp. Wealth has its own poetry, embodied for all time in Florence and Venice. There is no necessary opposition, as some people imagine, between commerce and art, no necessary connection between the wealth begotten by commerce and vulgarity. The merchant princes of Venice, the great bankers of Florence, belie such an assertion. It is not wealth that vulgarizes, but Puritanism, with its deep-rooted hostility to all forms of art and all true civilization. It is Puritanism, not commerce, that has given England those middle-class Philistines of whom Matthew Arnold held eloquent discourse, "with their narrow range of intellect and knowledge, their stunted sense of beauty, their low standard of manners." So too it is Puritanism, by destroying or impairing civilization, that must be held responsible for the tasteless extravagance of American Silver Kings, the descendants of the Pilgrim Fathers, from which, in the British Empire, the Peerage and its influence largely preserve us.

No censure can be more unjust than that which condemns the House of Lords as a plutocracy, and never was the Peerage more spiritual than at the present time. Literature and science are to-day accorded a position which they never held before. The peerage conferred since the beginning of the present year (1892) upon Lord Kelvin, by the advice of the Salisbury Administration, is the first of a purely scientific origin. The peerage conferred upon Lord Tennyson was the first ever bestowed upon a man of letters simply as such; for Lord Macaulay and the first Lord Lytton were also prominent politicians; and Lord Houghton, if not a politician, was a member of the House of Commons, and a Yorkshire squire. These peerages give us the high-water mark of literature and science in the public estimation. Men of literary genius had before this attained to seats in the House of Lords, as they had also held high office in the State, but only on condition of their previous participation in the warfare of current politics. These peerages form the first explicit recognition on the part of the Britannic State of the immense services of literature and science to the welfare and greatness of the nation. It does not do for the State to go too far in advance of public opinion, and not so many years back such peerages as these would have been scouted. The vulgar contempt for literature which inspired the English *bourgeoisie* in former days, and the widespread fear of the irreligious conclusions supposed to result from the discoveries of physical science which was carefully impressed on all classes with brutal violence by the ignorant zealotry of ecclesiastics, have given way before a gradual awakening of the public mind. Never since Puritanism poisoned the springs of the national life have literature, science, and art, and their various professors, occupied so high a place in general esteem. And the State, taking prompt advantage of this laudable change in public feeling, has enrolled the Poet Laureate and a man of science of acknowledged eminence as members of the House of Lords. Is this a homage afforded to wealth: or a recognition of the aristocracy of intellect and culture? For the first time in the history of the Imperial Parliament literature and science have found their direct representation in the Peerage, and the comment of Professor Bryce is that "a plutocracy has replaced the ancient aristocracy of our country."

The Baronetcy, which in his own day was considered a

sufficient recognition of the genius of Sir Walter Scott, has grown in ours into the Barony bestowed upon Lord Tennyson. This, at least, and the companion peerage of Lord Kelvin, can scarcely be considered mere vulgar adulation of new and undeserving riches, mere grovelling in the mire before Sir Gorgius Midas. But these do not stand alone. In the steadily increasing number of peerages bestowed on eminent public servants, whether at home, or as Governors in India and the Colonies, or as diplomatists in foreign countries; whether serving the country as civilians or as naval and military commanders; whether officers of the executive or members of the judicature ;· may be read a very different tale from that propounded by Professor Bryce. The institution of life peerages for the Lords of Appeal is by itself a sufficient answer to the criticism which he puts into the mouth of his Transatlantic friends. There are two tendencies which are clearly discernible in the Peerage system at the present day. One is a tendency to confer what are in reality life peerages on distinguished public servants without children, to whom an "hereditary legislatorship" might prove a burdensome inheritance. The other tendency is to the absorption of the Scottish and Irish Peerages in the Peerage of the United Kingdom. The "ancient aristocracy" of Scotland, so far as it may be said to be represented by a Peerage in which the last creation or promotion is of necessity more than a hundred and eighty years old, instead of being "replaced by a plutocracy," was never more vigorously holding its own.

Do such peerages as those of Lord Cairns, Lord Cottenham, Lord Selborne, Lords Ashbourne, Bramwell, Brougham, Campbell, Chelmsford, Coleridge, Esher, Field, Halsbury, Herschell, Hobhouse, Moncrieff, Monkswell, O'Hagan, Penzance, Truro, Romilly, represent mere wealth, or are they an honourable tribute to judicial eminence and the just meed of service to the Realm? Do such creations as those of Lord Strafford, Lord Gough, Lord Hardinge, Lord Hill, Lord Wolseley, Lord Alcester, Lord Roberts, Lord Keane, Lord Sandhurst, Lord Seaton, Lord Raglan, Lord Napier of Magdala,—do these commemorate illgotten and misused wealth, or the most honourable form of service that subject or citizen can render to the State? Does the Marquisate of Lord Dufferin; do the Earldoms of Lord Cowley, of Lord Iddesleigh, of Lord Lytton, of Lord Northbrook, of Lord Russell; do the Viscounties or Baronies of Lord Cranbrook, Lord Cross, Lord Halifax, Lords Hampden, Sherbrooke, Aberdare, Ampthill, Carlingford, Elgin, Ettrick, Emly, Hampton, Lawrence, Knutsford, Stanley of Preston, Monck, Meredyth, Lingen, Monteagle, Norton, Savile,—do such as these embody a vile worship of ignoble riches, or do they record the service to the nation of Ambassadors, Secretaries of State, Speakers, and other such ministers of the Commons or the Crown? Or, again, are we to find the parvenus and upstarts who have replaced our ancient aristocracy in Lord Howard of Glossop, or Lord Stanley of Alderley? in Lord Egerton of Tatton, or Lord Montagu of Beaulieu? in Lord Cromarty and Lord Ellesmere, or Lord Stalbridge and Lord Ebury? in Lord Lamington, or Lord Penrhyn, or Lord Wantage? in Lord Leigh, or Lord Sackville, or Lord Chesham? All these are peerages of the present reign.

A small number of Peers have been created with fortunes of comparatively recent acquisition, and these are forthwith erected into a proof that a plutocracy has "replaced the ancient aristocracy of your country." It is not difficult to imagine how, if new wealth had been rigorously excluded, the fact would have been dwelt upon *ad nauseam* as evidence that the Peers were "out of touch with modern conditions," that they had "no comprehension of the spirit of their age," that they represented dead, not living, eminence, and so forth, in all the varying keys of current cant. Because the Peerage is not a caste, its very liberality is brought up as a charge against it. Because it is an order, not a noblesse, it is arraigned as an ignoble plutocracy. But just as the Peerage has saved the nation from a noblesse of the Continental fashion, so it has saved the nation from a plutocracy. Its openness and breadth have compelled both birth and wealth to submit themselves to the supremacy of the Crown, and in the supremacy of the Crown to the supremacy of the nation. It has prevented birth and wealth alike from setting up an exclusive claim to predominance, and thus from coming into conflict with the public welfare and with one another.

The Peerage has saved the nation, not from a nobility, which exists both in it and beside it, but from a noble caste. "The growth of the Peerage," wrote Professor Freeman, who had at least no Tory bias, "with its comparatively harmless privileges, hindered the real nobility [all who bear coat armour by good right] from keeping or winning privileges which would have been anything but harmless. To the existence of the Peerage, more than to any other cause, England owes its happy freedom from the curse of a really privileged class, the happy equality in the eyes of the law of all men not actually Peers.... The privileges of the actual Peerage have been a small price to pay for such a blessing as this."

And in the same way the Peerage has saved the nation from an unquestioned rule of wealth. Instead of having been captured by the plutocracy, the Peerage has controlled and tamed the plutocrats. What a plutocracy means we can see from the example of America. In no other country in the world is the power of capital carried to such insolent heights of tyranny as in the United States. In no other country in the world is a rich man so absolutely secure from all the consequences of crime, so absolutely free to commit crime with impunity. By thus recognizing the claims both of birth and wealth in a reasonable form and subject to well-defined conditions, the Peerage has kept either principle from the excesses to which it might otherwise have given rise, and has bound them both to the chariot wheels of the State. And this accessibility, which in the eyes of our Radical aristocrats constitutes so grave a defect in the British Peerage, is recognized by the political scientists of the European Continent as a main source of its vitality and strength.

"The Roman aristocracy," says Bluntschli, "obtained its greatness, and the English aristocracy has preserved its influence and respect, because both remained in living union with the life of the people, and constantly derived new vigour by recruiting themselves from the classes below them. Exclusiveness is the cardinal fault of every aristocracy.

The privileges of the ruling class are founded on its qualities; but in the endeavour to secure the former by the strong defence of hereditary succession, it has often lost sight of the latter altogether."

And he lays especial stress on the accessibility of the Peerage as the principal cause of its permanent prosperity. Instancing as parallel causes the fusion of races in the British Isles, and the early power of the English Crown, he lays stress on the fact that a peerage was confined to one heir, that is to say, that the Peerage never was a caste.

"The early association (afterwards severed) of a peerage with a definite castle, estate, or office, gave rise to the important principle that only one of the sons or relatives of the deceased lord could take his seat in Parliament. Thus on the one hand the dignity and wealth of the great families remained concentrated in one head, while on the other the easy transition from one class to another served to minimise the distinctions of birth. Further, a Peer was not bound to marry into a noble family. This principle has not lessened the dignity of the nobility, while it has done far more to secure it from attack than the caste-like principle of equality of birth, to which the German nobility cling so closely. Finally, the Peerage was from time to time enlarged and enlivened by the creation of new Peers. . . . This constant supply of new and really aristocratic forces saved the English aristocracy from the danger of stagnation and incapacity." *

Thus this German professor of political philosophy, bringing to the consideration of the subject a dispassionate, judicial, and scientific mind, selects for especial eulogy those very points in the British Peerage system of which Professor Bryce falls foul. "If we look as a whole," he concludes, "at these characteristics of the English nobility we need not wonder why it alone has preserved its existence undisputed, while in every Continental country the aristocracy have either entirely disappeared, or only maintain a struggling and precarious existence."

If the Peerage had held obstinately aloof from the plutocracy, it would have converted both the latter and itself into a source of danger to the State. Instead of this it captured the plutocracy, civilized and educated it, forced it to feel ashamed of its own deficiencies, and to recognize the aristocracy of birth and breeding, of genius and culture, of intellect and manners. By doing so, by encouraging the new wealthy

* "Theory of the State."

classes produced by nineteenth-century material prosperity to form themselves on its own model, by holding out to them reasonable hopes of being eventually admitted by slow degrees and on good behaviour to its own level, it has sent forth a wave of civilizing influence that is felt throughout the British Empire. It has preserved the British Isles and largely purified the British Colonies from those "wealthy low orders" of whom a Chief Justice of Victoria once spoke with complaining mention, and who openly lord it in the United States. It has curbed the insolence of wealth in the most effective manner by frankly recognizing its reasonable pretensions and just claims.

"Honours," exclaims Mr. Neuchâtel in Lord Beaconsfield's "Endymion,"—"honours are inestimable to the honourable, and great wealth is a great blessing to the man who knows how to use it." This is the great question both for a man and for a nation with regard to wealth, as with regard to all other forms of power—how to use it. Where the power of intellect is used well and wisely, and to the public advantage, that power deserves public recognition; and where the power of wealth is used well and wisely, and to the public advantage, that power too calls for public honour and respect. There may be as much vulgarity in a sneer at wealth as in a gibe at poverty.

"The advantages secured to wealth do not exclude respect for birth, but work into it." But to this description of the modern Peerage system must be further added that the advantages secured by it to wealth work, not only into respect for birth, but also into respect for character, intellect, and genius, whether displayed in the public service, civil or military, or in the fields of literature, science, and art. No plutocracy has replaced the ancient aristocracy of the country, but the ancient aristocracy welcomes every new element of aristocracy, and has subdued and educated the new plutocracy. The tame elephant has caught and civilized the wild one.

What again can be more untrue or more monstrous than the assertion that modern peerages "are not associated, like the ancient titles, with the history of the nation"? We saw, in

CHAP. I.] EXAMINATION OF DR. BRYCE'S CRITICISMS. 97

an earlier chapter, that out of four hundred and eighty-eight peerages of England, Great Britain, and the United Kingdom, sixty-six had their origin in naval and military, sixty-six in judicial, and one hundred and seventeen in other civil services to the Empire, and of these the majority are peerages of the United Kingdom or Great Britain. Such peerages as those of Lord Eldon, of Lord Mansfield, of Lord Rosslyn, of Lord Thurlow, of Lord Kenyon, of Lord Cowper, of Lord Camden, not to cite instances from those previously quoted, carry history written on their face. Such titles as those of Wellington, Marlborough, Clive, Nelson, Mahon, Duncan, Amherst, Cadogan, Bridport, Hood, St. Vincent, Abercromby, Rodney, Hawke, can only be without historical associations to those who are in as complete ignorance of the history of the world as of the history of the British nation. It would be possible from a careful investigation of the Union Peerage from 1707 to reconstruct the history of the British Empire from that period, its wars and conquests, its internal changes and domestic policy.

The assertion, like the companion charge before considered, that the families of the Peers are "mostly new," is based on nothing but the grossest ignorance or carelessness, an ignorance pardonable perhaps in Americans, but a carelessness wholly inexcusable in the Oxford Regius Professor who adopts their unfounded assumptions as his own. If Dr. Bryce had devoted to a study of the House of Lords, in a dispassionate spirit, one-hundredth part of the time and trouble that he has given to the Constitutions of the United States and the Holy Roman Empire he could never have allowed himself to be betrayed by party prejudice into such ill-considered and unwarrantable statements. He says that "Pitt in England and Napoleon in France prostituted hereditary titles," and that these have therefore "ceased to be either respectable or useful." But did Pitt "prostitute hereditary titles"? Pitt became First Lord of the Treasury and Chancellor of the Exchequer late in December, 1783, and continued in office till succeeded by Addington in March, 1801. In May, 1804, Pitt came back to office, and his Administration lasted till February, 1806, when he was replaced by Lord Grenville. Among the peerages created on Pitt's advice were the Baronies of Kenyon in 1788, Thurlow in 1792, Loughborough in 1795, Eldon in 1799, the Earldoms of Camden in 1786, and Mansfield of Caen Wood in 1792,—all bestowed on judges, some of them the most eminent that have sat upon the English bench; the 1786 Barony of Dorchester bestowed on a Governor-General of Canada; the 1788 Baronies of Howe and Amherst, the 1795 Barony of Hood, the 1797 Viscounty of Duncan,—all created for those who had sustained the fortunes of the Empire by land or sea; the 1784 Barony of Eliot created for the representative of the "Patriot" Sir John Eliot; the Barony of Somers revived in 1784 for a representative of the Whig Chancellor and statesman; the 1788 Barony of Malmesbury, the 1793 Barony of Auckland, the 1797 Barony of Minto, conferred upon diplomatists. What "prostitution" is there here? Or if we look to the family of Pitt's Peers, we find that the Lord Braybrooke of 1788 was the fourth Lord Howard de Walden; the Earl of Carnarvon of 1793 a cadet of the house of Pembroke; the Lord Cawdor of 1796 descended from thanes and barons of remote antiquity; the Viscount Lowther of 1797 of a family which had a peerage in 1696; the Viscount Newark of 1796 the nephew and heir of the last Duke of Kingston; the Lord Bradford of 1794 descended in the male line from a keeper of the Great Seal, and in the female representing the Newports, Earls of Bradford in 1694; the Lord Dundas of 1794 a member of an illustrious and historic Scottish family.

Does Professor Bryce find fault with the creation of the first Lord Carrington in 1779, of the ancestor of the Earl of Kimberley as Lord Wodehouse in 1797, of the ancestor of the Earl of Morley as Lord Boringdon in 1784? Does he refer to the Earldom of Abergavenny conferred in 1784 on a Baron of Abergavenny dating from 1392, to the Earldom of Uxbridge conferred in 1784 on a Lord Paget dating from 1552, or to the Earldom of Talbot conferred in 1784 on a Peer representing a Chancellor of Great Britain and since united with England's premier Earldom? to the Marquisate of Stafford given in 1786 to the ancestor of the Dukes of Sutherland, or the Earldom of Grosvenor given in 1784 to the ancestor of the Duke of Westminster? to the Earldom of Strange given in 1786 to a Duke of Athole, or to the Marquisate of Lansdowne given in 1784 to the second Earl of Shelburne of a family dating in the Irish Peerage from the year 1200? to the Barony of Stuart of Castle-Stuart bestowed in 1796 on an Earl of Moray, the legitimate descendant in the male line of a Scottish King, or to the Barony of Stewart of Garlies bestowed in the same year on an Earl of Galloway, the descendant of a line that had branched off from the House of Stuart before it ascended the Scottish throne? to the Marquisate of Salisbury (1789) or to the Marquisate of Bath (1789)? to the Marquisate of Abercorn (1789) or to the Marquisate of Bute (1796)? to the Earldom of Fortescue (1789) or to the Earldom of Mount Edgcumbe (1789)? to the Earldom of Cadogan (1800) or to the Earldom of Nelson (1805)? or to the Earldom of Powis bestowed in 1804, on the son of Clive and the husband of a wife representing the Herberts of Powis?

The Whig legend, dished up by Professor Bryce with Yankee seasoning, is one which finds no countenance from history. Pitt "prostituted" nothing. His great crimes were that he assisted his royal master to break down the power of the Whig oligarchy, and restore the national character of the Constitution; that he combated, first that anarchic Parisian Revolution which threw back the cause of Parliamentary reform in Britain for more than forty years, and afterwards the military despotism which, ensuing upon it in due course, threatened the freedom of all Europe; that he completed that concentration of Imperial authority in the British Isles which was at once requisite to the creation and existence of the modern British Empire, and the indispensable preliminary to any scheme of Home Rule, Irish, English, or Scottish, not inconsistent with that Empire's union. For this great work, threefold in detail, but in principle and in conception one, his character has been persistently assailed and blackened ever since. The calumnies and invective launched against his memory to-day are but the faint echo of the Whig abuse of the earlier portion of the century and the attacks made upon him in his own lifetime. Those who support Gladstonian Home Rule, and the exclusion of Irish members from the House of Commons, may consistently regret the abolition of the old independent Irish Legislature, and the rejection of that measure of 1886 which would have been the first step towards its revival. But to those capable of taking a somewhat larger view, of appreciating the fact that neither the world nor the Empire have stood still since the last Parliamentary Union, the final abolition of an independent Ireland in 1800 will appear the most conclusive reason for the ultimate delegation, under adequate securities, of the local affairs of the British Isles to local assemblies in Ireland, as in Scotland, and in England, subject in each case to the absolute supremacy of the one Sovereign Parliament. To condemn Pitt is to acknowledge that what you mean by Home Rule is in reality the repeal of the Union.

That Peerages were given to secure the Union is true, but this unavoidable departure from his usual policy does not prove that Pitt "prostituted hereditary titles." Have peerages never been given before or since to reward the hardly gained support, or the tardy conversion to his measures, of the followers of a Whig or Liberal statesman? What of the wholesale creation of Peers threatened by the Whigs to secure the passing of the first Reform Bill? It is impossible to condemn Pitt and to acquit Lord Grey and his colleagues. The consent of certain Irish Peers and borough-mongers was necessary by the letter of the Constitution to a great and pressing measure itself of Imperial necessity. If these people had not been bribed, they would have required to be bayoneted. Pitt took the mildest and most conciliatory way out of a difficulty which was none of his creation. The fault lay, not with Pitt, but with the whole past history of Ireland, and in particular with the Whig party which for nearly a hundred years had tyrannized over that unfortunate country. The guilt, if guilt there be, of the measures taken to secure

the Union, is not in Pitt, but in Elizabeth and Cromwell and
William of Orange, in Protestant fanaticism and Anglo-Saxon
misrule, in those who had wantonly and wickedly destroyed
the major part of Ireland's ancient aristocracy, and replaced
them with Puritan adventurers. Yet even so both the nature
and the extent of the corruption have been grossly exaggerated. No law, written or unwritten, compels a ministry to
abstain from rewarding its own spontaneous supporters, and
among the Irish Peers then created or promoted some were
unquestionably men of family. The Earl of Antrim so
recreated in 1785, and the Lord Castle-Stewart advanced to
an Earldom in 1800, have been mentioned in earlier pages.
The Lord Adare of 1800 was the chief of an old Irish clan.
Two Irish Peers were English Admirals, the Lord Bridgeport
of 1794, the Lord Hotham of 1797. The Earl of Lucan
(1795) was descended in the female line from an elder brother
of the noblest hero Ireland has produced, the loyalist and
patriot Patrick Sarsfield, Earl of Lucan. The first Marquis
of Waterford (1789), already second Earl of Tyrone of the
new creation, had succeeded in 1769 to the Barony of la Poer
created in 1375.

Pitt did not ruin or corrupt the Irish Peerage. All through
the eighteenth century political inferiority had carried with
it a social disparagement. The degradation of the Irish
Peerage was long anterior to the Union and Pitt: beginning
under Elizabeth, it was completed at the battle of the Boyne.

The peerages created to secure the Union never seriously
affected the Peerage as a whole. That it has not diminished
the respect in which hereditary titles are held at heart by
the Liberal party is shown by the vast number of Liberals
who in the present reign have accepted them. A few
unworthy creations from time to time could not permanently
diminish the prestige of a body pre-eminently illustrating
that unbroken historic continuity which is the boast and
strength of the British constitution. For Professor Bryce,
when, carried away by his repugnance to the House of Lords,
he couples Pitt's creations with Napoleon's attempt to
fortify his throne with a nobility, is guilty of a very false,

inexact, and unhistorical comparison. Napoleon's nobility dated from himself, but no section of the British Peerage was dependent on the personality of Pitt. Pitt did not "prostitute hereditary titles," and it was not in Napoleon's power to prostitute them. That great man well understood the value of the hereditary principle which the theorists of our own time and country endeavour to persuade themselves that they despise; he knew well its enduring and endearing hold upon the memory and imagination of mankind. "If I had been my own grandson," he is reported to have said, "I could have rallied from the foot of the Pyrenees." He attempted to avail himself of the hereditary principle, to create a new nobility, dating from himself, which should lend its support to his dynasty and throne. But his nobility, without root in the past, had no power other than which it had derived from himself, and with its creator the creation perished.

The collapse of the Napoleonic nobility with the Napoleonic system, though far from so dismal and contemptible a failure as that of Cromwell's House of Lords, is of no value whatever as evidence against the British Peerage. "The Peerage as it exists in the three British Kingdoms," wrote Dr. Freeman, "has nothing in the least degree like it elsewhere." The old French nobility before the Revolution bore no resemblance to the British Peerage, and the nobility which Napoleon created bore no resemblance to it. What Napoleon's failure proves, and what Cromwell's failure had proved before him, is the impossibility and folly of usurpers. Like Cromwell, Napoleon was in a radically false position, from which there was and could be but one issue. His nobility rested on himself, and when he fell there was nothing to sustain it. "The title in itself of chevalier, count, duke, or prince," writes M. Taine, "carries along with it an idea of social superiority: when announced in a drawing-room, when it precedes the first sentence of an address, those who are present do not remain inattentive; an immemorial prejudice inclines them to award consideration or even deference. The Revolution tried in vain to destroy this power of words and history: Napoleon does better; he confiscates it; he arrogates to himself the monopoly of it; he steals its trademark from the old régime; he himself creates forty-eight thousand chevaliers, a thousand barons, three hundred and eighty-eight counts, thirty-one dukes, and four princes: furthermore he stamps with his own mark the old nobles whom he introduces into his nobility; he coins them anew and often with an inferior title: this or that duke is lowered a notch and becomes simply a count: taken at par or discount, the feudal coin must, in order to pass, receive the imperial stamp which gives it its recognized value in modern figures. Duc de Montebello or Prince de la Moskowa is equivalent in the imagination of contemporaries to a Duc de Montmorency or a Prince de Rohan; for if the prince or duke of the Empire is without ancestors he will be an ancestor himself." *

But to all this there was the one fatal drawback that Napoleon was a usurper. If a Monarch—it was inevitably asked—why not the real Monarch? if a nobility, why not the old nobility? "To keep the republic within bounds," as Thackeray neatly expressed it, "a despotism is necessary; to rally round the despotism, an aristocracy must be created; and for what have we been labouring all this while? for what have bastiles been battered down, and Kings' heads hurled, as a gage of battle, into the face of armed Europe? To have a Duke of Otranto instead of a Duke de la Tremouille, and Emperor Stork in place of King Log." Just in the same way people in England had resented the imposture set up by Cromwell. If the House of Lords had been abolished it was not to make room for "the Lord Richard Cromwell" and "the Lord Henry Cromwell," the "Lord Charles Fleetwood" and the "Lord John Claypole, Master of the Horse," the "Sir Thomas Pride" and the "Sir John Hewson," whom the Protector raked together as "somewhat to stand between me and the House of Commons." The few Puritan Peers nominated as members of this ridiculous body refused to have anything to do with it, and the whole affair speedily collapsed.

* "The Modern Régime," bk. iii.

Professor Bryce might with as much reason quote Cromwell's House of Lords against the Peers as the Napoleonic nobility. Cromwell's lords and Napoleon's dukes and princes failed for the same reason: because they were the ephemeral creatures of a single man, the outcome of an isolated individuality. To quote either against hereditary titles is surely the very wantonness and insanity of paradox. They failed and fell precisely because neither they themselves nor their authors were hereditary, but brand new. To be incorporated in an old-established order or noblesse by an old-established Monarchy is one thing; and to be placed in a brand-new institution by a brand-new potentate is quite another thing. Cromwell's lords were laughed out of existence, and Napoleon's dukes and princes, in spite of their military distinction, were the derision of Paris; though a Prince Bismarck or a Lord Beaconsfield is not ridiculous. Each of the usurpers named above was in himself the embodied negation of heredity, since for either of them to have appealed to the hereditary principle would have been an act of intellectual and moral suicide. In fact, the career of both these soldiers of fortune provided the most striking testimony to the virtue and validity of the hereditary principle that can be conceived. They established the principle that a usurper of the greatest genius must inevitably hold a political position weaker in the long run than that of the feeblest and most incapable prince who ever ascended a throne by hereditary right. Politics have their own laws as imperious as those of nature, and a breach of continuity in the life of the great organism called a nation is visited with the severest penalties on those who dare effect it. But the enemies of the House of Lords must be hard put to it for an argument when they allege as an argument against the British Peerage, that a foreign military tyrant, of unequalled genius, failed to establish a new nobility on the ruins of the old French noblesse.

Professor Bryce, who is nothing if not an aristocrat, tells us in the same chapter (106) of his American Commonwealth, that "the English system of hereditary titles tends to maintain the distinction of an ancient lineage far less perfectly than that simple use of a family name which prevailed in Italy during the Middle Ages or in ancient Rome. A Colonna or a Doria, like a Cornelius or a Valerius, carried the glory of his nobility in his name, whereas any upstart may be created a duke." It is remarkable how a fanatical hostility to established institutions can dull and dim the clearest intelligence. The idea put forward is evidently that a title serves to conceal the family of its bearer, and we have seen already that this is so far true that the comparative novelty of a peerage often tends to obscure the real antiquity of a family. But would any other system be either desirable or possible? Clearly, whatever may have been the case in mediæval Italy or ancient Rome, where, by the way, a certain practice of adoption conflicted somewhat with the maintenance of "an ancient lineage" as that is now generally understood, "the simple use of a family name" would fail altogether to maintain such a distinction in our modern world. In the British Empire, if not in foreign countries, people are in practice permitted to assume any name they like. We are all familiar with the development of Moses into Moss, Manasseh into Massey, Morris into de Montmorency, and with the yet more startling transformation of Joshua Bug into Norfolk Howard. One may do as the Romans did at Rome, not at Liverpool or New York. Lucius Cornelius Sulla has a different sound from Ulysses Simpson Grant, Julius Cæsar from Elijah Pogram. Double-barrelled and treble-barrelled names are permitted in the British Empire, so that the trouble is often to discover which of all his names is really a man's own name—the name, that is to say, of his paternal ancestors. It must be admitted that Brown-Jones-Robinson is a little confusing, nor is the confusion lessened when we come upon Robinson-Robinson, or Brown-Brown. Those names which are commonly esteemed the most aristocratic are the most commonly assumed by actors and actresses, music-hall stars, and the numerous classes who hang on to their skirts. In a country where any one is at liberty to take any name he likes, it cannot be said that the Dukedom of Wellington does not serve to maintain the distinction between a genuine Arthur Wellesley and an Arthur Wellesley of opera bouffe. In Scotland the greater a name the wider was its extension. There are Stuarts, not only in the Peerage, from Galloway to Moray, and hence originated the proverb, "A' Stuarts are no sib to the King." The names of Campbell, Murray, Graham, Scott, Hamilton, Gordon, Kerr, Hay, and Douglas are not unknown as those of Scotsmen, and these are also the names of the four Marquises, and six out of the eight Dukes, in the Peerage of Scotland. "Three great families in succession held the lordship of Lorn," writes Mr. E. W. Robertson, "and all Argyleshire is still full of MacDougals, Stewarts, and Campbells, offshoots of the families in question. The same may be said of Atholl, in which the Robertsons, the Stewarts, and the Murrays, names long prevalent in the district, represent the families which held the earldom, one of them still holding the dukedom. Many a Sutherland has branched off similarly in the north, and the western coasts are peopled with the descendants of different Lords of the Isles. The greater the name in Scotland the more numerous is it, and the more widely spread."* So General Stewart of Garth tells us in his book on the "Highlanders of Scotland," that there were more than a hundred Hugh Mackays to be found at one time in a certain Highland regiment.

It is obvious that in such circumstances "the simple use of a family name" would be no distinction at all. Hence there has arisen in modern times the greatly extended use of what are known as double-barrelled names. These are not invariably due, although they may be sometimes due, to ostentation or to snobbishness. A "Smith," for instance, may well be excused for putting "Payne" or "Goldwin" before it. An alleviation of this state of things would be found in the adoption of a greater variety of Christian names. But in the meantime it cannot reasonably be contended that their titles do not distinguish the Duke of Norfolk and the Earl of Effingham, both from one another, and from the countless multitude of persons who now bear the name of

---

* "Scotland under her Early Kings," vol. ii., appendix R.

Howard. It is quite certain to any one who considers the facts that an hereditary title "tends to maintain the distinction of an ancient lineage" not far less, but far more, perfectly, than any other system which as yet has been discovered. The conditions of the modern world differ beyond all comparison from those either of ancient Rome or of an Italian republic in the Middle Ages. What became of the Colonna and Doria whom Professor Bryce mentions? To-day they are dukes and princes and grandees of Spain. The "Almanach de Gotha" of 1892 gives us—

(1) "Giovanni-Andrea, prince Colonna, prince et duc de Palianoet Tursi, duc de Marino, prince d'Avello et Sonnino, etc., prince assistant au rône du St. Siége, grand d'Espagne de 1ère classe ;

(2) "Gioacchino Colonna, 6ème prince de Stigliano, prince d'Aliano, Marquis de Castelnuovo, grand d'Espagne de 1ère classe ;

(3) "Maffeo Barberini Colonna di Sciarra, prince de Carbagnano, Roviano, et Nerola, duc de Bassanello, Montelibretti, et Auticoli-Corrado, marquis de Correse, etc., comte de Pallazuolo, etc., baron et seigneur de San Stefano, etc., etc. ;

(4) "Giovanni-Antonio-Francesco-Giorgio-Landolfo Colonna, duc de Cesaro, duc de Reitano, marquis de Fiumedinisi, comte de S. Alesio, baron de Joppolo, Giancascio, etc.;

(5) "Alfonso-Maria Doria-Pamphily-Landi, prince de Melfi et de Valmontone, duc d'Avigliano."

We saw in an earlier chapter that the existence of the Peerage does not preclude the concurrent existence of a nobility independent of royal grant. But it cannot be maintained that this latter nobility is in the same secure position as the nobility founded on the Peerage. It rests on social opinion, and the opinion of society, using that word in its largest sense, is in a constant state of change. Popular opinion tends largely to identify the Peerage families with the nobility, and although this is but a vulgar error, there is considerable danger of its finding general acceptance. A Peerage is something definite and tangible, obvious to all men as a public recognition on the part of the State, but social opinion is an impalpable entity. An ancient family of the untitled aristocracy which retains possession of some portion at least of its estates will continue to enjoy some portion at least of its former social consideration ; but when the estates and the family part company it is highly probable that the social consideration will desert the family also. An hereditary peerage preserves a family and holds it together better than anything else. "Any upstart," says Professor Bryce, "may be created a duke." It would be interesting to obtain a statistical return of the upstarts who have been created Dukes in our history from first to last. But without harshly insisting upon fact in opposition to theory, "any upstart" may purchase an estate and may assume, if he does not already bear, the name of some historic family which possessed it. The law affords no protection to the bearers of historic names. But the impostor who should assume a peerage would be at once detected and exposed.

The complaint of Professor Bryce is in effect that the Peerage is an order, not a caste, a Baronage, not a noblesse. And this is true enough. Titles and primogeniture and the royal power of creating peers have made the Peerage an order, not a caste. But a complaint of this sort is out of keeping with the charge that the House of Lords oppresses the people. A complaint of this sort goes far to show that, in spite of all disclaimers, new Radical is but old Whig writ large. Professor Bryce attacks the House of Lords in the spirit of the Peerage Bill of 1719. A man could only be born a Colonna or a Doria. That the King, that is to say the nation, can make any one a Duke is far more democratic. What to the eyes of Professor Bryce are the demerits of the British Peerage, in the disinterested judgment of foreign political philosophers constitute a unique claim to public consideration, both popular and scientific, and the true secret of its enduring strength. The Peerage gives representation to aristocracy in a reasonable and practicable form. By the very limitations which it has imposed on the aristocratic principle it has preserved the aristocracy from running into vicious excess, and from meeting the fate which such vicious excess has entailed upon it in other countries. It has made aristocracy compatible with Monarchy and compatible with democracy, and in doing so it has preserved the balance of the Constitution.

The peerage has not ceased to be aristocratic, to be "either respectable or useful." If it had no other use than to preserve us from such an unchecked rule of irresponsible wealth as exists in the United States this alone would completely justify its existence. But it does much more than this. It gives a reasonable scope to ambition, and minimizes discontent. It is a great object of ambition with most prosperous men to found or continue a family, and a peerage preserves a family better than anything else. At a future date peerages even of the present time may have come to possess a venerable antiquity. There is nothing, but the natural decay of families, to prevent a peerage founded four hundred years ago from lasting for four hundred more. It gives a reasonable scope to ambition. The personal element cannot be altogether eliminated from public affairs. There is good ground for supposing that had Oliver Cromwell been made Earl of Essex there would have been no Commonwealth. A man who accepts a peerage binds himself to the established order of things. But a great general uncompromised by such a pledge may at any moment of popular dissatisfaction take advantage of it to become a military tyrant. The Peerage is of use because it saves us from a plutocracy and from a caste, from the unqualified rule of birth and from the unqualified rule of wealth. Where there is no State-regulated aristocracy the latter of these principles commonly prevails. Some one must go out of the room first. It may be very annoying to a learned historian to give place to some young whipper-snapper fresh from school or college, but if he did not he might have to yield precedence to the local "dry goods" person or some one even less acceptable.

That the peerage is "respectable" is shown by the fact that the men most respected by the nation never hesitate to accept titles, hereditary or personal, or if they refuse them do so on personal, and not on public grounds. One can understand and sympathize with the great Irish chiefs who flung aside Elizabeth's titles, but these princely leaders of Celtic and Celto-Norman clans were of other stuff than your nineteenth-century placeman and modern millionaire.

"Honours are inestimable to the honourable." Did Sir Walter Scott refuse a title, or Byron for all his Liberalism think little of his peerage—Byron whose constant allusions to his family and order won for him at school the nickname of "the old English Baron"? It is well known that Burke would have anticipated Disraeli in the title of Lord Beaconsfield but for the death of the only son in whom his hopes were centred. "Had it pleased God to continue to me the hopes of a succession," he wrote, in his "Letter to a Noble Lord," "I should have been according to my mediocrity, and the mediocrity of the age I live in, a sort of a founder of a family."

If we turn for an opinion from Professor Bryce to Lord Nelson, who lived in the very age when Pitt was "prostituting hereditary titles," what do we hear from his biographer? After the battle of the Nile, Nelson was made a Baron.

"When the grant (of £2000 a year) was moved in the House of Commons, General Walpole expressed an opinion that a higher degree of rank ought to be conferred. Mr. Pitt made answer that he thought it needless to enter into that question. 'Admiral Nelson's fame,' he said, 'would be coequal with the British name: and it would be remembered that he had gained the greatest naval victory on record, when no man would think of asking whether he had been created a baron, a viscount, or an earl.' It was strange that, in the very act of conferring a title, the minister should have excused himself for not having conferred a higher one, by representing all titles on such an occasion as nugatory and superfluous. True, indeed, whatever title had been bestowed, whether viscount, earl, marquis, duke, or prince, if our laws had so permitted, he who received it would have been Nelson still. That name he had ennobled beyond all addition of nobility: it was the name by which England loved him, France feared him, Italy, Egypt, and Turkey celebrated him; and by which he will continue to be known while the present kingdoms and languages of the world endure, and as long as their history after them shall be held in remembrance. It depended upon the degree of rank what should be the fashion of his coronet, in what page of the red book his name was to be inserted, and what precedency should be allowed his lady in the drawing-room and at the ball. That Nelson's honours were affected thus far, and no farther, might be conceded to Mr. Pitt and his colleagues in administration: but the degree of rank which they thought proper to allot was the measure of their gratitude, though not of his services. This Nelson felt, and this he expressed, with indignation, among his friends."*

---

* "Life," by Southey, ch. v.

"Honours are inestimable to the honourable." "Ribbons, and regalia, and rubbish," as Sir Wilfred Lawson, decorated himself with a self-bestowed Blue Ribbon, once styled the honours granted to its servants by the Crown, were to the greatest naval hero whom England has produced precious almost beyond their real value. Let us turn to another chapter (nine) of his Life.

"He wore that day [the day of Trafalgar], as usual, his admiral's frock coat, bearing on the left breast four stars, of the different orders with which he was invested. Ornaments which rendered him so conspicuous a mark for the enemy were beheld with ominous apprehensions by his officers. It was known that there were riflemen on board the French ships; and it could not be doubted but that his life would be particularly aimed at. They communicated their fears to each other, and the surgeon, Mr. Beatty, spoke to the chaplain, Dr. Scott, and to Mr. Scott, the public secretary, desiring that some person would entreat him to change his dress or cover the stars; but they knew that such a request would highly displease him. 'In honour I gained them,' he had said, when such a thing had been hinted to him formerly, 'and in honour I will die with them.'"

It would be impossible to give an instance of a great naval or military commander who refused a Peerage, though some generals and admirals have freely expressed their dissatisfaction that no such honour had been offered them. And what was accepted by Clive and Wellington, by Howe and Hawke and Rodney and Duncan and St. Vincent in their own day, has not been refused in ours by Lord Wolseley and Lord Roberts, Lord Clyde and Lord Strathnairn, Lord Alcester, and Lord Napier of Magdala. Peerages form a cheap reward for naval and military services. The practice of awarding them to distinguished officers forms such a "custom" as Bacon advocated in his Essay, "Of the True Greatness of Kingdoms and Estates," for "adding amplitude and greatness to a Kingdom." "The wars of later ages," he regrets, "seem to be made in the dark, in respect of the glory and honour which reflected upon men from the wars in ancient time." He dwells on the paucity of distinctions offered to generals in modern times, and urges the fullest employment of such as were in existence. "But in ancient times the trophies erected upon the place of the victory, the funeral laudatives and monuments for those that died in the wars, the crowns and garlands personal, the style of emperor, which the great Kings of the world after borrowed, the triumphs of the generals upon their return, the great donatives and largesses upon the disbanding of the armies, were things able to inflame all men's courages : but, above all, that of the triumph amongst the Romans was not pageants or gaudery, but one of the wisest and noblest institutions that ever was." Peerages and orders of Knighthood are almost our only rewards for successful soldiers and sailors, and that they are appreciated has been seen. So, too, in civil life it is "sublime mediocrity" that esteems its own services beyond reward and above recognition, not the inspired genius of the Heaven-sent Minister. The great Parliamentary middleman may refuse the highest honour that it is in the power of his Sovereign and country to bestow, but the Great Commoner becomes the Earl of Chatham.

We are told that the Peerage is not aristocratic, and when we ask for proof, we receive the answer that this ancient body, coeval with the first beginning of our Parliamentary institutions, and in origin far earlier, has recruited its numbers from those most eminent for power, distinction, and ability in each succeeding generation, and by so doing has diminished its own lustre and prestige !

CHAPTER II.

THE RADICAL CASE AGAINST THE HOUSE OF LORDS AS A SECOND CHAMBER.

THE Radical charge against the Peers, as a constituent element directly or indirectly of the House of Lords, that as an aristocracy they are not aristocratic, has been examined at some length, and we have seen that if the British Peerage does not reproduce the transcendent glories of the German and Hindu caste systems, it has at least the humbler merit of representing the men of Trafalgar and Waterloo. It remains to consider the other objections, partly practical, partly theoretical, that the House of Lords is a House of "hereditary legislators," and that hereditary legislators are absurd and wrong in principle; that the House of Lords oppresses the people; and that the presence of the Bishops in the House of Lords, though they do not in any sense owe their seats to a right hereditary in their family, is an aggravation rather than an alleviation of the other evils of the Upper Chamber.

To take the theoretical objection first, it has been seen already that the House of Lords, even without the Bishops, is not an assembly exclusively composed of "hereditary legislators." Putting aside the Prince of Wales and Duke of Clarence as extraordinary members, we found that in January, 1892, there were three hundred and eighty Lords Temporal who had inherited their seats; one Lord who, having been summoned in anticipation of his inheritance of his father's seat, must also be ranked as an hereditary legislator; and one hundred and thirty-two Lords Temporal who owed their seats to the nomination of the Crown or to election by their fellows. A House in which fifteen members held their seats for the duration of a single Parliament, in which seventy members were in effect members for life only, in which one hundred and fifty-six members did not owe their seats to "the accident of birth," is not to be fairly or accurately described as "a House of hereditary legislators." It is a House which contains hereditary legislators, but which also contains many other legislators who are not hereditary.

The charge, then, that the Upper Chamber is one of hereditary legislators applies in reality only to a portion of the Lords Temporal. The accusation against these hereditary legislators, so far as it is possible to extract any definite statement from the loose language of the Radicals on this point, appears to be that they stand condemned by the intrinsic absurdity of an hereditary right to legislate. Assuming that the justification for the existence of these Peers is based on the hereditary principle, the Radicals proceed to argue that the hereditary principle as applied to politics is without justification. But the Tory contention is just the opposite: it is not that the hereditary principle justifies the House of Lords, but that the House of Lords justifies the hereditary principle. The Lords Temporal, the English Peers as they stood before the Unions, were not called into being through a belief in hereditary legislators. They had their origin in the system of land tenure, and they were the greater vassals of the Crown. The Peerage rests upon no dogma. The Lords Temporal, like the Lords Spiritual, and like the Commons, grew up with and out of the nation. They were never summoned into existence at any given date through a belief in the virtue of hereditary legislators. That a peerage descended to one person only at a time was due to the foundation of the Baronage upon the land system of the country, Peers were summoned to Parliament as great landowners, and as an estate went to a single heir, or was divided among coheirs, so also went the Barony. Peers inherited their peerages, as the whole nation inherited its Parliament. The justification of the Peerage is, not in the hereditary principle, but in history. The intrinsic absurdity of an hereditary right to legislate does not come into the question. The abstract fitness or unfitness of hereditary legislators has no bearing on the case. But in truth no such intrinsic absurdity exists. There is no more absurdity in the hereditary right of one class of men to sit in a House of Parliament than in the hereditary right of an Englishman to trial by jury. There is nothing more absurd in the abstract in hereditary legislators than in elected legislators. Whether hereditary legislators are worse or better than elected legislators or nominated legislators, whether hereditary legislators may not work as well in one Chamber as elected legislators in another,—these are points to be tested by actual experience, not to be decided off-hand on *à priori* grounds.

The assumption of an intrinsic absurdity in hereditary legislators is based on another assumption, than which nothing can be more absurd, namely, that all men are born equal. Of all the contemptible platitudes promulgated by the French and American Revolutions this is perhaps the one most universally discredited. Science has established nothing more clearly than the infinite variety and diversity of the races of mankind, and that all men are not born equal. For the assumption that all men are born equal is one which, if it is to have political application at all, cannot be restricted to a particular nation. That all men are born equal does not mean merely that all Englishmen are born equal, or that all Englishmen, Scotsmen, and Irishmen are born equal. It means, if it means anything at all, that all Englishmen are born the equals of West Indian negroes or Bengali Baboos, of Kalmucks and Chinooks, Kurds and Kroomen. The necessary inference from the postulate of human political equality is not merely that the House of Lords should be abolished, but that India should be governed like the United Kingdom or the United Kingdom like India. All men are equal as human beings, but they are not equal in their capacity for self-government, nor in their capacity for governing others. And as one body of men, called a nation or a race, differs in this respect from another such body of men, so in a nation or a race one body of men called a class differs in this respect from another class. To say that all men are born equal is to enunciate an obvious truism or a transparent fallacy. We do not require to be told that all men are equally human, nor to be reminded that one dog is not more canine than any other dog, that all vegetables are vegetables and that not even a few of them are minerals. But if the phrase is intended to convey that all men are physically, morally, or intellectually equal, then it passes from an empty platitude into a mischievous fiction. We see this distinctly enough in the case of nations. We are all familiar with the weakness and the strength in the national character of the various peoples of Europe. And the character of a nation is the collective character of the men who compose it, the summary and general average of their weakness and their strength. We are familiar, too, with the persistence of national characteristics and their endurance from century to century. An heredity of qualities is freely acknowledged to exist in a nation. Why should it not exist, what "intrinsic absurdity" is there in supposing that it does exist, in a section of a nation? Far from there being any absurdity in hereditary legislators, considered in the abstract, the idea of such a class would be in entire conformity with the teaching of science. Nothing could accord better with antecedent probability than that a body originally composed of the rulers of the nation, and reinforced in each age by men distinguished for ability and force of character, should show an eminent capacity for the work of government and legislation. If there is anything absurd in the idea of hereditary legislators, it must be owing to its variance with nature. But, when we turn to nature, natural science gives the strongest assurance of the hereditary transmission of qualities, whether moral, physical, or intellectual.

But the House of Lords does not rest on the hereditary principle. It does not invoke science for its vindication, though if the Radicals appeal to nature as revealed to us by science, unto science they must go. The House of Lords rests upon that political experience of nations which is known as history. It has sprung up out of the past history of the

British nation, and it can point with confidence to the history of many other lands. It can point to the parallel case of Monarchy, and the fatal effects of the substitution in this case of the elective principle for the hereditary. It can point to the partition of Poland and to the disintegration of the Holy Roman Empire. It was the elective character of the Polish Monarchy that gave the foreign enemies of Poland a perpetual excuse and opportunity to interfere in her internal affairs, and that, by making the most national of institutions the standing object of domestic dissensions and foreign intrigues, ultimately occasioned the forcible dissolution of the Polish nation. It was the adoption of the elective principle that caused the break up of the German nation, not to be reunited till our own time. Let us on this point appeal from Philip the party politician to Philip the historian, and hear the judgment of that severe critic of the Peers, Professor Bryce.

"As the Germanic Empire is the most conspicuous example of a monarchy not hereditary that the world has ever seen, it may not be amiss to consider for a moment what light its history throws upon the character of elective monarchy in general, a contrivance which has always had, and will probably always continue to have, seductions for a certain class of political theorists. First of all, then, it deserves to be noticed how difficult, one might almost say impossible, it was found to maintain in practice the elective principle. In point of law, the imperial throne was from the tenth century to the nineteenth absolutely open to any orthodox Christian candidate. But as a matter of fact, the competition was confined to a few very powerful families, and there was always a strong tendency for the crown to become hereditary in one of them. Thus the Franconian Emperors held it from A.D. 1024 till 1125; the Hohenstaufen, themselves the heirs of the Franconians, for a century or more; the house of Luxembourg (Kings of Bohemia) enjoyed it through three successive reigns, and when in the fifteenth century it fell into the tenacious grasp of the Hapsburgs, they managed to retain it thenceforth (with but one trifling interruption) till it vanished out of nature altogether. Therefore the chief benefit which the scheme of elective sovereignty seems to promise, that of putting the fittest man in the highest place, was but seldom attained, and attained even then rather by good fortune than design. . . . No such objection can be brought against the second ground on which an elective system has sometimes been advocated, its operation in moderating the power of the crown, for this was attained in the fullest and most ruinous measure. We are reminded of the man in the fable who opened a sluice to water his garden, and saw his house swept away by the furious torrent. The power of the crown was not moderated but destroyed. Each successful candidate was forced to purchase his title by the sacrifice of rights which had belonged to his predecessors, and must repeat the same shameful policy later in his reign to secure the election of his son.... The electors, aware of the strength of their position, abused it to assert an independence such as the nobles of other countries could never have aspired to." *

The Electors converted themselves into Sovereign Princes, and Germany from an Empire became "an aristocratic federation." The decay of the Crown, as is always the case, was accompanied by the disintegration of the nation, and the decay of the Crown was directly due to the elective principle. So much for the elective principle as applied to Monarchy. Let us hear what the author of the American Commonwealth has to say of it as a means of securing eminent ability in high posts. If the position of Emperor was open in theory to every Christian, so the position of President of the United States is open to every native-born American citizen. And with what result?

" Since the heroes of the Revolution died out with Jefferson and Adams and Madison some sixty years ago, no person except General Grant has reached the chair whose name would have been remembered had he not been President; and no President except Abraham Lincoln has displayed rare or striking qualities in the chair. Who now knows or cares to know anything about the personality of James K. Polk or Franklin Pierce? The only thing remarkable about them is that being so commonplace they should have climbed so high. Several reasons may be suggested for the fact, which Americans themselves are the first to admit. One is that the proportion of ability drawn into politics is smaller in America than in most European countries. Great men are not chosen President, first, because great men are rare in politics; secondly, because the method of choice does not bring them to the top; thirdly, because they are not in quiet times absolutely needed." †

The method of choice does not bring them to the top. And thus in a century which has witnessed such European Sovereigns by hereditary right as the Emperor William and the Emperor Frederick, Victor Emmanuel and the Emperor King Francis Joseph, the only ruler that the loudly vaunted

* " Holy Roman Empire," ch. xiv.
† " Democracy in America," ch. viii.

American system can set beside them as having exercised a beneficial influence approximately equal on the fortunes of his country is President Lincoln.

If we look from the Holy Roman Empire to another great example of elective Monarchy, the Holy Roman Church, what do we see there? In theory the Papacy is as open as was the Empire to all members of the Roman Church, and the Holy Roman Church, unlike the Holy Roman Empire, with adherents in every country of the globe, may well claim to be œcumenical. The Papacy may be but "the ghost of the Roman Empire sitting on the grave thereof," but its spiritual Empire embraces worlds the eagles never knew. What can be more august, more sublime, than the idea of the Papacy, open in theory to every member of the Roman Church? But in practice no one is ever chosen Pope but an Italian Cardinal: none but an Italian has been chosen for generations past. So, too, it was the Italianism of the Popes that caused the great schism of Western Christendom. The Popes had sacrificed their spiritual Empire to their Italian principality, and their spiritual Empire was rent in twain. In theory any orthodox Christian, but in practice a German prince. In theory any member of the Church of Rome, in practice an Italian Cardinal. After Charles V. there was no great Emperor, and for the last three centuries at least there has been no great Pope. It may be doubted whether there is a past President of the United States of name familiar to an educated European, other than Washington and Lincoln. What President of a French Republic has left a name that will be remembered other than the President who, as "the nephew of his uncle," became Napoleon the Third? The application of the elective principle to the chief of the State is the enthronement of mediocrity.

If, on the other hand, we ask of the hereditary principle what it has to show in modern times, we are given Henry of Navarre and Gustavus Adolphus, the unjustly decried Louis the Fourteenth, whose acquisitions for France proved more enduring than those of Napoleon; his great antagonist the third William Prince of Orange, and two Sovereigns out of those three to whom alone, since Charlemagne, the usage of the world confirms the name of Great.

Clearly therefore, it is the elective principle, not the hereditary, that requires to stand on its defence. It is the elective principle that is condemned by science and finds no countenance from history. It is the intrinsic absurdity of elected legislators, if of any, that gives good ground for derisive comment.

If we turn to the great Republics of history, we find that the only two which succeeded in establishing a lasting dominion, Rome and Venice, were both eminently under the influence of the hereditary principle. Venice is the extreme type of aristocracy in its excess. The Shutting of the Great Council at Venice excluded from power and office in the State all but the descendants of those who had held office previous to the Shutting. Rome continued an aristocratic commonwealth in fact, though not in law, down to the last days of the Republic. *Fato Romæ fiunt Metelli consules.* The triumph of the Plebs over the Patriciate for the time replaced a nobility of birth with a nobility of office, but the nobility of office grew into a new nobility of birth.

"The Roman Plebs, so largely composed of the inhabitants of allied and conquered cities who had been admitted in a mass to the plebeian franchise, naturally contained many families which were, in wealth and nobility of descent, the equals of the proudest patricians. When the great magistracies were opened to the plebeians it was mainly by plebeians of this class that they were filled, and out of them combined with the old patriciate a new nobility arose. Every descendant of a curule magistrate, whether patrician plebeian, was *nobilis*; he had the *jus imaginum*, the right of exhibiting the images of the forefathers who had held high office, the number of which formed the measure of his nobility. Thus grew up a noble class, clothed with no legal privileges, but which gradually became as well marked in practice as ever the old patriciate had been, and which looked on the great offices of the commonwealth as its exclusive right. In the latter days of the commonwealth the consulship of, a new man, a man whose forefathers had never held curule office, though forbidden by no law, and though the man might be Caius Marius himself, seemed as strange as the consulship of a Lutatius or a Licinius once had been." *

This oligarchy only disappeared to make room for the Cæsars.

* Freeman.

The hereditary principle may appear absurd to persons who have never taken the trouble to consider it, or who are mentally incapable of doing so, but to students of history the great science of comparative politics teaches the lesson that either a strong and powerful Monarchy, or else a strong and powerful aristocracy, is absolutely indispensable to the welfare and greatness of a State. The hereditary principle in one form or the other, or in both, is the most vital element of political power and national existence. All the great States, that have not been great Monarchies, have been great oligarchies. If in our Constitution the democratic element has played a larger part than in those of most great States, this is because the Monarchy has never succeeded in destroying the aristocracy, nor the aristocracy in abolishing the Monarchy. The hereditary principle, dual in its embodiment, but undivided in essence, has through its twofold expression made room for a third partner in the State. Through the balance of the Constitution we have obtained an official nobility in no danger of stagnation and decay, and a Crown whose continuous efficiency is independent of the genius or the want of genius in any individual Sovereign. The hereditary principle in this double form has been so skilfully limited in either by its twin expression as to give it within and by virtue of those limitations redoubled force and a perpetually renewed vitality. Without the Baronage popular liberty might never have been won at all: without the Monarchy it must infallibly have perished beneath the unimpeded growth of oligarchical ascendency.

The testimony of history rebukes the foolish and unfounded expressions of contempt lavished upon hereditary legislators. The favourite Radical assumption of hereditary unfitness in a class of hereditary nobles is one without corroboration from outside, and refuted by the facts of our own history. It is not uncommon to hear the Peers attacked on the ground that peerages descend in the order of primogeniture, with an implied suggestion that the eldest son is always the fool of the family. The teaching of science on heredity might possibly apply, it is asserted, to the Peerage, if it were a caste instead of an order, might possibly apply even to the Peerage families, but cannot be adduced in favour of the Peerage itself. But the people who make use of this argument leave out of sight the obvious fact that it is not always, or nearly always, the eldest son of the last Peer who succeeds to a peerage. Sometimes it is the eldest surviving son, sometimes it is a brother, an uncle, or a nephew. Frequently it is a far more distant relative. Examples have been previously given of junior branches of Peerage families founding peerages of their own, and afterwards succeeding to the honours of the elder line. But many more examples might be given where a junior branch of a Peerage family that has not founded a peerage of its own has succeeded, after considerable length of time, to the representation of the family and its Peerage. Peers are not all eldest sons; they are selected by nature from the whole body of persons, sometimes several hundreds in number, in the line of succession to any given peerage; and the doctrine of heredity does not therefore apply to them to its full extent. But, supposing that all Peers who had inherited a peerage were the eldest sons of its last possessor, what of that? All eldest sons are not idiots, neither are all the eldest sons of Peers. No one would seriously advance the assertion that every firstborn son is a fool, or that first-born sons are as a rule inferior to the younger members of a family, and what is true of firstborn sons in general is true of the firstborn sons of Peers. What has given rise to the argument under consideration is the circumstance that the eldest sons of Peers, being as a rule the heirs to large landed property, have no occasion to make their own way in the world, and consequently have few opportunities of showing what there is in them. But the absence of an occasion or an opportunity to prove military, or diplomatic, or forensic ability does not prove the absence of the ability. The fact of a Peer succeeding as a rule to large landed estates, and the duties and business falling to landed proprietors, tends to debar them and their eldest sons from achieving the distinction so often attained by junior members of their family. A landed proprietor is not in the position of a fund-holder, or other such unattached capitalist, who can transport himself anywhere free from all ties of residence and local obligation. His estates belong to a great landed proprietor, but he also belongs to his estates. They are in themselves a profession, a business, an occupation. Every landed proprietor has his appointed place in the unpaid local government of the country. It is impossible for a man to be discharging the public duties of a resident landlord in Cumberland or Cornwall, and at the same time to be taking part in an expedition against Indian hill tribes, or writing a report on the condition and prospects of Parliamentary institutions in Bulgaria. The Imperial Parliament is at present also a local Legislature for Great Britain and Ireland, uniting, as it were, the functions of a Dominion Parliament (to the power of three) with such as are exercised by the Imperial German Bundesrath and Reichstag, and, so long as this highly anomalous arrangement continues, the knowledge of local wants acquired by Peers in the fulfilment of their local duties is no unimportant contribution to the enlightenment and efficiency of the Legislature as a whole. The absorption of many Peers in the local affairs of various portions of the British Isles might not of itself justify their presence in a purely Imperial Senate, but it cannot be said to tell against their sitting in the Upper House of a Parliament which deals with the local affairs of England, Scotland, and Ireland. The Lord Lieutenant of a country is to the smaller unit of the British Isles what the Lord Lieutenant of Ireland or the Governor of New Zealand is to the larger, and the true, unit of the world-wide British nation.

But, notwithstanding the fact that they are much hampered by local obligations, a large number of Peers in each generation show their inherited capacity for high affairs, not merely in Parliament, but in the official service of the nation. To those who complain, as the opponents of the Peerage have been known to complain in the press, that the second Duke of Wellington was not a great general like his father, no answer is possible save that what they demand is not in nature. Two Wellingtons or two Napoleons, father and son of equal genius, would be as great a portent as two Shakespeares, two Raphaels, or two Mozarts. Genius of the first order is not a mercantile investment to be conducted with a "Company" or "Sons." But that a high capacity, a talent only short of genius, is transmissible in families has been proved by innumerable instances. And it is this high capacity for affairs that is required in the members of a select assembly, and not the genius which from the nature of things is ever isolated and unique. Now the current belief, diligently propagated by Radical orators and writers, that the Peers are wanting as a whole in this kind of ability is entirely baseless. It is a superstition, nothing else. The old Whig doctrine that a King must necessarily be a fool, but a Whig Duke a being of divine intelligence and virtue, has been developed by the Radicals into the doctrine that Whig Dukes are fools too, if not something worse, and that the true quintessence of perfection is to be found in the editor of a society journal. A generation that has witnessed the establishment of the Kingdom of Italy and the resurrection of the German nation stands in no need of further disproof of the first assertion, and that hereditary legislators are not hereditary fools we shall see by a reference to the facts given in Appendices C and F.

The examples given there of hereditary genius in some of our noblest families may suffice to show the falsity and absurdity of the charge of hereditary incapacity advanced against the hereditary legislators. Such charges have their rise in nothing better than an angry intolerance of opposition, or a desperate endeavour to explain the embarrassing and inconvenient circumstance of a disinterested condemnation. It is asserted that hereditary legislators are wanting in political capacity, and the only evidence that is offered in support of the assertion is the fact that they have presumed to differ with the Liberal party in Great Britain. The attack on "the hereditary principle," like the charge that the Peerage is not aristocratic, is a mere missile of party warfare, recklessly launched without consideration or reflection. It is natural enough that the persistent opposition offered to their proposals by the House of Lords should cause annoyance, and, it may be, some secret uneasiness, to the more intellectual Liberals, and that they should endeavour to console themselves for this with the vain imagination that it is no true aristocracy, that a real nobility, or an ideal nobility, would hasten to further all their wishes. But such a theory will not hold water. Judged by all the canons of political science the Peerage must be pronounced one of the most truly aristocratic bodies that have ever existed. Indeed the impartial judgment of German political philosophers would appear to go even beyond this. And still less will the rash and startling assertions, born of sheer ignorance and haste, of the unintellectual Liberals pass muster. Their misdirected shafts of clumsy ridicule can only serve to demonstrate the strength of the position they assail. Their charges against the hereditary principle are based on nothing else than their personal assertions, and are flatly contradicted by history and science—by science as regards antecedent probability, by history as regards the proof of facts. Seek as they may to vary the ground of their attack, their charges all ultimately reduce themselves to this, that the House of Lords is, in the opinion of advanced Radicals, " a Tory caucus," or, as it is variously expressed, that it is " out of touch with the democracy," and that it " oppresses the people."

Now, that there is a great and growing divergence of political opinion between the majority of the members of the House of Lords and the Liberal party in Great Britain, is admitted on all hands. But that the House of Lords, therefore, oppresses the British people, is an inference which requires to be established. At the same time, there is a directness and a comparative rationality about the charge which entitles it to more respect than can be extended to such obvious after-thoughts and idle trivialities as the attack on the hereditary principle, and the allegation that the Peerage is not aristocratic. If the House of Lords really oppressed the people, that, as has been said, would be a reason more than sufficient for the drastic reform, or, if such reform proved unavailing, then for the abolition, of the

House of Lords. The majority of those who advance this charge say further that the cause of this oppression of the people is to be found in the peculiar constitution of the House of Lords. They do not urge that every Second Chamber must of necessity oppress the people, but only that this particular Upper Chamber does so, and they urge as the reason of its doing so that it is principally composed of hereditary Peers. It cannot be said that this charge is wanting in plausibility. As we have seen, aristocracies have again and again oppressed the people. They have oppressed the people by depriving them of all power in the State, and they have oppressed the people by destroying their national union. Thus at Venice the nobility gradually ousted the people from all political power. Beginning as an elective body, the Great Council converted itself by degrees into the closest of close corporations. First the change was introduced that none but the descendants of former councillors could be elected; next, election itself was abolished, and all descendants of former councillors became members on attaining their legal majority.

"The optimates of Venice did what the optimates of Rome strove to do: they established a nobility where the one qualification was descent from those who had held office in former times. This is what the nobility of office, if left unchecked, naturally grows into." *

All those families, and all those branches of families, which were not represented on the Great Council at the time of the Shutting, which was effected by a series of changes between 1297, and 1319, were excluded for ever from the political power and privilege of the ruling class which thus established itself, and this although some of them were as noble as the families and branches of families then represented on it. The office of Doge became a byword for weakness, the nobility established a monopoly of power, and the people were excluded from all voice in the State.

This is one way in which a nobility may oppress the people. Again, a nobility may oppress a people by destroying or disintegrating the nation, either by breaking up the State or

* Freeman.

Kingdom into a number of smaller States or principalities, or by depressing the Crown, which is the centre of national union, or by both processes together; for where the first of these courses is pursued the second necessarily follows. In Germany the nobility of the Empire became dynastic and territorial; bit by bit they extracted from the weakness of elected Emperors all the rights and powers of Sovereign Princes, till, with the Peace of Westphalia, national disintegration became complete. So dire and deep-rooted was the disease, so fell and pernicious its effects, that even to this day Germany has scarcely recovered full national union. The Imperial Bundesrath, with the representatives of four Kingdoms, six Grand Duchies, five Duchies, and seven Principalities, if it commemorates the national resurrection of Germany, is also a standing memorial of her national decay.

"The tendency to sovereignty," writes Bluntschli, "was characteristic and powerful, and had a disastrous effect on the Empire. It led the most eminent families to sacrifice the majesty of the Empire to the claims of the Papacy, to weaken and cripple the German monarchy, completely break up the national unity, and make German territory subject to foreigners."

As they had made use of the Pope in the Middle Ages against the Emperor, so afterwards, when the progress of the Continental Reformation had brought these old enemies together, they made use of Protestantism against them both. The enlightened policy of a great French statesman, a Prince of the Church of Rome, eagerly grasped the opportunity of striking a death-blow at the power of the Empire. From the Peace of Westphalia the German nation remained in a state of dissolution down to the present day. In their unrivalled selfishness, the German Princes never shrank from allying themselves with France against the House of Austria, till at length under Napoleon the very name of the Empire vanished into space. Napoleon, besides causing Francis the Second to declare the Holy Roman Empire dissolved, as a consequence of the Confederation of the Rhine, secularized the ecclesiastical principalities, and mediatized seventy-two secular princes and lords. At the same time, he created the Elector of Bavaria a King, and soon after raised the ruler of

Wurtemberg to the same dignity. The rulers of Brandenburg had before this become Kings of Prussia, but the province from which they derived this style was a non-German possession of the Hohenzollern dynasty. The Electors of Hanover had also for nearly a hundred years occupied the throne of Britain, and an Elector of Saxony had become King of Poland. Now, however, the Kingdoms of Saxony, Bavaria, and Wurtemberg proclaimed the utter ruin of the German nation as the result of the ambition of its nobles. Thirty-four sovereign princedoms were recognized by the German Confederation in 1815, besides many princely families of sovereign rank. The number has since been reduced by voluntary resignation, natural extinction, and annexations, the spirit of German nationality, so long disembodied, having become incarnate in the Hohenzollern Monarchy; but twenty-one principalities survive, beside the Kingdom of Prussia, as a perpetual monument of the disasters that may be brought upon a nation by the unrestrained predominance of a nobility.

France had gone through the same process of disintegration at an earlier period, though the natural hatred of parochialism in a Celtic people of Latin civilization enabled them to recover earlier and more completely from the ravages of the disease.

"The Carolingian Mayors of the Palace," writes Bluntschli, "put themselves at the head of the powerful military nobility. They helped to confirm the nobles in their domains, and with their aid they drove out the degenerate Kings. This movement found its main and constant support in Northern France, in Austria, where the Germans were dominant, and which was hence called Francia Teutonica, as opposed to the Roman France of the South. The nobility of office and service became more and more a feudal nobility of Barons, Seniores, and Vassals, each of whom learned to feel his independence within his own sphere. Thus the transition was made from the hierarchy of royal officials to the independent sovereignty of Seigneurs: and the new nobility became hereditary with their fiefs."

The natural consequences were those indicated by Professor Freeman and other historians who have described the Feudal System. The empire of Charlemagne was broken up into a

number of fiefs ; the nominal ruler of France was only the
first among the great lords of his kingdom, and his own
authority, as well as the liberties of his people, were completely overshadowed by the new counts and dukes, who were
absolute masters of their own provinces and threatened the
existence of the monarchy itself.

More than one of the Plantagenet Kings of England held a
larger portion of France under his rule than the French King.
The first of them, Henry II., held Normandy, Maine, Touraine,
Anjou, Poitou, Guienne, and Gascony, having acquired some
of these possessions from his parents and others with his wife.

By slow degrees the French Kings restored the shattered
fabric of French unity, and in this way or that, by war, by
contract, or by succession, recovered the lost provinces.
Vermandois was recovered by Philip Augustus in 1183;
Gothia and Toulouse by Philip III. in 1270. In 1285
Champagne fell by marriage to Philip IV. In 1453 Gascony
and Aquitaine were conquered and annexed by Charles VII.
Anjou was annexed by Louis XI. in 1474, and Burgundy in
1479 by the same Monarch. Brittany came by marriage to
Francis I. in 1552, and Louis XIV. claimed and took South
Flanders in 1667. The victory of the King and the nation
over feudal oligarchy and disintegration was practically completed by Louis XI., though feudal privileges, apart from
feudal power, lingered on down to the Revolution. Louis XI.
broke down the territorial and dynastic nobility. The figure
of Charles the Bold, Duke of Burgundy, is in French history
what the Kingmaker is in English, the embodiment of
expiring feudalism. But, just as in Germany the great
nobles took advantage of the Continental Reformation to
complete their victory over the nation and convert themselves
into sovereign and practically independent princes, so in a
less degree was it in France. Just as in England those Peers
who sought to revive the old bad ways of feudalism in a novel
form allied themselves with a *bourgeoisie* who wished to
substitute the Continental for the Anglican Reformation, so
in France great nobles availed themselves of Calvinism for a
final onslaught on the Crown.

K

"The Huguenots were a small fraction of the nation. Whatever importance they possessed they derived from their rank, their turbulence, and the ambition of their leaders. In a few towns of the south and southwest they formed a majority of the population. But everywhere else they were mostly noblemen, full of the arrogance and reckless valour of their class, anything but Puritans in their morals, and ready to destroy the unity of the Kingdom for political no less than religious objects." [*]

It was this disloyal, unpatriotic, and anti-national attitude of the French Puritans, strongly contrasting in these respects with the English Roman Catholics, that roused the fierce hatred of the French people, shown in the Massacre of St. Bartholomew, and occasioned that lasting resentment which brought about the Revocation of the Edict of Nantes. The French people, never inspired with the Gothic or Semitic intolerance of Spain, persecuted the Huguenots not as heretics but as traitors, and it is undeniable that no body of religionists ever did more to deserve the name.

The miseries suffered by France under the feudal oligarchy, never afterwards forgotten, account for the enthusiastic devotion of the French nation to their Kings before the Revolution, for the passionate ardour with which all traces of provincial autonomy were finally swept away at the Revolution, and for the strong centralized administration which survives all changes in the outward form of government. "France one and indivisible" had a meaning for French ears, such as "England one and indivisible" could never convey to the more fortunate people of a land united for ever by that greatest of national blessings the Norman Conquest.

The history of Venice furnishes us with an example of the way in which a nobility may thrust out a people from all place or power in the State. The history of Germany and the history of France show us how a nobility by depressing the Crown may break up a nation. The history of Poland, —were it worth while to proceed,—might show us how by a steady pursuance of the same policy it is possible for a nobility to obliterate a nation. Our own history shows us how a section of the Peers struck a heavy blow at the union of the three nations. First, they contrived to expel

[*] E. S. Beesly, "Queen Elizabeth."

LOSS OF THE AMERICAN COLONIES.

the national dynasty of Stuart, and in doing so injuriously affected the Crown not only as the centre of union in each nation but as the centre of the union of all three. No thanks or praise are due to those Whig statesmen who projected and pressed on the Parliamentary Union of Great Britain, for it was the Revolution alone that had made it a necessity. Under the old Constitution the concentration of Imperial power in the person of the Monarch rendered an Imperial Parliament superfluous. Home Rule, in an enlarged sense of the expression, could well exist in this effectual, though rough, Imperial Federation. When the King in Council was superseded by the King in Parliament then came the necessity for that concentration in a new form of Imperial authority in the British Isles, of which the previous embodiment had been destroyed. At the cost of repeated civil wars a remedy was discovered for the evils wrought by the Revolution, which remedy was itself in some respects little better than the disease. To the expulsion of the Stuarts we owe the Irish difficulty existing at the present day, and, as a point of constitutional law, the loss of the American Colonies. The American Provincials rebelled, so they claimed, perhaps with dubitable sincerity, not against the lawful authority of the King, but against the usurped authority of the Parliament of Great Britain. They contended that their Legislatures stood in the same relation to the Crown as the Parliament of Scotland had occupied before the Union. It is manifest that but for the limitations of the prerogative introduced by the Revolution it would have been perfectly possible for the British Sovereign to act as King of America without violence to his constitutional relation to the parent lands. Among the many random and reckless charges brought against that great Monarch and admirable man, King George the Third, none is more unjust than the indictment that by his restoration of the Monarchy he lost America. It was the very intensity of his loyalty to his engagements, of his unswerving fidelity to the conditions on which he had received the Crown, that closed to him a line of policy which an unscrupulous Sovereign might have followed with success. Instead of taking advantage of this great opportunity to undo the Revolution settlement, he honestly and honourably asserted the supremacy of Parliament; and it was this, the assertion of Parliamentary supremacy on the part of Great Britain, which the Americans put forward as the final pretext of their separation.

The Revolution of 1688, as a matter of constitutional law, caused the loss of the American Colonies. It also created the Irish difficulty as it exists at the present day. To the triumph of the Whigs we owe it that there is at the present day in the Parliament of the three Kingdoms a body of legislators, elected not hereditary, the constitutional representatives of the Irish Commons, whose open hostility to the British Empire is hardly to be allayed by the prospect of Irish legislative autonomy, and of whom some have publicly expressed a desire for Irish independence. To the triumph of the Whigs we owe it that wherever the Irish race is to be found throughout the world, within or without the Queen's dominions, there also exists a just and burning resentment of the wrongs inflicted upon their country by England in the past, and, in too many cases, a passionate longing for revenge. Scotland alienated till the accession of King George the Third, Ireland alienated down to the present day,—such was the effect on the national and natural union of the three peoples of the British Isles of the triumph achieved by the Whig oligarchy in the expulsion of the Stuarts.

Having succeeded in effacing for a time the national character of the Monarchy, the great Whig nobles went further, and attempted to subvert the national character of the other elements of the British Constitution. Of the three Estates of the Realm they attacked with the greatest virulence the English Church as the former ally of the Monarchy. In Scotland the Revolution swept the Church away, and established Presbyterianism in its stead. In Ireland the Anglican Church exaggerated all the abuses brought by Whig dominance on the Church in England. Described by Swift as no better than highwaymen, the Irish prelates find their true example in Archbishop Stone of Dublin, a man fitter to be the high priest of some Pagan mysteries than a Christian bishop. In England the constitutional organ of the Church's voice was silenced. Convocation was suppressed, and Whig Bishops were appointed, of whom the Churchmanship of most stood in no need of denial, and the Christianity of not a few was with too much reason suspected. Dissent became rampant, and for the first time in her history the Church of England ceased to be regarded as before everything the Church of the people.

The House of Lords, as has been seen, they endeavoured to convert into a close corporation of the then existing Peerage, a body almost as hermetically sealed against all outside influence as the Great Council of Venice itself. Foiled, happily, in this attempt by the internal dissensions of the Whig party, and the jealousy of the great Peers felt by Sir Robert Walpole and his bourgeois supporters, they were more successful in their attack upon the Commons. Partly by the operation of the Whig Septennial Act, partly by the elaborate system of national corruption instituted by Sir Robert Walpole, partly by the general influence of Whig ascendency, and partly by the causes which had made the establishment of that ascendency possible, the "people's Chamber" was converted into an assembly which, if not aristocratic in any true sense of the word, was anti-popular and anti-national. Instead of protecting the people from the oligarchy, it became a buttress and outwork of oligarchic power. It was the storm of this stronghold of the Whig families by the resuscitated nation under George the Third that first turned their attention to the cause of Parliamentary reform.

It appears, then, that the charge against the Peers, or the House of Lords, that it or they "oppress the people," has in it nothing farfetched or improbable. We have seen from the examples of foreign lands that it is perfectly possible for a nobility to bring the greatest misery and ruin on a people, even to the extent of destroying their national existence. And we have seen further that the particular body of nobles known as the Whig Peers did as a fact inflict great loss and suffering on the three nations of the British Isles, that they brought evils upon the commonalty and the whole body politic which are still felt at the present day. If it be said that the House of Lords has oppressed the people, there are few who would be venturesome enough to dispute such an assertion. If it be said that the Peers at the Revolution, and afterwards, under George the First and George the Second, sought to destroy the constitutional liberty of the nation and to found a governing oligarchy on the ruin of the power of the people and the Crown, few will be foolhardy enough to challenge such a statement. Undoubtedly the House of Lords has oppressed the people. But does it oppress the people now? Is it possible to maintain with truth and justice that it has oppressed the people at any period since the reforms effected in its composition by King George the Third? These are questions to which an affirmative answer must be given before the Radical charge can be considered proven. That the House of Lords oppressed the people under the first monarchs of the House of Hanover is no better reason for its abolition now, than is the oppression practised by King John for the abolition of the Monarchy, or the oppression practised by the House of Commons in the time of the Great Rebellion and the Interregnum for the abolition of the House of Commons.

It is not pretended by the most intemperate critics of the House of Lords that the Peers are engaged in breaking up the British Empire into a number of independent Principalities or semi-independent fiefs. They are not charged with aspiring to the position of a Nizam of Hyderabad or a Begum of Bhopal, a Maharaja of Gwalior or a Maharaja of Mysore. The Whiggiest of Whig Dukes is not employed in erecting his estates into a Duchy of Burgundy or a Duchy of Brunswick. Instead of disintegrating the Empire, the Peers act as connecting links between the peoples of its various lands. The knowledge displayed in the debates of the House of Lords of foreign and Imperial affairs is notoriously far greater than that displayed in the debates of the House of Commons; and Imperial affairs, the affairs of the

Empire, are for the most part the affairs of the Colonies and India. On these subjects the Peers, with no fear of the constituencies before their eyes, can speak with a freedom, and a detachment from the local prejudices of the British Isles, which is impossible to members of the House of Commons. The experience acquired by many Peers, either as Colonial and Indian Governors, or in the United Service when quartered in the Colonies and India or on naval stations, or by travelling and contact with distinguished and influential persons in the Colonies and India, enables them to speak not only with freedom, but with judgment—a judgment which often strikingly contrasts with the ill-informed and ill-considered utterances of speakers in the House of Commons. The House of Lords is beyond dispute the Imperial branch of the Legislature, both as regards composition and as regards views. Instead of disintegrating the Empire, the Peers largely assist to hold it together.

Neither is it said, nor could it be said with any show of reason, that the Peers are attempting to tread in the footsteps of the Venetian nobles or our own Peerage Bill and Revolution Peers. So far are they from endeavouring to convert their order into a caste, or a close corporation, that it is actually made a reproach to them, by persons who doubtless believe themselves to be sound democrats, that they are not sufficiently exclusive. They are taunted with according too ready and generous a recognition to the new elements of aristocracy that from time to time appear upon the surface of the nation's life. "If you were only like the Colonnas and Dorias," it is hinted to them, "you might oppress us as much as you chose, and nothing should be said about it: but you *will* take into your ranks *parvenus* and *nouveaux riches*." They are attacked by Liberals for their too great liberality, and denounced in the same sentence for not being aristocratic and for being out of harmony with democratic feeling.

It is clear that, if the House of Lords is oppressing the people, it is not oppressing them in any of the ways that one might look for from the example of French, or German, or Venetian, or our own history. The Lords are not attempting to change the dynasty; they have not essayed to put a stop to further additions to their number; they do not indulge themselves at stated intervals in the luxury of an academic debate as to the propriety or otherwise of the elective principle in the constitution of the House of Commons. If the Lords are oppressing the people it can only be in one way, and that is by their legislative action as an Upper Chamber. The accusations of their enemies are not remarkable for coherence or lucidity. It appears, however, to be admitted that they are not charged with an active policy of aggression, but with offering too stubborn and prolonged a resistance to the measures sent up to them by a Liberal majority in the House of Commons.

It is said with truth that the Peers have opposed, and in some cases greatly retarded the passage, of nearly every measure that has been brought forward by the Liberal party and passed into legislation from the early years of the present century. It is claimed that they have persistently obstructed every Liberal reform, and that, while experience shows them to have been wrong in the past, they are still pursuing the same policy to-day. And it is undeniable that the Peers offered a stubborn opposition to the first Reform Bill, and that they greatly retarded the removal of religious disabilities, or rather of civil disabilities, on account of Religion. If we believe that because the Peers were once wrong they must always be wrong, or that because the Liberal party was once right it must always be right, we shall have little hesitation in condemning the House of Lords. It must be allowed that the Liberal party, with whatever motive, did a great and beneficent work in that liberalization and democratization of our institutions which was a necessary condition of nineteenth-century colonial expansion, and the indispensable basis of the full union in the future of the British nation throughout the world. Whether democracy is in itself wise or unwise, a bad or a good form of government, it is the natural and inevitable outcome of the social conditions of the age, and, for the present at least, indispensable. It were an unedifying task to consider the motives from which the

Whigs introduced the first Reform Bill, though it is neither uncharitable nor inaccurate to suppose that they did so principally in the hope of recovering their lost ascendency, and with little idea of the far-reaching consequences of that measure. But by the introduction of the Reform Bill began the gradual extension of the franchise, while by the removal of Roman Catholic and Nonconformist disabilities the State became free to all without distinction of religion. These measures of reform were opposed by the Peers, and it is said that they thereby constituted themselves the enemies of progress and of the people.

With a large number of persons the mere fact that the Peers were unsuccessful in their opposition to these measures is taken to show that they were wrong. But, to put the matter on rather higher grounds, it may be said that, inasmuch as the State embraces all citizens, it is sound policy to give a direct voice in public affairs to as many of them as is possible without hazarding the existence or welfare of the State, and at the same time to assert the supremacy of the State over all religious denominations by ceasing to identify a share in its government with the membership of any one of them. If these premises be accepted it will be seen that the Peers were wrong in opposing these reforms, but that they were not altogether wrong. Events have on the whole falsified their anticipations of resultant evil, but they have also proved that in some respects their fears were thoroughly well founded.

In considering the probable effects of any suggested change or reform in politics, it is impossible to exclude altogether from consideration the political antecedents of those who bring it forward. It is true that many political changes are attended by results the very reverse of what their authors either desired or foresaw. But the majority of men, always prone to identify political principles with a party or a person, naturally look for some personal or party motive in the advocates of every change, and are apt to estimate its probable effects from the sanguine anticipations of its promoters of whom they judge by their past public conduct. Now, at the time of the first Parliamentary Reform agitation the antecedents of the Whig party were as bad as they well could be. At the time of the great struggle with Napoleon their attitude had been one of open sympathy with the foreign enemies of their own country. Sober reflection has probably convinced the majority of those who took part in it, that the "Bulgarian atrocities" agitation is an incident for which English and Scottish Liberals have good reason to blush. But imagine the "Bulgarian atrocities" agitation carried on in the height of the Crimean War, and a Crimean War in which the forces of Austria and Prussia were joined to those of Russia and Britain was without a single ally, and you get a faint idea of the extremity of bad citizenship and anti-patriotism shown by the Whigs during the great contest with Napoleon. They stood before the country as an anti-national and anti-British party which had not failed for want of effort to lay the nation at the feet of the French Emperor. Fox had not scrupled to defend some of the most infamous excesses of the Revolution, and the sympathy felt by the Whigs with the Revolutionists had passed into sympathy with Napoleon. A section of the Whigs in whom patriotism prevailed over party had given in their support to Pitt, but of the Whig party as a whole it cannot be disputed that their sympathies lay with France as against their own country. Their sentiments, which they did not deign to conceal, are to be found in the "Memoirs of Lord Holland," and in the vilification of the Duke of Wellington which Byron inserted in "Don Juan." To them Napoleon, until his downfall, had been an object of the same hero-worship and enthusiastic admiration as the "divine figure from the North" to Liberals of a later day. They stood before the country, then, as a discredited party, a party which had never before displayed itself so openly or so unblushingly as disloyal, unpatriotic, anti-national. Their foreign policy had been one which the English language could not supply words to describe, and, in the mere description, to condemn. Morally treason, intellectually madness, had it been carried out, it would have sacrificed the life and existence of the nation, destroyed the last stronghold of human freedom, the last centre of resistance to French arms, and made Napoleon the tyrant of Europe and the master of the world. "Tremble," said Talleyrand, as reported by Madame de Rémusat,—" tremble at the Emperor's success over the English, for if the English Constitution is overthrown, the civilization of the world will be shaken to its very foundations." It was this end that the Whigs had exerted themselves to secure. In the extremity of the national need they had sought to betray the national cause. In a supreme crisis of the country's fortunes they had proved false, "faithless they, amidst the faithful faithless only found."

Thus there was abundant reason for regarding every proposal of the Whig party with the utmost suspicion and distrust. But, further than this, the public mind of Britain had received a great shock from the French Revolution and the Napoleonic despotism, from which it took many years to fully recover. That Revolution put back the course of Parliamentary reform in Britain for more than forty years. It created in the minds of many men zealously attached to British freedom a contempt for the cause of freedom, on the Continent a deep-rooted conviction that foreigners were unfit for free institutions, and a positive sympathy with Continental autocracy. Just as the German Revolution which is called the Reformation provoked the Spanish or "Catholic" Reaction, so the French Revolution provoked a movement in favour of authority, real or supposed, in its most unreasonable forms. As always, one fanaticism by a natural repulsion gave rise to another, a counter fanaticism as irrational and pernicious as the first. The wild absurdities and frantic criminalities of the Revolutionists had brought their unerring penalty of a military despotism, and at the time it seemed that only the severest measures of repression could cope with the anarchic tendencies to which the Revolution had given birth. The unfortunate, and not only unfortunate but grossly culpable, language of the Whig leaders, the reckless incendiary speeches of which Fox and his friends had been guilty, had created an unfavourable and perhaps unjust impression as to their real policy and aims. Himself the most violent of partisans, than whom Shaftesbury was not more unscrupulous, Fox had damned the Whig party for a generation. But the uneasiness which he had created in the public mind long survived him. The French Revolution was still in men's thoughts, estranging them on both sides from those national traditions which might have quieted their apprehensions or sobered their ambitions. And, as though to complete the justification of the suspicion with which they were widely regarded, the Whig leaders in the Reform agitation made both threats and use of mob violence. If, in these circumstances, the Tory aristocracy viewed Parliamentary reform with wholly unwarrantable dread of its consequences, no candid or ingenuous thinker will be disposed to blame them.

Pitt, who had pressed forward the question of Parliamentary reform when the Parliament and the nation were alike indifferent to it, recognized that there is a time for all things, and when the storm of Revolution burst suddenly on Europe his sense of fitness and the opportune convinced him that the time for reform was not now. If to have an ideal, a distinct aim and policy, as opposed to the hand-to-mouth devices of politicians who, being unidea'd, flatter themselves that they are therefore "practical,"—if this is to be an idealist, then Pitt was an idealist. But, as a statesman, not a fanatic, he recognized that even for the realization of an ideal there is an opportune moment and an inopportune, and so soon as he had unwillingly convinced himself of the danger to the world held out by France, he resolutely referred the execution of his most cherished schemes to a more favourable season, and prepared at once for the supreme task of saving British empire and European freedom. That a representative assembly which is not representative was a mockery, a delusion, and a snare, none saw more clearly than Pitt. But he also saw, what by the wilfully blind he has been blamed for seeing, that the greatest of national institutions is the nation itself. A time when the existence of the nation was at stake was no time for discussing the niceties of Parliamentary reform. Had Pitt's vision of these truths been less clear and penetrating, it is both possible and probable that long ere the date of the first Reform Bill there would have been no British Parliament left to be reformed, nor any Whig party to reform it.

But the still liberal Toryism of Pitt which had reluctantly postponed for the time his early policy of conservative reform hardened in other men, his successors, into an obscurantist policy of mere negation. A Tory party grew up which sought to maintain all the abuses originally introduced by the Whigs, even now that the Whigs themselves had come to acknowledge the necessity for their abolition. A Tory party grew up which had nothing in common with historic Toryism, which was without principles, without aims, without vitality,—a Tory party which has given Toryism its bad name; a Tory party which promoted not conservation but stagnation. Pitt is not responsible for the men who came after him and traded on his name, who held up this champion of reform as against the progress dearest of all things to his heart. Just so there are men now who seek to trade upon the memory of Lord Beaconsfield, and who, while he was alive, spoke of him as a Jew adventurer and mountebank; who then said that he never spoke the truth except by accident, and now endeavour to employ the authority and prestige of his name against the consolidation of the Empire. A crass, lifeless, and unintelligent Toryism came into being— a Toryism which consisted in stupidly resisting all change good or bad until it was too late, and then, by a stampede, converting reform into revolution and defeat into rout; a Toryism which alternated the malignant obstruction of Lord Liverpool with the tardy and useless surrenders of Sir Robert Peel.

Thus, on the one hand, there was a large and influential party which, in the violence of the reaction against the French Revolution, had flung aside its own historic principles, and adopted a policy of stolid resistance of inevitable change. And on the other hand, there was a party condemned by its own antecedents, and the object of well-warranted distrust. The right measures were brought forward in the wrong way and by the wrong men. The right men, in opposing the wrong men, opposed also the right measures.

Of the political timidity, and the undue, not to say extravagant, caution, begotten by the reaction of which Burke was the prophet, the Duke of Wellington was a conspicuous example. By birth a member of that Anglo-Irish aristocracy, which, with few exceptions, never identified itself with the people of the land of its adoption, and belonging to the profession of arms, the Duke was ill-fitted by nature and by training to sympathize with, or even fully to comprehend, popular movements and popular reforms. This great man has been unjustly held up as a friend of Russian autocracy and the military governments of Central Europe. No accusation could go wider of the mark. The principle which the Duke constantly advocated with regard to foreign policy was that of non-intervention in the domestic affairs of other countries. He was held in no greater favour by the reactionaries of the Holy Alliance than by Continental revolutionists. Neither abroad nor at home was Wellington a fanatic of reaction. What the antagonist of Napoleon steadily kept in view was the national necessity of a permanent and stable government. What he dreaded in the Reform movement was the unfitness for political power of those on whom it was proposed to bestow it. Knowing the complex and intricate machinery of the Britannic State, he feared with good reason that the establishment of a middle-class ascendency would prove, if not fatal, at the least prejudicial in the highest degree, to the political society called the British Empire. He believed that the reign of the *bourgeoisie* would operate as a menace to the worldwide union of the British realms, and in this belief he was thoroughly justified. He foresaw that those great possessions in four continents which had been acquired for the British people by their hereditary chief and natural leaders, and confirmed to them at Waterloo and Trafalgar, would stand in imminent danger and rash and wanton alienation at the hands of the vestrymen and beadles whom middle-class ascendency would place in power.

That the Duke was thoroughly right in this dismal forecast of the future, subsequent events have abundantly established. That the British Empire exists in its present form to-day, that Canada, South Africa, and Australia are not independent Republics, is no result of the first Reform Bill, but due to a natural force of things that makes for union. The Empire exists, not as a consequence of that middle-class rule in the Old Country which began with the first, and ended with the last Reform Bill, but in spite and in defiance of it. That the extension of the franchise was as much a matter of practical necessity at Home as it has been in the Colonies, cannot be doubted. But between the process in the old countries and in the new there was this essential and all-important difference, that in the former case it conveyed a right, not merely of domestic self-government, but of determining the fate and fortunes of the whole Empire. Now the use to which the middle classes put their newly acquired power was to sever as far as possible every bond of union between the United Kingdom and the Colonies. To-day there is much talk of Imperial Federation, and the promoters of the movement have been advised by a British Premier to consider in the first place, as an essential preliminary to further steps, the feasibility of a Military Union and a Customs Union, a Kriegsverein and a Zollverein. But it is the fault of middle-class ascendency, of the Liberal party in Great Britain, that these are not already in existence. A Customs Union, whether with foreign countries or among the Colonies, is universally regarded as the indispensable condition of political and Parliamentary union. Yet to-day we have men both in Canada and Great Britain discussing without surprise or inquietude the commercial annexation of Canada by the United States. That Free-trade is economically the best policy for the country which pursues it is not to be questioned. But can it be seriously pretended that Free-trade, as practised by the United Kingdom, has not had, both in itself and in the time and manner of its adoption, a disintegrating influence on the relations of the British Isles to the British Colonies? No one acquainted with the facts will belie his own character for intelligence and candour by attempting to ignore the fact that the Free-trade fanaticism of the Mother Country, and the Protectionist fanaticism of Colonial democracy, are at the present time among the principal obstacles to the true political union of the British Isles and Colonies.

Economically Free-trade may have done wonders for the manufactures of Great Britain, while at the same time depopulating the agricultural districts, swelling the number of destitute poor in the great cities, aggravating Irish discontent, and rendering the United Kingdom liable to be starved into surrender in time of war. But politically it has reduced the British Isles and Colonies to a number of discordant atoms. And this result was neither unforeseen by, nor unwelcome to, those great apostles of Free-trade in England, Messieurs Cobden and Bright. One may even say that they deliberately projected this result. They looked forward to the immediate and universal adoption of their principles, to the conversion of the whole world to Free-trade as a consequence of the conversion of the Liberal party in Great Britain. And they also looked forward to the secession of the Colonies; they expected, invited, and incited Canada, Australia, and the Cape to follow the example of the United States. It is not unfair to say that the cardinal principle of their policy, on which all the rest of it depended, was the disintegration of the Empire. Contemplating such a result, and eagerly expecting it, the party then in power scouted all proposals to relax, however slightly, the rigid orthodoxy of the new economic policy of Great Britain in favour of the Colonies. No consideration was shown for the Colonial interests to be affected by the new departure, and the Colonies, without being allowed a voice in the matter, suddenly found themselves cut adrift. The policy of isolation, then adopted in the lively expectation of events that have not, and never will, come to pass, has since been erected into a dogma held with all the devout superstition of the middle-class Dissenter. To question, not merely the economic orthodoxy, which no one ever doubted, but the political value, of the Cobden system, has called forth an anger, not to say a fury, comparable only to the indignation and the horror with which a pious heathen might hear aspersions cast upon his favourite fetish. Not only were the Colonies thus peremptorily severed from the economic system of the centre of the Empire, but when their inhabitants presumed to assert the same liberty of individual action which the Mother Country, without warning, had asserted for herself, they were denounced as traitors by the very men who had constantly incited them to break from their allegiance to the Crown. Few spectacles have been witnessed more amusing than that of Mr. Bright arraigning the loyalty of Sir John Macdonald on the ground of the active disbelief of Canada in the infallibility of Manchester Free-trade which was adopted by the Mother Country without a thought of the Colonial interests to be affected, and when the Colonies, isolated by no action of their own, fell back on a system of Colonial Protection, they were denounced with angry invective or subjected to grandmotherly remonstrance. It is the fault, not of the Colonies but of the Old Country, and in particular of the Liberal party in Great Britain and Messieurs Cobden and Bright, that Free-trade does not exist throughout the Empire. That great bond of political union, commercial union, was by the Free-trade prophets in their arrogance and ignorance destroyed. They looked forward to the universal adoption of Free-trade, and they indulged in rash predictions not more reliable than Mother Shipton's prophecies. Their forecast of the economic future of mankind has failed not less completely than they, in making it, exhibited their ignorant contempt for the motives that rule the foreign and domestic policy of nations. The monopoly of the markets of the world which they looked to for British manufactures is now threatened on every side, both by Government action and private competition. The Colonies, first despised, and afterwards reviled, have taught a lesson which has received a striking acknowledgment in the recent efforts for British expansion in Africa. And, as though to emphasize the œcumenical rejection of the principles of Bright and Cobden, and to point the contrast between English Liberalism and Colonial Democracy, the ruling party in Australia proclaims itself at once Protectionist and Liberal.

The adoption of Free-trade, in the manner in which it was adopted, dealt a great blow to the union of the Empire. And that result was viewed, not only without disfavour, but with approval by those who at the time and since have been most active in support of Free-trade policy. These men believed in the disintegration of the Empire, and they used their utmost efforts to secure it. If self-government in purely local matters was conceded to the Colonies, it was with the direct view of getting rid of them, and as the prelude to separation. They were given broadly to understand that the sooner they took themselves off, the better they would please the ruling class (the middle class) in Great Britain. Cobden denounced the Colonies as existing solely for the benefit of the aristocracy; to Mr. Bright the Colonies appeared as useless, if not as dangerous, as India; while to Mr. Gladstone the worldwide expansion of the freest of free peoples has ever seemed of a piece with Napoleonic schemes of conquest. It is no exaggeration, and no partisan malice, to say that the most trusted leaders of the Liberal party in Great Britain have to this day remained entirely out of sympathy with the Colonial idea. No other Liberal leader has enjoyed the confidence reposed in Mr. Gladstone, and Mr. Gladstone, addressing the Cobden Club in 1890, could find nothing better to say of the Australian democracy than to attribute their partial exclusion of the Chinese to an incurable propensity for loafing, and a fatal addiction to strong drink. This want of sympathy with the Colonies on the part of Mr. Gladstone is admitted to be a failing by those of his followers who have acquired more modern notions of the world and discarded the old-fashioned primers of political geography.

But Mr. Gladstone is not singular in this respect among the members of his party. Mr. John Morley has taken the trouble to attempt to disprove the possibility of that closer union of the British Colonies and Isles commonly called Imperial Federation, and, as a necessary inference, since the present relations of those Colonies and Isles are from the nature of the case transitional, to prove the certainty of disintegration. It is not so long ago since the word "Imperialist" was to the Liberal party in Great Britain the bitterest reproach that could be launched against a politician, and the impression still lingers on in certain quarters that the Colonies and India are but a wicked fiction of Lord Beaconsfield's too picturesque imagination. Strange as it seems, if we consider how largely the Colonies have in many respects realized the Radical ideal, they have never been really popular with the Liberal party in Great Britain. And *per contra* the Liberal party in Great Britain has never been really popular in the Colonies. Whatever may be the opinions of a Colonist with regard to the domestic affairs of his own, or of the Old Country, in nine hundred and ninety-nine cases out of a thousand it is the Tory policy, and not the Liberal policy, that finds favour with him as regards Imperial affairs. And the reason for this is sufficiently obvious. It is no sympathy with Dukes and Duchesses, with hereditary legislators or Established Churches, that takes him over to the Tory side. It is the plain and simple fact, palpable to all persons, foreign or British, not resident in the British Isles, that the Liberal party in Great Britain, the Whigs and the *bourgeoisie*, the party of which the English Nonconformists are the backbone, is and always has been out of sympathy with both Colonies and India, and has never for a single moment so much as attempted to realize their overwhelming importance. India, indeed, to the Nonconformist mind, so influential in the Liberal party, presented the attractions of a mission field and a field for experiments of a doubtfully philanthropic character. And South Africa provided abundant opportunities for endeavouring to place the black man on an artificial and unnatural footing of equality with the white. But Canada and Australia could address no such appeal to the enthusiasm of Exeter Hall. The wealth and the population of the United States, perpetually advertised, forced themselves on the meanest understanding, and hence arose the singular delusion that it was a greater and more glorious thing to have lost, than it would be to have kept them. Those, who were loudest and most fervent in depreciating the Colonies and advocating the dissolution of the Empire, were the most noisy in setting forth the countless virtues of a Republic with so many dollars and so large a population.

In the day of its power the Liberal party in Great Britain, both by word and deed, did its best to detach the Colonies from the Empire as a useless encumbrance. Conceded self-government in purely local matters, with a reluctance tempered with delight at the imaginary prospect of their consequent departure, their wishes with regard to all matters of Imperial policy were systematically disregarded, and their interests systematically sacrificed whenever these came into conflict with the demands of any foreign Power.

The fears, then, of the Tory Peers for the British Empire, as they are to be found expressed in the correspondence and conversations of the Duke of Wellington, their nervous apprehensions as to what might result from middle-class ascendency, were thoroughly well founded. Where it would have been possible to bind the whole Empire together by a well-considered commercial policy, with very slight infractions of Free-trade, the opportunity was deliberately rejected, nominally from fidelity to economic principle, really from the short-sighted selfishness of the English manufacturers. As a consequence we see Canada and Australia wedded to Protection, and the constant stream of British emigration which should have enriched the former increasing the strength of the United States. Where it would have been possible, by a simple compliance with Colonial offers, to establish a "War Union" and gradually bring into being an organization of the whole armed force of the nation for the defence of the whole nation throughout the world, the power of the Empire is paralyzed for want of concentrated effort and frittered away in useless expense for want of one supreme direction and design. Lastly, as regards Imperial policy, it only requires a glance at the map to recognize the grievous shortcomings of the Mother Country in providing for the future of her children. Canada, cheated again and again out of her legitimate frontier by American address and British imbecility and indifference; South Africa, with Germany and Portugal encamped upon her skirts and retarding her full union; Australia, with her Hinterland of the islands in the Pacific converted into outposts of Germany or France, and with the United States threatening to become a third intruder,—all alike proclaim the patriotism and wisdom of the Peers in questioning the policy of the first Reform Bill. Necessary and unavoidable as may have been the extension of the franchise, the result was to place the middle class in power,—power, not only over the future of the British Isles, but over the future also of the British Colonies. And the use that they made of that power, as regards the Empire, was to detach the Colonies from the Isles by every means short of actual violence. Now, indeed, when all but the veriest Rip van Winkles of Radicalism are beginning to awake to the stupendous importance of the Colonies, and the unique position which they give the British people in the present politics and the past and future history of the world, it is ingeniously pretended by the apologists of middle-class policy that the Colonies were abandoned to their own devices with the farsighted and statesmanlike purpose of securing a loyalty born of their free will. But this is not the view of the past which is held in the Colonies themselves. Their memory is not so poor as to permit them to stomach such an artless fable. They know well that when they were grudgingly conceded self-government in purely local matters, and left to protect themselves as best they could, it was with the avowed purpose of paving the way for separation. They were not thought worth keeping, and though the younger members of the Liberal party in Great Britain may evince a natural and pardonable anxiety to consign so unpleasant a circumstance to oblivion, it is a fact not likely soon to fade from the Colonial consciousness. The quarrel of the Colonies has been with the Colonial Office—that is to say, with the House of Commons; and the House of Commons during by far the greater portion of the present reign has been dominated by a Liberal majority.

No people of the modern world are in some respects better qualified for self-government than the people of the British Isles, but they are not qualified to govern other Britons. This is in fact the task which the middle class essayed, and the result was a lamentable failure. They failed with the Colonies, as they failed with Ireland, and as they would have failed even with India had they attempted a like interference in Indian affairs. That the Empire is in its present chaotic state of disconnection and disorganization, that, instead of an orderly system in which all the parts discharge their several functions in unison and harmony, we have a loose confederation of which the indefinite conditions occasion a perpetual friction, this is the work of the first Reform Bill. The anarchy in the relations of the United Kingdom to the Colonies, and of the Colonies to one another, is crushing evidence of the political incompetence of the English middle class, of their unfitness for Imperial rule.

Just as the Duke of Wellington pointed out with prophetic accuracy, many years before the event took place, the evils that would be brought on Europe by a German annexation of Alsace-Lorraine, just as he foretold that peace with France after such a cession could never be more than a mere truce, so his judgment nowise played him false when he trembled for the existence of the Empire if the middle class should be installed in power. And, as we have seen, this middle-class ascendency, everywhere, and of set purpose, promoted the disunion of the British people, and the break-up of their dominions. When the people in a former day had lost their first Colonial Empire, a Tory King and a Tory aristocracy had immediately resolved, and carried out the resolution, to create for them a second. When the great Whig Peers and their middle-class supporters came into power, they acted on the directly contrary principle. Because the first Colonial Empire had gone, they declared with rash ineptitude that the second must go likewise; and when their Colonial fellow-countrymen exhibited a natural reluctance, they did their best to force them into separation.

The Peers were doubtless wrong in their opposition to the

first Reform Bill, but they were right, and entirely right, in believing that middle-class ascendency would prove dangerous, if not disastrous, to the British Empire. Necessary and desirable as the extension of the franchise may have been, having regard solely to the domestic affairs of the British Isles, it was unhappily accompanied by a partial dissolution of the Britannic State, and an unwise and wanton isolation of the British Isles from those British Colonies which together with them constitute the British nation.

That there was a section of the Tory party which offered a bigoted and purblind opposition to all change, has been acknowledged. But there was also an enlightened and patriotic Toryism, represented by the Duke of Wellington, which opposed the first Reform Bill from a fear that middle-class ascendency would bring about the destruction of the Empire as a worldwide State. This fear has been entirely justified by subsequent events. That the Colonies are still united, however loosely, to the Mother Country, is due to nothing else than the determination of the Colonies not to be forced and driven into separation. To those, indeed, since there are such yet to be found, in the ranks of the Liberal party in Great Britain, who still deplore the growth of the British people and their free institutions in three Continents, and who alternately deride and deprecate the idea of their banded union with the British Isles for the defence of universal freedom, it must appear the highest merit of the Liberal middle class that it attempted to destroy the Empire and dissolve the nation. To such philosophers as Mr. Morley, and such patriots as Mr. Goldwin Smith, this alone may seem the sufficient vindication and the distinguishing glory of English bourgeois rule. But to the remainder, and now at last to the great and overwhelming majority, of the British people, even in England itself, it must appear not less unpatriotic than insane. Those who are capable of appreciating the incalculable benefits derived by the British Isles and the British Colonies from their mutual connection, and the still greater and more lasting benefits that would accrue to both and to the world at large from their fuller, stable, and perpetual union, will not think harshly of the Peers for pausing ere they hazarded the committal of a priceless heritage to the weak hands, faint hearts, and dull intellects of those whose incompetence for ruling an Empire is written on every page of Canadian, of Australasian, and of South African history. The greatest of national institutions is the nation itself. A measure that threatens the existence of the nation is a measure, not of progress, but of retrogression, and to hesitate ere entrusting the *bourgeoisie* of Great Britain with a power, not only of wrecking the Empire, but of shattering the nation into a thousand fragments, commensurate with the desire of their leaders and orators to do so, is neither an opposition of the people nor "out of harmony with democratic feeling." If the existence of the Colonies as a portion of the British Empire is of benefit both to themselves and to the British Isles, that is to say to the British nation; if it is of benefit above all to the British labourer or working man, then the conduct of the Peers in questioning the wisdom of bringing into power those who sought to expel the Colonies from the Empire, was not an oppression, but a protection, of the people, and conceived in the best and highest interest of the Colonial and Home democracy. Had that which the Peers resisted been the mere extension to the middle class of a share in the self-government of the British Isles, they might with propriety and justice be condemned. But with this self-government there was bound up the power of governing other people, of controlling the destiny and dominating the future of the new nationalities within the Pan-Britannic nation, the Canadian, the Afrikander, the Australian. To be admitted to the exercise of the less important functions was impossible without concurrent admission to the exercise of the more important. Imperial power was bound up with domestic self-government. The fault lay, not with the Peers, but with the over-centralization of our institutions.

The Peers were not altogether in the right, but still less were they wholly in the wrong. They opposed themselves to that necessary stage of constitutional development, the reign of the middle classes in Great Britain, but they did so from an honourable solicitude for the maintenance of the British Empire, and the existence and union of the British nation.

So much, then, for the opposition of the Peers to the first Reform Bill. If it can scarcely be adduced in their favour, still less can it, with truth or justice, be adduced against them. It was prompted by considerations that do equal credit to their patriotism and foresight, and that their anticipations of disaster have proved to be excessive, has been due, not to the policy of the Liberal party in Great Britain, but to the new power, unforeseen either by Tory aristocrat, or Whig oligarch, or Liberal *bourgeois*, of Colonial democracy. The charge against the Peers, that by opposing the Reform Bill they oppressed the people, is one which it were wiser to withdraw, since, if pressed, it justifies a severe and damaging rejoinder. To urge the point is to call evidence which can only injure the cause it is expected to support. And as this charge falls to the ground, if it does not recoil on those who make it, so too the charge against the Peers that, by opposing the removal of religious disabilities, they oppressed the people, is one which suffers from investigation. Now, the imposition of civil disabilities on account of religion, viewed in the abstract, is clearly contrary to all sound policy. It subordinates the State to the Church, and perverts the former into an instrument for the propagation of religious dogma. It is founded on an altogether wrong conception of the rights of the Church, and of the duty and functions of the State. Viewed in the abstract, the imposition of civil disabilities on account of religion must be unequivocally condemned. But when we descend from the general to the particular, and from the abstract principle to its concrete application, we shall see that, as regards the Protestant Dissenters, civil disabilities were not imposed without cause, nor maintained without reason. The imposition of civil disabilities on the English Protestant Dissenters was a measure for the protection of the National Church and national freedom. To grasp this fully, we must recall those supreme facts of British history, the Parliamentary Unions of England with Scotland, and of Ireland with Great Britain. The Parliament of Great Britain and Ireland was formed by a union of the Parliament of Great Britain with the Parliament of Ireland; and the Parliament of Great Britain was formed by a union of the Parliament of England with the Parliament of Scotland. Before the Union with Scotland, the Parliament which met at Westminster was the Parliament of England only, and in law and constitutional theory the English Church was co-terminous and co-extensive with the English State. Before the unfortunate squabbles of the sixteenth century, every one had belonged to the same religion, for there was then only one religion to belong to. It no more occurred to an Englishman to reject the authority of the English Church than it now occurs to an Englishman to reject the authority of the English State. With the exception of a few heretics, "cranks" or prigs in modern idiom, who were promptly suppressed, sometimes with undue severity, the legal theory corresponded with the actual fact. But with the changes initiated by Henry the Eighth came in fresh national dissensions, though these did not finally take formal shape till a considerably later period. The purpose of Henry the Eighth was simply to get rid of the Pope and make the Church thoroughly national. His secularization of the lands held by the monasteries was no more due to Puritan sympathies than the secularization of Church lands in modern times, in Italy and Spain, was due to the adoption of Protestantism by the rulers of those countries.

"Separation from the see of Rome," says Professor Freeman, "was not meant to carry with it any change of doctrine, or to imply any breach of communion with the Churches which remained in the Roman obedience. It was strictly a scheme of ecclesiastical independence, and no more.

"But the acts of Henry put on peculiar character from the circumstances which led to his ecclesiastical changes, and from the way in which many of them were carried out."

"The policy of William the Norman," writes Professor Thorold Rogers, "was to establish an independent Church, ruled by his nominees." It was this policy that Henry revived and put into force against Rome. He asserted the autonomy of the kingdom in ecclesiastical matters against the Pope, as he asserted its autonomy in political matters against the Emperor. In the "Act for Restraint of Appeals to Rome," it is recited in the preamble that, "By divers and sundry old authorities, histories, and chronicles, it is manifestly declared that this realm of England is an Empire, and so hath been accepted by the world." And the Act was avowedly designed to keep "the Imperial Crown of this realm from the annoyance as well of the see of Rome as from the authority of foreign potentates." The aim of Henry was to assert his independence of the Papacy and Holy Roman Empire, not to cut himself adrift from the universal belief of Catholic Christendom. His position was not Lutheran or Calvinist, but Russian or Byzantine. So in the East the Church of Russia asserted its national independence of the Patriarchate of New Rome; but in breaking from Constantinople it did not lay aside its true historic character, or forfeit its position as an integral portion of Orthodox Christendom. So likewise in our own time, with the emancipation step by step of the Balkan nationalities, the national Churches of Servia, Bulgaria, Roumania, and the Hellenic Kingdom have asserted their independence of Byzantium, but they did not therefore become "Protestant." Protestant in the sense of the English law, Protestant as protesting against the claims of the Papacy, they were before, and Protestant in this sense they remained. But Protestant, in the sense unrecognized by and unknown to the English law, Protestant as rejecting historic Christianity, they did not become.

This was the position assumed by the English Church under Henry, and which it still maintains. There is nothing in the changes, effected by the Anglican Reformation, which does not find its parallel in historic Christendom elsewhere. The translation of the Bible into English, which is triumphantly exhibited by some as an adoption of foreign Protestantism, was a plagiarism from the Church of Rome. It is the first step that costs; and the true originality was in the translation of the Bible into Latin. The substitution of English for Latin in the Anglican liturgy has its counterpart in the substitution of Slavonic for Greek in the services of the national Churches of the East. From the time of Elizabeth the marriage of the clergy was tacitly connived at; but in the East every parish priest is required to be a married man. Henry the Eighth had no sympathy with the German Revolution: the antagonist of Luther never became a Lutheran. Nothing could be further from his mind than the national adoption of foreign Protestantism. But the unfortunate influence of the Continental Reformation extended in time to England. Just as the French Revolution in politics unsettled the reason of many persons at a later date, so the German Revolution in religion created a party of religious fanatics in England, who sought to substitute foreign revolution for national reform. These people did not propose to themselves their organization in altogether novel bodies. What they sought was, in American phrase, "to capture the machine," to get possession of the Church of England, and demolish its historic character. Under Edward the Sixth they came within measurable distance of success, and their intolerant fury provoked the formidable Spanish and Roman reaction of the following reign. Under Elizabeth, the State, on the one hand, sought to compel conformity to the National Church; and the Church, on the other hand, made great and injudicious concessions to the Puritans to induce them to conform. While the Pope, by forbidding his sympathizers to attend the parish churches any longer, called into existence the new body of religionists now known as Roman Catholics, the Puritans split up into a number of sects, mutually hostile, but all agreed in enmity towards the Church of history.

Those of the Puritans who had with doubtful honesty conformed, the ancestors of the modern Low Church party, constantly agitated for further and destructive change, while the non-conforming sectaries, or Nonconformists, attacked the Church from without. At length the Puritan party triumphed, they seized the Church endowments, and the

Church of England was proscribed. They no longer attempted to "capture the machine," but followed the same course as the foreign Protestants. They swept away the historical Church of the country, and set up a perfectly new body in its stead. At the Restoration the Church had its own again, and the Nonconformists, as a necessary precaution, were placed under rigorous restraint. But it was not the Church alone that had suffered in the Reign of the Saints. Each and every one of the national institutions had been swept away by these religious monomaniacs in the hope of setting up a Semitic theocracy on the ruins of English freedom. If the Great Rebellion was in the rebel Peers an attempt to revive feudalism in a new disguise, it was in their Puritan allies the attempted resuscitation of Judaism misunderstood. And if Cromwell, as autocrat, filled in the Commonwealth the part of the Oriental despot whom Calvinism set up for its Deity, too effectually to give the saints full play, his tyranny was nevertheless based on the essential condition that he should permit his followers to tyrannize over other people. The whole nation had suffered from the Puritan Inquisition, and the whole nation resented it. An active and unscrupulous minority, full of the desperate zeal of religious fanatics, had subjected the whole nation to an iron rule of dervishes, and the nation was determined to preclude the possibility of its recurrence. England stood aghast at the debasing servitude from which she had escaped, the depths of humiliation to which a proud and free people had been dragged down by a daring crew of crazed but crafty enthusiasts. The reign of the saints had had its trial, and it had shown its entire incompatibility with law and liberty no less than with loyalty, with civilization no less than with national and individual freedom. Never again would the nation descend into such an abyss of degradation, and, to secure this end, it was unavoidable to adopt timely precautions. Not for the protection of the Church only, but for that of the nation's freedom, it was necessary to have recourse to safeguards against those who had so unmistakably established the nature of their aims and the absolute lack of conscience with which they sought to attain them. The strange but undoubted connection between religious insanity and homicidal mania, since seen in the Taepings of China, and the Hau-hau fanaticism of Maoris in New Zealand, had been brought home to the public mind on a colossal scale rarely to be witnessed in the history of nations. The men of the Restoration had to deal with remorseless and unscrupulous fanatics, nor is it wonderful that the nation had resort to such natural measures of self-defence from sudden and pitiless assault as we now adopt against the lunatic and criminal. The civil disabilities imposed on the English Protestant Dissenters constituted a measure, not of religious persecution, but of national insurance. Against the enemies of the State, the State perforce stood on its guard. The civil disabilities of the English Nonconformists had their origin in that reign of the saints which was a reign of terror.

The English Church, as it has been seen, was in law and constitutional theory co-terminous and co-extensive with the English State. But by the Revolution of 1688 and the Parliamentary Union of Great Britain two very important changes were made in Church and State relations. By the Revolution of 1688 the supremacy over the Church of the King in Council was replaced by the supremacy of the King in Parliament. By the Union with Scotland the State of England became merged in the State of Great Britain. While the power of Parliament over the Church was augmented, the nation no longer consisted in theory of English Churchmen. The Parliament of England which, with the exception of the Bishops, was entirely composed of Anglican laymen, was now sunk in a Great British Parliament, which avowedly included a large contingent of Scottish Presbyterians. A change so sweeping in the relations of the Church and State had excited on both sides of the Border misgivings and forebodings, and by the Acts of Union it was sought to make the maintenance of the Established Church in each country an essential and fundamental part of the Union. A similar provision was inserted in the Irish Union, and it was sought to give the Irish Church Establishment additional security by "uniting" that with the Church of England. Thus, before the removal of any religious disabilities, the Church of England was no longer in relation to a Parliament of England only, but had fallen under the power of a Parliament of Great Britain and Ireland, and membership of this Parliament was not restricted to English Churchmen. If the civil disabilities of Roman Catholics were removed, then to the body of Scottish Presbyterians already sitting in Parliament would be added a large number of Irish Roman Catholics. If the civil disabilities of the Protestant Dissenters were removed, then to the Scottish Presbyterians, and the Irish Roman Catholics, would be added a considerable number of English Protestant Dissenters. Such a result could not be viewed with complacence or indifference by those who had the interests and welfare of the Church at heart. There was no longer any serious or immediate danger that the English sectaries would endeavour to re-enact the scenes of the Rebellion. But there was great and most considerable danger that they would employ any power they might obtain to the disadvantage of the Church, whether by legislation further infringing her spiritual rights and constitutional liberty, or perhaps destroying or impairing her historic character, or by the confiscation in part or whole of her temporal endowments. By the Unions the relations of Church and State underwent a complete alteration, and the Union security for the Church of England has since become inoperative. At one time only tolerated sectaries, the Dissenters gradually acquired full political rights. It was impossible to admit them to full citizenship under the conditions then existing, without at the same time admitting them to a right of interfering in Church matters. Morally and in equity, since the freedom and self-government of all Dissenting bodies has long been acknowledged, they ought not to exercise this right to the detriment of the Church of England. But they can so exercise it, and they do so exercise it, and that as a matter of course.

"It is admitted by all the authorities of the Church of England," writes Sir Charles Dilke, "that some legislation is needed in Church matters;

but it is difficult to obtain this legislation from a House of Commons in which there is a large Roman Catholic and Presbyterian and a large Nonconformist element, and in which only a small minority are interested in ecclesiastical matters. The result of the impossibility of legislating about the Church of England in the House of Commons must inevitably be, sooner or later, the disestablishment of the Church."*

Without concurring in the lugubrious, if somewhat indefinite, prediction of the last sentence, it may be said that we have here, from an eminent Radical authority, a plain confession of the injury done to the Church of England by the removal of Nonconformist disabilities. For neither the Irish nor the English Roman Catholics have ever shown themselves at all forward in attacking the Church of England, whatever action the former may have taken with regard to the Anglo-Irish Church now disestablished. Nor is it probable that any Scottish members would assail the English Church but for the co-operation of her Southron enemies. The injury is done to the Church by the English Nonconformists, and this injury is also an injustice. Let us hear Mr. Gladstone on this point.

"We are thus brought to consider," he wrote in his letter to Bishop Blomfield on the Royal Supremacy, "the second great change adverse to the Church which has so greatly changed to her disadvantage the position defined for her at the Reformation, namely, the change of the personal composition of the Nation and of the State. She then contracted with a State of whose policy it was a capital part, that all its members should be her members too : and her members, moreover, not by a nominal profession only, but through a membership tested in the most searching manner by periodical participation, subject to public discipline, in her highest ordinance. And that this circumstance entered essentially into the considerations upon which she made her bargain, we may well judge not only from the writings of her divines bearing upon the subject, but from the tenacity with which her governors resisted the toleration of Dissenters and their admission to political privilege. . . . It is obvious that what they resisted was a claim, not merely to civil privileges, but to the exercise of powers that included much control over her own destinies. . . . While the pretensions of the State have been in constant growth, its composition has rendered it progressively unfit to exercise even the qualified functions it had before possessed. Divisions of opinion have multiplied ; the nation is broken up into many sects and religions :

---

* " Problems of Greater Britain," part iv. ch. 1.

all claim the equal exercise of political power, and nearly every claim has been admitted."

Thus we have it on the evidence of Mr. Gladstone that the opposition of the Peers and others to the removal of Nonconformist disabilities was to a great extent a policy of self-defence on the part of English Churchmen against future aggressions which have since actually come to pass. Just as it was impossible to admit the middle class to a power, which was, in fact, ascendency, without imperilling the existence and relaxing the union of the British Empire, so too it was impossible to admit the Nonconformists to the full rights of citizens without injuring and endangering the English Church. Had it been a question of admitting the Protestant Dissenters to power in all matters not ecclesiastical, then the opposition of the Peers to their enfranchisement might be deservedly stigmatized as illiberal and bigoted. The advance of the nation, and of the world, in civilization and enlightenment, had rendered a second Commonwealth, a repeated reign of the saints, an impossible anachronism. There was no need to fear the success of an effort, no matter how vigorously renewed, to govern the British Isles on the political principles of Judaism or Islam. Had power in non-ecclesiastical matters alone, been that to which the Protestant Dissenters claimed admission, then to oppose their enfranchisement in the nineteenth century would have been sheer intolerance. Had it ever been a question of admitting them to a Legislature of England only, then power in ecclesiastical matters also might have been conceded to them with safety, and, if not with justice, at least with generosity. But to admit them to a Parliament of Great Britain and Ireland was to place the Church of England at the mercy of an English minority which could secure the co-operation of the Scottish and Irish members in attempting to injure her. It was to lay the Church of England open to every assault of her enemies. It was opposed with right and reason by the English Bishops and the Tory Peers as a surrender of the key to the position occupied by the Church of England, and a virtual infraction of the Acts of Union.

They predicted that the English Nonconformists, not content with political equality, would adopt a policy of active aggression and essay the disestablishment and disendowment of the Church. And the prediction has come true. Emboldened with their success against the Church of the English Pale in Ireland, the Nonconformists have pressed on, and are now urging the confiscation of English Church property in that portion of the kingdom of England of which the counties are collectively described as Wales. This they put forward as an object of immediate legislation, but they do not hesitate to avow that they regard " Welsh Disestablishment" as only a step towards, and a first instalment of, the confiscation of Church property throughout South Britain. Things have been brought to the pass described by Sir Charles Dilke, and, not only to that pass, but far beyond it. The ecclesiastical legislation required is deliberately obstructed with the open and declared purpose of assisting the cause of Disestablishment.

Now, if an English Parliament were in existence charged with the supervision and control of all matters of purely English interest, it is probable that the Church of England would stand in no danger. The Church of England is still the Church of the majority of Englishmen, and even among those who for a variety of reasons are not enthusiastic Churchmen, the greater portion would prefer the continuance of Anglican " ascendency " to a possible ascendency of " the Nonconformist conscience." It is not for nothing that the English Protestant Dissenters cause Great Britain to stand alone among all the British Dominions in taking no religious census. They put forward no conscientious objection to stating their numbers in any portion of the British Empire where no Established Church exists. The working of the Nonconformist conscience would appear to be kept under masterly control. In Great Britain, where they are actively attacking the Church Establishments in North and South Britain, a tender scrupulosity does not permit them to be counted, but in Canada and Australia, where there is no Church in direct connection with the State, this modest diffidence is non-existent. It is impossible not to admire a conscience of such manifest political utility.

If an English Parliament were in existence, it is so probable as to be all but certain, that the English Church would stand in no danger. If, then, it should ever come to be disendowed and disestablished, this will be brought about by the combination of an English minority with the Scottish and Irish members of the House of Commons. By virtue of the Unions of 1707 and 1801 a direct breach will be effected in the express stipulations and the most solemn terms of the Acts which alone give those Unions their legal validity. It was made an essential condition of each Union that the Church Establishments then in existence should be left uninjured. By the Irish Church Act, 1869, this condition was violated in the case of Ireland, and now it is proposed to extend the same treatment to Scotland and England. One wrong, however, does not make two rights; and this line of policy cannot be carried out without most grievous injustice to the English and the Scottish peoples. It was laid down by Mr. Gladstone, in the course of his famous Midlothian campaign, that the question of Scottish disestablishment was one to be decided by the Scottish people, and this statement was subsequently endorsed by Lord Hartington, now Duke of Devonshire. If this statement be accepted, then it follows by necessary inference that the question of English disestablishment is one to be decided by the people of England, and not by the people of Great Britain and Ireland. Yet, contrary to both letter and spirit of the Acts of Union, and to the express declaration of Mr. Gladstone, the Gladstonian Liberals are now engaged in endeavouring to effect the disestablishment, both of the English Church and of the Presbyterian body known in law as the "Church of Scotland," in and through the Parliament of the United Kingdom.

The Church of England in no way affects Irishmen or Scotsmen. Its boundaries, considering it as an establishment, are co-terminous with the Kingdom of England, plus those ancient possessions of the English Crown, the Channel Islands and the Isle of Man. The Church of England, in the larger sense, of the Anglican Communion, extends throughout and beyond the British Empire. But the Church of England, viewed as an Establishment, considered an Estate of the Realm, is, to quote Macaulay, " an institution as purely local as the Court of Common Pleas." Yet the decision of the future of this institution, entirely peculiar to England, exclusively belonging to the sphere of her domestic interests and internal affairs, is by those who, forsooth, style themselves Home Rulers, referred to the adjudication of a body in which an English majority may be overruled by an English minority acting in conjunction with the representatives of Scotland and Ireland.

The Church of England and the "Church of Scotland" are bodies of entirely different origin. They hold their property by an entirely different title. The "Church of Scotland" is a body which dates back no further than some three hundred years. The Church of England was in existence before the English State, before there was a King of England, before there was an English nation. The "Church of Scotland" holds its property in virtue of an Act of the Scottish Parliament passed as a consequence of the Revolution of 1688. The Church of England acquired the property which it holds, through various corporations, at no given date, and by no Act of Parliament, but by the countless benefactions, spread through centuries, of individual Churchmen. The little that the Church of England has received, at intervals few and far between, from the State, would make a beggarly set-off against the wealth extorted from her by the Tudors. Why should the fate of the Church of England, as an Establishment, be made to depend upon that of the Presbyterian Establishment in Scotland? Why should an institution with which the vast majority of Englishmen are satisfied be swept away because the Scottish Free Church persists in keeping up a feud with the Scottish Established Church, of which the original cause has been removed and is by most people in a fair way to be forgotten?

It may be allowed that the Peers in opposing the removal of the disabilities of Protestant Dissenters oppressed the

English Nonconformists as citizens; but it must also be allowed that the only alternative to this oppression of the Protestant Dissenters by the Peers was—that which is now visible before us—the oppression of the English Church by the Protestant Dissenters, and of the English people by the English Nonconformists. When there was no longer any danger of Nonconformist supremacy, of a second Puritan Commonwealth, then there would have been no longer any necessity for Nonconformist disabilities, had things remained *in statu quo*. But in the meantime the Anglo-Scottish and the Irish Unions had completely altered the situation. It was impossible to do justice to the English Nonconformists without doing injustice to England. Of two undoubted evils the Peers would have preferred the less. That the English Church should be subject to the legislation of English Nonconformists, Irish Roman Catholics, and Scottish Presbyterians, would have been and is a grievance and an injustice to all English Churchmen. That the fate of a purely English institution should be dependent on the votes of the representatives of Scotland and Ireland, would have been and is an injustice to all Englishmen. The State had already violated its compact with the Church. It was now proposed that it should violate that compact further. This proposal was ultimately carried out with the disastrous consequences that we see to-day. The Peers held with good reason that the civil disabilities imposed on a small section of the English people formed but a trifling injustice by comparison with the enormous wrong that would be done to the whole people by the wanton ruin and destruction of that immense system of organized philanthropy, of tender solicitude for the spiritual and material welfare of the masses which England possesses in her National Church. They foresaw that the Protestant Dissenters, not content with political equality, would proceed to advance the specious demand of " religious equality ;" in other words, that the English Nonconformists, not satisfied with exercising a control over the Church, which State and Church alike long ago abdicated with regard to the sects, would set themselves to coerce the Irish members of the

House of Commons, and cajole the Scottish, into conspiring with them to achieve the overthrow of a vast work of public beneficence, the loss of which all the other religious bodies of the English Kingdom put together would be unable for a single instant to make good.

The removal of the Nonconformist disabilities, taken in conjunction with the Unions of Great Britain and the British Isles, effected a complete change in the position of the Church of England. That Churchmen, well knowing the nature of the Nonconformist conscience, should seek to avert future danger by opposing the removal of those disabilities, may present itself in the light of a grievance to political Dissenters; but to any person with a sense of justice, its unpleasantly, but unavoidably, harsh character will be amply redeemed by the knowledge that such opposition was intended to secure fair play both to the English Church and to England as a whole. Nor will those consent to stamp that opposition with the name of oppression who call to mind why and how those disabilities originally came to be imposed, and what has since been the result of their removal.

No Home Ruler, no one who has an intelligent grasp of the Federal principle, can in consistency or logic blame the Peers for endeavouring to secure to England a supreme voice in English affairs, even though by the disagreeable, but necessary, means of the maintenance of Nonconformist disabilities. No Unionist who takes his stand on the essential and fundamental conditions of the Unions can condemn the Peers for endeavouring to enforce the moral guarantees of union. If Scotland is entitled to keep her Scots Law, no matter what Englishmen or Irishmen may think about it—and he would be a venturesome politician who would dare to assail it,—then the opinion of England, and of England only, should prevail on the question of the English Church.

But while the civil disabilities of the Protestant Dissenters were originally requisite as a measure of police, and, latterly, the alternative to an oppression of the English people by a persecution of the English Church, it is impossible to discover the shadow of an excuse for the civil disabilities imposed by the Puritans and Whigs upon the Roman Catholics. These were never required as a measure of national protection, but, on the contrary, opposed a perpetual impediment to the union of each of the three nations and to the union of them all. The loyalty of English, of Scottish, and of Irish, Roman Catholics, under circumstances of the grossest provocation, must excite in equal degrees the astonishment and the admiration of every dispassionate student of our history. Unfortunately for the Roman Catholics, and for the nation, the dissolution of the monasteries had brought into existence a party in Great Britain, which had a vested interest in representing every approach to toleration, or lull in persecution, as part of a deep-laid scheme for the restoration of Papal supremacy. It was by the bugbear of Romish aggression and pretended Popish plots that such astute and unscrupulous politicians as Pym and Shaftesbury worked upon the fears and fanaticism of the English trading classes, and secured their co-operation to the great nobles in a common attack upon the Church and Throne. In Ireland, where the National Church never accepted either the Anglican or the Continental Reformation, Puritan "adventurers," as they correctly styled themselves, fastened on the Catholicism of the nation as a fresh pretext for forfeitures and confiscation, while the Church endowments were transferred to an episcopate and clergy who, by the mass of the Irish people, were regarded as schismatical intruders. Finally, by the expulsion of the last Stuart King *de facto*, and the ruin of his hopes in Ireland, the cause of liberty and toleration was, for the time being, lost. It is probable that William of Orange, who, to give every one his due, was no Orangeman, would have willingly accorded toleration to the Roman Catholics. But he had to gratify the malignant passions of his supporters, and to insure them, so far as possible, from the consequences of their evil deeds, not less than to minister to their, and to his own, cupidity. The immense forfeitures of Irish land which scourged the Irish people for their loyalty, were fittingly accompanied by those hideous penal laws which form the everlasting reproach of

England and the perpetual excuse of present Irish disaffection.

The penalties on the exercise or profession of the Roman Catholic religion in course of time were gradually removed, but the civil disabilities of Roman Catholics remained. It had been Pitt's purpose to follow up the Union by the removal of these disabilities, and, as part of his general scheme for the pacification of Ireland, to establish at the same time a State provision for the Roman Catholic and Presbyterian clergy. Had this grand policy been carried out, the Union would have presented itself in a very different light to the people of Ireland from that in which they ever since have seen it. Unfortunately a variety of circumstances conspired to prevent this policy from being carried out, and when Roman Catholic Emancipation at last became a fact, it was unaccompanied by any measure such as Pitt had projected for placing the priesthood in a position of independence towards their flocks. The honourable and conscientious scruples of King George the Third, skilfully worked upon by treacherous and designing men, for long formed an insuperable obstacle to Emancipation, while the religious fanaticism revived by the Methodist movement, and sustained and strengthened by the Evangelical, threw fresh difficulties in the path of concurrent endowment.

What the Tory Peers had reason to fear as regards Roman Catholic Emancipation was not only that, as in the case of the Protestant Dissenters, it would introduce into Parliament a body of religionists who, if not so actively hostile to the English Church as the English Nonconformists, were at least strongly antagonistic to her, but the peril to which it would expose the Anglo-Irish aristocracy, the Anglo-Irish Church, and the Great British and Irish Union. Roman Catholic Emancipation was Irish Emancipation. There was good reason for anxiety as to its effect on the social institutions and established order of the sister Kingdom. For generations the masses of the Irish people had been ground down in the most cruel and pitiless slavery that ever nation has had to undergo. Could it be supposed that they were so incapable of resentment as to refrain from using their newly acquired power against the descendants and representatives of their former tyrants and oppressors? Could it be supposed that, when their moral assent to the Irish Union having been obtained by the prospect and promise of attendant relief from their disabilities, they had afterwards found themselves, if not deceived, altogether disappointed, their first use of Emancipation when at last it came would not be to turn the power it brought against the Union?

That these were no unreal or imaginary dangers we have the irrefutable testimony of the present and the past. The Peers would have sought to ward them off by coming to an understanding with the Church of Rome, and enlisting the vast moral influence of that society in Ireland on the side of order and the Union. But the Protestant fanaticism of Orangemen in Ireland, and of the Nonconformists and others in Great Britain, the natural dislike of Irish agitators to every form of civil or ecclesiastical control, and the traditional Whig hatred of every form of historic Christianity, combined to prevent this laudable and desirable result. Roman Catholic Emancipation, as it ultimately passed, was but a maimed and mutilated version of Pitt's policy, deprived of the safeguards which he had judged essential and which every State of Europe, Protestant or Roman Catholic, has found it necessary to adopt.

The Tory Peers who opposed Roman Catholic Emancipation did so for the most part in the belief that it would endanger the Irish Church Establishment, the Irish landed proprietors, and the Irish Union, unless it was accompanied by safeguards and precautions which were not forthcoming. And since Roman Catholic Emancipation was carried out without these safeguards and precautions, every danger that they foresaw has come to pass. The Irish Church Establishment has been swept away. Unable, and in some cases perhaps unwilling, to obtain a State endowment for their own religion, chiefly in consequence of English Nonconformist opposition, the Irish Roman Catholics fell back in the next place on the alternative policy of secularizing the endowments held by the Anglo-Irish Church, officially styled the Church of Ireland, and assisted the English Nonconformists to carry out this eminently narrow and provincial scheme. As the Peers who opposed Roman Catholic Emancipation feared and foresaw, the Irish Church Establishment has been swept away. But though the Irish Church Establishment has been swept away, it is more than doubtful whether the Irish Church question has yet found its solution. The same statesman who framed the Irish Church Act and secured its passing, thought it necessary to insert in his scheme of Home Rule a provision debarring the Irish Parliament from establishing or endowing the Roman Catholic religion ; that is to say, from settling the Irish Church question in accordance with the views and wishes of the great majority of the Irish people, rather than in accordance with the views and wishes of English Puritans and Scottish Presbyterians. And that this statutory provision was not adopted without cause has been shown by the constant anxiety displayed on the subject by the Presbyterians and Nonconformists on both sides of St. George's Channel. The policy of concurrent endowment advocated by Pitt, and by the Tory Peers, as the true solution of the Irish Church question, was rejected in deference to the provincial and sectarian prejudices of the English political Dissenters, and a policy of disestablishment was adopted in its stead. But although there is no possibility that the disestablished Church, not "of Ireland," but of the English Pale, will ever be restored to its position by an Irish Parliament, although so far the policy of disestablishment is likely to hold good, there is every possibility and no little probability that an Irish Parliament, should such an assembly be brought into existence, will in one form or another subsidize the Church of Rome. Thus, as the ultimate result of Roman Catholic Emancipation, passed without the safeguards which the Peers deemed essential, the Anglican Church Establishment in Ireland will have been swept away only to put a Roman Catholic Establishment in its place.

If the people of Scotland are entitled to settle the question of Scottish disestablishment, if the people of England are entitled to settle the question of English disestablishment, then surely in reason and justice it cannot be disputed that the people of Ireland are entitled to settle the question of Irish establishment. Had a policy of concurrent endowment been carried out in a way fair and reasonable to those concerned, such an arrangement might with well warranted confidence have been expected under all circumstances to endure. But the entire absence of consideration for Irish sentiment, the absolute contempt for the opinions and desires of those who were alone affected, shown in the policy of disestablishment, has created no claim upon the Irish majority for deference to the wishes or the prejudices of the Protestant minority. And through the absurd course of affecting to ignore the position of the Church of Rome in Ireland as *de facto*, if not *de jure*, the National Church of Ireland, a grave injustice has been done both to the Irish priesthood and the Irish people, while the possessors of an influence of incalculable power have been forced into an attitude of at least apparent antagonism to the Union and the Empire. Those who are the guides, and should have been the leaders, of the people, have been driven to compete with village demagogues and Americanized agitators in pandering to their ignorance and passions, and a great spiritual force, which everywhere else is actively exerted in the cause of social order, has in Ireland been perverted to assist the propaganda of political disaffection and agrarian revolution.

The Irish Church Establishment has, as the Tory Peers anticipated, been swept away, as a consequence of the unstatesmanlike and unscientific method of Emancipation. But no finality was attained by the Irish Church Act, 1869, and the statesman who proposed and passed that measure has been obliged to confess as much by repeatedly declaring his intention to withhold from any Irish Legislature that power of dealing with religion which in the case of the Scottish Church Establishment he has explicitly asserted for the Scottish people as apart from, and distinguished from, the people of England and of Ireland. At the same time the Irish clergy, despairing of recognition at the hands of the

Parliament at Westminster, have been compelled to look for that which they regard as justice to an Irish Legislature.

The Anglo-Irish Church as an Establishment has fallen as a consequence of the impolitic and incomplete measure of Emancipation which Puritan fanaticism enforced on those who effected it. In itself, Roman Catholic—that is to say, Irish—Emancipation was both right and necessary, but the actual form which it took under the pressure of ultra-Protestant bigotry was pernicious and disastrous. It was a half measure carried at the wrong time and in the wrong way—a moiety of justice reluctantly conceded to agitation and shorn of everything that could induce the Irish people to forget and forgive the past. The Anglo-Irish Church Establishment has therefore perished: and the Anglo-Irish aristocracy have also suffered greatly. It would be easy to dwell upon the defects of the Anglo-Irish aristocracy and to point a moral from their fate in the style in which historians of the French Revolution are wont to edify their readers with highly flavoured descriptions of the wickedness of a nobility weak enough to succumb to such a movement. Leaving, however, such an ungracious and ungenerous task to the profound, candid, and philosophic observers for whom the successful always is the right, it is enough to say, that the Anglo-Irish aristocracy had never discharged, nor so much as sought to discharge, the primary and essential function of every aristocracy, that of identifying its interests with those of the people. As a Monarchy in ceasing to be national loses the one sole reason of its existence, so the aristocracy which declines its natural and inalienable duty of the leadership of the people seals the warrant of its own destruction. The Anglo-Irish aristocracy, taken as a whole, had always remained a caste apart from the people, a conquering and foreign caste, "alien in race and religion." Sometimes it had been English in its views and sympathies, sometimes Anglo-Irish, never Irish. Its very excellences and merits contributed to bring about its downfall, and its fidelity, as it conceived, to England made it the more impossible in Ireland.

From the mind of the Irish masses the forfeitures, confiscations, and plantations of successive English Governments had effectually removed all idea of sanctity attaching to property in land. They knew only that the land which had once been held by Irishmen had been violently transferred to invading settlers in punishment of Irish loyalty and Irish fidelity to the Roman Catholic faith. In the time of Elizabeth, of Cromwell, and of William of Orange, they had been looked upon as aborigines by English colonists, and treated in a fashion by comparison with which the dealings of the United States Government with the Red Indians might well seem the mirror of justice and mercy, probity and honour. Now that they were enfranchised, it would have been more than wonderful if they had abstained from seeking to recover that which they recognized as rightfully their own.

But though the Anglo-Irish aristocracy had little enough claim upon the Irish people, they had every claim upon the country which had planted them in Ireland as an English garrison. If the policy, deliberately adopted and affirmed with reiteration, in pursuance of which they had been originally planted in another land, and which had been bolstered up by disabilities and penal laws,—if this policy, having failed beyond redemption, was now to be abandoned and reversed, then England was bound by every principle of justice to protect and secure the interests of those whose chief fault was that they had loved her too well. If it was necessary to expropriate the Irish landlords, then this process should have been carried through at the cost of the country in whose cause their ancestors had ventured their fortunes in a strange land. If it was requisite that the representatives of English policy should be bought out, they should have been bought out at English expense. But instead of this, the unfortunate Irish landlords, placed between two fires, have been sacrificed by the one country in the vain hope of appeasing the anger and discontent of the other. The "garrison," which should have been marched out with all the honours of war, has been perfidiously betrayed to the enemy, only to arouse contempt and renewed hostility by this open display of the vacillation of English counsels and the shamelessness of English infidelity. The Irish landlords have been ruined by instalments, and the measures of land-purchase at last brought forward have been too late to stave off disaster from many families whose great crime was that they represented English policy in the past.

Thus the dangers which the Peers anticipated to the Anglo-Irish aristocracy and the Anglo-Irish Church from a half measure of Emancipation have been abundantly realized, nor were their fears for the Union excited with no less reason. The "Liberator" O'Connell, the central figure in the story of Emancipation, also led for years an agitation for the Repeal of the Union, and although this great orator and undoubted champion of the Irish people in his last days discarded Repeal for Federation, the Home Rule agitation of a later time has had many supporters who avowedly meant by Home Rule the Repeal of the Union, and few of prominence who favoured Federation. Home Rule is an alluring phrase of vague import, and may cover either of two very different ideas. The first idea, Imperial, Federal, or Pan Britannic, is that of the concession of local legislatures for local affairs to England, Scotland, and Ireland, concurrently with, or as a preliminary to, the representation of Canada, Australia, and perhaps the Cape, in an Imperial Parliament thus left free to deal with Imperial affairs. Under such a scheme the supremacy of the Imperial Parliament over the British Isles would be preserved in its integrity, while as regards the British Colonies then represented in it its actual power as a political fact would be brought into coincidence with its nominal power in law and constitutional theory. On the other hand, the freedom of self-government of each local nationality, Kingdom, or Dominion, in all matters not of Imperial importance, would be sufficiently assured by the common interest of each one of them in resisting the undue interference of the central Executive and Legislature. Such an idea may be, and has been, called chimerical, and it has been pronounced incapable of realization by some persons whose judgment is entitled to respect, as well as by others whose patriotism, intellectual power, and practical acquaintance with the different portions of the Empire do not qualify them to give an opinion. But whether it is practicable or impracticable, not Mr. Goldwin Smith himself could pretend that such a scheme, if carried out, would prove fatal to the Union of the Empire. The scheme may err in the magnitude of its conception, but it cannot be alleged that it errs on the side of want of patriotism and loyalty. This is one idea which may be covered by the phrase Home Rule, and which is in fact Imperial Parliamentary Federation. This scheme of Home Rule is in reality an adaptation of the Unions of 1701 and 1801 to twentieth-century conditions.

But there is another, and a very different sort of Home Rule, and it is this which has always been put forward by the Irish Parliamentary party, and which since 1885 has received the support of the Gladstonian Liberals. This scheme of Home Rule is applied to Ireland by itself, without reference to the British Colonies, or to the other portions of the British Isles. Under it an Irish Parliament would be established, while the present Parliament at Westminster would remain the Parliament of the Empire, but at the same time become again, what it was before the Irish Union, a local Legislature of Great Britain. Whether or not Irish members were retained, permanently or for a time, in the Imperial Parliament, the same state of things would be reproduced as existed before 1782, when there was an Irish Parliament dependent on the Parliament of Great Britain. Now, under such a system as this one of two things might be the case. Either the Imperial Parliament would lose all control over Ireland, even in matters of Imperial importance, or Irish affairs would be constantly referred from the decision of the Parliament at Dublin to the decision of the Parliament at Westminster, in which case the Irish legislature would be an empty mockery. It is impossible to doubt that in either event the final result would be the formal, as well as the practical, Repeal of the Union by some such Act of Renunciation as was passed in the last century, and a revival of the conditions that existed from 1782 to 1801 when Ireland and Great Britain were united only through the Crown—a union which, under existing constitutional practice, is no real or effective union at all. Home Rule of this sort is an impossible anachronism. It was found impossible a century ago, and it is a hundred times more impossible to-day. Home Rule as a detail in a general scheme of Britannic Federation, Home Rule for Ireland as for England, for Scotland, for Canada, for Australia, for the Cape,—Home Rule, in short, all round, with representation in the Imperial Parliament all round likewise,—this would be a natural and constitutional development, the fulfilment of the two great principles of our political growth, the consolidation of Empire and the expansion of local self-government. But Home Rule for Ireland only, Home Rule in the Gladstonian sense, would be no constitutional development but an antiquarian revival, a measure not of progress but of retrogression, a step not of evolution but reversion.

It is preposterous to attempt to justify such a proposal by the example of the Colonies. Nothing can be more certain to any one who has devoted an hour's consideration to the subject than that, unless some means are discovered for bringing those Colonies in which responsible government is fully established within the Imperial Parliamentary Union of the British Isles, the outcome must sooner or later be their separation from the Empire. Unless the Imperial Parliament, the present Sovereign of the British Empire, is to be abolished, and a new body set up in its stead, that Parliament must be so reformed as to admit of the presence of their representatives. Canada has passed, Australia is passing, Afrikanderland will pass, from a colony or group of colonies into a nation, and it rests principally with the people of the British Isles to determine whether these new nations shall be nations with the Greater British nationality or without it. The example of the Colonies proves above everything the necessity for full and formal Union, a Union, not only " of hearts," but of swords and purses. And the only permanent and constitutional form of such a union lies in the reform of the present Parliament of the British Isles into a Parliament of the whole worldwide British nation, local Legislatures being everywhere preserved or established for the transaction of purely local business.

The example of the Colonies proves nothing in favour of Gladstonian Home Rule, and the example of Ireland herself in the last century disproves the possibility of its success. No matter how strenuously it may be sought to conceal the fact, there can be no reasonable doubt that this sort of Home Rule is in effect, if not in name, the Repeal of the Union. This is the Home Rule that has been sought by the Irish party formerly under the leadership of Mr. Parnell, and now, as it would seem, under the influence of Archbishop Walsh; and this is the policy to which Mr. Gladstone was converted, and to which he converted the Gladstonian Liberals. And the demand for it is the direct effect of Roman Catholic Emancipation passed in the manner to which the Tory Peers objected. The Anglo-Irish Church Establishment has been abolished, though no definite settlement of the Irish Church question has for certain been arrived at: the Anglo-Irish aristocracy have been despoiled contrary to every principle of justice: and the Union is threatened, not only by the constitutional representatives of the greater portion of the Irish nation, but by a large body of Scottish and English Liberals. In short, with every sympathy with Ireland for her wrongs of the past, with no antipathy against the Irish people, the Roman Catholic religion, or the Celtic race, one must yet acquit the Peers of the charges of religious intolerance and oppression of the people, and confess that in their opposition to an unscientific, unconditional, and incomplete Emancipation they were animated by the highest and the purest patriotism, and discerned only too clearly in advance the danger to the Union which would arise from it, and has arisen.

Reviewing the action of the Peers in the three great instances alleged against them—their opposition to the first Reform Bill and to the unconditional removal of Roman Catholic and Nonconformist disabilities,—it is evident that, if their action pressed hardly in some few particulars on certain sections of the British people, it was nevertheless prompted in the main by a zeal for the welfare and greatness of the nation as a whole, and for the Parliamentary Union of the British Isles and the political union of the British Empire. It is quite true that they were not altogether in the right, but neither, on the other hand, were their opponents. Each party was then in a manner the complement of the other, and the dangerous extremes into which the Liberals were led by a creditable, but not seldom indiscreet and unseasonable, passion for individual freedom, were counteracted by that farsighted determination of the Peers to preserve at all hazards the unity and greatness of the State which at times rendered them unduly blind to immediate political necessity. In fact, to all who have ceased to accept the superstition, fallen of late years into some disfavour, of an omniscient and infallible Liberal party in a House of Commons existing by divine right, the patriotism and prevision of the Peers in the cases cited will appear not less evident than the narrowness which marred the length and accuracy of their view, and the futility of their struggle with the inevitable march of events; if, then, no impartial jury would return a verdict of "Guilty" on these great stock charges of oppression of the people advanced against the House of Lords, how much more must the most skilled and practised advocate fail to establish a substantive case against them on any of the minor pleas of the indictment.

It is said with some truth that the Peers have retarded the passage and limited the scope of many Liberal enactments, and to those who still hold the decadent and death-stricken dogma of an omniscient and infallible House of Commons—always with the proviso of a Liberal majority—which ought also to be omnipotent, such an assertion of authority seems blasphemous. But this charge is brought, and brought with truth, not only against the House of Lords, but against Second Chambers all over the world; against a House wholly consisting of nominated legislators, no less than against a House partly composed of hereditary legislators; against a Second Chamber of elected legislators, no less than against a Second Chamber of nominated legislators. Everywhere and always a Second Chamber is a check upon a First.

The delay and minimization of change are the necessary conditions of its permanence. If legislative changes were not delayed and minimized, on the accession to power of the party in opposition they would be repealed. Liberals in Great Britain may dilate as they please on the tyranny exercised by the Peers; but a foreign or a Colonial observer would be struck by their self-restraint and moderation. It is alleged against the House of Lords that, in the matter of Mr. Gladstone's Irish Land Acts, it behaved as a House of landlords, and that its members selfishly consulted their interests as a class. But to a citizen of the United States, commonly held up by English Radicals as the ideal of democracy, the wonder would be, not that Peers should be found to oppose such measures, but that any one should be found to propose them. The House of Lords passed them with considerable reluctance, but in the United States they never would have passed at all. For by the fundamental articles of the United States Constitution all such legislation, in violation of contracts, is forbidden both to the Federal Government and the States, and, if passed, would be treated as null and void in the courts of law. This "Tory caucus," this House "of hereditary legislators," which is "out of harmony with democratic feeling," consented to legislation against landlords which, in the American Republic, would be impossible.

When it is said that the House of Lords, being a Chamber "of hereditary legislators," opposes itself to the will of the people, as expressed by the House of Commons, it becomes necessary to inquire how far the House of Commons represents the people. Now, it is obvious, in the first place, that any Bill sent up to the Lords by the Commons, which is a subject of party contention, has been passed, not by the whole House of Commons, but only by a majority of its members. These members, again, represent a majority of the constituencies; but a majority of the constituencies is not the same thing as a majority of all the electors of the country. A very small difference of votes in each constituency is sufficient to return a large majority of members of one political complexion, while leaving a minority almost as numerous wholly unrepresented. Parliament is a rude and imperfect contrivance for expressing the will of the nation. By an established convention, a majority in the House of Commons is held to represent a majority of the nation on the particular question, if any, on which it has been returned; but this is merely a convention—nothing more. And, even accepting this convention, nothing can justify the assumption that the majority in the House of Commons represents the nation, but the fact that the particular legislative change at issue has been expressly submitted to the nation at a general election. Where this is the case, where a majority of the constituencies have decided in favour of a policy distinctly and unequivocally placed before them, there the House of Lords, if it has previously opposed such a policy, now gives way, as it did on the Irish Church question. But how often can this be said to be the case? A political party appeals to the constituencies with not one, but twenty projects of legislation. On which of all these projects, often disconnected, sometimes inconsistent, can the judgment of the people be fairly said to be taken? The House of Commons does not represent the people of the British Isles at all on questions of foreign and Imperial policy. It represents them only by convention on questions of internal and domestic policy.

Take the question of Home Rule and the countless side-issues and irrelevant topics which have been mixed up with it. One member is returned as a Home Ruler, not because his constituents are in favour of Home Rule, but because they desire Welsh or Scottish Disestablishment. Another Home Rule member has been returned as pledged to support Local Option, not because a majority of his constituents are in favour either of Local Option or of Home Rule, but because one minority, by banding itself with another minority, has converted itself into a majority.

Various remedies have been suggested for evils which are universally admitted. Proportional representation, the second ballot, *scrutin de liste*, and so forth, all embody attempts to redress such a state of things, and to secure a true and real representation of the people. But until one or other of these remedies has been successfully applied, it is idle to talk of the House of Lords overriding the will of the people. The accusation is an echo from a bygone day, when there was only one party line of demarcation running throughout Great Britain, and the Irish members were an inconsiderable and unorganized minority. The old notion of two parties, each of which was entitled to an innings, and, when it got its innings, to fair play from the Crown and House of Lords, is one which will not do at all in these times. Parliamentarianism, in the old sense, has had its day, and is now disappearing as a necessary consequence of the extension of the franchise. There are no longer two parties only in the House of Commons, but some half a dozen. The old division into Conservative and Liberal fails altogether to embrace the combinations of the latest politics. The Liberal party, always divided into Radicals and Whigs, has been further sub-divided into Unionist Whigs and Gladstonian Whigs, Unionist Radicals and Gladstonian Radicals. There are the Irish Nationalists, roughly placed under the two heads of Parnellites and anti-Parnellites, but with countless subdivisions. There are the Welsh Particularists; the Labour party; the crofter members; the normal Scottish Radicals, as distinguished from the normal English. In this maze of local politics, how can it be said that this or that chance kaleidoscopic combination represents the deliberate will and well-considered purpose of the people on any given question?

The superstition of a House of Commons representing the "will of the people" with mathematical accuracy and automatic regularity has lately been attacked by the Radicals themselves. They have urged with right and reason that seven years constitute a period much too long for the duration of a Parliament; that a House of Commons, elected six or seven years before, even with the relief of by-elections, has long ago ceased to represent the constituencies. But if a House of Commons does not, cannot, represent the constituencies for seven years, for how long does it represent them? And if, in a mechanical way, it represents a chance majority in each constituency for a few months after each election, does it ever really represent the people as a whole?

The House of Commons, it must be repeated, is but a rude and imperfect contrivance for the representation of the Commons of Great Britain and Ireland. That large portion of the British nation which has transferred its residence from the British Isles to the British Colonies, it does not even pretend to represent at all. And among the people of the British Isles it represents only that portion of the electors who record their vote, and those under conditions which enable a mechanical majority in each constituency to defeat a majority of the electors as a whole. So that, in fact, the House of Lords, instead of defeating the representation of the people, secures to some extent that they shall not be misrepresented. It has it in its power, either to prevent a measure from becoming law, or to insist that it shall be submitted to the judgment of the nation. The Radical complaint amounts to this, that when they have managed to get together a majority in the House of Commons, nominally representing the people, it is a hardship that the decision of this majority should be upset or overruled at the polling-booths by the people themselves. Professing to speak in the popular interest, they dread and denounce an appeal to the people.

The House of Commons, like the House of Lords, is a human institution, and therefore imperfect. The Radicals themselves insist that in two or three years from its election it ceases to represent the electors. At the best, therefore, it represents for a brief period of time only a given section of the nation. But the Monarchy, and in a less degree the House of Lords, represent the nation always, not by direct election, but by permanent assent. They represent, not a majority of majorities in the constituencies at a particular election, but the nation as a whole, its life and history in the past as well as its hopes and interests in the future. They represent, not a spasmodic burst of unreal sentiment, but the settled policy and purpose of the country ; not the adroit and successful manipulation of fanatics and fads, but the fixed and unalterable characteristics of the State as an organic whole.

If the House of Lords had not, or were to abandon, this right of challenging an appeal to the country on any grave matter in dispute between itself and a majority of the House of Commons, the majority of the House of Commons would become absolute. It is impossible to suppose that the royal veto would be exercised on a measure that had passed the two Houses, for under present constitutional practice the Ministers of the Crown are selected from those who can command the support of the Lower Chamber. If the check provided by the House of Lords were to be destroyed or weakened, a Ministry secure of its following in the House of Commons could propose and carry measures on which the constituencies had never been consulted, or of which they had never even heard. It follows, therefore, that the power of the House of Lords to force a Ministry to dissolve, or else retreat, is a necessary protection of the minority. It ensures that measures shall be laid before the people before they are presented in the people's name, and, far from conflicting with democracy, it secures to the people a direct voice on all great proposals of legislative change. It combines all the advantages of the referendum with none of its drawbacks or demerits.

The complaint against the House of Lords that as a Chamber " of hereditary legislators " it acts in the exclusive interest of its class, is one which loses any weight it might otherwise possess when we reflect that all over the world, and throughout the British Empire, every Second Chamber, no matter of what constitution, is regarded with impatience by those who have secured, perhaps with difficulty, a temporary triumph in the First.

The House of Lords is attacked as a body of hereditary legislators ; but if it were composed of nominated or elected legislators, it would fare no better at the hands of its Radical assailants. Where the Upper House is composed of nominated members, the nominations must be with a limit or without one. Where they are limited in number, as in Canada, complaints are constantly heard that the nominees are all of one political complexion. Where they are without limit, as in New South Wales and New Zealand, the Upper Chamber is swollen beyond all natural dimensions by the successive additions of competing Ministries, and the Crown is engaged in a constant struggle with its advisers to restrain them from outraging all decency, by the length of the list of their new nominations. A Second Chamber, composed entirely of elected legislators, would put forward claims very different from any that have been advanced on behalf of the House of Lords. If there is one point more clearly demonstrated than another in the instructive work of Dr. Bryce, it is that in the United States Constitution the Senate plays the part which is borne by the House of Commons in our own. To convert the House of Lords into an elected Assembly is an intelligible proposal; but it was surely never put forward in the interest of democracy. A Second Chamber of elected legislators may mean the formal abolition of the House of Lords, but it would also entail the practical abolition of the House of Commons.

The experience of Canada, as of the Australasian Colonies, shows that an Upper House exclusively composed of Crown nominees is neither powerful nor popular, and a Second Chamber of popular election is a contradiction and nullification of the First. The hereditary legislators, far from being a blemish on the House of Lords, are its principal excellence, and the secret of its moderated strength. The "hereditary principle" gives a body too powerful to be dependent on a passing Administration, but not powerful enough to constitute a permanent obstacle to necessary change. It hits the happy mean between the extreme weakness and inefficiency of a House consisting of life nominees and the dangerous and excessive strength of an American Senate. The existence of so large a body of its members whose seats are independent of the Crown preserves the House of Lords from subserviency to Ministers; the fact that they are none of them indebted for their seats to popular election precludes the possibility of the Second Chamber attempting to take up the position of a rival or superior House of Commons.

The House of Lords is accused of oppressing the people, and when the charge is examined it is found that the oppression consists in requiring that the direct vote of the people shall be taken in all matters of legislation gravely affecting the people's interests. It is said that the Peers are "out of harmony with democratic feeling;" and when we ask for proof, it is admitted that their true offence lies in their assertion of the essentially democratic principle of the *plebiscite* or *referendum*. But, as a matter of fact, the real fault of the House of Lords, from a Radical point of view, is that it is Conservative, not Liberal. But whose fault is that? How is it that the peerages created by Liberal Ministers for their supporters in one generation are held by Conservatives in the next? If it were only in matters of domestic legislation that the House of Lords differed with the Liberal party in Great Britain, there would be good reason for suspecting that the House of Lords was in the wrong. But the difference between them is not more emphatic on a Land Act than on questions of foreign and Imperial policy. Imperial policy is, for the most part, Colonial and Indian policy, and on all Colonial questions the opinion of the Colonies is with the House of Lords, and against the Liberal party in Great Britain. On all questions of Indian policy the opinion of the rulers of India is with the House of Lords, and against the Liberal party in Great Britain. It would be easy to find in the Colonies and India many men who have no belief in Established Churches and no superstitious veneration for hereditary legislators; but it would not be easy to find one man of intelligence and information who approved of either the foreign, or the Indian, or the Colonial policy of the Liberal party in Great Britain.

Nor is this all. It is conceivable that the Liberal party in Great Britain might be altogether fallible as regards Imperial policy, but infallible as regards domestic policy. But if we look to the Colonies we shall find no support for this suggestion. The Liberal party in Australia is as fanatically Protectionist as the Liberal party in Great Britain is fanatically Cobdenite. Between these rival Popes, the English and the Antipodean, each equally convinced of his own infallibility, equally intolerant of opposition, who is to decide? One thing is certain that both cannot be right, and there is at least a possibility that both may in different ways be wrong. Finally, it may be said that, if on the one hand the House of Lords has often resisted the will of the Liberal party in Great Britain, on the other hand the Liberal party in Great Britain is not the British people in any use or acceptation of the term.

As for the Bishops, their presence in the House of Lords is, as we have seen, a relic of the time when the Imperial Parliament was only the Parliament of England, and when the English Church was co-terminous and co-extensive with the English State. Their removal from the Upper Chamber would not of itself affect the local position of the Church of England, although in one sense it would be a measure of Disestablishment. But why should they be removed? It is not asserted that they "oppress the people." They are not of necessity members of the landlord class, and they take so small a part in current politics that they can scarcely be accused of injuriously affecting the fortunes of Liberal legislation. They are the only life members of the House of Lords who are not also Peers. Their presence formed in a way a precedent for the new position of the Lords and ex-Lords of Appeal. Since the Anglican priesthood, like the Roman Catholic clergy and ministers of the Established Church of Scotland, are excluded by law from sitting in the House of Commons, the Bishops are the only official representatives of the English Church in Parliament. Their removal might take place without Disestablishment, but without Disestablishment it would be as unnecessary as unwise. If literature, science, and art deserve representation in the Upper Chamber, how much more must that great department of thought and action, philosophy and feeling, which forms the principal interest in the lives of a large portion of mankind, and which has its own unique and incomparable literature, its subtle theologic science, its admirable art. Their presence can only offend those who on every ground are utterly undeserving of consideration, insolent and aggressive secularists: and the mere fact that it offended such people would be its sufficient and entire justification, for if there is anything more contemptible and odious than religious fanaticism it is the fanaticism that is anti-religious. As for the objection that it is a violation of "religious equality," admitting for the sake of argument the objection to be well founded, the remedy surely lies, not in the removal of the Bishops, but in the admission to the House of Lords of the representatives of the principal religious bodies which now exist side by side with the Anglican Church. But this it will be more proper to consider later in the volume.

PART III.

RADICAL REMEDIES.

CHAPTER I.

THE ABOLITION OF THE HOUSE OF LORDS.

WE saw in an earlier chapter, when dealing with *The Radical Case against the House of Lords*, that the periodical conflict between that body and the Liberal party in Great Britain, giving rise to bitter Radical complaints, has caused those whose wishes have been thus frequently frustrated to put forward a demand that the House of Lords shall be "ended or mended." With some the demand is for the abolition of the bicameral system, and the reduction of Parliament to a single Chamber—that is to say, to the House of Commons. Others, of a more lively fancy, exercise their ingenuity in devising varied schemes for the more moderate "mending" of the Upper Chamber with expedients borrowed from all the constitutions of the world, from the United States to Switzerland, and from Germany to Japan. With one man the idea is to convert the House of Lords into an assembly of the chairmen of the English County Councils, a Gaiety burlesque of State representation in the American Senate: while another gentleman, whose imagination takes a wider field, appears to think that, by enticing the Australian Agents-General into the House of Lords, the Upper Chamber will eventually emerge as a sort of Bundesrath or Federal Council, the House of Commons and its proceedings in the meantime being loftily omitted from consideration. These fanciful schemes, agreeing only in their entire lack of respect for the historic continuity of the Constitution, may be discussed later. For if the House of Lords is to be "abolished," it would be a waste of time to consider its "reform." If it is to be "ended" rather than "mended," the cobbler does not need to be called in.

It is remarkable that among the Radical politicians who have been most conspicuous in demanding the abolition of the House of Lords there should be included Sir Charles Dilke, a politician who, by the confession of both friends and foes, stands almost alone among the members of his party in his acquaintance with foreign, Colonial, and Indian affairs. With the outlook, and to some extent with the instincts, of an Imperial statesman, Sir Charles Dilke is content, and even anxious, to father a design which, but for his adhesion and persistent advocacy, would seem likely to commend itself to none but the veriest Bumbles and Chawbacons of English vestry politics. It is strange that a politician who has shown so keen an interest in the Colonies, and an extensive, if not a profound or accurate, knowledge of their aspirations and affairs, a politician who, if not committed to Imperial Federation, is very far from desiring the disunion of the Empire, should ignore the obvious effect on the outlying portions of the Britannic realms of so grave a change in the constitution of the governing body of the Empire. The constitution of the Imperial Parliament is a matter of interest to the whole Empire. Sir Charles Dilke favours the abolition of the House of Lords, and the reduction of the Imperial Parliament to a single Chamber consisting of the House of Commons. But has he thought for one moment of the effect of such a change on the relations existing between the British Isles and the British Colonies and India? The Queen is the Queen of all her subjects, Insular or Oceanic, European, African, American, Asian, Australasian. The House of Lords contains many members of Indian, Colonial, and other Imperial experience, and all its members are exempt from direct local responsibility. But the House of Commons is elected by the constituencies of Great Britain and Ireland : it represents them, and it represents nothing else. And to abolish the House of Lords is to remove one of those checks on the dominance of the electors of the British Isles over the remainder of the Empire which alone render the present situation endurable and possible. One democracy has no belief in, and no respect for, another democracy; and the supremacy of the Mother Country over the self-governing freemen of her Colonies could not long continue, if that supremacy were nakedly and undisguisedly translated into a supremacy of a local-party majority in the House of Commons. The quarrel of the Colonies has been with the Colonial Office, that is to say with the House of Commons. If the will of the House of Commons were set free from all restraint the quarrel would be renewed more bitterly than ever, and that in a form disastrous to the Empire.

Sir Charles Dilke forgets that, in the Colonies, it is the Whig and Liberal policy in Imperial affairs that is disliked, and the Conservative policy that finds favour. This feeling is not peculiar to the Conservative sections of Colonial society. It prevails throughout the length and breadth of the community, and is nowhere more vigorously expressed than in ultra-democratic journals. The only difference is that, whereas in all who cherish the Imperial connection the Liberal policy excites mingled shame and pity for the Old Country, with those of narrower and more provincial sympathies it is apt to be regarded as an unmistakable symptom of her decadence and approaching fall.

"It would be one thing," declared the *Melbourne Age* some three years back, "to part company with the men who made a small country great: it is another, and a very different thing, to part company with men who are making a great country small."

These are the words of the organ of the Liberal party in the leading Colony of democratic Australia.

Sir Charles Dilke seems to have forgotten that it is the Liberal party in Great Britain that is responsible for the presence of the Germans in New Guinea, and the encroachments of the French in the Pacific; for the annexation of the West African Coast between the Orange River and Cape Frio by Germany, and for her intrusion into Zanzibar. But, although these inconvenient facts may have escaped his memory, they are not forgotten in the Colonies, and in

O

combination with the anti-Russian feeling of Australasia, and the Russophile antecedents of the Liberal party in Great Britain, they have aroused in the Colonies for the Imperial policy of that party a sentiment of indignation blended with contempt.

Sir Charles Dilke recently attempted to create party capital out of the attitude of the Salisbury Administration towards Newfoundland; and Lord Rosebery and other Liberals, striving to be more Colonial than the Colonies, denounced the cession of Heligoland. But the views that they expressed found no echo in any Colony except perhaps Newfoundland itself. The press and the public of Australia, as of Canada, are not so blind as to be unable to distinguish between the course of putting pressure on a recalcitrant and unreasonable Colony, in whose interests the resources of diplomacy had been exhausted, to conform to the general requirements of the Empire, and such an unwarrantable interference in the local affairs of a self-governing Colony as has been since attempted by the English Liberals in the case of Queensland. And in the case of Heligoland, Sir Charles Dilke and Lord Rosebery, striving to be more Colonial than the Colonies, failed to be Colonial at all. They showed that they had failed to grasp the true Colonial idea, which is, not that wherever the British flag has been unfurled it can never be withdrawn (for in that case we might be obliged to fight for districts of the Arctic regions or perhaps for the nearest point yet gained to the North Pole), but that wherever Britons go *and stay*, and settle, they should carry Britain with them. We ought always to be ready to exchange a mere possession or dependency, a coaling station or trading settlement, for a more valuable or more convenient possession elsewhere (as we did with the Dutch upon the Gold Coast); always provided that such ceded possession is neither a colony of the British people, nor an adopted colony of some other European nation, nor inhabited by those to whom, as in the case of the peoples of India, we stand in a parental and fiduciary relation, being their guardians and trustees. Nothing can make a British colony but British colonization, or the political adoption of a colony of another European nation. Anything else is a mere possession or dependency, not an extension of the British nation. Britain has no moral duty to Aden or Gibraltar; she holds them at her own pleasure for her own convenience; and the extravagant declarations of the English Liberals in the matter of Heligoland were heard in the great self-governing Colonies with impatience and amazement.

Notwithstanding these attempts to create local party capital out of the difficulties of the whole Empire, it is the Liberal policy, not the Conservative, that is looked upon in the Colonies with angry apprehension. Now, the proposal of Sir Charles Dilke to abolish the House of Lords is a proposal to give that Liberal policy full play, to render the Imperial Parliament less Imperial and more insular than it is already, by reducing it to the House of Commons. The House of Lords is the Imperial branch of the Supreme Legislature, both as regards representation and as regards views. Sir Charles Dilke, therefore, as an Imperialist Radical, suggests as his contribution to the solution of the problem of the consolidation of the Empire, that the Imperial branch of the legislature should be swept away. But it is easy to foresee that the abolition of the House of Lords, and the adoption of the single-Chamber system in place of the bicameral—even supposing that such a change was imperatively necessary on domestic grounds—could not fail to prove disastrous to the Empire. It would alienate the Colonies; it would imperil India.

Members of the Liberal party in Great Britain who have never been out of the British Isles, or who having been out of them have been careful to take with them and bring back with them the Insular Liberal mind, may perhaps cherish the illusion that in their disagreements with the House of Lords they carry with them the "moral sympathy" of Colonial democrats, that "the great heart of the People" in the Colonies is throbbing to "join hands with them across the sea." But in this pleasing belief they are entirely mistaken. The House of Lords is no grievance to the Colonies. It is not the House of Lords that seeks to interfere in their local affairs, but, on the contrary, the Liberal party in the House of

Commons. And as regards foreign affairs, Imperial policy, the House of Lords is in substantial agreement with the Colonial democracy. It is not the House of Lords that is peculiar or eccentric in its views of Imperial policy. Those it shares with ninety-nine Britons out of a hundred in every portion of the Queen's dominions save the British Isles. If any one feels inclined to question the truth of this assertion, a residence of a few months in the greater Colonies will quickly rid him of his doubts. A peace-at-any-price policy, a Russophile policy, is no policy of the democracy. The Imperial policy of the Liberal party in Great Britain, Imperial as concerning the Empire but in no other sense, is due in part to the personal idiosyncrasy of Mr. Gladstone; but it is also and far more a mere survival, a relic of the days when that party was a party mainly composed of merchants, manufacturers, and tradesmen, engineered by Whigs. The ideas and the policy of such persons in the sixties or the seventies, with a strong Nonconformist flavouring, differ *in toto* from the ideas and policy of the Colonial democrat. With the Liberal party in Great Britain matters of Imperial policy are habitually subordinated to the demolition of Established Churches. But the Colonial democrat has no Established Churches to demolish, his atmosphere is far from Nonconformist, and instead of swearing by Messieurs Cobden and Bright he is usually a bigoted Protectionist.

As regards the affairs common to the whole Empire—that is, chiefly foreign policy—the House of Lords is in substantial agreement with the Colonial democracy; and as regards the local affairs of the Colonies, it is not the House of Lords, but the House of Commons, that attempts to interfere. The change projected by Sir Charles Dilke would not be popular in the Colonies, but the reverse; for, so far as they can be affected by the Imperial Parliament, it would place them at the mercy of a party majority in the House of Commons. The House of Lords includes men of Colonial experience, who can afford to tell the truth without fear of the consequences. But in the House of Commons every member is responsible to his constituents, and goes in dread of the countless societies of fanatics and sects of faddists who hover round the field of politics and attempt to blackmail every candidate for Parliament into a promise to support their absurd and mischievous proposals. Few members of the Lower House can afford to speak the whole truth, and it is fewer still who have the courage to do so. The House of Lords, now, like the Crown, serves to break the force of any conflict of opinion between the Colonial and Home democracies. But for the Crown the British Empire could not hold together for a single week. The abolition of the British Monarchy would be the signal for the immediate and irretrievable break-up of the British dominions. And as the Crown is the centre and keystone of union, so the House of Lords, though in a less degree, serves to support the edifice of Empire. That independence of the House on Insular electors, which places its members at some disadvantage in dealing with purely Insular affairs, places it at a far more than commensurate advantage in dealing with all affairs that are not purely Insular. The House of Lords is a protection and defence of the Colonies from possible encroachments of the House of Commons. And, this being so, it is a matter of absolute indifference to the Colonial democracy how, or of whom, the House of Lords may be composed. For all they care the House of Lords might be a House of Ladies, a Chamber of Peeresses, if only it held out a sufficient measure of protection to their interests.

The wrongs or rights of the Liberal party in Great Britain in its warfare with the House of Lords do not interest the people of the Colonies. What interests them is, in the first place, the safety of the Empire, that is to say, their own, contingent on the adoption of a sound foreign policy; and, in the second place, the perfect freedom of their self-government in local affairs. Neither of these is threatened by the House of Lords, and the former it perpetually urges. But the Liberal party in the House of Commons ignorantly flouts the one, and with rash temerity assails the other. And if it does so now, when the voice of the House of Lords can constantly go forth to the British Isles in warning and remonstrance, what would it do when that voice was silenced and the House of Commons knew no check or curb but its own will? Of the illicit influence of private societies and persons, and the irresponsible power in the hands of certain individuals, a striking example was given when, at the instance of the Salvation Army, the House of Commons superseded the system of local self-government established in the country in the case of Eastbourne. A House of Commons even now liable to fall under such influences, would stand in danger, when all effective check was removed, of committing blunders fraught with ruin to the Empire. Such a body, looking only to the Home electors, might seek to force upon the Colonies some such scheme of immigration as that propounded by "General" Booth; might seek to establish in the midst of free Australia a Salvationist Paraguay, administered by dervishes, and governed by a Mahdi. The issue of such an experiment cannot be doubted.

The composition of the House of Lords is to the Colonies a matter of indifference, provided only that it affords some measure of protection to their interests. They have no superstitious veneration for hereditary legislators; they have no superstitious prejudice against them. Nor do they entertain a superstitious veneration for the House of Commons. They have Parliaments of their own, composed, always in part, sometimes altogether, of elected legislators, but never, either in whole or part, of hereditary legislators. In the general publicity of small communities they are freely admitted behind the scenes; they see the working of the wires that move the puppets, and they know that legislators, and in particular elected legislators, are mortal, very mortal, not divine. The judgment that they form of their own legislature they largely transfer to the House of Commons. They look upon it, rightly or wrongly, as a body of precisely the same nature as their own Legislative Assembly, only on a larger scale. The real reverence that they entertain for the Crown would be seriously damaged, the deference that they indubitably feel for the Imperial Parliament would quickly disappear, when they saw the authority of both monopolized by a single Legislative Chamber, exclusively composed of the representatives of the electors of Great Britain, or of Great Britain and Ireland. The Imperial element in the Parliament of Westminster would be altogether eliminated, while the local element would be emphasized and enlarged. Such a preponderance of local over Imperial interests in the Supreme Legislature, such a degradation of the Imperial Parliament into a grand vestry of the British Isles, could only be effected at the price of sacrificing the Empire.

One democracy feels no reverence for another democracy, no disposition to consult its pleasure, to defer to its possibly superior wisdom. This is true of the democracy of the British Colonies, and it is true also of the democracy of the British Isles. Short of the abolition of the Monarchy, no measure could be contrived more certain to bring those democracies into dire and disastrous collision than the abolition of the House of Lords. One free people is utterly unfit to rule another, and Sir Charles Dilke and his friends, could they realize their scheme, would find that in gratifying a childish spite against the House of Lords they had made shipwreck of the British Empire. Indeed, it must be admitted that Sir Charles Dilke, in his *rôle* of an Imperial statesman and a would-be interpreter of the Liberal party in the Colonies to the Liberal party in Great Britain, is singularly unfortunate in his suggestion for dealing with the Imperial Parliament. He displays a curious ignorance of Colonial thought and feeling, or a curious contempt for them. The Colonies certainly would never consent to be ruled, or even directed, by an Imperial Legislation consisting of one Chamber. Their complaint is not that the Upper House of the Imperial Parliament is too strong, but that it is not strong enough; not that the Imperial element is excessively developed in the constitution of the governing body of the Empire, but that it obtains in far too scant proportion. If, in negotiating a scheme of Imperial Federation, they demanded the abolition of the House of Lords, it would be with no view of establishing the supremacy of the House of Commons, but, on the contrary, to effect the practical supersession of that body by the creation of an Upper Chamber, modelled on the United States Senate. A time is coming when, if Imperial Federation is to be seriously thought of, the House of Commons will require to be either " ended " or " mended," abolished or reformed. A large number of those persons in the British Colonies, who favour the perpetual union of the Colonies with the British Isles, are in favour of the abolition of the House of Commons and the substitution of an entirely new body in its stead. But, at the risk of being condemned as a reactionary, one may still cling to the belief and hope that it is not even now too late for its reform.

The reduction of the Imperial Parliament to a single Chamber, the transference of the sovereign authority of the Empire to a local and temporary majority in the United Kingdom, would preclude the possibility of Imperial Federation. But, long before the stage of Imperial Federation had been reached, it would, in all human probability, have fatally and finally severed the British Isles from the British Colonies, and caused a calamitous explosion in the Indian Empire. Jealous as the Colonies already are of Old Country interference or dictation, if it once took the form of the undisguised interference of a party majority in the British Isles with the freedom of Colonial self-government, on such terms they would refuse to remain any longer members of the Empire. As for India, with an absolute rule of the majority in the House of Commons, there would be no possible security against the careless adoption, at the instigation of Exeter Hall, of some resolution that would set by the ears every Hindoo and every Moslem in the dominions of the Empress, and light up the world with the grand and never-equalled spectacle of the inextinguishable conflagration of the great fabric of British rule in Asia. To reduce the Parliament of the Empire to a local legislature of the British Isles is for the people of the British Isles to abdicate their Empire. As well might the United Kingdom be ruled by the Common Council of the City of London as the Empire continue to acknowledge the supremacy, or even the ascendency, of a Parliament shorn of all that was Imperial, and cut down to the dimensions of a single Chamber representing nothing, and no one, but the constituencies of Ireland and Great Britain.

Sir Charles Dilke, in advocating his plan for the reduction of the Imperial Parliament to the House of Commons, does not scruple to draw arguments from the example of the Colonies. He points to the Provinces of Ontario and Manitoba in the Dominion of Canada as having Legislatures consisting of a single Chamber. But though Sir Charles Dilke may put such an argument before the public of the Old Country, he could not advance it to a Canadian audience without the certainty of being laughed at and jeered off the platform. "There is a river at Macedon, and a river at Monmouth." Is Ontario a United Kingdom of three great, ancient, and powerful nations, or is it the Province of a Dominion which is itself a Colony, dependent upon the parent lands? Are the powers and functions of the Legislature which meets at Winnipeg one and the same with the powers and functions of the Legislature which meets at Westminster? Has Manitoba Colonies in every quarter of the globe? Or has Ontario an India? None can know better than the author of " Problems of Greater Britain " that the case of Ontario and the case of Manitoba are not cases to the point. The Legislature of each is a purely local body, discharging strictly defined and limited functions, liable even in the exercise of those functions to find its legislation on the subjects expressly assigned to it by the Canadian Constitution disallowed by the Dominion Government. What possible comparison can there be between such a body and the Parliament of the United Kingdom, whose power over the Empire is in law without limit or control? With equal cogency, and perhaps with greater candour, Sir Charles Dilke might adduce the example of an English County Council. A Canadian Province, in strict subordination to the National Legislature and Executive at Ottawa, can dispense with a Legislative Council, in addition to its Legislative Assembly, almost as well as an Indian Province can dispense with a Legislative Assembly, in addition to its Legislative Council. But where no such National or

Dominion Government exists, it would be impossible to find a single Colony in the possession of responsible government where the Legislature is limited to a single Chamber. Newfoundland, the Cape, New Zealand, Tasmania, Western Australia, South Australia, Victoria, New South Wales, Queensland, differing among themselves in their preference for nomination or election, are all agreed in an adhesion to the bicameral system. Two or three, perhaps even four Canadian Provinces — for Prince Edward Island, a territory of less extent that the West Riding of Yorkshire, has lately proposed to follow the example of Ontario, Manitoba, and British Columbia—may dispense with a Second Chamber; but in the Parliament of the Canadian nation there is a Senate of nominated members, as under the scheme of Australian Federation there was to be in the Australian Parliament a Senate of elected members returned by the federated Colonies. The polity of Canada or Australia as a Dominion, or a nation, is surely of greater import and significance than the local arrangements existing in a Canadian Province. It is difficult to imagine that Sir Charles Dilke is serious in recommending that the Imperial Parliament should frame itself anew on the model of the Legislature of Manitoba, but on any other supposition it would be impossible to acquit him of taking a rather cruel advantage of the dense and deplorable ignorance of Colonial affairs existing in his Radical disciples. Sir Charles Dilke must indeed have found arguments scarce that would tell in favour of his proposal, when he dragged into the controversy a matter with no more bearing on the constitution of the Imperial Parliament than has the form of government in a Crown Colony.

But if we are to look around for example and instruction, if the Mother of Parliaments who has planted her children in every British land, and whose copies in so many foreign countries attest the admiration of mankind, is now in her old age to take lessons from her offspring and from those who hitherto have sought to ape her, we shall find, wherever we may cast our eyes, that the bicameral is the prevailing Parliamentary system. Not in the Colonies only, but in the

United States; not in countries with institutions of directly British origin only, but in Mexico and those South American Republics which have endeavoured to frame their constitutions with more or less success on the model of the United States; not in the New World only, but the Old; the bicameral system is the well-nigh universal Parliamentary type. In Austria as in Hungary, in the Prussian Kingdom as in the German Empire, in France, in Italy, in Spain, in Portugal, in Belgium, in the Netherlands, in Denmark, in Switzerland, in Sweden, the Legislature is made up of two Chambers. Monarchy or Republic, Federal State or Unitarian, it is the same.

"On the Continent of Europe," wrote Sir Henry Maine, "there are no States without Second Chambers, except three—Greece, Servia, and Bulgaria,—all resembling one another in having long been portions of the Turkish Empire, and in being now [1885] very greatly under the influence of the Russian Government." *

Sir Charles Dilke, who thinks it worth while to quote Manitoba, who proposes the example of British Columbia for the imitation of the British Empire, may appeal for support to the Hellenic Kingdom, which, like British Columbia, is unicameral, and, like Manitoba, has neither Colonies nor India. But even Sir Charles Dilke, it is to be supposed, would hesitate to quote Bulgaria, where the new Parliamentary institutions are apparently administered in the "fearless old fashion" of the Turk, or Servia, where the members of the Opposition are at times subjected to the chastisement of naughty schoolboys in the Parliamentary recess.

Since the judgment of Parliamentary mankind confirms our own past national experience, it is not immodest to prefer the teaching of history and comparative politics to the empirical schemes of revolutionary theorists. When we find a Federal Empire like Germany, and a unitarian Republic like France, a Federal Republic like the United States, and a unitarian Kingdom like Italy, all concurring in the necessity of a Second Chamber, we may take it that States, with

* "Popular Government," essay iii.

constitutions so essentially diverse, are not for nothing in this one particular agreed. Everywhere a Second Chamber is a check upon the First, and everywhere it is confessed that such a check is needed. Against Canada it is idle to quote Manitoba; against France, Italy, and Germany it is idle to quote Bulgaria, Servia, and Greece. The example of Manitoba may be of some interest and use to Athabasca or Assiniboine, but it is of no interest or use whatever to the Empire as a whole. The example of Bulgaria may be of interest and use to Armenia; but it is of no use, and of but slight and severely scientific interest, to those older political nations of the West who have never had to struggle out of the thraldom of Muscovite or Turkish Orientalism. The universal judgment of modern political mankind in every State of standing, with institutions approximately free, asserts the necessity of a Second Chamber as a check upon the First.

"'If,' wrote Sir Henry Maine, 'it [the Radical argument] runs, a Second Chamber differs from the First it is mischievous; if it agrees it is superfluous.' It has perhaps escaped notice that this saying is a conscious or unconscious parody of that reply of the Caliph Omar about the books of the Alexandrian Library which caused them to be burnt. 'If the books,' said the Commander of the Faithful to his lieutenant, ' differ from the book of the Prophet they are impious; if they agree they are useless.' The reasoning is the same in both cases. It takes for granted that a particular utterance is divine. If the Koran is the inspired and exclusive word of God, Omar was right; if 'Vox Populi, Vox Dei,' expresses a truth Siéyès was right. If the decisions of the community, conveyed through some particular organ, are not only imperative but all-wise, a Second Chamber is a superfluity or an impertinence. The advocates of a Second Chamber do not assert that the decisions of a popularly elected Chamber are always or generally wrong. But it is impossible to be sure that they are right. . . . What, then, may be expected from a well-constituted Second Chamber, is not a rival infallibility but an additional security." *

That such a security is everywhere considered necessary has been seen. But what few people seem to grasp is, that in our own case it is more necessary than in almost any other. Not only have we Imperial interests at stake greater than those of any foreign country, but our Constitution stands almost alone in its unlimited liability to change, and

" Popular Government," essay iii.

in the simplicity of the means required to effect change. In nearly every foreign country the Constitution is hedged round with elaborate safeguards and precautions to preserve it from the danger of reckless and hasty innovation. In nearly all countries the Constitution is placed among the fundamental laws, and can only be changed by an elaborate process involving the fullest discussion and a sufficient period of delay. But the Britannic Constitution could be changed by an Act of Parliament, passed in a single session. There are no limits to the legal omnipotence of Parliament; it is the absolute Sovereign of the British Empire; and it could change or abolish every institution in that Empire with as much ease, and no more delay, than it passes an Act to legalize a marriage where some trifling formality has been omitted. Abroad it is quite different. In France, as in some other Continental countries, a broad distinction is drawn, not only between those laws that are "fundamental," and those laws that are not, but between a legislative and a "constituent" assembly. The Parliament of France has no power to change the French Constitution in the casual, off-hand fashion in which the Imperial Parliament can change the British.

"The French Parliament," says Professor Dicey, "is not a sovereign assembly, but is bound by the law of the Constitution in a way in which no law binds our Parliament. The articles of the Constitution, or 'fundamental laws,' stand in a totally different position from the ordinary law of the land. . . . These laws cannot be changed by the ordinary Legislature acting in its ordinary legislative character. The two Chambers, in order to effect a change in the constitutional manner, must, in the first place, each separately resolve that a revision of the Constitution is desirable. When each has passed this resolution, the two Chambers meet together, and, when thus assembled and voting together as a National Assembly, or Congress, have power to change any part of the Constitutional laws. . . . The various Constitutions [past and present] of France," concludes Mr. Dicey, "which are in this respect fair types of Continental polities, exhibit, as compared with the flexibility of English institutions, that characteristic which may be conveniently described as rigidity. . . . The flexibility of our Constitution," he explains, "consists in the right of the Crown and the two Houses to modify or repeal any law whatever; they can alter the succession to the Crown or repeal the Acts of Union, in the same manner in which they can pass an Act enabling a company to make a new railway from Oxford to London. . . . The rigidity," on the other hand, "of the Constitution, say of Belgium or of France, consists in the absence of any right on the part of the Belgian or French Parliament, when acting in its ordinary capacity, to modify or repeal certain definite laws termed constitutional or fundamental."

In Belgium "the ordinary Parliament cannot change anything in the Constitution; it is a legislative, not a constituent, body; it can declare that there is reason for changing a particular constitutional provision, and having done so is *ipso facto* dissolved. The new Parliament thereupon elected has a right to change the constitutional article which has been declared subject to change."

"In Switzerland no change can be introduced in the constitution which has not been submitted for approval or disapproval to all male citizens who have attained their majority. . . . No legal revision [of the Constitution] can take place without the assent both of a majority of Swiss citizens and of a majority of the Cantons. . . . Even an ordinary law which does not involve a change in the Constitution may, after it has been passed by the Federal Assembly, be submitted on the demand of a certain number of citizens to a popular vote, and is annulled if a vote is not obtained in its favour."

In Germany "the Constitution may be changed by the Imperial (Federal) Legislature in the way of ordinary legislation. But no law amending the Constitution can be carried, if opposed by fourteen votes in the Federal Council (Bundesrath). Certain rights, moreover, are reserved to several States which cannot be changed under the Constitution except with the assent of the State possessing the right." In the United States "changes in the Constitution require for their enactment the support of three-fourths of the States." *

In all these countries, great or small, the amendment or revision of the Constitution is no such easy matter as it is with us, no such trifle as it seems to Sir Charles Dilke. With us no laws are constitutional or fundamental in the sense that they cannot be changed. In foreign countries, even with a Second Chamber, it is still thought necessary to defend the Constitution from attack, to insure it from hazardous and needless change, with an elaborate apparatus of safeguards and precautions. But from us, who have no safeguards for our Constitution whatever, save the personal courage and wisdom of the Monarch, and the intelligence and patriotism of the House of Lords, it is proposed to take away even such a bulwark of the Constitution as we possess

* "Law of the Constitution."

in our second Chamber. In Monarchical Belgium, as in Republican France, with the Constitution hedged round with guarantees and fundamental laws, a Second Chamber is still deemed essential to the public safety. But in Britain, where there are no such guarantees and no such laws, where one law is just as sacred, just as "constitutional," just as "fundamental," as any other law, where all laws alike can be repealed by an Act of Parliament, hurried through the Houses at the fag-end of a session, Sir Charles Dilke proposes with a light heart to deprive us of that security against revolution and subversive change which is provided by the House of Lords.

In our case the "additional security" spoken of by Sir Henry Maine is perhaps more needed than in any other. It is needed on account of the extraordinary variety and complexity of our national and Imperial interests, far transcending those of any foreign State. It is needed on account of the exposed and undefended position of our Constitution, left open to attack unlike any other, and for which it is impossible to adopt the Continental methods of defence without fatally abridging and impairing the supremacy and Sovereignty, and by consequence also the efficiency, of the Imperial Parliament.

But it is possible to go farther than Sir Henry Maine. Whether the voice of the people is the voice of God, is a point best left to theologians. It were more immediately profitable to inquire whether, and how far, the voice of the House of Commons is the voice of the people. It has been remarked before that the method by which members are returned to the Lower Chamber is unsatisfactory in the extreme as regards the representation of the people, altogether inadequate to express the national will on any other than some few test questions which have been forced on the attention of the constituencies at a general election. Questions arise which were never foreseen when the members were returned. Subjects come up for discussion which were then unknown. It is acknowledged that in many constituencies the election turns, not on the national issues submitted to the electors, but on some matter of purely local and temporary interest, a wrongful arrest by a policeman, or the refusal of a Home Secretary to censure or remove a judge, whose attitude in a sensational trial has provoked the displeasure of an evening paper. How can it be said that electors who deliberately choose their member on such a principle as this, have expressed a decision on the great national questions that are brought before Parliament? Again, the political programme of a party may embrace a dozen different items, with no more connection between them than exists between Scottish Disestablishment and Irish Home Rule, between marrying one's deceased wife's sister and the enfranchisement of leaseholds. The unfortunate elector who favours any item of the programme has to vote for all or none, or else to lose all voice in the matter by refraining from voting. Even were elections triennial, instead of septennial, there would still be no absolute security that the country had clearly expressed itself, save on the condition that one question, and one question alone, had been put before it at a general election..

It is notorious that politicians, both in the British Isles and elsewhere, in order to gain votes, pledge their support to measures and principles in which they have no faith, because they know or believe that these will not be carried. A Parliamentary candidate might now cheerfully promise to vote that the sun goes round the earth, but he would hesitate ere doing so if he knew that such a resolution would be carried, and, if carried, would occasion a great convulsion in the solar system. In the same way members of the House of Commons have been known to lend their support to principles and measures that they heartily repudiated, with well-warranted confidence that the action of the House of Lords would avert the evils that would otherwise certainly arise from their unscrupulous behaviour. Thus the quack proposals of the various societies that now exist for the suppression of individual freedom receive an outward countenance from Parliament which they would most assuredly fail to obtain from the electors.

In the uneventful conduct of ordinary business the House of Commons may represent the people fairly enough; but in dealing with all other matters the voice of the House of Commons is not the voice of the people in nineteen cases out of twenty. Whether or not we are prepared to deify Demos, some method must be devised for his more exact and faithful representation before a majority in the House of Commons can be entitled to say in the magnificent style of the Nicene Council, "It has seemed good to the Holy Ghost and to us."

Abroad, as we have just seen, and in the British Colonies, the bicameral system is well-nigh universally adopted in Parliamentary countries; quite universally, it may be said, if we include those countries only that are in any degree comparable with the United Kingdom. And if we look back on the history of the British Isles, we shall find no warrant in it for any belief in the value and efficacy of a single Chamber. The Scottish Parliament, it is true, was restricted to a single Chamber; but it was a single Chamber in which hereditary legislators sat side by side with elected. The Scottish Parliament bore no resemblance to the modern House of Commons. If all the members of the House of Lords were entitled to sit in the House of Commons, this would give but a faint notion of the non-democratic character of the old Scottish Parliament.

In England the House of Lords was "abolished" in 1649 by a vote of the House of Commons; but the success, whatever that may have been, of the Protectorate and Commonwealth was in no sense due to the single Chamber of the House of Commons. When the House of Lords had been abolished, what followed?

"The Commonwealth," says Mr. Inderwick, Q.C., "proceeded to elect a body more powerful than the House of Lords, whose dominion became actually, though not nominally, supreme over Parliament itself, which issued its orders and its edicts, and though professing to attend the decisions of Parliament did in fact transact the entire business of the nation. The Council of State, known at first by the high-sounding title of the Lords States General, in whose records, far more than in those of Parliament, is to be found the full history of the times, was constituted in

February, 1648-49, and consisted of forty-one members, of whom nine were a quorum. They had the dignity of a House of Parliament, a Great Seal of their own; their officer carried a mace similar to that of the House of Commons; they elected their own Speaker or President. . . . The Council of State occupied a stronger and, if possible, a more independent position than the American Senate. Without such a body as this the government of the country could not have been carried on." It "transacted every important matter of business during the twelve years of the Commonwealth. . . . During the whole of the Interregnum," continues Mr. Inderwick, "owing to the want of patriotism and the impracticability of the Commons, power and authority were necessarily vested in Cromwell and his Council of State, although they both openly endeavoured to make Parliament responsible for much of the miscarriage of government business."*

To the cynic it would appear something of a waste of labour on the part of the friends of a single Chamber to put their whole soul into the abolition of the House of Lords, merely that "power and authority" may be "necessarily vested" in a "Cromwell and his Council of State." In the search for simplicity, it is possible to proceed still farther in the abbreviation of Parliament than the abolition of the House of Lords; and the system of one Chamber passes by a natural transition into the system of one man.

Whether we accept the reading of Mr. Inderwick, conceived perhaps somewhat too exclusively from a lawyer's point of view, and regard the Council of State as a body stronger and not less independent than the American Senate, or whether we look upon it as a mere emanation from the autocracy of Cromwell, necessary to his assistance and relief in his stupendous task of personal government, the single-Chamber system is on either assumption equally condemned.

"Although in the French Republic of 1793 Government by one Chamber was proclaimed," significantly remarks the same author, a strong Cromwellian and no partisan of the House of Lords, "yet the period of that Government was notorious for the most fearful access of fury, savagery, and brutality that has ever disgraced the annals of Europe."

Whether we look to Republican countries, such as France, Switzerland, and the United States, or to democratic countries

* "The Interregnum."

such as the Australian Colonies, the rule is everywhere the same, and in many of these countries the Second Chamber exercises powers to which the House of Lords puts forth no claim. Neither in the actual world around us, nor in our own past history, can any warrant whatsoever be discovered for a belief in the beneficence, or even in the possibility, of the single-Chamber system.

The explanation of the demand for a Parliament of one Chamber is to be found in a desire that a majority in the House of Commons should hold absolute power, that legislation should no longer consider the hostile or reluctant minority, no longer represent the compromise dear to English minds, but embody all the prejudices and passions of a triumphant faction. But in that case legislation, instead of being accepted by the defeated party, would be repealed so soon as they could get into power. A system of reaction and counter-reaction, of retaliation and reprisals, would be instituted, ending probably in alternate proscriptions of each faction by its opponents, till some strong-minded soldier put a stop to the whole thing as an intolerable nuisance.

If the House of Lords were to be abolished, and no new Second Chamber erected in its stead, nothing would stand between the nation and the House of Commons but the Crown. It is easy to imagine the position of the Monarch in such case. With the whole work of the House of Lords cast upon his shoulders, he would either neglect it and become a mere dupe in the hands of his Parliamentary advisers, to be discarded as useless, like all dupes, when he had served his turn ; or, making a stand against the tyranny of the majority in the single Chamber, he would find himself involved in a struggle in which the Monarchy, or else the Chamber, would be for ever overthrown. Either the single Chamber would destroy the Monarchy, or the Monarchy would destroy the single Chamber. Thus the abolition of the House of Lords would bring in its train the abolition of the House of Commons or the abolition of the Crown, the abolition of the British Empire or the abolition of our constitutional freedom, or the abolition of both.

When the Crown was either abolished or reduced to a cypher, the last remaining check upon the majority for the time being in the House of Commons would be gone. There would be nothing to prevent the single Chamber from voting itself " in permanence," and resolving to sit on till the crack of doom. One Parliament in our history has earned everlasting infamy by extending the term of its own duration from three years to seven ; but the single Chamber, once elected, could extend the years of its existence unto seventy-times seven. Nor would there be any remedy against such a proceeding save armed rebellion. The single Chamber might, it may be safely said it would, declare itself permanent. It might also by a single vote sweep away that whole system of the supremacy of the law on which all freedom and all property ultimately rest, by declaring that its resolutions should have the force of an Act of Parliament. There would be nothing to gainsay it ; all power would be already in its hands. Thus for that supremacy of the law, which is the boast and basis of our Constitution, we should acquire in exchange the arbitrary and capricious tyranny of some three or four hundred Czars directed by an inner Junto of some half-dozen Sultans.

The general who should free the nation from such a yoke as this, even though merely to substitute his own, would be welcomed indeed as a saviour of society. We should then enter upon a cycle of revolutions and reactions, and might hope in time to rival the success of the French as "the ablest architects of ruin." Such is the alluring prospect which Sir Charles Dilke holds out to us, such the effect of the proposed change which he champions, and which, in the face of America, Europe, and Australia, he persists in calling democratic. Could a more striking proof be given of the insularity of the Liberal party in Great Britain, and the provincialism of the most Imperialist statesman whom the English Radicals are able to produce? In the interest of the Empire and the Monarchy, of liberty and law, of minorities and of the nation as a whole, the reduction of the Imperial Parliament to the single Chamber of the House of Commons cannot sufficiently be deprecated. But above all, and more than all, must it be deprecated in the interest of the House of Commons. No enemy could do it so great a disservice as he, who could succeed in persuading it to endeavour to install itself as the sole ruler of the Empire and the nation. Grasping at omnipotence, it would in the end lose all the power that it now possesses. An interval of anarchy and chaos would be followed by the resurrection of the Tudor Monarchy, or the rise of a Napoleonic or Cromwellian despotism.

Just as the limitations imposed upon the Crown by the existence of a Parliament and Peers have within those limits strengthened its authority, and placed it beyond the hazard of a predominating personality in the Monarch, so the limitations imposed upon the House of Commons by the existence of the Crown and House of Lords are the necessary conditions of its unimpaired vitality, and the essential safeguards of its vigorous life. To abolish the House of Lords would, for the House of Commons, be a step more fatal than the enactment of the Peerage Bill of 1719 would have proved itself to be for the Upper Chamber itself.

Those who, in the parochialism of their insularity, despise alike the example of foreign countries and of the British Colonies, will also, in the temporal provincialism of an ephemeral policy, reject with scorn the witness of our history, though the Long Parliament rose from the grave to bear its testimony. But to minds careless or incredulous of disaster to the Empire, and indifferent or pleased at the prospect of the destruction of the Constitution, and to men who regard politics as a game, and a game in which all rules, all laws of sport, may be safely and honourably disregarded, it may not be amiss nor altogether without use to endeavour to bring home some few of the inconveniences and the misfortunes which the abolition of the House of Lords would inflict upon the Liberal party in Great Britain. If they refuse to accept the picture just drawn as an accurate or faithful delineation of the events that would surely come to pass, if they obstinately hug the strange delusion that revolutionary measures can be carried out free from all the unfailing concomitants of revolution, they should at least weigh, before taking a step that could never be retraced, the minor, and the alternatively certain, consequences of their action.

In the first place, then, as one result of the abolition of the House of Lords, the Liberal party in Great Britain would suffer an immense defection from its ranks. All those men who have hitherto been content to support Liberal measures in the knowledge that the rights and interests of minorities, would be protected by the House of Lords, would find themselves compelled to reconsider their position and transfer their weight to that side which, by acting as a drag on Liberal legislation, secures the permanence of legislative measures once enacted. All those men of family, and established or inherited position, who hitherto have been content to act with the Liberal party in the hope of moderating extreme counsels, guiding Radical enthusiasm into safe, or comparatively safe, channels, securing that desired changes shall be effected gradually and take their least offensive form, and generally maintaining the concord of all classes of society, would now be forced to fight under another standard. Instead of lending their countenance to Liberal measures, and thus gaining for the Liberal party wide support among the nation at large, they would be driven over to the opposite party, and thus leave their former friends to look for leaders among a set of politicians whose names were as little known in the country as they themselves were little loved and little trusted. A herd of turbulent demagogues, adventurers in the worst sense, would replace the Peers, the country gentlemen, the men of business, who have led the Liberal party in its better days. Fortunate it would be indeed, if, here and there, among a crowd of ignorant and reckless agitators, there could be discovered any one entitled to so much respect as a dreamy man of letters who had mistaken his vocation, or a bookish pedant who, from writing history, had in an evil moment turned to make it.

The abolition of the House of Lords would expunge from the Liberal party every conservative element yet left in it; it would destroy every liberal sympathy cherished by Conservatives. The two great parties would be brought into more violent and bitter opposition than at any previous period. Whether it would gain for the Liberal party an increased support among the "masses," whether it would not rather drive large numbers of them over to the Tory side, may be matter of dispute. But this is absolutely certain that of the "classes" the whole body would henceforth range themselves as Tory. From a political party the Liberals would become a social, and a Socialist, party, a party of social discontent; and against the party of social anarchy and social tyranny all who had anything to lose would hasten to stand shoulder to shoulder in the cause of liberty and order. It is no far-fetched or irrational hypothesis to presume that the Liberal party would become a Labour party. Now Labour, when content to act through the agency of Conservatives or Liberals, can exercise great influence, but so soon as it stands aloof, and attempts to form a party of its own dominating the others, it unites all sections in society and politics against it. This is the case in foreign countries, and this is the case in the British Colonies, and this will be the case also in the British Isles. Labour is never so powerless as when most threatening, never so certain of defeat as when most thoroughly organized. Whenever, therefore, the Liberal party in Great Britain becomes a Socialist or Labour party, it will give the signal for its own immediate collapse and final extinction.

Not only would the abolition of the House of Lords, and the adoption of the single-Chamber system, have a deterrent effect on those who in the past have been the best and most valuable supporters of the Liberal party, the solid guarantee of its integrity and character, and its bailsmen to society, but it would also deprive the Liberal party of the adhesion of those members of the "classes" who have been accustomed to support it in the hope of some day receiving their reward by being enrolled in the Peerage. Peers of Scotland since the Union have ceased to be created. The creation of Irish Peers is subject to definite limits: no Irish peerage has been created since 1868; and for a still longer period no Irish peerage has been bestowed on any but an Irishman.

The Peers that remain are the Peers of England, Great Britain, and the United Kingdom. Now, a peerage of this kind is essentially an office, dependent on the existence of the House of Lords.

"In an English peerage," says Professor Freeman, "the primary idea is political power; rank and privilege are a mere adjunct. The Peer does not hold a mere rank which he can share with his descendants; he holds an office, which passes to his next heir when he dies, but which he cannot share with any man while he lives."

The Peer is "not a mere noble, but a legislator, a counsellor, and a judge." The House of Lords is not identical with the Peerage; but the Peerage has no meaning apart from the House of Lords. All hereditary legislators might be excluded from the Upper Chamber, and their place be taken by elected legislators or nominees, and the House of Lords would still remain. But if the House of Lords were to be abolished, it would be absurd and impossible to go on creating Peers. The Peers, as a body, would lose their corporate position; but the political and social influence of individual Peers would be enormously augmented. And while the Liberal party was deprived by its own action of that power of conciliating opinion among the "classes" with which the exercise of the Crown prerogative of creating Peers on the advice of responsible Ministers now invests it, the whole of this vast, social, and political influence would be arrayed against it. Under the Commonwealth, though the House of Lords was abolished, Peers were permitted to retain their rank and titles. But even if these, too, were taken from them by Act of Parliament, it would be impossible to enforce the prohibition in practice. Titles have been "abolished" in France; but the only effect has been to create a manufacture of spurious titles, and the jobbery for the Legion of Honour under the Third Republic. Titles are prohibited by law in the United States; but the effect has been to create an inordinate and insatiable appetite for worthless titular distinctions. It has become a proverb that the Judges and Colonels of America would suffice to meet the needs of all the armies and all the courts of justice in the world. There one becomes a Professor by going up in a balloon; and the members of a widespread organization, in happy ignorance of the phrase "chevalier d'industrie," have sonorously dubbed themselves the Knights of Labour. Nothing is more remarkable than the extravagant importance attached to rank and titles in countries where they do not exist. In the British Colonies, where there are no hereditary legislators, the practical weight of rank and title in the British Isles is apt to be grossly over-estimated; while in a Republican country, like the United States, the travelling Peer is literally worshipped.

Peerages could not be abolished, no matter what the wording of an Act of Parliament; but a monopoly could be established in favour of the existing Peers, by debarring the Crown from their future creation. The Peerage would become a close corporation, closer even than the Whigs sought to make it in 1719. And the vast social influence of this body, placed by the abolition of the House of Lords beyond the reach of legislation, would be uniformly exerted against the Liberal party. Every one with social pretensions, every new man who desired to make good a position in society, would be compelled to enlist himself as an enemy of Liberalism. The ostracism of a society whose influence extends far and wide beyond its highest circles, and would then extend still farther, would be the unfailing penalty of Liberal opinions.

If the House of Lords were to be abolished, the creation of peerages would inevitably come to an end; the existing Peers would become the leaders of the general body of the titled and untitled nobility; and the Liberal party would have aroused the untiring and implacable hostility of a popular and powerful aristocracy, set free from all State regulation and control.

Furthermore, under the Commonwealth, when the House of Lords had been abolished Peers were made eligible to the House of Commons. The Lord Salisbury of the day sat in the single Chamber for Herts. If the House of Lords were again abolished, and the eligibility of Peers to the Lower

Chamber revived, a Lord Salisbury of our own day might be elected a member of the House of Commons. With such a system the comparative importance of the leading Commoners would be greatly lowered and diminished. The presence even of men uniting force of intellect or character with the prestige and glamour of a great position in so eminent a degree as Lord Salisbury and the Duke of Devonshire, the late and the present Lord Derby, could not indeed affect to any great extent the position of statesmen of the first rank, such as Mr. Disraeli and Mr. Gladstone, but ordinary politicians would be at once thrown into the shade. The existence of the House of Lords acts as a duty for the protection of able Commoners. If the arrangement indicated were adopted, many men who now cut a great figure in the Lower House would then become very small fry. None can be more deeply interested in the preservation of the House of Lords than those who sit, or hope to sit, on the Treasury bench in the House of Commons.

If the House of Lords were abolished, it would be impossible to refuse to allow Peers to be elected to the House of Commons. Otherwise they would stand alone among their fellow-subjects in their disability, or with the clergy, if the clerical disability were not at the same time removed. In this case the state of things would be established that existed in the fourteenth century in Florence, where, says Hallam, "the distinction of high birth was that it debarred men from political franchises and civil justice."

"For a certain class of citizens," comments Professor Freeman, "to be condemned by virtue of their birth to political disfranchisement is flatly against every principle of democracy. The Florentine democracy was in truth rather to be called an oligarchy, if we accept the best definition of democracy (Thucydides, vi. 39), namely, that it is the rule of the whole, while oligarchy is the rule of the part only."

Some years ago it was the fashion to argue that, on the Commonwealth terms, the abolition of the House of Lords would actually operate as a Conservative measure by flooding the Lower House with Peers. To suppose, that constituencies that had assented to such a measure would hasten to stultify themselves by converting the House of Commons into a House of Lords, is not less paradoxical than the idyllic pictures drawn—before it came into existence—of a London County Council, under the presidency of the Duke of Westminster, in which the ground landlord should lie down with the Social Anarchist. But although a revolutionary measure is not, and never can be, anything else than a measure of revolution, enough has been said to show that the abolition of the House of Lords, while disastrous to the Empire and the Constitution, would possess at least the solitary, but scarcely compensating, merit of causing grave personal inconvenience to some of those who in their haste most loudly advocate it. It has been made clear, too, that the abolition of the House of Lords is no such simple process of removing from their path an unwelcome obstacle to the realization of their will, as it appears to the majority of Radicals; that, were it feasible, it could not be accomplished without involving consequences which, if in no higher interest, at least in the interest of their party, should give them food for the most serious reflection.

After all, it is perhaps a waste of time and labour to discuss a proposal which can never come " within measurable distance of practical politics." Even if there were an overwhelming Liberal majority in the House of Commons, even if that majority were united in a determination to make an end of the Upper Chamber, there would still remain two parties whose consent is indispensable to the abolition of the House of Lords, the Monarch and the House of Lords itself. Without the consent both of the Monarch and of the House of Lords that body cannot be abolished save by a revolution. It is unlikely in the extreme that any normal Monarch could be induced to yield his consent to such a proposition. No Monarch who wished to play the part of what is called a " Constitutional" Sovereign would consent to such a total and subversive change in the Constitution. No Monarch who did not harbour ulterior designs, unfavourable to popular government and public liberty, could fail to feel the want expressed by Cromwell of "somewhat to stand between me and the House of Commons." Cromwell, as we have seen, had his Council of State, and later, in 1658, attempted, though in vain, to revive or create a House of Lords. If even to a man in the position of Cromwell a Second Chamber presented itself in the light of a necessity, how much more must it appear indispensable to an ordinary and "Constitutional" Sovereign. No Monarch not possessed by an insane desire for absolute and uncontrolled power would consent to the abolition of the House of Lords, and a Monarch, afflicted with such a mania for autocracy, would consent to it only as a needful preliminary to the abolition of the House of Commons.

But supposing, for the sake of argument, that the consent of the Sovereign could be obtained, there would still be wanting the consent of the House of Lords itself. It is unnecessary to suggest that this would not be given as a mere matter of form. The House of Lords cannot be legally abolished without its own consent. The only way, therefore, in which this consent could be obtained, if at all, would be by the creation of some five hundred Peers all pledged to put an end to their own existence, and created for that specific purpose. Nothing else but such a *reductio ad absurdum* would be sufficient. No mere threats of creating Peers could avail to terrify the House of Lords into putting an end to its own existence. To vote for its own abolition is a very different thing from yielding a reluctant assent to a measure for the reform of the other Chamber of the Legislature. It is probable that the House of Lords would fight its guns to the last; if it did not, it would deserve to be abolished. It is probable that it would, literally, die but not surrender. Nothing but the doubling of its numbers by a creation of new Peers could secure the consent of the Upper Chamber. The Monarch who thus strained his powers, and the House of Commons who compelled him thus to strain them, would in doing so announce that thenceforth the rule of the country was at the disposal of any one skilful enough and unscrupulous enough to seize it. No venerable past, no Constitutional sanctity, could from that time onward be alleged on their behalf against the Cæsar who dared to pass the Rubicon. In a contest, where violence has once been admitted, it is the civilian who must infallibly go to the wall; and the throne and sceptre in their fullest and uttermost reality would fall to the first soldier who had the spirit and the enterprise to take them.

Without the consent of the Monarch and the House of Lords, the abolition of that body is in law impossible. Even though the consent of the Monarch should be forthcoming, it would still be of no avail unless he were prepared to go farther, and accord his active personal co-operation to the party that attempted the destruction of the Upper Chamber, and that to the full extent of creating a body of Peers, if men could be discovered to accept such peerages, more numerous than all the members of the House of Lords. No Monarch would dare in this way to imperil his own throne or to give the signal for the downfall of all established institutions.

The abolition of the House of Lords, unless as a detail of a revolution, is a mere *brutum fulmen*, an insolent, but an empty, and an idle menace. The abolition of the House of Lords, save by a triple consent which in two cases at least never would be given, can only be effected by a revolution. And as for that, as for a revolution, there is the army, and there is also the hangman.

CHAPTER II.

A UNITED STATES SENATE.

JUST as the charge that the House of Lords oppresses the people, however ill founded, is in itself better deserving of attention and consideration than the idle and obviously malicious suggestions that the Peerage is not aristocratic, or that the Upper House, being (as it is not) exclusively composed of hereditary legislators, therefore rests on some disproven dogma; so the pleading of those who, while disapproving of the House of Lords as it exists, admit the necessity of a Second Chamber, carries more weight, and is entitled to a more patient and careful hearing, than the mere sneers or invective of the fetish-worshipping iconoclasts, who would abolish the bicameral system in favour of the absolute rule of the majority of the hour in the House of Commons. With those who complain that the House of Lords is an obstructionist body it is possible to reason, but not with the high-flying aristocrats who affect a disappointment that every member of the Peerage is not descended in direct male line from William the Conqueror or Alfred the Great. And in the same way with those who put before the world their own ideal of a Second Chamber it is possible to some extent for the friends of the Constitution to meet on common ground, as it is not with the revolutionary fanatics who threaten the Empire with a single Chamber, though they prudently refrain from setting forth how such a consummation can be brought about.

Owing to that "flexibility" of the Constitution which is at

once its chief danger and among its principal merits, there is no scheme of a Second Chamber, however different from the present House of Lords, that could not be carried out in all its main and essential features without the abolition of the House of Lords, by the reform and transformation of that body. The substitution of elected legislators for hereditary legislators in the House would no doubt be a radical change, but it is favourably distinguished from the single-Chamber scheme in this, that, however radical, it would not be revolutionary.

Accordingly, a variety of plans have been put forward for the conversion of the House of Lords into an Assembly wholly or partially elected—elected, that is to say, not in the manner of the Scottish or Irish Representative Peers, but by the outside public. Thus it has been suggested that the members of the House of Lords should be chosen by popular election from among the whole body of the Peerage; that the House of Lords should be elected by the House of Commons; that it should be elected wholly or in part by the English and Scottish County Councils; that the Agents-General for the Colonies should immediately be brought into the House of Lords in order that it may hereafter become an elected Assembly on the model of the United States Senate.

And if no House of Lords were already in existence, and the task of framing a Second Chamber of the Imperial Parliament had devolved upon the present generation, much might be said in favour of an Upper House of elected legislators. If, putting the Imperial Parliament aside, we were framing a local Legislature for a portion of the British Empire inhabited, not by Africans or Asiatics, but by the British people, still more might with justice be advanced on behalf of the elective principle. While there are no considerable foreign States, being Parliamentary, that dispense with a Second Chamber, there are not a few who base that Second Chamber in whole or part upon election.

All the world is familiar with the conspicuous example of the United States Senate, and the brilliant success claimed for that body in imparting stability to American institutions.

"The Senate," we are told by Professor Bryce in his long glowing panegyric of the "American Commonwealth," "consists of two persons for each State, who must be inhabitants of that State, and at least thirty years of age. They are elected by the Legislature of the State for six years, and are re-eligible. One-third retire every two years, the old members being thus at any given moment twice as numerous as the new. As there are now thirty-eight States, the number of Senators, originally twenty-six, is now seventy-six. As there remain only eight Territories which can be formed into States, the number of Senators will not (unless indeed existing States are divided, or more than one State created out of some of the Territories) rise beyond ninety-two. This is of course much below the present nominal strength of the House of Lords, and below that of the French Senate (300) and the Prussian Herrenhaus (432)."

Since the publication of Professor Bryce's work, some of the possibilities he glanced at have been translated into fact, and there are now, in 1892, eighty-eight Senators representing forty-four States.

In the German Empire, the Upper House of the Federal Legislature consists of fifty-eight members, who, inasmuch as they are appointed, not by the Emperor, but by the different States of the Empire, may in a way be said to be elected. These, however, are not allotted on the American principle of two to each State; Prussia, for example, appointing a much larger number.

In the Herrenhaus of the Kingdom of Prussia there are a few elected members. Otherwise the House chiefly consists of life members, but includes also the Princes of the various branches of the House of Hohenzollern, the chiefs of the mediatized princely families, and fifty heads of the territorial nobility.*

In Switzerland, the Upper Chamber, or Ständerath, consists of forty-four members, two, on the American principle, elected by each Canton.*

In the Netherlands, the Upper Chamber consists of fifty members, elected by the Provincial States (*i.e.* Assemblies) from among the most highly assessed inhabitants of the eleven Provinces, or certain high functionaries.*

In Denmark, the Landsthing consists of twelve members appointed for life by the Crown, and fifty-four indirectly elected by the people.*

* "Statesman's Year-Book," 1890.

In Sweden the Upper Chamber of the Diet consists of one hundred and forty-five members, who are elected for nine years and required to possess a property qualification. They are elected by the twenty-five Landtags, or Provincial Assemblies, and by the corporations of four towns not represented in those Assemblies, viz. Stockholm, Malmö, Göteborg, and Norrköping.*

Roumania has a Senate consisting of one hundred and twenty members elected for eight years, besides eight bishops. A small property qualification is required in electors. A Senator must be forty years of age, and possess an annual income of about £400.*

In Belgium the Senate is elected by the same electors as the Chamber of Deputies. It is elected for eight years, one-half of the Senators retiring every four years, unless there is a dissolution, when all go.*

In France the Senate is elected for nine years, and consists of three hundred members, one-third retiring triennially. The Senators must be forty years old.

"They are elected indirectly by an electoral body composed (1) of delegates chosen by the Municipal Council of each Commune, in proportion to the population, and (2) of the Deputies, Councillors-General, and District Councillors of the Department. There are 225 Departmental Senators. By the law of 1875 there were also 75 Senators elected for life by the united Chambers; but by the Senate Bill of 1884 it was enacted that vacancies arising among the Life Senators would be filled up by the election of ordinary nine-year Senators."

Of the three Departments of Algeria each returns a Senator.*

In Spain, by the Constitution of 1876, the Senate includes a hundred and eighty members elected by the Corporations of State, *i.e.* by the communal and provincial States, the Church, the Universities, etc., and by the largest taxpayers. They are renewed by one-half every five years, and altogether every time the Monarch dissolves this Chamber of the Cortes. On the other hand there are a hundred Crown life nominees and a number of other members, who with the nominees must not exceed one hundred and eighty in all, and who are known as Senators in their own right (*Senadores de derecho propio*).

* "Statesman's Year-Book," 1890.

These Senators in their own right are (1) Princes of the Blood near in the line of succession to the throne ; (2) "grandees in their own right with an annual rent a of 60,000 pesetas (£2400);" (3) Captains-General and Admirals in the navy; (4) the Patriarch of the Indies, and the Spanish Archbishops; (5) the Presidents of the Council of State, the Supreme Tribunal, and the Tribunal of Cuentas del Reino.*

In Portugal, "under a new law of 1885, the hereditary Peers are to be gradually extinguished, the Camara dos Pares consisting for the future of (1) one hundred Life Peers ; and (2) fifty elective" (over thirty-five years of age), of whom five are to be indirectly elected by the University of Coimbra and other learned bodies, and the remainder by the administrative districts of the country.*

Thus in the American, German, and Swiss Federations, in Sweden, France, the Netherlands, and Belgium, the Second Chamber is wholly constituted of elected legislators. In Denmark and Roumania elected legislators form an overwhelming majority in the Upper House, while in Spain they constitute one-half of the Second Chamber, and in Portugal they are to constitute one-third.

They appear, however, in but scant number in the Prussian House of Lords ; and in the Austrian Herrenhaus, the Hungarian House of Magnates, and the Italian Senate they are altogether wanting.

In British Colonies, with the Parliamentary system fully developed, examples of an elected Second Chamber are to be found in South Australia, Victoria, and Tasmania. In South Australia the members of the Legislative Council are elected for nine years, one-third retiring triennially. In Tasmania the eighteen members of the Upper House are elected for six years. But the most noteworthy example of an elected Second Chamber in the British Colonies, and therefore in the British Empire, since no institution of the kind exists in India or, at the present time, in the United Kingdom, is undoubtedly the Legislative Council of Victoria. This body consists of forty-eight members.

* "Statesman's Year-Book," 1890.

" They are now," writes Mr. Jenks, in chapter xxvii. of his valuable work on the Government of Victoria, " distributed among fourteen provinces, of which six return four members each, and the remaining eight each send three. Each member elected upon a vacancy caused by an effluxion of time holds his seat for six years. Members elected to fill extraordinary vacancies hold for the unexpired terms of their predecessors. The Legislative Council can never be dissolved, but its members retire in rotation on the expiry of their tenures. Periodical elections are held in every province in each second year, at which the oldest member retires, and, in addition, in the provinces which send four members, a periodical election is held every sixth year, which does not, apparently, coincide with any of the biennial elections. All members are eligible for re-election. To be qualified for membership of the Council a candidate must be a male of the age of thirty years, either a natural-born subject or naturalized and resident in Victoria for ten years, and must have been beneficially entitled to a freehold estate in Victoria of the clear annual value of £100 for one year previously to his election. A declaration as to his property qualification must be made by the elected candidate before he takes his seat, and if he parts with the property without making other provision for his qualification he forfeits his seat. The following persons are entitled to vote for the election of members of the Legislative Council in that electoral division of the rolls in which their names appear: (1) the owner of a freehold estate rated in a municipal district or districts in one province at the annual rate of £10; (2) the owner of a leasehold estate created originally for five years, similarly rated at the annual value of £25; (3) the occupying tenant or licensee of land similarly rated at the annual value of £25; (4) the graduate of a British University, and the matriculated student of the University of Melbourne; (5) the barrister-at-law, solicitor, or conveyancer; (6) the legally qualified medical practitioner; (7) the duly appointed minister of any Church or religious denomination; (8) the certificated schoolmaster; (9) the officer or retired officer of Her Majesty's land or sea forces. Provided that these persons are (1) males of the age of twenty-one years, and (2) natural-born subjects, or persons who have been naturalized for three years, and resident in Victoria for the twelve months previous to the 1st of January or July in any year. Joint owners, lessees, and occupiers of qualifying land may claim as many rights in respect thereof as the value will cover. All voters except those who claim in respect of property must take out elector's rights in the electoral divisions."

The eminent success, upon the whole, of the Victorian Legislative Council as a strong and stable Second Chamber in a purely local and territorial Legislature is the justification for thus inflicting on the reader the details of its constitution *in extenso*.

In the scheme of an Australian Parliament, drawn up by

the Sydney Federal Convention, the Upper House or Senate
was to consist of eight members for each Colony represented
in the Federation. These eight Senators were to be chosen
by the local Legislature of their Colony, and to retire by
sections at the end of each three years. They were required
to be thirty years of age ; to be natural-born British subjects
or naturalized subjects of not less than five years' standing ; to
have resided for five years within the limits of the Federation ;
and to possess the qualifications required of an elector for
the Lower Chamber or House of Representatives. No person
could sit at the same time in the National or Federal Parliament and in the local Legislature of any Colony forming
part of the Australian Commonwealth or Federation. It is
obvious that this scheme was suggested in its main features
by the United States Senate ; but its adoption was due, not
so much to admiration of the American example, as to the
jealousy felt by the smaller Australian Colonies of New
South Wales and Victoria, and by New South Wales and
Victoria of one another. As there were only six Colonies
actually proposing to take part in the Federation when
formed (New South Wales, Victoria, Tasmania, South Australia, Western Australia, and Queensland), to have adhered
to the number allotted to each of the States in America
would have produced a Senate ridiculously small. Provision
was made in the scheme for the establishment of new
"States" or Provinces within the Federation, and, with
Australian Federation or without it, Queensland will probably be broken up at an early date into three Provinces.
South Australia will some day part company with her
Northern territory, while the vast region of Western Australia must ultimately be cut up into some three or four
political divisions. But this process will never be carried
so far as to produce the number of States existing in the
American Republic, and consequently the rule of two
Senators apiece could never have produced a sufficiency
of members of the Upper House.

Turning back to the elected Second Chambers now actually
in existence in Australian Colonies, and in particular to the

Legislative Council of Victoria, it is easy to see that, admirably as such a body may fulfil the functions of an Upper House in a purely local and territorial Legislature, it would be entirely out of place as the Senate of an Imperial Parliament. Wisely or unwisely, the Australians themselves apparently hold such a conception to be too purely local to supply the fitting basis even for the Upper House of their Dominion Parliament, itself a local and territorial body. Much more, then, must it be unsuited to form the groundwork of the Second Chamber in that Supreme Legislature, the jurisdiction of which, confined to no particular locality, ranges over the whole British Empire and the whole British nation. The Legislature of Victoria, owning at present no superior authority but that of the Imperial Parliament, is indeed somewhat better deserving of attention and consideration than the Provincial Legislature of Manitoba, crushed out of all importance or significance by the overwhelming weight of the Dominion Parliament. It may furnish useful limits for the construction of an Upper House in a purely local and territorial Legislature of Ireland, Scotland, or England. But it is altogether out of place in a discussion of the appropriate elements of a Second Chamber in the supreme governing body of the Empire.

Once more retracing our steps, we come to the formidable array of foreign countries with an elected Second Chamber; and here it might seem at first sight as though their authority, if it be accepted, must condemn the constitution of the House of Lords. And, certainly, one must expect to be accused of special pleading in laying down that, while their example teaches the necessity of a Second Chamber, the fact that their Second Chambers consist of elected, not hereditary, legislators, may be safely disregarded. Partial as such a statement must appear to all but the unbiased, it is nevertheless the simple expression of the truth. That States with conditions so widely divergent from our own concur with us in the necessity of a Second Chamber, is evidence in favour of a Second Chamber. But that in the composition and constitution of that Second Chamber they should depart so far from the Britannic model, is the necessary and inevitable outcome of their widely varying conditions. That a Second Chamber is adopted by all but the entirety of the countries that have a Parliament at all, is proof that in the judgment of Parliamentary mankind a Second Chamber is a necessary feature of any legislative body with the pretensions of a National Parliament. But the fact that many of these countries base their Second Chambers on election is no evidence at a l that, if they were in our place, they would not maintain the existing House of Lords, that with our conditions they would reject our system. And the importance of many of these countries is too inconsiderable to make a minute comparison of their system with our own of any value. In the great principle of a Second Chamber they are agreed with us. In the details of the application of that principle they disagree with us, partly from necessity, partly from a choice to which it would be easy to attach extravagant importance.

Now, to begin with, it may be as well to remember that we are not in the position of Japan, searching the world for the materials of a Constitution. To regard the Parliamentary institutions of foreign countries as beneath our notice, to regard their study as a condescension, would be not less illiberal than foolish; but it is no mere display of Chauvinistic bigotry and arrogance to recall the fact that these institutions, in nearly every case, were borrowed from our own. In social civilization we have, no doubt, learned much from foreign countries, especially Italy and France, and may have yet more to learn. But in political freedom it is we who have taught them. They have adapted our Constitution to their circumstances, and their circumstances are wholly different from our own. In considering the example of foreign countries, it is necessary to discriminate. No one but the most rabid English Radical would urge the example of Russia in favour of Autocracy; and it would be cruelly severe to cite the South American Republics as telling against Parliamentary institutions. Putting the United States for a moment on one side, we shall see that it is only the Great Powers of Europe who are really in any degree comparable with ourselves. It is they alone who have anything remotely answering to our conditions. The example of Roumania or Denmark might be of service to an independent Ireland, but it has no bearing on the present case. The Netherlands and Belgium, Portugal and Switzerland, and even Sweden, exist only under the protection of the public law of Europe, and by the grace of the Great Powers. But for the suspicion and fears entertained by each of the Powers with regard to all the rest, these little countries would soon be snapped up and absorbed into their powerful neighbours. If the incurable and not unwarranted distrust of each of the great military Powers of the European Continent by all the others could be so far suspended as to permit of their arriving for a time at an agreement, the smaller States would go as Poland went before, for it is more than doubtful whether we should any longer interfere singlehanded to protect them. One constant effort of the diplomacy of Europe at the present time is to prevent Russia from swallowing the Balkan States in the face both of the British Empire and the Triple Alliance. These small States exist only on sufferance; and although both in international law and political science the smallest State possessed of independence, even though that independence should be merely technical, is the equal, theoretically, of the greatest, every one should be able to perceive that it is almost as absurd to suggest the details of the practice of the Netherlands and Belgium, of Denmark and Sweden, of Roumania and Portugal, for the imitation of the British Empire in the application of an accepted principle, as it is to quote the examples of Manitoba and Ontario, of British Columbia and Prince Edward Island, as a reason why that principle should be rejected. And the example of Switzerland is still more irrelevant, since that country, like the United States, and like the German Empire, is a Federal State in which the sovereign authority is vested in the Constitution, and power legally divided between the component States and their whole, whereas with us the King in Parliament is the absolute Sovereign of the Empire.

Dismissing, then, the small Powers of Europe, as useless for the purpose of comparison with ourselves in any but the broadest features of their politics, we are left with the Great Powers, and with Spain, which, if too inconsiderable to be reckoned a Great Power, is too considerable to be classed with the small Powers. Of the Great Powers one—Russia—except in the Grand Duchy of Finland, is altogether destitute of Parliamentary institutions.

Eliminating Russia, we have left France, Germany, Austria-Hungary, Italy, and Spain. Of these France is a Republic; Germany is a Federation; and the Dual Monarchy, as Austria-Hungary is not uncommonly styled, is really two countries bound together in a manner so peculiar as to form a State—if State it can be called—bearing no resemblance to our own. Italy and Spain are the only two considerable Powers that, being at once Monarchical and non-Federal, can be compared with exactness with the United Kingdom.

In Spain, as we saw, one-half of the Second Chamber is made up of elected legislators, but the other half is nearly equally divided between what may be called Life Peers and a heterogeneous assemblage of Royal Princes; Lords Spiritual; eminent judges, soldiers, and sailors, who might also be described as Life Peers; and grandees possessed of a certain property qualification.

In Italy, the Senate is composed of the Princes of the House of Savoy who have attained their majority, and an unlimited number of Crown life nominees. The latter must be forty years of age, and fulfil the condition (1) of holding high office; or (2) of having acquired fame in science, literature, or "any other pursuit tending to the benefit of the nation;" or (3) of paying taxes to the annual amount of 3000 lire (£120). In 1886 there were three hundred and fifteen Senators.* The examples of Italy and Spain, therefore, if taken together, tell rather in favour of Life Peers than of a Second Chamber based upon election. But neither Italy nor Spain has anything approaching to our Empire. Italy has no Colonies at all; and Cuba is the only

* "Statesman's Year-Book," 1890.

real Spanish Colony; while the Philippines are scarcely a sufficient set-off against India. If Canada, South Africa, Australia, with Tasmania and New Zealand, and the Indian Empire, were taken out of the British dominions, then what was left, excluding, of course, the British Isles, would be a rough equivalent of the Spanish "Colonies" or transmarine Empire. It is evident that Spain can afford to localize the Upper Chamber of her Parliament in a way which is impossible, or, if possible, would be unwise in the extreme, for us.

Italy has no Imperial interests to consider, and her example, therefore, could only with justice be cited in the case of a Legislature which, if National, was at the same time purely local. But we need not go out of the British Empire to find a Parliament which, if not National in the same full and unqualified sense of the expression as is the Italian Legislature, represents a nation within the Pan Britannic nation, and is also purely local. The Senate of the Canadian Dominion is, like the Italian Senate, a body of life nominees, though it does not, like the latter assembly, include Princes of a royal family. And the Canadian Senate is commonly reputed to be neither powerful nor popular. But whether or not the Italian example is worthy of imitation by those already provided with a Second Chamber less dependent on the Crown, it supplies no argument in favour of elected as opposed to hereditary legislators.

One-half of the Spanish Upper Chamber roughly resembles the House of Lords in composition, though not in constitution. The other half is best, though inadequately, imagined as the Chairmen of the County Councils of Great Britain, plus the lay Ecclesiastical Commissioners, the members for the Universities, and perhaps the Presidents of the Royal Academy and Royal Society. If one-half of it tells for a Second Chamber of elected legislators, the other half of it tells for the present House of Lords. Our " Patriarch of the Indies" is the Archbishop of Canterbury. Our " President of the Supreme Tribunal" is the Lord Chancellor. And there are few of our "grandees in their own right"—Peers, that is, of England, Great Britain, and the United Kingdom without "an annual renta of sixty thousand pesetas." One-half of the Spanish Upper House tells in favour of the House of Lords, speaking roughly. And the other half, with its strong representation of local interests, does not tell against it. For Spain, having nothing, with the exception of Cuba, in the least degree resembling the greater British Colonies, can without hazard grant a direct dual representation to her Home interests. But with us, whatever direct representation in the House of Lords was given to the British Isles, would be indirectly taken from the British Empire. The House of Commons is already more than sufficiently parochial. If the House of Lords were either abolished or localized, the Imperial Parliament would, as regards representation, sink into a purely local Legislature. If it is imperative that the English County Councils should elect somebody to something, it should be to the Upper House of a purely local and territorial Parliament of England. It is to this that the Spanish practice points, not to the localization of the Upper Chamber of a Legislature which embodies the Imperial Union of three historic nations, and has the custody of the Imperial interests of nations yet three more, their common offspring in their common Colonies. If the Parliament of Westminster is to pass into the Parliament of the British people throughout the world, if it is to continue for all time the Parliament of the British Empire, then we must proceed in the direction not of further localizing it, but of its Imperialization. The example of Spain partly corroborates the Conservative belief in the excellence, though not in the divinity, of the House of Lords, and partly illustrates a system which might work well enough in the Upper House of a Dominion Parliament for the local affairs of the Kingdom of England, but would be altogether out of place in the House of Lords of the Imperial Parliament of the United Kingdom of Great Britain and Ireland.

From Italy and Spain we get but small encouragement to transform the House of Lords into a Second Chamber based upon election. Nor can the example of Italy be fairly said to tell against those hereditary legislators of whom so large a portion of the House of Lords consists. It involves no disparagement of a great, and, on the whole, a friendly people to say that in politics it is rather for Italy to take lessons from us than we from her. The greatness of Italy, since the time at least of the Emperor Constantine and the adoption of Christianity as the State religion of the Roman Empire, has lain in other spheres than that of politics. The marvellous efflorescence of Italian genius in the period of the Renaissance had for its chief fields literature and art. The debt of humanity to the wonderful people who discovered the New World and recovered the Old, who placed us in living relations with the Athens of Pericles and the Rome of Cæsar, it would be difficult, if not impossible, to over-estimate. Nor is it easy to forget the brilliant reigns of many Popes and Princes, the long and gorgeous tale of Venice, and above all the lofty triumph of Italian genius in the Papacy. But the incontestable political genius shown by many Italian City-States and rulers was uniformly exercised for selfish and unpatriotic ends, for the aggrandisement of classes or of individuals, but never for the union of the nation. The Papacy itself, that superb memorial of Italian pride, intellect, and ambition, has been denounced by patriotic Italians from the days of Dante and of Machiavelli to those of Carducci and Cavour as the principal agent in Italy's political disunion. With the political intellect the Italians were abundantly, and superabundantly, supplied, but they were wanting in the political character. If intellect alone had been sufficient, they might have stood at the head of all the nations of the earth; but they were deficient in those grave and solid moral qualities which, far more than mere intelligence, are requisite to political greatness and success. They lacked the capacity for self-sacrifice, for self-subordination, the concentrated public spirit, the absorbing devotion to the political community, which had given Rome her victory over the far more acute and brilliant Greeks, and the presence of which, however inarticulate and unexpressed, in the humblest and rudest British soldier gives him his ineffaceable superiority over the most polished, learned, and subtle of Hindoos. The obstacles to the union of nations are not physical obstacles, not even intellectual obstacles, but moral obstacles. The Italians had none of that political faith which can move mountains into the sea, and it was their unhappy lot to remain divided down to the last half of the nineteenth century.

Italy as a political whole is a creation of our own time, and among modern nations of the Western World Italy and Germany were last, and by far the latest, to be reunited or united. Italy, therefore, as a nation, as an organic whole, has not our political experience, has not our political conditions. Our Parliament, the House of Lords no less than the House of Commons, springs out of our national history, has its roots deep in our past national life. The House of Lords is no conscious or deliberate creation, but an outcome and a growth. It had its origin in the system of land-tenure under the Norman kings. It is at once a cause and an effect of the non-existence in England of a titled and privileged *noblesse*. It would have been impossible for Italy, had she desired it, to reproduce our House of Lords without reproducing our whole history. "The Peerage as it exists in the three British Kingdoms," wrote Professor Freeman, "has nothing in the least degree like it elsewhere." Everywhere else the people "entitled to bear coat armour" grew into a caste. Sir Henry Maine has given the explanation of the fact that the House of Lords has not been "more extensively copied in the constitutions of the Continent" in "the extreme numerousness of the nobility in most Continental societies and the consequent difficulty of selecting a portion of them to be exclusively privileged." An Italian Duke or a French Marquis as often as not resembles the British Duke or Marquis in nothing but the name. In Russia a Prince may be a cabman. It would be impossible for any foreign country to have a Second Chamber exactly like the House of Lords, for they have none of them anything exactly like the Peerage. In Italy the multitude of Dukes and Princes would probably have rendered any attempt to set up such a body altogether vain. But in the Austrian Empire and the Prussian Kingdom there is a Herrenhaus; in Hungary there is a House of Magnates. Louis XVIII. established a Chamber of Peers in France, though it was first altered and then swept away. That the Italian Senate, apart from the Princes of Savoy, consist of nominated legislators, rather than hereditary, may be in some measure the result of choice; but it is also, and far more, a matter of necessity.

France at the present time is a Republic, and the German Empire is a Federation. In Austria-Hungary the existence of the Delegations, and their control of the affairs common to the Empire and the Kingdom, make the Dual Monarchy a State, if it can be called one, impossible to compare in strictness with our own. It is, as though, speaking very roughly, our three kingdoms, each retaining its own Sovereign Parliament, were united only, apart from the possession of a common Monarch, in a War Union, an entirely voluntary Customs Union, and a common Foreign Office. Whatever may be thought of this extraordinary, but, no doubt, necessary form of government, the Upper Houses of both Austrian and Hungarian Parliament are clearly suggested in idea by the House of Lords. The Herrenhaus of the Austrian Reichsrath consists (1) of those Archdukes who are of age (twenty in 1889); (2) of "a number of nobles in whose family the dignity is hereditary by nomination of the Emperor" (sixty-six in 1889); (3) of life members (one hundred and nine in 1889); and (4) of ten Archbishops and seven Prince Bishops (making a total of two hundred and twelve in 1889).* The House of Magnates is a much larger body. It consisted in 1889 (1) of the twenty Hapsburg Princes who had attained their majority; (2) of "all hereditary Peers" paying 3000 florins a year in land tax (about £300), who were then two hundred and eighty-six in number; (3) of eighty-two Life Peers appointed by the Crown; (4) of forty Prelates of the Greek and Latin Churches; (5) of eleven clerical and lay representatives of the Protestant confessions; (6) of seven *ex-officio* members (State dignitaries and judges); and (7)

* "Statesman's Year-Book," 1890.

of three delegates of Croatia-Slavonia : making in all four hundred and fifty-nine, of whom nearly two-thirds were "hereditary Peers."* In both of these bodies, as in the Prussian House of Lords, may be traced a strong desire to reproduce as far as possible the British Upper Chamber. In Austria and Hungary we can see both Lords Temporal and Lords Spiritual, the singling out of the Prince Bishops for representation along with the Archbishops recalling the manner in which the Bishops of London, Durham, and Winchester are bracketed with the two Archbishops to the disparagement of their other suffragans.

France is a Republic, and in a Republic of the modern-time type there is no place for hereditary legislators ; although in the sense in which the Bishop of London is a hereditary member of the House of Lords, the Senators for New York are hereditary members of the American Senate, the hereditary right of representation attaching in the one case to the diocese, and in the other to the State. But for "hereditary legislators" in the sense of Peers there is no place in a modern Republic, although at Venice, as was seen before, there were no legislators who were not hereditary. And France is not only a Republic, but a democratic Republic, and considerably more democratic than Republican. In such a State there is obviously no room for hereditary legislators. Even under a powerful Monarch there would probably be great difficulty in introducing a Peerage into France, on account of the hatred still felt for the old *noblesse*, from whom such a body would almost necessarily be in part recruited. Under a President— and the career of the Napoleons has induced the French to confine Presidential powers to very narrow limits—a Peerage would be clearly impossible. A Second Chamber of nominees would be equally out of the question, since neither a President nor a Premier could be safely entrusted with their nomination. There remains, therefore, only the course which the French have actually adopted. Of the Senate three-fourths are elected by local electorates, and the balance by the two Chambers acting as one Assembly. It is this latter feature

* "Statesman's Year-Book." 1890.

that has probably given rise to the grotesque suggestion that the House of Lords should be elected by the House of Commons. The suggestion is of course ridiculous, because the whole *raison d'être* of a Second Chamber is as a check upon the First, and a House of Lords elected by a House of Commons every three years, sometimes more often, would be no check at all or an exceedingly imperfect one. But as a matter of fact the French Senate is not elected by the Chamber of Deputies. Three-fourths of the Senate is wholly independent of the Lower Chamber; the rest is elected, not by the Deputies alone, but by the two Houses acting together.

Any Second Chamber, other than one of elected legislators, would be impossible for the French Republic, and, given an elected Second Chamber, the French could hardly have chosen the electors other than they have done. They could not have turned their Upper House into an American Senate without breaking up France into American States, a course which no citizen of that country is sufficiently unpatriotic to desire. They have, therefore, from necessity localized their Upper Chamber, but they have not localized it to the same extent as the House of Lords would be localized, if three-fourths of it were returned by the County Councils of Great Britain, or of Great Britain and Ireland. For the three Departments of Algeria each return a Senator. Now, Algeria is the only French possession in the faintest degree resembling Australia or Canada. In the strictest exactitude it rather resembles a British possession at the other end of the Dark Continent, the Cape Colony, having a very large African population, and a large number of European colonists who are not of French origin. But still, such as it is, Algeria is the only real French Colony, and in the representation of localities in the French Senate Algeria is included. The example, therefore, of the French Senate is one that cannot be quoted in favour of a proposal to destroy the Imperial character of the House of Lords with an inundation of the elect of English, Scottish, and, one may suppose, Irish County Councils. France has only one Colony, as distinguished from a mere possession or dependency, and that Colony is treated in this respect as part of France. But no one proposes that the Shire Councils, let us say, in the Colony of Victoria should return members to the House of Lords. No one proposes that they should return members to the Australian Senate, nor even to the Victorian Legislative Council. Yet the true British counterpart of the French system would be that all the County Councils of the British Empire should return members to the House of Lords. The example of the French Senate is good for this or it is good for nothing.

In truth, it is equally futile and absurd to argue from the example of foreign countries in the constitution of their Senates. There is not one of them with our conditions. There is not one of them with anything approaching either the Colonies or India in magnitude, in diversity, and in importance. There is not one of them with a Parliament which is at once a local and territorial Legislature for three nations bound together in an union Federal in spirit, though unitarian in form, and at the same time the legal Sovereign of some hundred millions of Asiatics and three great territories held by European settlers having local Legislatures of their own. To quote the localization of the French or Spanish Senates, not to recur to minor examples, as against the House of Lords, is as preposterous as it would be to deride the French Republic for going without Peers, or to scold Italy for not inviting the College of Cardinals to form a part of her Second Chamber. They know their own business best, and we know ours best. They have shown their good sense in not attempting a slavish and mechanical copy of our Parliament, and we can pay them no higher compliment than by admiring and emulating the justice and nicety of their discrimination. They have shown their true feeling for the historic principle in not attempting the exact reproduction of the House of Lords, as we can show ours by preserving the House of Lords in all its main and essential features. A Second Chamber is a desirable and indispensable check upon the First, but the minute details of the composition of that Chamber must be determined by the political and social circumstances of each nation. No supporter of the House of

Lords contends that the Canadian Senate or the Australian Upper Chamber should be made up of Lords Spiritual and Lords Temporal. For the social circumstances of Canada and Australia at the present time differ as widely from those of the British Isles as the powers and functions of a purely local and territorial Legislature differ from those of the Imperial Parliament. At one time and in one place hereditary legislators may be best, and at another time and for another place nominated or elected legislators may be advisable. And it is one thing to preserve an Assembly the outcome of the peculiar history and institutions of a country, and another to expect that such an Assembly should be literally reproduced in countries of quite other history and of institutions essentially diverse. Where we can with profit follow foreign countries is, not in the mechanical details, but, at times, in the spirit, of their arrangements. Thus we can with advantage take a hint from Spain, and make the rank of a Field Marshal or an Admiral of the Fleet a qualification for a life peerage, in the same way as a Lordship of Appeal. We can note the care of France for her Colonies, and emulate the enlightened ecclesiastical policy of the Apostolic Kingdom, respecting and recognizing the venerable ministers of every creed that urges man to the Ideal, of every altar raised to the Unseen.

The German Empire is a Federation, like Switzerland and the United States, and differs therefore essentially from a State like the United Kingdom, which, however Federal in spirit, and with whatever solemnly enacted guarantees for the right of each of the three ancient nations that compose it, is nevertheless unitarian in form. Germany is a nation composed of Sovereign States. We are a Sovereign State composed of nations. The German Bundesrath represents twenty-six States—the Kingdoms of Prussia, Bavaria, Saxony, and Wurtemberg; the Grand Duchies of Oldenburg, Hesse, Baden, Saxe-Weimar, Mecklenburg-Schwerin, and Mecklenburg-Strelitz; the Duchies of Brunswick, Anhalt, Saxe-Altenburg, Saxe-Meiningen, and Saxe-Coburg-Gotha; the Principalities of Waldeck, Lippe, Schaumburg-Lippe, Schwarz-

R

burg-Rudolstadt, Schwarzburg-Sondershausen, Reuss-Schleiz, and Reuss-Greiz; the Hanse towns of Hamburg, Bremen, and Lubeck; and the Reichsland of Alsace-Lorraine. It is the Second Chamber to the Reichstag (of 397 members) which represents Germany as a nation; just as in America the Senate represents the States, and the House of Representatives the people. And if in the British portions of the British Empire there existed a King of Ireland and a Grand Duke of Lancashire, a Duke of Ontario and a Prince of New South Wales, all Sovereign potentates, the example of the German Bundesrath might be of great service and instruction to us. If there were still with us a King of Leinster, a Welsh Prince of Wales, and a Norse Jarl of Orkney, as semi-independent feudal rulers, and if the system of mediæval anarchy which Shaftesbury and Locke attempted to plant in Carolina, had firmly taken root in the New World, like the rabbit in Australia, we might do much worse than follow the German precedent in attempting to combat and subdue this monstrous and gigantic evil. But by the blessing of Providence the only Sovereign of the British people is the Queen. Whatever may be the exact legal status of the Indian Princes their case is not apposite to the matter under consideration, since India does not even possess self-government, and will never be called upon to take part in the government of the British Empire till the end of the Empire is at hand. The only Sovereign of the British people is the Queen, and consequently the arrangement by which the four Kings, seven Princes, etc., etc., of Germany have been brought to act together is for all British purposes entirely useless. The means adopted to combat Asiatic cholera are of no instruction for countries which are neither attacked nor threatened by that pestilence. The Federalism of Germany is the half-way house from feudalism to full national union. If it was impossible for Germany to traverse, like Italy, the road from complete disunion to complete union in the space of a single generation, that circumstance cannot render her example of any greater profit to those more fortunate lands, in which feudalism has long been extinct and the fullest union years ago established.

But it is only due to the advocates of an elected Second Chamber to gratefully acknowledge that it is not the example of the German Bundesrath that they commonly bring forward. The inspiration of all these schemes for such an Upper House, whether elected by the House of Commons or the County Councils, by local constituencies in the British Isles or, in a manner, by the Colonies, is ultimately derived from the United States Senate. The quaint conceit of a House of Lords elected by the House of Commons is no doubt based, as we have seen, on a misunderstanding of the French Senate. But that misunderstanding would never have arisen in minds that were not influenced by a hazy and indistinct recollection that Senators in the American Republic owed their seats to the choice of inferior legislative bodies. The example of America, however, gives still less support or countenance to such a proposal than the example of France. The Senators for each State are elected by the Legislature of their State, not by the House of Representatives, and this as an essential part of the United States Constitution. Nothing could have been further from the thoughts of the men who drew up that Constitution than to make their Second Chamber a mere creature and echo of their First. What says Professor Bryce?—

"The Senate has succeeded by effecting that chief object of the Fathers of the Constitution, the creation of a centre of gravity in the government, an authority able to correct and check, on the one hand 'the democratic recklessness' of the House [of Representatives], on the other 'the monarchical ambition' of the President. Placed between the two, it is necessarily the rival and generally the opponent of both. The House can accomplish nothing without its concurrence. The President can be checkmated by its resistance. These are, so to speak, negative or prohibitive successes. It has achieved less in the way of positive work, whether of initiating good legislation or of improving the measures which the House sends it. But the whole scheme of the American Constitution tends to put stability above activity, to sacrifice the productive energies of the bodies it creates to their power of resisting changes in the general fabric of the government." *

The Second Chamber in the United States is not based upon election in order to bring it into closer harmony with the

* "American Commonwealth," part i., ch. ii.

House of Representatives, but on the contrary to make it as independent of that House as possible. That the House of Lords should be elected by the House of Commons, is a puerile proposal which its authors can never have taken the trouble to think out, or to think twice about, and which is entirely undeserving of any serious attention.

As for the proposal that the members of the House of Lords should be chosen by popular election from among the Peers in existence, it is not indeed marked by the infantile fatuity of the suggested change last considered; but if the popular electorates in question are to be restricted to the British Isles, then it is open to the same objections as the election of the House of Lords by the County Councils of Ireland and Great Britain. And if the popular electorates are to be extended through the whole British nation, then it must be said that the Colonies would consider such a scheme, if at all, only as a detail in a much larger and more extensive scheme of Imperial Federation. They would not consent to be formally and directly represented in the House of Lords unless they were at the same time formally and directly represented in the House of Commons; and in either case they would require as an essential preliminary that the local affairs of the British Isles should be delegated to local Assemblies. It is possible, no doubt, but not probable, that Canada would seek admission to the Imperial Union of England, Scotland, and Ireland by herself; but until the Australian Colonies are formed into a nation—until, that is to say, Australia exists—it is not only premature, but absolutely impossible, to propose Imperial Federation for the acceptance of Australia. Australian Federation is not the antithesis of Imperial Federation, but its necessary antecedent.

As a step towards Imperial Federation a gentleman in the Colonial Office has lately revived a proposal, which he can scarcely claim as original, that the Agents-General for the Colonies and, it may be supposed, the Canadian High Commissioner, should be accommodated with seats in the House of Lords. Looking upon the House of Lords in its present form as antiquated and useless, he urges that these functionaries should be introduced into it, in what precise capacity it is not clear, on the chance that it will somehow and some day be evolved through the magic of their presence into a Federal Council or a Bundesrath or a United States Senate, something or other of a Pan-Britannic or Imperial character, while the House of Commons, flying off through space, descends to earth as a purely local and territorial Legislature. It is to be feared that this ingenious proposal has little chance of being attended with success. In the first place it is not at all certain that it would meet with the approval of the Colonies. In the opinion of Sir Charles Tupper, the present High Commissioner for Canada, the proper place for a Canadian High Commissioner is not in the House of Lords, but in, or in close attachment to, the Cabinet. He evidently regards himself as a rudimentary Secretary of State for Canada. This, of course, does not exclude the idea of a seat in the House of Lords. On the contrary, it almost necessarily involves a seat in one or other House of Parliament; for, with the best of wills in all concerned, the effective representation of the Colonies in the Imperial Executive will in the long run be found to be impossible without their representation in the Imperial Legislature. But a seat in the House of Lords, or in either House, is not, in the view of Sir Charles Tupper, an important, or even necessary, part of his proposal. He does not propose it. His patriotic ambition for the young nation which he represents soars beyond the House of Lords to the Imperial Cabinet.

Canada, therefore, has other views for her London representative. With regard to the Cape the writer cannot speak. But it can be affirmed with confidence of the Australian Colonies that the proposal would meet with favour from no one except, possibly, the Agents-General themselves. Is it proposed to make the Agents-General Peers during their continuance in office? Because, if so, such a proposal might meet with reasonable opposition from the Sovereign and the House of Lords. It would certainly tend to diminish public respect for the Upper House, both in the United Kingdom and the Colonies. Much has been written by Mr. Froude of the unworthy appointments to Governorships made in former times, and some of the Colonies have shown themselves not a little disposed to be hypercritical in judging later selections of the Home Government. They are not equally fastidious in the choice of their Agents-General, nor can it be said that in some recent appointments they have exhibited a morbid sensitiveness to social opinion in the Old Country, or an exaggerated regard for their own public reputation. An Agent-General is appointed by the Ministry of the Colony which he represents; the Home Government has no control over his appointment; and to make such an official an *ex-officio* member of the House of Lords would be to invest a Colonial Ministry with the uncontrolled exercise of an essential branch of the Queen's prerogative. Even an Imperial Ministry cannot make the most estimable of men a Peer without the personal concurrence of the Monarch. Much more, then, is it out of the question that a Colonial Cabinet should exercise such power at its sole discretion.

If, on the other hand, the office of an Agent-General should be a qualification for, but not a title, to such an official peerage, and the choice among the Agents-General rested, as it would rest, with the Colonial Office, then, whatever might be the Colony or Colonies whose Agent or Agents-General were favoured, his or their selection would cause jealousy and heartburnings in all the others. Moreover, before the favoured Agent-General had had time to take his seat, some change might take place in the Administration of his Colony as an effect of which he would be recalled. The plan proposed would bring the House of Lords and the Peerage into contempt, and would fail to gratify the Colonies. It is founded on an entire misapprehension of the position of an Agent-General. It is the fashion nowadays to speak of an Agent-General as an Ambassador. He is nothing of the kind. An Ambassador represents one Sovereign to another Sovereign. An Agent-General represents a purely local and territorial, subordinate and dependent, Legislature to the Colonial Office. An Agent-General, as the general agent for the Colony, fills a highly important and responsible position. But to speak of him in the vein of King Cambyses, to call him an Ambassador, is impolitic; for it provokes unkind people to remember that, except that he is an agent in borrowing, instead of lending, money, he is much more like a money-lender's tout. An Agent-General is not an Ambassador; but, if he were, he would be accredited to the Sovereign, not the House of Lords.

Probably, with Australian Federation, the number of Agents-General will be reduced, and Federated Australia, like Federated Canada, will content herself with a single representative. In that case the Colonies with responsible government would be represented by a couple of High Commissioners for Canada and Australia, the Agent-General for the Cape, and an Agent-General apiece for Newfoundland and New Zealand. Even if all of these were brought into the House of Lords, the Upper Chamber would not be much more like a Bundesrath or an American Senate than it is at present; unless, indeed, they had the whole House to themselves. To have filled the office of Agent-General for a term of years with credit and success should be a sufficient qualification for a life peerage, without at all constituting a title to receive one. But to make the Agents-General *ex-officio* members of the House of Lords could be attended by no good result whatever.

The notion that the House of Commons would consent to be degraded into a purely local and subordinate Legislature for Great Britain or the British Isles, relinquishing to a transformed House of Lords the Sovereign powers of the Imperial Parliament, is not less far-fetched and unpractical than the notion that the House of Commons as a single Chamber could successfully maintain for the Legislature of Westminster the position of the supreme governing body of the Empire. To propose a severance of the two Houses and a degeneration of the Lower House into a local Assembly, shows as great a contempt for the historic continuity of the Constitution as the proposal for the abolition of the House of Lords. The House of Commons as a single Chamber would infallibly break the existing bonds of union between the British Isles and British Colonies; and the House of Lords as a single Chamber, even though it contained nobody but Agents-General, would not unite them one hairbreadth more closely. It was no single Chamber, popular or Federal, that united England with Scotland, and Ireland with Great Britain. It is no single Chamber, popular or Federal, that unites the people of the Canadian Dominion. The single Chamber of a Federal Council altogether failed to unite the people of the Australian Colonies. And it is no single Chamber, popular or Federal, that will unite Canada and Australia with the British Isles. The union of Parliamentary peoples must be a Parliamentary Union. What is required is, neither the abolition of the House of Commons nor the abolition of the House of Lords, but that each should be reformed on the existing lines of the Constitution by the systematic and logical development of principles already imbedded in its structure.

The apparent success of the United States Senate, and its undoubted stability as a Second Chamber, have made a powerful impression on the British mind; and, in the customary British fashion, natural in a land where all principles of criticism, æsthetic or political, are neglected or unknown, a number of people are rushing headlong to persuade the nation to adopt it, without pausing to inquire whether the success of the American Senate may not be the failure of the American Constitution, and whether stability may not be purchased at too dear a price. The idea seems to have gained ground in certain quarters, that at all costs we must manage to get a United States Senate. Thus, on the one hand, we have the County Councils put forward as supplying the unit in the British Isles which in America exists in the State Legislature. And, on the other hand, we have correspondents of the *Pall Mall Gazette* writing to thank the Editor of that Journal for "teaching them" that "what is wanted" is the conversion of the House of Lords into an assembly elected by all the local Legislatures of the Empire.

Gratitude, it would seem, is not so difficult to come by as cynics have supposed. Of this political Revivalism which offers us "Salvation full and free, here and now," if we believe in a United States Senate, it must be said that, like ecclesiastical Revivalism, it is emotional and nothing more. If keeping our nerves well under control, instead of yielding to hysteria, we look the facts fully and fairly in the face, we shall see that it would be impossible for us to get a United States Senate without destroying the Constitution, and endangering the nation and the Empire, and that this impossibility need not distress us, since we are very much better off without one.

It is impossible, we repeat, for us to manufacture a United States Senate without destroying the British Constitution. The American Second Chamber is no isolated feature of the American system. An American Senate is the natural and necessary complement or outcome of an American President, an American Lower House, and American States. "The American plan" (*i.e.* of a Second Chamber), says Dr. Bryce, "is grounded on and consonant with the political conditions of America." But the political conditions of America are not the political conditions of the United Kingdom and the British Empire; and it is impossible for us to reproduce the political conditions of America without sacrificing the existence of the Empire, and hazarding the union of the United Kingdom. We have for our chief of the State an hereditary King, not an elected President. The Ministers of that King sit in Parliament, and are responsible to Parliament. The Ministers of the President are responsible neither to the House of Representatives, nor to the Senate. The Senate is founded on the doctrine of "State rights." It had its origin in the independence of the States which came together to form the American Commonwealth. It has its justification in the fact that each of those States, and the other States now in the Union, is a Sovereign State, except in so far as its powers have been expressly limited by the Constitution.

"Every State in the Union," says Professor Dicey, "can claim to exercise any power belonging to an independent nation which has not been directly or indirectly taken away from the States by the Constitution."

"The Senator," says Professor Bryce, "was—to some extent, is still—a sort of Ambassador from his State." The name of the United States is no senseless and unmeaning jingle. They are, literally, States, once altogether independent, which have been United. America, like Germany, is a nation composed of Sovereign States. We are one Sovereign State composed of nations. The American Senate is the direct product of the American States. Therefore, in endeavouring to reproduce it, we are confronted with the initial difficulty that we have no States.

In India, it is true, there are the dominions under the direct rule of Indian Princes that are known as native States. But none of these are States in the American sense. They are all under the immediate supervision and control of the Indian Government, and the ultimate supervision and control of the Government at Westminster. Not even the correspondents of the *Pall Mall Gazette*, scarcely even the electors of Finsbury, would propose that our United States Senate should exist for the representation of the native States.

Wherever we may look throughout the British dominions, it is impossible to discover any counterpart of the American States. The King in Parliament, as Professor Dicey is never tired of affirming, is the absolute Sovereign of the British Empire. The United States Government and Congress are the creation of the Sovereign and independent States which came together to form the American Federal Republic. But with us, except the Tynwald of the Isle of Man and the Assembly known as the States in Jersey and in Guernsey, every local Legislature in the British Empire is the creation of the Imperial Parliament in modern times. The Colonial Legislatures, in which the gushing Radicals of the *Pall Mall Gazette* find the equivalent of the American State Legislatures, are altogether different from the latter in origin and history, in character and functions. In America the central Government is the creation of the local Legislatures, but with us the local Legislatures are the creation of the central Government. Since the Union with Ireland on January 1, 1801, there has been only one Sovereign authority in the British Empire. The old Irish Parliament had successfully asserted its independence in 1782, and in the following year an Act of the Imperial Parliament had recognized Irish independence. Thenceforth till 1801 the King, Lords, and Commons of Ireland were in Ireland what the King, Lords, and Commons of Great Britain were in Great Britain, absolute and Sovereign. But there is no Legislature now in existence, which stands in the same relation to the Parliament of Great Britain and Ireland, as the Parliament of Ireland between 1782 and 1801 stood in to the Parliament of Great Britain. The formerly individual and isolated Sovereignties of England, Scotland, and Ireland have all been merged and blended in the common and collective Sovereignty of the United Kingdom. But the Legislatures of Canada, Provincial and Dominion, are not and never have been Sovereign; the Legislature of the Cape Colony, the Parliaments of Newfoundland, and New Zealand, and the Australian Colonies, all alike derive their existence from the will, and hold their powers by the gift, of the Imperial Government. Their Constitutions are in each case founded on an Act of the Imperial Parliament, and by an Act of Parliament they are liable in each case to be suspended or repealed. The Imperial Parliament can at any moment step in and supersede the local Parliament, and any Act of a Colonial Legislature running counter to Imperial legislation is *ipso facto* null and void. It is easy to comprehend that the Australian Legislatures, each with its jurisdiction limited to its own Colony, are no Sovereign Legislatures. But this is equally true of the Dominion Parliament of Canada. The legislation of the Dominion Parliament, like the legislation of the Provincial Parliaments, derives its whole and sole validity from the British North America Act, 1867. Canada and the Australian Colonies and the Cape of Good Hope are no Sovereign and independent States, but merely political subdivisions of the British Empire endowed by the Imperial Parliament with certain limited powers of territorial legislation and local self-government.

And, if the equivalent of the American States does not exist in those British Colonies which possess responsible government, still less is it to be found in the County Councils of Great Britain. A County is a mere administrative district of the United Kingdom, and the Council is charged with its administration. A County Council bears no more resemblance to an American State Legislature than the Melbourne Board of Works bears to the Czar of Russia. It is not the fact that the Senators are elected by geographical divisions of America that has given the American Senate its strength, but the fact that these geographical divisions are, subject to the Constitution, Sovereign States. It is impossible to have an American Senate without American States. Therefore, if the British Isles are to be taken as the unit, to arrive at a United States Senate the County Councils must first be converted into American State Legislatures. Or, if the British nation is taken as the unit, then Acts of Renunciation must be passed endowing the Canadian Parliament, the Cape Parliament, and each of the Australasian Parliaments with all the rights and powers of Sovereign and independent Legislatures; in other words, the British nation must be shattered into fragments on the chance of their voluntary reunion. To turn the United Kingdom into a United States with the State represented by the County, is a project only fit for the discussion of the debating society of Hanwell Asylum. Deliberately to substitute for the King, Lords, and Commons of the United Kingdom, as the Sovereign of the British Empire, the King, Senate, and Commons of Canada, the King, Legislative Council, and Commons of New South Wales, and so forth, is to dissolve the Empire on the pretext of its consolidation. A King, Lords, and Commons of Scotland, and a King, Lords, and Commons of England, had been found incompatible with union before 1707. A King, Lords, and Commons of Ireland, and a King, Lords, and Commons of Great Britain, had been found incompatible with union before 1801. A King, Senate, and Commons of

Canada, and a King, Lords, and Commons of Great Britain and Ireland, would be equally incompatible with union now. So long as the Colonial Legislatures remain in subordination to, and dependence upon, the Imperial Parliament, the present union, slight and attenuated though it be, may still endure. But when once those Legislatures have been placed on a footing of equality with the Imperial Parliament, then, as in the case of Ireland, there would arise the immediate necessity for Parliamentary Union or total separation.

An American Senate is impossible without American States, and in the British Empire American States do not exist. But to endeavour to create American States out of the self-governing Colonies would not, as the writers of the *Pall Mall Gazette* appear to imagine, further the union of those Colonies with the United Kingdom. When Canada and Australia concur in a project of Britannic Union they will enter such a union as nations, not as States. If the Canadian Provinces were still disunited; if, instead of the Dominion as a unit, we had to deal with New Brunswick, Nova Scotia, and the rest one by one; if, in like manner, the Australian Provinces were to remain for ever disunited, and we had Queensland, Tasmania, and so forth, for our units; then the provinces to be united would present a superficial and delusive resemblance to the American States. But, if there is one thing certain about Canada, it is that, whatever course she may adopt in the future, whether she seeks a closer union with the United Kingdom, or admission into the United States, or independence, she will go or stay as a united whole. If there is one thing certain about the Australian Colonies, in the belief of all Australians, it is that a united Australia is an indispensable preliminary to further political development, whether in the direction of coalition with the British Isles or independence. Just as the union of Mercia and Northumbria, East Anglia and Wessex in the one realm of England; the union of Alban and Strathclyde, Lothian and Galloway in the one realm of Scotland, were necessary steps in advance to the eventual Union, however long subsequent, of England and Scotland with each other; so the union of the Maritime Provinces, Ontario, and Quebec in the one realm of Canada, the union of Victoria and New South Wales, Queensland and South Australia in the one realm of Australia, constitute the necessary preface to the union of Canada and Australia with Ireland and Great Britain and with one another. Whenever Canada and Australia concur in a scheme of Pan-Britannic Union, they will enter neither a United Empire nor a United States, but a United Kingdom; but a United Kingdom in which each nation, whether in the Colonies or Isles, retains or receives a Dominion Legislature for the settlement of its local affairs. In an Imperial Union, constituted on such a basis, Canada and Australia will be entities too powerful and great to require, or to desire, for the defence of their local liberties the elaborate protection sought for the Swiss Canton or American State. The establishment of local Legislatures in the British Isles will at once restore to Englishmen, to Scotsmen, and to Irishmen the security for local rights sought in vain to be provided by the Acts of Union, and reassure Canadians and Australians as to the safety of their local institutions by giving to Insular Britons a common interest with themselves in resisting possible aggressions of the central Government. Thus we shall obtain all the advantages of Federalism without forfeiting the Sovereign character of the Imperial Parliament.

An American Senate is no necessary or desirable element in any scheme of Pan-Britannic Union; and it is impossible without American States which do not exist, and the creation of which would almost certainly dissolve the Empire. It is also impossible without a fundamental change in the character of Parliament. The Senate, as Dr. Bryce tells us, was devised as a check on the President and the House of Representatives, and a most effectual check it has proved. "Placed between the two, it is necessarily the rival, and generally the opponent of both." Do we want a Second Chamber of the Imperial Parliament which will be "necessarily the rival" of the House of Commons, and "generally the opponent" of the King? Do the Radicals of the *Pall Mall Gazette* desire such an Assembly, at the thought of which every Tory true to Tory traditions must shudder. If they do desire it, they may be Radicals, but, of a surety, they are no democrats. Can any one but the most old-fashioned and reactionary Whig enjoy the prospect of a Second Chamber such that the House of Commons "can accomplish nothing without its concurrence," and the Crown "can be checkmated by its resistance"?

An American Senate is impossible without an American President, American Ministers, and an American House of Representatives. We must adopt the whole of the United States Constitution or else none of it at all.

"The United States," writes Dr. Bryce, "is the only great country of the world in which the two Houses are really equal and co-ordinate. Such a system could hardly work, and therefore could not last, if the Executive were the creature of either or both." Accordingly, as a necessary consequence of the independence of the Senate, "the Ministers do not sit in Congress. They are not responsible to it, but to the President, their master. An adverse vote of Congress does not affect his or their position. . . . An American Cabinet resembles not so much the Cabinet of England or France as the group of Ministers who surrounded the Czar and the Sultan."*

An American Senate means, therefore, American Ministers, and an American House of Representatives. It means the abolition of responsible government. Now, responsible government is not the same thing as party government, though a dishonest attempt is sometimes made to confound them. Party government exists nowhere in greater force and virulence than in the United States, where, as we have just seen, responsible government is unknown. Party government in the old English sense does not exist in the German Empire, and there responsible government is fully established —the responsibility of the Minister to the people, Parliament, and Sovereign. Party government in the old English sense was only possible when the House of Commons, and politics generally, had running through them one broad line of demarcation. Now the old party system is crumbling away. Instead of two parties only we have more than half a dozen,

* "American Commonwealth," chs. xviii., vii.

and may expect as many more. Party government, originally invented by the Whigs for their own purposes, will shortly disappear, and we shall see a powerful Minister, strong in the personal confidence of the people and the Monarch, successfully hoodwinking and browbeating all the venomous and discreditable factions in the House of Commons, knocking their heads together, and employing each in turn to spoil the game of all the others. Party government will disappear, but responsible government will become more vigorous than ever, the responsibility of the Minister, not to those parties which formerly usurped the place and power of the nation, but to the nation itself. As the extension of the franchise has broken up the old party system, and the establishment of more frequent Parliamentary elections will cause its disappearance altogether, so the break-up and disappearance of the party system will bring both the Crown and its Ministers into far more intimate and confidential relations with the people. But with an American Senate the process would be exactly reversed. Party government would be brought back in its utmost virulence of renewed and intensified vitality, while responsible government would be abolished. An American Senate means American Ministers.

American Ministers mean an American House of Representatives, a House of Commons deprived of nine-tenths of its power and importance, a House of Commons to which the Ministers of the Crown are not responsible, a House of Commons with virtually no control over the Imperial policy of the nation. This is the true meaning of American Ministers and an American Senate. They mean the nullification of the representation of the people in "the People's Chamber" by a second elective Assembly expressly based on a principle of inequality. How is the Senate of the United States composed?

"Every State," replies Professor Bryce, "be it as great as New York or as small as Delaware, sends two Senators, no more and no less. New York is thrice as large as Scotland. and as populous as Scotland, Northumberland, and Durham taken together. Delaware is a little smaller than Norfolk, with about the population of Bedfordshire. It is therefore as if Bedfordshire had in one House of a British Legislature as much weight as all Scotland together with Northumberland and Durham a state of things not very conformable to democratic theory. Nevada has now a population about equal to that of Caithness (40,000), but is as powerful in the Senate as New York. This State, which consists of burnt-out mining-camps, is really a sort of rotten borough for, and controlled by, the great 'silver men.'"

An American Senate is impossible without American States, and States of the American type are happily unknown in the British dominions. But supposing that it were possible for us to create such a body without destroying the Constitution and the Empire, we should have for our Second Chamber an Assembly in which the vote of Jersey or the Isle of Man carried exactly equal weight with that of Canada or Scotland. What possible protection could such a body really hold out to Colonial interests? Australia would never dream of offering to New Zealand an equality of power and representation with herself in the Upper House of an Australasian Parliament. And it is absurd to ask either for Scotland or for Ireland, or, till their wealth and population have enormously increased, for Australia or Canada, an equality of voice and vote with England in determining the common policy of the whole Empire. In the Parliament of the whole British nation the British nation must be represented as a whole. Its ports, the minor and internal nations of England, Canada, Australia, and the rest, will for all local purposes have their Dominion Parliaments. But as regards that Imperial Parliament, the true principle of equality is not that Canada or Australia should be the equal of England, much less the equal of the British Isles, but that a Canadian or Australian should be the equal of any other Briton.

The principle underlying the United States Senate, if we leave out of view the fact of the original equality of the States as States, is the equality of things essentially unequal, and the practical result of their representative system, as Dr. Bryce expresses it, "is as if Bedfordshire had in one House of a British Legislature as much weight as all Scotland together with Northumberland and Durham."

S

This body, exercising such enormous power, is a representation of the few to the disadvantage of the whole. The United States Senate does in fact represent an oligarchy, not of Sovereign Princes, but of Sovereign States. And, representing an oligarchy, it exercises its power at the expense of the constitutional forces which, in our own case, are known as the power of the Crown and the power of the people. A United States Senate, were that possible in the British Empire, would not check the House of Commons in the sense in which the House of Lords checks it. It would not check the House of Commons merely, but practically supersede it. Both the powers actually vested in the House of Commons, and those powers of the Crown that are exercised on the advice of Ministers possessing the confidence of the House of Commons, would be either appropriated to itself or altogether abridged by this anti-popular, anti-national, oligarchical Assembly. This is the remedy which the Radicals of the *Pall Mall Gazette* put forward in the name of democracy for the terrible and inhuman oppression practised by the House of Lords. They complain that the House of Lords oppresses the people, and, to put an end to this, they urge the creation of a Second Chamber which would reduce to a nullity the representation of the people in "the People's Chamber."

An American Senate means American States, American Ministers, an American House of Representatives. It also means an American President, a Monarch who, while he keeps American Ministers irresponsible to an emasculated House of Commons, is deprived *en revanche* of the most striking and essential attributes of a Britannic King. In the British Empire the power of making peace and war, the power of making treaties, the appointment of Judges, Ambassadors, and Ministers, are all vested in the King.

"But," says Professor Bryce, of the United States Senate, " its executive functions are : (*a*) to approve or disapprove the President's nomination of Federal officers including Judges, Ministers of State, and Ambassadors ; (*b*) to approve by a majority of two-thirds of those present of treaties made by the President, *i.e.* if less than two-thirds assent the treaty falls to the ground. . . . The Senate," he continues, " through its right of confirming or rejecting arrangements with foreign Powers secures a general control over foreign policy. . . . The Senate may and occasionally does amend a treaty and return it amended to the President. There is nothing to prevent it from proposing a draft treaty to him, or asking him to prepare one, but this is not the practice. For ratification a vote of two-thirds of the Senators present is required. This gives great power to a vexatious minority, and increases the danger, evidenced by several incidents in the history of the Union, that the Senate or a faction in it may deal with foreign policy in a narrow, sectional, electioneering spirit.' As for the other executive function of the Senate, though "the appointments to Cabinet offices are confirmed as a matter of course," and " those of diplomatic officers are seldom rejected, their right of confirming nominations submitted to them by the President has been used by the Senators to secure for themselves a huge mass of Federal patronage : by means of this right a majority hostile to the President can thwart and annoy him."

Thus in the most essential attributes of Monarchy, the British King would be dethroned. Nor is it even certain that the Ministers spoken of just now as irresponsible, however independent they might be of the House of Representatives or Commons, would be the Monarch's own. In this particular our hereditary ruler would be at a disadvantage compared with the elected ruler of the United States. Unlike the President, he could not point to a popular election as a public decision in favour of his policy. Probably his Ministers, while irresponsible to the House of Commons, would be imposed upon him by the Second Chamber. He would lose all the distinguishing prerogatives and powers of a British Monarch without acquiring those of a President of the United States. The power of the Crown and the power of the people would together sink to a lower depth than they reached under the first two Georges. The House of Commons would in effect be superseded ; the King would in effect be dethroned. For oligarchy is inconsistent with Monarchy, and with democracy ; while aristocracy is the support and the defence of both.

Such would be, so to speak, the internal effect of an American Senate upon the British Empire. The external effect would not be less serious.

"No European State, no British Colony," comments Professor Bryce, "entrusts to an elective assembly that direct participation in executive business which the Senate enjoys." No British Colony, it should be unnecessary to observe, has the power of making treaties, or the power of making peace and war. No British Colony keeps naval or military forces, except for local defence. No British Colony employs a Diplomatic Corps. A British Colony is not a case in point, but it is very true that no European State adopts the course of the American Republic, and no European State could afford to do so, nor could America herself afford to do so had she for her neighbour in Canada a Power of less long-sufferance and loving-kindness than the meek and forbearing British Empire. No European State adopts the course, or could afford to do so, and least of all could a State like our own, which is not only European, but also American, Asiatic, African, and Australasian. The intimate and indissoluble connection between the Empire and the Monarchy could not in this case, or in any other, be with impunity disregarded and despised.

"The problems," writes Dr. Bryce, "which the Foreign Office of the United States has to deal with are far fewer and usually far simpler than those of the Old World. The circumstances of England" (i.e. Great Britain and Ireland) "with her powerful European neighbours, her Indian Empire, and her Colonies scattered over the world, are widely different."

The observation is a just one. America, though with an African question in her midst in the sphere of domestic politics, has, like the European Powers, whose case was previously considered, nothing in the least resembling the Colonies and India. She does not, indeed, as Dr. Bryce declares, "stand unassailable in her own hemisphere;" but she is unassailed, and that for the sufficient reason that the only neighbour who could successfully assail her is, in despite of constant provocation, bent on peace.

But can any educated adult, in the possession of his mental faculties, cheat himself for a single moment with the belief that the Foreign Office of the British Empire could cut such capers as the Foreign Office of the United States without some dire and instantaneous catastrophe? Could a Power with such tremendous interests as our own allow the national dignity to be perpetually sacrificed, the national safety to be daily imperilled, by a body capable of performing such ridiculous antics as the United States Senate? That the American Republic has escaped the natural consequences of her policy of meanness and arrogance, temerity and bluster, with no worse penalty than the world's contempt, is due to the fact that, while we are her only formidable neighbour, "she is unassailable in her own hemisphere" by any Power but ourselves. But can any one imagine that we, with ships and commerce to be attacked on every sea, with Russia, Germany, and France for neighbours in Africa or Asia, with but a tiny strait between the European Continent and the heart and centre of our Oceanic realms, could with a like safety set at nought the law of nations, the principles that regulate the intercourse of civilized States, the national amenities and public courtesies of the civilized world? Could we afford an affair of New Orleans or an embassy of Chili? Could we undertake with a light heart to dictate to the Great Powers of Europe in the conduct of their domestic affairs and internal policy?

The safety of the United States is the safety of buccaneers in their den. But the baron with lands to be ravaged could not follow the course of the bandit whose refuge lay in the impenetrable forest, or the brigand whose sure defence was in the unknown path to his far mountain lair.

The mischief already wrought by reckless questions in the House of Commons sufficiently jeopardizes the success of our Imperial policy, and, in that, the safety and the existence of the Empire. If the power of the Crown in these matters were limited by a United States Senate, if every treaty underwent public discussion by such a body, if every ministerial and diplomatic appointment required its sanction, a foreign policy of any kind would become impossible. Already placed at tremendous odds, as compared with countries for which it is possible to pursue a scientific foreign policy, acting at an enormous disadvantage, since in no country but the British Empire, and in no portion of that Empire but the governing portion of the British Isles, is patriotism regarded

as a reproach, if not a crime, we should then be unable any
longer to continue the unequal struggle. As an American
Senate means the effacement of the House of Commons, and
the obliteration of our constitutional freedom, so also it
means the effacement of the Monarchy, and the obliteration
of our worldwide Empire. Instead of uniting, it would destroy the Empire; and it would free the House of Commons
from a moderate, reasonable, conditional, and temporary
check, only to crush it beneath the overwhelming weight of
a colossal and all-powerful oligarchy.

This is the reality of the Beatific Vision which the correspondents of the *Pall Mall Gazette* thank its Editor for
"teaching" them "to work for." This is the Earthly Paradise
in which they wish to land us. To get rid of the House of
Lords they are ready to obliterate the Crown and efface
the House of Commons, these Pharisees who strain at the
House of Lords and would greedily gulp down an American
Senate!

Fortunately, to convert the House of Lords into a United
States Senate would be a feat as impossible to accomplish as
to sweep away the Second Chamber altogether. The abolition
of the House of Lords, were it demanded by the unanimous
voice of the House of Commons, would still require the consent of the Lords and the Crown. But the conversion of the
House of Lords into a United States Senate would meet
the united opposition of Commons, Peers, and Monarch.
Neither the Commons nor the King would consent to be
thus quietly put upon one side. There is no room in the
same Parliament for two such bodies as the British House of
Commons and the American Senate. The place which is
taken by the House of Commons in our Constitution is filled,
and more than filled in the American, necessarily not in
every detail of an exact comparison, but still substantially,
by the Senate. The part of King Lear is one which is never
played by a legislative body save under stress of actual compulsion. For the creation of a Council of State there is
necessary in the first place a Cromwell. The man of pleasure
who in a cynical old age asked as to the House of Commons,

"Does that still go on now?" would scarcely have taken the trouble to inquire whether it had ceded its powers to an American Senate.

The probability that a Monarch would assent to a measure for the establishment of such a body may be measured by the change that it would effect in his position. The King has yet to be discovered who would willingly be reduced to a position less powerful and less dignified than that of a modern President of the French Republic. Not only would the Monarch lose the essential attributes of Sovereignty in regard to making treaties, peace, and war. He would also be deprived of his power of creating Peers. For the conversion of the House of Lords into a United States Senate, though it would not necessitate the abolition of the House of Lords, would, like the abolition of the House of Lords, require the abolition of the present Peerage as a political body. A Second Chamber from which the existing Peers were not as such excluded would not be a United States Senate. A body half composed of "hereditary legislators," and half of legislators representing States, would bear no likeness to the Upper House of the American Congress. Although by enacting that for the future the House should consist exclusively of Lords Temporal, and that those Lords Temporal should receive a writ of summons as a consequence of their election in a given fashion, and hold their seats and Peerages only during their continuance in office, the formal abolition of the House of Lords could be avoided, the character of the House would be none the less vitally affected. The present Peers would lose their membership, actual or potential, of the Upper Chamber, and no more Peers, of any other kind than that before described, would be created. To the latter change the Crown would offer a vigorous resistance, threatened as it would be with the loss of a great source of power and influence; while to their own abolition the Peers would extend an opposition not less pertinacious, unrelenting, and determined, than to the formal abolition of the House of Lords.

The abolition of the House of Lords is conceivable only as

a measure of revolution, but the conversion of the House of Lords into a United States Senate is not conceivable at all. Before Cromwell called into existence a Council of State, the House of Lords had been abolished. For the abolition of the House of Lords there is required a revolution. But for the establishment of a United States Senate as the Second Chamber there is requisite, first the abolition of the House of Lords, and then a revolt from the system of a single-Chamber; first a revolution, then a reaction; first a Long Parliament, and then a Cromwell. It is difficult to believe that a Cromwell of our own time would show himself the magnanimous and disinterested statesman of Mr. Inderwick's history—or imagination.

So much, then, for the project of an elected Second Chamber. Elected by the people of the British Isles it would destroy the Imperial character of the Imperial Parliament. Elected by a British nation, split up into American States, it would substitute for the British the American Constitution, a polity incompatible with the existence of the British Empire.

The example of foreign countries, to the discriminating full of instruction, is to the crude and hasty a delusion and a snare. If France had retained Canada and Louisiana and peopled them with French colonists, Canada and Louisiana would with France be represented in both Chamber of Deputies and Senate of a Common Legislature. Could Spain win back Mexico and South America, she would not be so blind and mad as to expect the allegiance of Chili and Peru, Bolivia and Argentina, to be given to a Parliament of which the Lower Chamber was in whole, the Upper Chamber was in part, localized in the Kingdom of Spain. That the Constitution of the United States is no model for our imitation, Professor Bryce himself may teach his friends, if, before raving of the American Senate, they will condescend to find out what it is. If America possessed our Colonies and India, she would be forced to give them up, or to give up her Constitution.

Far afield as the enemies of the House of Lords may travel, search high, search low, they will find no Second

Chamber based upon election that, without destroying the Empire or the Constitution, could replace the present Upper House.

But although the House of Lords is as little likely to be transformed into a French or an American Senate as it is to be abolished altogether, there is another change entirely feasible, entirely constitutional, neither revolutionary nor even radical, which would give to the Liberal party in Great Britain complete relief in all domestic affairs from its grievances, real or imaginary, against the House of Lords. It is strange that, while they ransack the universe for examples to support their case, while they allege instances so entirely inapplicable as a Provincial Legislature of Canada and the Second Chamber of a Federal Republic, they should overlook the simple, obvious, and efficacious remedy of Insular Home Rule. Let local Legislatures be established in each of England, Scotland, and Ireland, and the House of Lords becomes at once divested of its immediate control of local policy and legislation. If, as the Radicals have constantly maintained from 1886 to 1892, Ireland is fit for a Home Rule Parliament notwithstanding Irish flightiness and disaffection, with how much greater safety could England and Scotland each receive a National Legislature, and the Imperial Parliament, thus delocalized, be set apart for Imperial affairs. The House of Lords could not remain the Upper Chamber of the Imperial Parliament, and at the same time form a part of any of these local Legislatures. No one proposes to restore the Irish House of Lords in any Irish Parliament. In these purely local and territorial Legislatures, exercising no Imperial functions, the Second Chamber might well be based upon election. It might with advantage be framed on some such plan as the Legislative Council of Victoria. To such a body, and to its Lower Chamber, Peers equally with Commoners might be elected.

It would be impossible, were it desirable, to restore the old English, Scottish, and Irish Peerages as they stood before the Unions, impossible to determine the exact proportion of the English, Scottish, and Irish elements in the Union Peerages of Great Britain and Great Britain and Ireland. There are many Irish peerages held by Englishmen and Scotsmen. There are some Scottish peerages held by Irishmen and Englishmen. There are Union Peers taking their titles from places in England, and also from places in Scotland. The Earl of Rosslyn is Lord Loughborough; the Earl Dudley is Lord Ednam. The Duke of Leeds is Viscount Osborne of Dunblane. The Earl of Mansfield is Viscount Stormont. The Duke of Athole is Lord Strange; the Duke of Buccleuch is Earl of Doncaster. The Duke of Abercorn and the Earl of Verulam are Peers of Scotland, Ireland, and Great Britain. The Scottish Barony of Herries has passed into the Yorkshire family of Constable; the Scottish Earldom of Orkney into the Irish family of Fitzmaurice; the Earldom of Mar and the Earldom of Dysart into the families of Goodeve and Tollemache. The Irish Lord Macdonald is the chief of a clan in the Scottish Highlands. The Irish Lord Hotham and Lord Downe belong to Yorkshire. If the Earl of Cawdor, who is Viscount Emlyn, were entitled to a seat in an English or a Scottish House of Lords, he would be entitled to a seat in both. The Peerage as an institution of each nation has become lost and merged in the Peerage as an institution of all three.

It would be impossible that the Peers should constitute a House of Lords in each local Legislature. Even were it possible to distinguish among them for that purpose, no Liberal would consent to this proposal, no Conservative of any powers of foresight and calculation would be sufficiently foolish to propose it, and the Peers themselves would probably refuse their assent to a change which would necessarily entail their departure from the Upper House of the Imperial Parliament.

Home Rule all round, for England and for Scotland as for Ireland, would altogether remove the Radical grievance, real or supposed, against the House of Lords, as regards the domestic affairs of the British Isles. As to Imperial affairs and the Foreign, Indian, and Colonial policy of the Liberal party in Great Britain, on that the House of Lords would still express the censure of Foreign Powers, the Colonies, and India. But in all matters of internal policy and local legislation the Liberal party would thenceforth be free from the control and supervision of the House of Lords.

It is difficult, even with the best of wills, for any man to liberate his mind wholly from the unconscious influence of inherited sympathies, and the prejudices and partialities of his education. Yet strive as one may to regard Liberal legislation in a perfectly impartial and dispassionate spirit, it nevertheless seems impossible in justice and reason to condemn the House of Lords for demurring to agrarian measures which in the Courts of the United States would have been held invalid, and which, by the confession of their authors, failed in each case to attain their end. Still it cannot be doubted that the House of Lords in dealing with agrarian legislation occupies a very false position. In origin a House of landlords, it is to a large extent a House of landlords still, and this fact will always bias the popular mind against it when a controversy over such matters arises between it and the Liberal party in Great Britain. If the man who is his own lawyer has a fool for his client, it seems a pity, and a mistake, that the House of Lords as a House of landlords should conduct its own case. It provides the Radical party with at least the semblance of a grievance, and as a matter of strategy it would be wiser to rely for the defence of landed property on a skilfully devised Second Chamber in each local Legislature. Where the great mass of the inhabitants of a country reside in towns and cities, representations of the fabulous wealth of the landed proprietors obtain an easy acceptance. To the ignorant artisan or envious tradesman it is useless to propound the truths of universal experience, to remind them that without capital labour is hopelessly inadequate to the successful cultivation of the soil, and that where there is no landlord there is a money-lender or a bank. To depict the state of things existing in the new countries of the United States and the

British Colonies to men thoroughly demoralized by the Irish example, would be labour wasted. As the Upper House of the Imperial Parliament the House of Lords may be strong enough; but as the Second Chamber of a local Legislature for the British Isles it is lamentably and perilously weak. And this weakness is due to the fact that in dealing with agrarian legislation the House of Lords appears to the multitude to be judging its own case. In origin the House of Lords was a House of landlords, and this, which was once its strength, is now its weakness.

The Liberal party in Great Britain, and the House of Lords, are in disagreement both on Imperial and local questions. With regard to the disagreement on the former, having in mind the unquestionable fact that the House of Lords is here supported by the democracy of the Colonies and the bureaucracy of India, it must be said without a moment's hesitation that the Liberal party in Great Britain is absolutely and altogether in the wrong. That it is also in the wrong with regard to domestic questions is clear to all Conservatives; but it is not certain that it would appear equally manifest to a perfectly impartial and unbiased observer, could such a one be found. We believe that the Liberal party has long ago fulfilled its mission; that it has done its appointed work in the liberalization and democratization of our institutions, and is now degenerating into a faction. But this, after all, is a belief, a matter of faith, not of knowledge. That the Imperial policy of the Liberal party is wrong we know as a literal and demonstrated fact, as incontestable as any ascertained truth of physical science. We should condemn that policy with even greater vigour were we Liberals. But we cannot, putting party aside, with an equally unfaltering confidence pronounce them wrong in domestic policy. It is possible that a perfectly wise and perfectly just man, were such a being accessible, would, on this point, deliver judgment in their favour.

If we consider, then, for the sake of argument, that the Liberals may have a grievance as regards domestic policy, here is the remedy. There is no need for them to abolish the House of Lords, still less to scheme for its conversion into a United States Senate. All they need do is to extend to Scotland, and to England, the same treatment that they propose for Ireland. If Home Rule is at once good for Ireland, and compatible with the maintenance of the Union, then Home Rule must be good also for England and Scotland. No one who accepts democracy as an inevitable fact, whether he welcomes it or not, can deny that the will of the English people will be far more clearly ascertained in regard to purely English questions when these questions are dealt with by themselves than when they are mixed up with Irish questions, Scottish questions, questions of foreign affairs, the Colonies, and India. The same, *mutatis mutandis*, is true of Scotland and Ireland.

If the grievance of the Liberal party against the House of Lords lies in the action of that body on domestic questions, then they have no right to demand the abolition of a Chamber admittedly sound on Imperial policy when all they have to do to get away from it is to obtain local Legislatures for local affairs. If, allied with this grievance, there exists a desire for the further Imperialization of the House of Lords, then, too, they should favour the relief of both Chambers of the Imperial Parliament of the burden and task of local legislation, since the delegation by those Chambers of their local functions to local Assemblies is an inseparable condition of the representation of the Colonies in the supreme governing body of the Empire. And if they covet a Second Chamber, based on popular election, an excellent and admirable system for the Upper House of a purely local Legislature, they might not impossibly conciliate Conservative opinion by including in the Local Parliament of each of the three ancient kingdoms a Chamber suggested in idea by the Victorian Legislative Council.

But, until the Liberal party in Great Britain declares itself distinctly and unequivocally in favour of Home Rule for each Kingdom in Great Britain, not less than for Ireland, the Radicals must not expect to be taken seriously in their attacks upon the House of Lords. It is too much to ask that the Upper Chamber of the Imperial Parliament should be demolished or altered beyond all recognition, on the ground that the House of Lords, in its domestic capacity, is a hindrance to Liberal local legislation, when the Liberal party has, and knows, its remedy, and obstinately refuses to apply it. The case against the House of Lords—if case there be—is a case, not for its abolition, nor for its conversion into a United States Senate, but for English, Scottish, and Irish Home Rule.

PART IV.
CONSERVATIVE REFORMS.

CHAPTER I.

THE NEED FOR REFORM.

THE foregoing chapters of this book have been devoted to a consideration of the House of Lords, of the charges advanced against it by the Liberal party in Great Britain, and of the remedies to which the members of that party would have resort as a consequence of its supposed evils. The history and constitution of the House of Lords were briefly reviewed, and it was seen that, while the Peers are in origin a Baronage, the House of Lords is very far from being exclusively composed of " hereditary legislators." The Radical case against the House of Lords was then examined, and the charges alleged against the Peers of a lack of aristocracy were found to be based on a misconception, both as to the nature of the Peerage, and the nature of nobility, and to be wholly disproved by the clear evidence of undisputed and indisputable facts. The charge that the House of Lords oppresses the people was next investigated, and on investigation resolved itself, so far as relates to the present day, into a mere expression of partisan intolerance and impatience. It was not denied that the House of Lords oppressed the people under the first two Georges, but it was shown that, since the reforms effected in its composition by King George the Third, this has never been the case; that the Tory Peers, in their opposition to the first Reform Bill and the removal of Nonconformist disabilities, were animated by high and worthy motives, and largely justified by well-founded anticipations of ensuing evils which have since come to pass; that

T

their opposition to the removal of Roman Catholic disabilities was not without extenuation or excuse; and that, far from oppressing the people at the present day, the House of Lords is a main security that the will of the people shall be clearly ascertained in order that it may afterwards prevail. The remedies proposed by the Radicals for the grievances from which they believed themselves to suffer were scrutinized in detail. It was seen that the two schemes alone calling for attention—the scheme for the abolition of the House of Lords, and the scheme for its conversion into a United States Senate—were alike crude, ill-considered, and impracticable; that the latter of these schemes postulates the previous adoption of the former; and that the adoption of the former postulates a revolution. Finally it was pointed out that, even admitting, for the sake of the argument, that the Liberal party in Great Britain may have a grievance against the House of Lords as regards domestic legislation, their true remedy for a state of things so deeply deplorable lies, not in wrecking the Constitution and the Empire, by laying rash hands on the Upper Chamber of the Imperial Parliament, but in the establishment of local Legislatures for English, Scottish, and Irish affairs, thus enabling the governing body of the Empire to become representative of the whole British nation, in the British Colonies no less than the British Isles.

But although the Radical case against the House of Lords breaks down completely on investigation, although their fanciful proposals for dealing with non-existent evils are not less undesirable than they are, happily, impossible, it does not therefore follow that the House of Lords stands in no need of reform. The divinity and infallibility of the House of Lords is not a doctrine of the Tory party any more than the divinity and infallibility of the House of Commons. These pages may be searched in vain for any trace of such a contemptible and baseless superstition, and in this they faithfully reflect the true spirit of historic Toryism. The old Tory party of Bolingbroke and Wyndham was a monarchical and democratic party.

"There can be no doubt," says Macaulay in his Essay on Lord Chatham, "that, as respected the practical questions then pending, the Tory was a reformer, and indeed an intemperate and indiscreet reformer, while the Whig was conservative even to bigotry."

The old Tory party was a monarchical and democratic, that is to say an Imperial, party. The only true Imperialism is Royalism, and the only true and historic Toryism is Tory Democracy. The man who puts the House of Lords on a level with the Crown may be a Conservative, but he has no right to call himself a Tory. Such a man is in reality a Whig, and it is as impossible for a Whig to be a Tory, as for an Orangeman to be a Tory, in any sense but the bad sense, and unfair sense, of a stagnationist and an obstructionist. In these days the Tory party is so much encumbered with proselytes of the gate, converted Whigs, and renegade Republicans, that it is necessary to insist upon the true facts of its history. The party of the House of Lords was the Whig party, the party of the Peerage Bill of 1719. The Tory party was a party of the Crown and the people. The doctrine of an infallible House of Lords which ought also to be omnipotent, of a House of Lords existing by divine right, is no doctrine of Toryism. The Tory party has never sought to abolish the House of Lords ; it has never sought to erect it into the sole power in the Constitution. The only reforms effected in the House of Lords since the sixteenth century and before the present reign, for the changes wrought by the Unions of 1707 and 1801 are not to be regarded as reforms, were the reforms effected by King George the Third, and King George the Third has been unceasingly abused by Whigs, Liberals, and Radicals, from his own time down to ours, as a Monarch who attempted to realize the Tory ideal of a Patriot King. The Tory party has never declared that the House of Lords was so bad an institution that it required to be abolished ; it has never pretended that the House of Lords was so good an institution that it could not be improved. It has never maintained that the House of Lords was beyond reform, still less that it was above reform. Nor again has it ever asserted that the House of Lords was the best of all possible Second Chambers in the best of all possible Parliaments. But what it has constantly said has, in effect, been this, that although the House of Lords is a fallible, human institution, like the House of Commons, we may depend upon it that a Second Chamber which has grown up with, and out of, our national life and Imperial existence, is in its main and essential features better suited to ourselves and our peculiar circumstances than any other that we could now devise. It has never denied either the necessity, or the desirability, of change in the House of Lords; it has always condemned radical change as dangerous and inexpedient; it has always condemned revolutionary change as treason to the nation's highest interests. This has been, and is, the attitude of the Tory party in general. This has been, and is, the attitude of the Tory party in the House of Lords. With right and reason the Tory Peers in the Second Chamber refused to concede to the Crown the power, claimed for it in the case of Lord Wensleydale, of swamping the House at a moment's notice with an unlimited number of Life Peers possessed of no definite qualification. With equal right and reason they have since conceded to the Crown the power of creating a limited number of Life Peers possessing a due, definite, and honourable qualification.

Change is the universal law of human life. All that is not progress is retrogression, and there is no radicalism so destructive as the radicalism of stagnation. We can see this clearly enough in the public life of nations. "The Power that ceases to take and begins to give up," said one of the greatest of the Makers of Germany, "is a *Puissance finie.*" Had England remained as she was in the days of the Tudors, instead of combining with Scotland and Ireland, in the Personal Union of 1603 and the Parliamentary Unions of 1707 and 1801, to form one United Kingdom of the British Isles, and, through the union of the British Isles, to create a worldwide Empire of the British people, she would not, indeed, have made any formal change, but the very abstinence from formal change would have fatally altered her relative position to the changing world around her. France in the time of the Great Monarch was a far greater power than she is to-day. This was due not only to the greatness of the Great Monarch, not only to the essential mediocrity of the institutions which she has since adopted, but to the fact that while Russia and Britain have enlarged their Empires, while Germany and Italy have been united, France has failed to permanently extend the boundaries which then limited her power. France has, on the whole, remained the same, but other Powers have altered, and in changing have changed France with them. That which changes the least in outward show may change the most in reality and essence. To maintain the same relative position it is necessary to be prepared for periodical readjustments. Those institutions and societies which never change, which refuse to adapt themselves to new circumstances and new conditions, may well boast their immobility, for it is the immobility of petrifaction.

Now, the House of Lords, as compared with the Crown and the House of Commons, has undergone but very slight change since the time of the dissolution of the monasteries. The House of Commons has been reformed again and again. The great feature of the Parliamentary history of the British Isles in the present century has been the removal of civil disabilities on account of religion and the extension of the franchise. Very considerable changes have taken place in the position of the Monarch in the last two centuries. For the supremacy of the King in Council there has been substituted the supremacy of the King in Parliament. The right of succession to the Crown has been vested in those descendants of King James I. and VI. who at the time of the limitation did not profess the Roman Catholic religion, to the exclusion, not only of the direct descendants, since extinct, of the issue of King James II. and VII. by his second marriage, but also of the numerous Roman Catholic descendants of King Charles the Martyr. Furthermore, persons in the line of succession to the throne are forbidden to marry members of the Church of Rome, or to join that society themselves, on pain of forfeiting their place in the line of succession, and the Monarch must adhere to the Anglican branch of the Church

Catholic. No changes so great and serious have taken place in the constitution of the House of Lords. The reforms effected by King George the Third were reforms in the composition of the House of Lords, not in its constitution: reforms that took the shape of a multiplication of the Union Peers, not reforms in the structure of the Second Chamber. The other principal changes, before the present reign, were those caused by the Parliamentary Unions. But though the Unions, in bringing in the Representative Peers system, implanted a valuable element of reform in the constitution of the Upper House, they did not affect Peers of England or the Union. They introduced elements of reform, but they were not reforms themselves. They were changes of addition to the House of Lords, not of alteration in its previously existing structure. They established two new classes of Lords Temporal, but they left the great body of Lords Temporal untouched. They in no way qualified or modified the tenure of their seats by the Peers of England, by the Peers of Great Britain who succeeded to the Peers of England, or by the Peers of Great Britain and Ireland who succeeded to the Peers of Great Britain. The only structural reform for many centuries in this great body of Lords Temporal has been that effected in the present reign by the institution of life peerages of the United Kingdom for the Lords and ex-Lords of Appeal. This is the only great constitutional change in the Lords Temporal that has taken place at all comparable to the changes in the Monarchy and House of Commons. For the peculiar representation of Scottish Peers was due to the peculiar circumstances recounted in the first chapter, and the Great British and Irish Union naturally followed the precedent of the Anglo-Scottish. The institution of life peerages for the Lords of Appeal is the only great constitutional change that has taken place in the Union Peerage, and even this is a reform of addition. A new class of Union Peers has been established, but the elder variety remains unaffected.

So, too, with the Lords Spiritual, the only constitutional change that has taken place has been the establishment of the new order of what may be called Prince Bishops, the differentiation of the sees of London, Durham, and Winchester from the other suffragan dioceses of Canterbury and York, and the reduction of the hereditary representation of these latter dioceses to an hereditary possibility of being represented. Anglo-Irish prelates were brought in by the Irish Union, and removed some seventy years later, but this is the only other change of any sort that has taken place in the Lords Spiritual. The only constitutional change has been that previously mentioned.

The changes in the constitution of the House of Lords from 1550 to 1892 have been comparatively trifling, and this fact alone should induce us to suspect the possible existence of a necessity for structural reform. In the last three hundred and fifty years the Monarchy and the House of Commons have changed greatly. The House of Lords has not changed with them.

But, although the House of Lords has changed little in constitution, it has changed greatly in character and composition. In origin a Baronage, the Peers of England at the Union of 1707 were reinforced by representatives of the Baronage of Scotland. At the Union of 1801 the House of Lords received a fresh accession in the representatives of the Baronage of Ireland. But ever since the accession of King George the Third the House of Lords has been steadily tending to become less and less of a Baronage, and more and more of a Senate. The Unions themselves invested the House of Lords with an Imperial character which had previously been less manifest in the Second Chamber of a Parliament which, although without superior in the way of a written Constitution, and exercising for long a paramount jurisdiction over Ireland, was at the same time a local and territorial Legislature. At the present time the House of Lords is beyond doubt the Imperial Chamber. But in the English Parliament, a territorial Legislature, the House of Lords, putting aside the Lords Spiritual, was an English Baronage, and a Baronage was before all things territorial. The Unions, being a consolidation of Imperial authority, emphasized the Imperial character of a Legislature which, before locally supreme, now stood without a rival, and in particular the Imperial character of the House of Lords. But the great multiplication of the Union Peers by George the Third, the long wars that took place in his reign, and the Imperial harvest of those wars in conquests and cessions, contributed still more to delocalize the Upper Chamber, and to substitute a Senatorial for a Baronial qualification in the modern Peerage. That Monarch had to contend with a resuscitated feudalism, and in an extension of the Empire he sought and found a support of the supremacy of the Crown. For the Second Chamber in the Governing body of the Empire a purely territorial Baronage was manifestly insufficient. George the Third broke down the power of the Whig families, and stormed their stronghold, by the obvious expedient of greatly increasing the number of Peers; and his Peers were taken not from territorial magnates only, but from men eminent in every department of the public service, Chancellors and Judges, Ambassadors and Ministers, Admirals and Generals, and Indian and Colonial Governors. Ever since the accession of the King in whose reign India, and Australia, and South Africa were added to the Empire, and Canada confirmed to it, this tendency of the House of Lords to put off the Baronage, and put on the Senate, has been progressing till it has at last found a formal acknowledgment in the creation of life peerages for the Lords of Appeal. Landed property is no longer regarded as a requisite in aspirants to the Peerage, and the connection between the House of Lords and the soil of the United Kingdom, once so intimate, is now rapidly approaching dissolution. A variety of causes have co-operated to bring about this result. The great increase in the number of different forms of wealth; the outburst of material prosperity in portions of Great Britain; the luxury and ostentation of modern society; the wide extension of the means of travel; the growing cosmopolitanism in taste and residence of the wealthier and better educated classes; the agricultural depression consequent on unrestricted foreign competition;—all have combined to detach the Peerage from the soil. A number of Peers have been created from men, often childless, with little or no property in land. Other Peers have in one way or another parted company with the landed estates that were formerly attached to their titles. Peers whose income, being derived from land, has shrunk through the general depression of the agricultural interest, or whose estates were greatly encumbered by the burdens laid upon them in more prosperous times, have been glad to escape with the remainder of their fortune, or, notwithstanding their reluctance, have been compelled to sell. More fortunate Peers, whose income, derived from other sources than agricultural property, has expanded instead of diminishing, have felt the force of those temptations to foreign residence and travel and the less provincial society of great capitals, which none but the most retired or bucolic are in this age wholly able to resist. The agrarian revolution in Ireland, and the menace held out to land by witless Jacobin capitalists, who have not the sense to see that all property is held by the same title, have shaken public confidence in landed investments, while the loss by landed proprietors of the political power which they formerly exercised, and modern changes in the law of Real Property, have all contributed to the same end. Land has become a far less desirable possession, and the social prestige and political power formerly attendant on land ownership have very largely disappeared. The impoverishment of some Peers, by the decline in agricultural values, has combined with the enrichment of other Peers, by the growth of villages into towns and towns into cities, to destroy the territorial attachment and distribution of the Peerage. That recognition of new forms of power which has given rise to so much annoyance and disgust in Professor Bryce and the high nobility of Boston, has brought into existence a class of Peers not primarily connected with the land, while the number of peerages bestowed in recent times on public servants has largely qualified the territorial aspect of the House of Lords, and imparted to it a tinge of officialism and bureaucracy.

Far more various in the elements of its composition than in the days of Whig ascendency, the House of Lords to some extent reflects the great growth of British interests beyond the British Isles, and the present abundance and variety of national interests within the Isles themselves. The House has steadily tended to become less of a Baronage, and more of a Senate, and the Peers in becoming more Imperial have of necessity become less local, as in becoming urban and modern they have also become less rural and feudal. The increased efficiency of the House of Lords as an Imperial Senate has been obtained at the inevitable cost of its decreased efficiency as the Second Chamber of a territorial Legislature. Before the Georgian and Victorian expansions of the Peerage, every Peer was as well known in his own locality as was the King in the whole kingdom. Every Peer was in a way a sort of little King. Each district had its territorial magnate in the House of Magnates, just as each district had and has its territorial militia. But all this has changed. The great soldiers and statesmen brought into the Peerage, the ambassadors and pro-consuls, belonged, for the most part, not to this or that locality, but to the whole nation. And in the affairs of the whole British nation, and the Empire which that nation rules, the House of Lords speaks with an authority, and is heard with a respect, which were never greater, or so great, at any previous period of its history. But in the territorial affairs of localities the authority and weight of the Peers have necessarily declined with the decay of their local influence and territorial predominance. Some Peers have no estates at all, while others have so many estates that they appear to be unable to localize themselves at any one of them. A Duke with many great estates has more concentrated power for good than a hundred country gentlemen. But one man, no matter how public-spirited and how laborious, cannot play the same part in local affairs that is played by a hundred men. The multiplication of the Peers, and the substitution of Senatorial for Baronial qualifications, have had for their inevitable consequences a decline in the power and popularity of the House of Lords as the Second Chamber of a local legislature. The House of Lords has not yet become sufficiently Imperial for the Upper House of a

Parliament in whose First Chamber Canada and Australia should be represented, while on the other hand it has become too Imperial to discharge its local functions with entire success.

Notwithstanding the incessant additions to the Peerage, made on the advice of Liberal Ministers in the present reign, the growth of the Peerage has not kept pace with the growth of the nation even in the British Isles, to say nothing of the British Colonies. Absolutely it has increased in numbers, but relatively it has diminished. Yet, even at the present rate of increase, the very number of the Peers entitled to sit in person in the House of Lords will necessitate some change in the tenure of their seats. The causes which checked the growth of the Peerage in mediæval times have almost entirely disappeared, like the causes which checked the growth of population. Now the British people have in the Colonies a boundless field for free expansion, and the growth of manufacturing industries in the United Kingdom has enabled the British Isles to support an immensely larger number of inhabitants. Now there are no longer the insurrections and rebellions, the raids and feuds, the civil wars and private wars, the forfeitures and attainders, which kept a constant current of change in personal composition running through the Peerage. Now there is nothing to prevent the House of Lords from growing into an unmanageable mob but an abrupt cessation of the creation of new peerages, and the consequent conversion of the House of Lords into a close corporation.

At the time of the Scottish Union it would have been unfair to the people of England if the Peers of Scotland had been admitted in a body to the Great British House of Lords. Now, there is no reason whatever why Peers of Scotland and Peers of Ireland should not represent themselves in the same way as Peers of England and Peers of Great Britain. Now, there is no danger whatever to English interests to be feared from an inclusion of the Scottish and Irish Peerages. Many Peers of Scotland or Ireland are Englishmen. Many Peers of Great Britain or the United Kingdom are Scotsmen or

Irishmen. The local character of each Peerage has been overshadowed by the Imperial character of the whole Peerage. Why should a Scottish gentleman, with a peerage created four hundred years ago, be without a right to sit in person in the House of Lords, when his next-door neighbour, whose father was created a Peer four years ago, has a right to sit in person? The distinction between Peers of Scotland and Ireland and Peers of England and the Union has become a distinction wholly unjustified by any real difference. Always invidious, it is now antiquated and fantastic. That this is felt to be so, is shown by the increasing number of United Kingdom peerages bestowed on Scottish and Irish Peers.

In recent creations there has been a strong tendency to substitute a Senatorial for a Baronial qualification, but no change has yet been made, except in the case of the Lords of Appeal, in the direction of substituting a Senatorial for a Baronial tenure. Yet, if the Peerage from Baronial is to become Senatorial, some change in this direction will be necessary. Heredity is of the essence of a Baronage: selection is of the essence of a Senate. If peerages are to be less exclusively associated with landed property, the rights attaching to them will require reconsideration. Genius cannot be entailed and settled in the same way as land or money. Talent is no doubt transmissible, but it is apt to be fitful and uncertain in its manifestations. A territorial family will always command a certain degree of respect, but, when a Poet Laureate has passed away, what of his successors? The Lord of Chatsworth or of Trentham will always be a personage of consideration, but, without endorsing the suggestion of Mr. Froude that "a Dukedom of Stratford-upon-Avon would be a cap and bells for Shakespeare's descendants," it is permissible to doubt whether it would be either to the honour of Shakespeare, or the advantage of the House of Lords, that his descendants should as such sit in the House *in secula seculorum*. Wealth is a form of power, and genius is a form of power, but they are not transmissible in one and the same manner. There are degrees and kinds of greatness. One man is great on account of his office, another is great on account of his estates, a third is great in himself. There is the greatness of a Lord Chancellor, the greatness of a Duke, and the greatness of a Bacon. A man may be great not only on account of his estates or office, but in himself; but this is not always the case. Now, even if the greatness of a Duke or a Bacon merits eternal representation in the House of Lords, this can scarcely be said of the greatness of a Lord Chancellor, a Home Secretary, or a Speaker of the House of Commons. It is right enough, and eminently desirable, that a Poet Laureate, or a Field-Marshal, should have a seat in the Upper Chamber. It is neither wrong, nor undesirable, that their descendants should enjoy the title, rank, precedence, and such few privileges as remain, of an hereditary peerage. But is it right, is it in the least desirable, that, fit or unfit, they should go on sitting in person through countless æons in the House of Lords? Why should they be privileged in this manner when Peers of Scotland or Ireland as such are not? A Field-Marshal may be a Duke of Wellington; or he may be something altogether different. A Poet Laureate may be a Tennyson; but he may also be a Pye. There are many men, again, who would themselves make useful members of a Second Chamber, but whose services are not so great and glorious, nor their genius so eminent, as to call for an everlasting recognition. This fact has been acknowledged in the number of peerages bestowed in the present reign on men of talent without children. But if a United Kingdom peerage were not of necessity hereditary, it would be possible to introduce a larger number of men of talent into the House of Lords without choking up the Second Chamber for all time with their landless descendants. The representatives of great or distinguished men are very fitting material out of which to form a Second Chamber, but it is material which requires to be submitted to a further test. It is improper and impolitic that a man, whose presence would both adorn and strengthen the House of Lords, should be compelled to decline a seat in it on the ground that a peerage, however acceptable to himself, would to his children prove a burdensome inheritance. A tenure unvarying in its Baronial character is incompatible with an extended adoption of Senatorial qualifications. The growing extension of peerages to families not basing their claims on great landed fortunes, and the growing disconnection with the soil of families formerly territorial, alike call for greater elasticity and a revised tenure.

The grievances commonly put forward by the Radical party against the House of Lords have been examined, and have been found, for the most part, to rest on no foundation. But the Radical party has a just ground for complaint in the callous and contemptuous treatment of measures that have passed the House of Commons at the hands of Peers who as a rule take no part in politics, and pay little or no attention to political questions. There are too many Peers who stroll down to a great Parliamentary discussion as they might to a general meeting of their club. It is this which arouses so vehement a sentiment of indignation in the Radical bosom. The real levity, and the apparent insolence, of such handling of great national questions is deeply and bitterly resented, nor is it possible to say that such resentment is unwarranted. This is a great blot on the House of Lords, and a very serious drawback to its efficiency and influence. The careless indifference to the affairs of the nation ordinarily exhibited by many Peers is set in a still more unfavourable light when contrasted with the zeal shown to discredit Toryism, and imperil the Constitution, by throwing out, for the occasion only, some Radical measure which some of them have not so much as read, and of which others have not the sense to understand the mischief. There are Peers whose only purpose in public life seems to be to embarrass their own party and give the enemy occasion to blaspheme. A Peer who steadily refuses to discharge the public duties of his order, ought to be debarred from interference in legislation at his sole whim and pleasure. There are mischievous and eccentric persons in the House of Commons, but they are there by the deliberate choice of their constituents. They represent, as it is intended that they should represent, the

CHAP. I.] DEFECTS OF THE HOUSE OF LORDS. 287

folly and ignorance of their electors, so that the Crown, in the pursuance of its designs, may know how far popular prejudice requires to be dissipated or consulted, how far popular ignorance requires to be dispelled. But the folly and ignorance that a foolish Peer represents are only his own. The House of Lords in a great debate on foreign policy would impress the bitterest Radical of any intellect, but the public respect for it is not promoted, when an Orange Peer jumps up and declares it a fixed article of the Conservative creed that the National Gallery should be closed on Sunday. A Monarch who feels himself unfit for the discharge of public duties can abdicate the throne. A Prince, on succeeding to the throne, can renounce his right to the succession. A Peer can only stop away, and in doing so give the impression of contemptuous indifference.

There can be no doubt that, owing, partly to the growing delocalization of the Peerage, and partly to the usual abstention from public business of many Peers, the House of Lords has greatly lost its hold on public opinion in matters relating to domestic affairs in the British Isles. The Second Chamber, based upon election, of a purely local and purely territorial Legislature would be able to do many things which the House of Lords only attempts in a half-hearted manner, and then, frightened at the sound of its own voice, runs away. The House of Lords cannot be changed into such an assembly without imminent danger to the Constitution and the Empire, and the abolition of the Peerage as a political body. No Second Chamber which includes hereditary legislators, or life nominees, can ever deal with legislation affecting property with the freedom and fearlessness of a Second Chamber based on popular election. Just as the constitution of the Imperial Parliament is an interest of the whole Empire, so a sufficiently strong Upper Chamber in the Legislature immediately dealing with the local affairs of England, Scotland, or Ireland, is a matter of concern to every property holder in each of the three kingdoms. But the House of Lords in these matters shows great weakness. No Second Chamber based upon election would have passed such measures of agrarian confiscation as Mr. Gladstone's Irish Land Acts. What is wanted is a Victorian Legislative Council as the Upper House of a local and territorial, subordinate and dependent, Parliament in each of England, Scotland, and Ireland. Insular Home Rule, carried through on such a basis, would provide a security against agrarian revolution which the House of Lords has entirely failed to supply in the past. Until some such security is obtained, landed property in the British Isles will continue to be in greater danger than landed property in any other portion of the British Empire. That landed property is exposed to no such risks in the ideal polity of the English Radicals, the American Republic, it is perhaps superfluous to mention.

The House of Lords, partly in consequence of its tendency to develop into an Imperial Senate, partly in consequence of the negligence and inertness of a portion of its members, has altogether failed as a barrier against local agrarian revolution. It is impossible to strengthen it for local politics without disastrously affecting the relation of the Imperial Parliament to the Empire, or working untold harm to the Constitution. But, although it has gone too far in the Imperial direction to remain any longer efficient as a territorial and local Chamber, it has not gone far enough for the Upper House of the governing body of the Empire. Just as the delegation of its local functions to an elected Second Chamber in each of three local Legislatures would deal the severest blow that could be dealt to the Jacobin cause in the British Isles, so this is also the essential condition of its remaining the Upper House in a Parliament of the whole British nation. The British people have in the last century and a half spread themselves over the vast possessions in three Continents won for them in those great wars which fools and fanatics have denounced as the idle and profligate amusement of the aristocracy. In Canada and Australia they have formed or are forming themselves into nations, and early in the twentieth century, if not sooner, the question will arise whether these new nations are to combine with the English, the Scottish, and the Irish nation, in the greater

British nation, or whether they are to follow the evil example of the United States. If they are to remain within the British nation, then one of two things is certain : either the British Constitution must be altogether changed, or the Parliamentary Union of Canada and Australia with Great Britain and Ireland must proceed on the same lines as the Union of Ireland with Great Britain, and the Union of Scotland and England, subject to the establishment or maintenance of a local Legislature for the local affairs of each minor nation in the Imperial Union. Any other scheme of Union than that of the representation of the Colonies in the Imperial Parliament, coupled with Insular Home Rule, necessarily implies the dethronement of the Imperial Parliament and its supersession by some rival or superior authority. That is to say, it implies a fundamental change in the Constitution. If, then, the British Constitution and the British Empire are to be alike preserved, this is the plan which will unavoidably be followed.

It is impossible in the nature of things that Canada and Australia, when once they have arrived at a full realization of their local nationality, should long remain content with a dependent and subordinate position. There will be three courses open to them : independence, union with the British Isles only through the Crown, and union through the Imperial Parliament. Of these courses, the second need not be considered, as it would infallibly end in either the first course or the third. If, therefore, the Colonies do not eventually separate from the United Kingdom, and the Constitution should remain unchanged in any vital particular, we may count on their representation in the Imperial Parliament. And if they are to be represented in the Imperial Parliament, then the House of Lords must be reformed. The representation of Canada and Australia in the House of Commons would be a comparatively simple matter. Canada, on the basis of its present population, would be entitled to about the same proportion of members as Ireland, and Australia, with New Zealand, to rather fewer than Scotland. But the representation of the Colonies in the House of Lords is an affair of greater intricacy. There is nothing, indeed, to prevent a Colonist from being created a Peer at the present time in the same way as any other British subject, though up till now only two such peerages have been created—the Barony of Mount Stephen conferred on Sir George Stephen, and the Barony of Macdonald of Earnscliffe bestowed on the widow of that distinguished Canadian and British patriot Sir John A. Macdonald. There is nothing to prevent a Colonist from being created a Peer, but there are comparatively few Colonists who could be created Peers with equal advantage to the Colonies and the House of Lords. The Colonies, indeed, contain many men of high culture and good family, and they also contain many rich men. But as a rule, to which there are of course exceptions, the men of family or culture are not rich, and the rich men are not of good family or high culture.

In the early stages of colonization, Colonial society is naturally and inevitably democratic. Men are really as equal as men ever can be in commencing life in an unsettled country, just as they are equal on a desert island or a raft. The tradition formed in the early days lingers on long afterwards, and is especially active at the outposts of settlement, gradually dying away elsewhere as society becomes more highly organized and complex. Then the old distinctions and divisions reassert themselves, though the publicity of Colonial life, and its ever-changing conditions, render the classes and sections of Colonial society more elastic and fluid than those of an old country. Just so, the limbs of a growing boy are not set like those of a man. An aristocracy recognized by social opinion is everywhere and at all times of slow growth, and not least in Colonial society. This is true of the revolted British Colonies known as the United States, and it is true of those Colonies which have remained loyal. No wise man would wish to see it otherwise. The ramifications and elaborations of Old World society would be as entirely out of place in the early stage of colonization, as the ceremony and courtesies of a State ball would be in a battle. The soldier, with his face blackened with smoke and his hands red with gore, is the noblest of all figures, and of the pioneers of the worldwide migration of the British people none but a fribble and a *petit maître* would demand the tone and manners of Lord Chesterfield. Still, sooner or later, an aristocracy begins to form itself, and where uncontrolled by higher authority it becomes, as we see in the United States, an aristocracy of wealth. In an industrial community wealth, if uncontrolled and unchecked, exercises undue predominance over the higher elements of aristocracy.

The British Colonies have not been wholly unconnected with the hereditary distinctions established by the Britannic State. King James I. and VI., who, as "the British Solomon," had a fair insight into the weaknesses of mankind, instituted the Order of Baronets, probably suggested to him by the minor Barons of Scotland, who retained that designation much longer than the corresponding class in England, and, indeed, have preserved it to this day. He established the Baronets of Scotland and Nova Scotia to aid the colonization of a land that has since become part of the great Scottish Colony of Canada, as he connected the Baronets of England with the Plantation of Ulster. Baronets have since increased and multiplied and replenished the earth throughout the British world, and, like the non-hereditary Order of St. Michael and St. George, have been not without a certain value in moulding and influencing political opinion. The profession of ultra-Radical opinions is not always dissevered from the aspirations of social ambition, whether in the British Colonies or British Isles; and such distinctions have without doubt a soothing influence on Colonial politicians, who, if left unnoticed, might fancy that their conspicuous merits had been intentionally slighted. Lord Carrington has proclaimed to the British Isles the immense importance attaching to the Order of the Bath in the mind of New South Wales; and the only Colonial politician, who has thought it worth while to place on record the fact that he had declined a knighthood, has also thought it worth while to insert his name and arms, or rather his name and address, and a not very ancient or illustrious pedigree, in Sir Bernard Burke's "Golden Book of the

Colonial Gentry." It is difficult to imagine George Washington refusing the K.C.M.G.

Although, however, only baronetcies and knighthoods have taken permanent root in the Colonies, attempts have been made at various times to connect these transmarine possessions of the Crown with the higher ranks of the State-recognized nobility. Sir William Alexander, a Scottish poet and Secretary of State, was in 1633 created Earl of Stirling and Viscount Canada, an arrangement of titles which at the present day must, to the most patriotic Scotsman, seem grotesque. Earl of Dumbarton and Viscount Australia, Earl of Selkirk and Viscount South Africa, or Earl of Peebles and Lord India would strike the ear as a somewhat curious combination. The style chosen by Lord Stirling for his second title cannot, however, be condemned as insonorous, and it is possible that it may have been suggested by the Dukedom of Ireland, bestowed by Richard II. on his favourite Robert de Vere, Earl of Oxford, whom he also created Marquis of Dublin. Peers in the seventeenth century sometimes settled in the Colonies, as in the famous instance of Lord Baltimore, and Peers have occasionally done so since. Many cadets of peerage families seek their fortunes in Greater Britain, and nothing is more natural than that some of these should from time to time succeed to the representation of their family. But, although at different periods it has been endeavoured to establish a Peerage peculiar to a given Colony or given Colonies, the attempt has fortunately failed in every case. The failure must be considered fortunate, for, had such an attempt proved successful, the Colonial Peerage so established would, like the Irish Peerage in the last century, have been politically inferior to the Peerage of Great Britain, and this political inferiority would, as in the Irish case, have carried with it a social stigma. The creation of a distinct Colonial Peerage must have presented another obstacle to Pan-Britannic Union, instead of assisting its accomplishment. In the reign of Charles II., the great Whig statesman Shaftesbury and the great Whig philosopher Locke drew up a Constitution for the Carolinas, which, although quite impracticable, is full of interest as a disclosure of the true Whig feeling. The Peer and the philosopher wished to plant a system of full-blown feudalism in the New World. A class of leetmen or serfs was to be established ; and these poor creatures, and their children after them for all generations, were to be bound to perpetual labour on the soil. In this Whig ideal polity the social edifice was naturally crowned by two orders of Peers, Landgraves or Earls, and Caciques or Barons. The Colony was to be divided into counties, and each county was to be made happy with one Landgrave and two Caciques. Such was "the cause for which Hampden died on the field, and Sydney on the scaffold." From the Whigs, with their complacent self-delusion that Whig principles were "of eternal truth and universal application," thus piously engaged in building up a Whig party on the other side of the Atlantic, it is a relief to turn to the greatest native-born politician whom Australia has yet produced, William Wentworth. This admirable man, of a high stamp not too common in the politics of any country, was so much impressed with the excellence of the House of Lords that he desired its reproduction in Australia. This, of course, would have been impossible, and Wentworth was fortunately saved from a great blunder by the opposition of a violent demagogue called Dr. Lang, of much notoriety in his day and in his own Colony, and of two politicians who afterwards became Sir Henry Parkes and Lord Sherbrooke.

No local Peerage exists in any portion of the British Empire outside the British Isles. The creation of new Peers of Scotland was forbidden at the Union, and the creation of Irish Peers, though still legal, has practically been discontinued. Every Second Chamber of a local Legislature in the Colonies consists of nominated or elected legislators. Had the Colonies wished to reproduce the House of Lords and establish a distinct local Peerage, they would probably have failed to do so, for in the Colonies, as in most foreign countries, the materials for a House of Lords in its present shape do not exist. These facts all point to the conclusion that the House of Lords, like the House of Commons, should relinquish its local functions to a local Chamber, and develop itself still further into an Imperial Senate. There are two tendencies clearly discernible in the Peerage at the present time. One is a tendency to life peerages, shown in bestowing peerages on men without children, and the subsequent extension of the Appellate Jurisdiction Act, 1876. The other tendency, shown in the increasing number of Union peerages bestowed on Scottish and Irish Peers, is to the amalgamation of the five Peerages of England, Scotland, Great Britain, Ireland, and Great Britain and Ireland, into one Imperial Peerage of the United Kingdom of the British nation. It is by following out the former tendency to a legitimate conclusion that we can arrive at an adequate representation of the Colonies in the House of Lords. At present the Colonies have comparatively few men qualified in every respect for hereditary peerages. It would be far easier and less hazardous, in the first instance, to provide for their suitable representation by means of a class of Life Peers. Afterwards, Colonists, like Englishmen or Scotsmen, could be from time to time enrolled in the hereditary Peerage. But to make a class of Life Peers of any effect for the representation of the Colonies, it would be necessary to decrease the number of hereditary Peers sitting in person in the Upper Chamber.

If that which is known as Imperial Federation is to become an accomplished fact without violence to the Constitution, both Houses of the Imperial Parliament must be reformed. The representation of the Colonies in the House of Commons would be a simpler matter than their representation in the House of Lords; but for that very reason the latter should be first attempted, and the way thus gradually paved to fuller union. That the House of Lords should be elected by the local Legislatures of the Empire; that the Agents-General should hold official seats;—are propositions which have been considered and dismissed. But although the House of Lords must, like the House of Commons, be reformed on the existing lines of the Constitution, the necessity for reform is none the less urgent. Though the thorough Imperialization of the House of Lords is impossible without the delegation of its local functions, much may be done in the meantime to fix a conception in the public mind of the House of Lords as the Senate of the Empire. This principle was directly and unmistakably asserted by the second Salisbury Administration when Lord Mount Stephen was summoned to the House of Lords. If the British nation, as Whigs are still found to contend, is limited to the British Isles, then the creation of a Canadian a Peer of the United Kingdom was an intolerable invasion of the right of the people of Great Britain and Ireland to manage their own affairs. On the assumption of the *Edinburgh Review*, that there is but one nation in the British Isles and that this nation extends no farther than the British Isles, the summons of distinguished Colonists to the House of Lords is wholly without justification. But this is not the view of the Duke of Devonshire, who speaks of England, Scotland, and Ireland as " the three nations that make up the British Empire," and thereby affirms that the people of the British Isles are both more than one nation and less. There are three British nations in the governing body of the Empire, and there are other British nations forming themselves outside it. The creation of the Mount-Stephen Barony was a distinct and unequivocal pronouncement in favour of the worldwide union of all the nations that compose the British people. If this example is followed up, it may be possible, before the time for complete union arrives, so to develop the House of Lords as to make further change unnecessary for the perfection of its Imperial character. And, if it be said that the presence of Colonists in any large numbers in a House of Lords with its existing functions would be a possible injustice to the people of the British Isles, it is sufficient to answer that this must be regarded as part of the price paid by them for their exclusive control over Imperial policy. If · it operated as a grievance, they could find relief at any moment by the establishment of local Legislatures for their domestic affairs.

There is only one policy really open to the House of Lords, that of its further self-development into an Imperial Senate—

a Senate after the style of the Roman Senate under Augustus, rather than after the style of the American Senate under Mr. Harrison. But if the House of Lords is to be so developed, then it must undergo a change not only in its composition, but its constitution; not a reform of addition only, but a reform in its existing structure. A Senatorial tenure must go hand in hand with a Senatorial qualification; an extended provision must be made for life peerages; and for the future those hereditary Peers who are personally without public distinction must be content to be represented by deputy, as the Scottish and Irish Peers are at present, though on an electoral basis better adapted to secure the representation of minorities. In this way the number of hereditary legislators can be further reduced without injuring the Peerage, while room will be made at the same time for an increase in the number of life members of the Upper House. The efficiency of the House as a legislative Chamber would be greatly promoted; the drawbacks to its hold on public esteem would be removed; and eminent men could be freely summoned to the House without entailing the formidable consequence of their descendants also sitting in it for all time.

It is sometimes argued by timorous friends of the House of Lords that it had best be left alone, and that no reform can be attempted without danger. But although the House of Lords may be left alone, no one need fancy that it will remain the same. Change it will, and the only real choice is, not between change and immutability, but between the change of reform and development, and the change of stagnation and decay. The frightened pessimists who dread discussion, by their opposition to the reform of the House of Lords, are playing into the hands of the men who openly avow that they shall oppose all attempts to reform it in the hope that it may ultimately be abolished. Peers, at present with seats in the House of Lords, may not like to be disturbed; but, in the first place, there is not the slightest occasion to disturb them, and, in the second place, the House of Lords exists for the nation, not the nation for the Peers. The House of Lords is not the King, but even to the Kingship a certain condition has been affixed, a certain qualification of personal fitness is required in the Monarch. The House of Lords is not the King, and its constitution can no more be considered fixed and final at any given moment than the constitution of the House of Commons.

It is not likely that any reform of the House of Lords would satisfy Radical extremists. No one likes to be deprived of a grievance, imaginary or real. But it would remove the chief ground of their complaints. And the people to be considered are not this crank or that merryandrew in the House of Commons, but the Imperial democracy. In fact, the worst revolutionists are those who refuse to accept timely reforms. It is a commonplace of history that very small reforms might at one time have averted the downfall of the French Monarchy, and the people who did most to provoke the Revolution were the first to run away from it.

The House of Lords has unavoidably lost much of its power as a local Legislature. There is now no possibility that a territorial Parliament of England, Scotland, or Ireland, would contain a Second Chamber in which the Peers, as Peers, found place. If the House of Lords is not steadily developed on the lines suggested, it is possible that it may also miss its chance as an Imperial Senate. As a body controlling domestic legislation, the House of Lords is neither powerful nor popular. Should it fail to maintain its Imperial position, and it can only maintain it by continuous advance, it may be that the idea of a United States Senate will acquire too firm a hold upon the public mind to be dislodged. It has been shown, indeed, that the abolition of the House of Lords, or its forcible conversion into something quite different from what it is, are no such easy affairs as the Radicals imagine. But, although it would be a difficult matter for the Monarch and the House of Commons in conjunction to formally abolish the House of Lords, it would not be so difficult for the House of Lords to practically abolish itself. From a struggle for existence it might perhaps emerge with triumph, but nothing can save it from degenerating into a State pageant, if it refuses to expand

with the Empire, to grow with the national life. Reasonably
or unreasonably, there exists widespread dissatisfaction with
the House of Lords as the Second Chamber of a local Legislature ; if it does not adapt itself to new circumstances and
changed conditions, if it does not anticipate new needs, a
similar dissatisfaction may arise with it in time as the
Second Chamber of an Imperial Parliament.

It is impossible to deny that the action of the House of
Lords in opposing the extension of the franchise, and the
removal of civil disabilities on account of religion, in the
actual shape which these measures assumed in the hands
of the Liberal party, have prejudiced the popular mind,
which is seldom discriminating, against the Second Chamber,
and predisposed the ignorant to the assumption that in any
dispute between the House of Lords and the Liberal party
in Great Britain the House of Lords must be in the wrong.
The absurd and extraordinary schemes promulgated by its
enemies for the "ending or mending" of the House of Lords,
show that this great national institution has lost ground,
since otherwise no one would dare to father such wild and
impertinent proposals. Now, the Radical complaint against
the constitution of the House of Lords is that it is a House
of hereditary legislators ; and the Radical complaint against
the composition of the House of Lords, is that it is a House
of landlords. If, therefore, in a reform of the Second
Chamber the hereditary element were subjected to further
qualifications, and a class of members introduced who were
neither hereditary legislators, nor even hereditary Peers, nor,
on the other hand, in the majority of cases landlords, at least
in the sense of territorial magnates, it would be impossible
for the Liberal party to oppose a measure embodying such
proposals without convicting itself of insincerity and levity.
The chronic Radical agitation against the House of Lords
has created in the public mind a vague feeling that it ought
somehow to be altered, together with a strong reluctance to
proceed to lengths against a proud and ancient institution
of the nation. A comprehensive scheme of reform put forward by the Peers themselves would probably be received

with acclamation. Were such a scheme adopted by the House of Lords to be rejected by the Liberal party in the House of Commons, the Liberal party would find itself in a very false position. The nation would know how to judge of the honesty and good faith of previous Radical complaints. It is probable that, if the House of Lords drew up such a scheme and passed it, the Liberal party would not have the audacity and effrontery to reject it. To do so would greatly damage their cause and character with the country. The public, which does not care for details, would note only that the House of Lords wished to be reformed, and that the Liberal party had prevented this. But if the Radicals did refuse to pass such a measure, then they would put themselves for ever out of court. If, after that, they complained of the landlords or hereditary legislators in the House of Lords, every one would remember that the Radicals had only themselves to thank for this, that they had been offered a liberal measure of reform, and had deliberately rejected it. Such a scheme would force the Liberal hand, and whether they accepted or rejected it, it would be favourably regarded by the country as a convincing and irrefutable proof that the House of Lords desired to place itself in thorough accord with the nation. If the Peers, while there is time, will undertake their own reform, they could compel the Liberal party to accept their terms, or to desist from all further agitation.

The patriotism of the Peers, and their self-interest as an order, are alike concerned in their reform. The constitution of the Imperial Parliament is of the utmost weight to the whole Empire. If the Lords Temporal and Spiritual adopt a scheme of real, not illusory, reform, then those who now seek to overawe and intimidate them, and excite popular odium against the House with baseless charges, will be forced to either accept such a concession, or for ever hold their peace.

CHAPTER II.

LIFE PEERS.

AMONG the reforms which have been suggested by men whose attachment to the House of Lords is beyond suspicion, has been the creation of Life Peers. Life Peers, it has been said already, were unknown in the original constitution of the Peerage, and had in fact no place in the Upper Chamber till, within the last few years, life peerages were established for the Lords of Appeal. The Irish Representative Peers were life members of the House of Lords, but hereditary Peers: and the Bishops were members for life of the House of Lords, but not Peers. The Lords of Appeal are the first Life Peers. Although, however, the Lords of Appeal are the only Life Peers, normal Peerages of the United Kingdom are frequently bestowed on men without heirs to inherit their titles; that is to say, such men are in effect created Life Peers. There is, therefore, already in the Second Chamber a class of legislators who are in everything but name Life Peers, above and besides the Lords of Appeal.

It has been said before that the hereditary character of the Peerage is that which has given the House of Lords its independence of the Crown and House of Commons. A House, entirely dependent on the Crown, would be unable to give the Crown any support worth having, and would constitute no serious check upon the Lower Chamber. A House entirely independent of the Crown would, like the United States Senate, be "necessarily the rival" of "the people's Chamber," and "generally the opponent" of the chief of the

State. The hereditary principle has given the House of Lords its strength, while the power of the Crown to create new Peers has kept the House from growing too powerful. A Second Chamber entirely composed of Crown life nominees is, as the experience of Canada and other Colonies has proved, neither powerful nor popular. Where there is a definite limit to its numbers, complaints are heard similar to those made against the House of Lords. Where there is no such limit, perpetual attempts are made to swamp it with fresh nominees, and the Crown, as Lord Onslow and Lord Glasgow have found in New Zealand, is brought into conflict with its Ministers.

A House of Lords entirely composed of Life Peers would lose all importance, without acquiring popularity. It would be unable to appeal to the historic principle, like the present House of Lords. It would be unable to appeal to the elective principle, like the United States Senate. It would, moreover, require the abolition of the existing Peerage as a political body, not less imperatively than some of the Radical schemes previously mentioned. It is clear, therefore, that a House of Lords entirely composed of Life Peers is out of the question. To discontinue the creation of hereditary Peers, and make no Peers but Life Peers for the future, is open to the twofold objection that it would eventually destroy the independence of the House of Lords, while converting the existing Peerage into a close corporation. To allow of the unlimited creation of Life Peers, would also tend to destroy the independence of the House of Lords, and would at the same time subvert the dignity of the Peerage. Men would be created Life Peers on probation, with the promise of hereditary Peerage if they faithfully adhered to their party. If the power of the Crown to create new peerages has been a check on the hereditary Peers, the fact that those new peerages are also hereditary has been a check on their creation. A permanent addition to the House of Lords and Peerage causes more hesitation than the allotment of a seat for life in a Second Chamber.

For the establishment of a class of Life Peers with safety

and success, two things are requisite : first, that the number of such Peers should be carefully defined and limited; and next, that each of such Peers should be required to possess a definite and fixed qualification. The experiment of the Lords of Appeal has been entirely successful, but had not the Wensleydale attempt to secure for the Crown an absolute and unlimited discretion in creating Life Peers been defeated, a very different story might need to be recorded. An unscrupulous, or, what is the same thing, a self-righteous Minister, whenever he found himself in danger of losing his measures in the Second Chamber, would put pressure on the Monarch to create the number of Life Peers necessary to give his Administration a majority. The number of Life Peers will require to be carefully limited, and it will be impossible to specify the nature of their qualifications too exactly. Such a description as that of " having acquired fame in science, literature, or any other pursuit tending to the benefit of the nation, or paying taxes to the annual amount of £120," is altogether too vague and indefinite. Following the example of the Lords of Appeal, it will be wise to state with the utmost detail and precision what offices, and what length of service in them, will qualify for a life peerage.

The holding, or having held, certain offices of State, is at the present accepted in practice as constituting a claim to an hereditary peerage. Thus, the Lord High Chancellor of the United Kingdom is usually created a Baron on appointment to that office, as in the case of Lords Westbury, Chelmsford, Halsbury, and Herschell, and others too numerous for mention ; and, should he hold office a second time, having before held it for any lengthy period, he is usually created an Earl, as in the case of Lord Cairns and Lord Selborne. So, too, any person who has held the office of a Principal Secretary of State, or one approximately equal to it in importance, is commonly created a Viscount, as in the case of Lord Sherbrooke, Lord Cranbrook, and Lord Cross ; and this practice extends to Speakers of the House of Commons, as in the case of Lord Eversley and Lord Hampden.

If, then, the having filled certain high offices is considered to establish a claim to an hereditary peerage, much more should it establish a claim to a life peerage. And, although it is not probable that in the majority of cases a life peerage would be preferred to one that was hereditary, it may not be wholly amiss to take such a contingency into account. It must be remembered that any Act enumerating the qualifications required for a life peerage would be permissive, not compulsory, in character; and it would be as well, therefore, to allow the Crown, within reasonable limits, the widest and amplest discretion.

In considering the nature of the qualification required for a life peerage, the first that naturally suggests itself is that of having held high office in the State. And among political offices those that at the outset strike the eye are the offices connected with that Executive of the United Kingdom which, at the present time, is partly Imperial, and partly Insular. It will be agreed without dispute that to have held the office, for ever so short a time, of Lord Chancellor of Great Britain; Lord Privy Seal; Lord President of the Council; Lord High Treasurer or First Lord of the Treasury; Lord High Admiral or First Lord of the Admiralty; Chancellor of the Exchequer; or Principal Secretary of State for Foreign Affairs, for War, for the Colonies, for India, or for Home Affairs, should constitute a sufficient qualification for a life peerage, since none, or very few, of these offices are bestowed on politicians of trifling importance, and nearly all are in themselves of utmost gravity. To this list it might perhaps be advisable to add the office of Lord High Chancellor of Ireland.

Descending in the scale of an Administration, we come to the offices of President of the Board of Trade, President of the Board of Agriculture, and President of the Local Government Board; Postmaster-General; Chancellor of the Duchy of Lancaster; Vice-President of the Committee of Council on Education: Junior Lord of the Treasury; Junior Lord of the Admiralty; Secretary for Scotland; and Chief Secretary to the Lord-Lieutenant of Ireland. The Irish Chief Secretaryship is now combined with the Keepership of the Privy Seal of Ireland, and the Secretaryship for Scotland with the Keepership of the Great Seal and Privy Seal of Scotland. It might be well to demand a tenure of any of these offices for a term of not less than two years as a security against possible abuses.

A large number of subordinate offices of importance in each department of the Government are partly Parliamentary and partly permanent. Such are those of the Under Secretary of State for War, Foreign Affairs, Home Affairs, the Colonies, and India; Under Secretaries for Scotland and Ireland; Secretaries to the Treasury, the Admiralty, the Board of Agriculture, and the Local Government Board. In this case it would be wise to exact a tenure of four or five years.

Passing from the Administration of the United Kingdom to the State officers with Viceregal functions, it would do no harm to enumerate the Viceroy and Governor-General of India; the Governor-General of Canada; and the Lord-Lieutenant General and General-Governor of Ireland; although, as a fact, these offices are commonly bestowed on Peers. When Australian Federation has been accomplished, the Governor-General of Australia might be added. The Lord High Commissioner to the General Assembly of the Church of Scotland is not now an officer of much importance, but, since, in the event of Scottish Home Rule, he would probably resume his former functions as Lord High Commissioner to the Parliament of Scotland, it might not be altogether purposeless to include his office. In all these cases it would be unnecessary to specify the length of tenure.

To include the Governorships of Gibraltar and of Malta would provide a qualification for some distinguished military officers. In Asia, the office of Governor of Madras, Bombay, Ceylon, the Straits Settlements, or Hong Kong should surely qualify for a life-seat in the Senate of the Empire, and, perhaps, too, the Governorship of British North Borneo. In Africa, the Governor of the Cape, the Governor of Natal, the Governors of the Gold Coast, Lagos, Sierra Leone, St. Helena, and Mauritius would be included. In America, the Governorships of Newfoundland, Bermuda, British Honduras, British Guiana, the Falkland Islands, the Bahamas, the Windward Islands, the Leeward Islands, Barbados, and Trinidad, should qualify; and so, too, should the office of Captain-General and Governor-in-Chief of Jamaica. In Australasia, the Governor of New Zealand, the Governor of Fiji, the Governors of New South Wales, Victoria, South Australia, Queensland, Western Australia, and Tasmania, should receive a similar recognition. It would be necessary to exact a tenure of not less than two years, and it would be wise to exact a tenure of not less than three or four. If it be said that some of these places are of small importance, it must be replied that a Life Peers Bill would be permissive, not obligatory, as to its details; would establish a qualification, not a title or a claim; and that a large field of choice should be thrown open to the Crown.

With like provisions, there might be included the Lieutenant-Governor of Jersey, the Lieutenant-Governor of Guernsey, and the Lieutenant-Governor of the Isle of Man; the Lieutenant-Governors of Bengal, the Punjaub, and the North-West Provinces and Oudh; the Chief Commissioners for the Central Provinces, Burmah, and Assam; and the Lieutenant-Governor of any Province of the Dominion of Canada. To these there could be added, on Australian Federation, the Lieutenant-Governor of an Australian Province.

From a Governor or a Governor-General one passes naturally to his Ministers. In the United Kingdom the Privy Council has largely lost the position that it once held. The committee of the Privy Council known as the Cabinet is an inner circle of the Administration; and the committee of the Privy Council called Judicial is the supreme Court of Appeal for the whole of the British dominions outside Great Britain and Ireland. Membership of the Privy Council, apart from civil or judicial office, has become a distinction chiefly honorary. The Administration has been before considered, and Judges in general will be considered later on. But membership of the Judicial Committee should be a qualification for a life peerage in the same way as a Lordship of

X

Appeal, the appellate tribunal known as the House of Lords being to the United Kingdom what the Judicial Committee is to the remainder of the British Empire. For non-judicial members of the Privy Council possessing no other qualification it would be necessary to prescribe a membership of not less than ten years, so as to debar a Minister from rushing undistinguished partisans through the Privy Council into the House of Lords. Members of the Privy Council in Ireland would require to be dealt with on the same conditions.

The Privy Council in Canada is limited to Ministers and ex-Ministers, and provides, therefore, a *bonâ fide* qualification. In this case a five-years' membership would be sufficient as a test.

The Privy Council of India is to be found in the Council of the Governor-General and the Secretaries to the Indian Government. As appointment to these offices is never dictated by a Legislative Assembly, and those who hold them are chosen for their experience and capacity, the shorter term of three or four years would probably suffice. The Council of India, which assists the Secretary of State in London, is also composed of men selected for their special talent for good government, not by mere Parliamentary caprice. In this case, too, a service of three or four years might be sufficient, but it would be necessary to provide that membership of the Council of India should cease with creation as a Life Peer. Otherwise, the public might be confronted with the unseemly spectacle of the head of a Government department engaging in Parliamentary conflicts with his official subordinates.

In the Australian Colonies there is no common or Dominion Executive, any more than there is a common or Dominion Legislature. Until the further union of Australia, a ten-years' membership of the Executive Council of New South Wales, Victoria, South Australia, Queensland, Western Australia, or Tasmania, might be the limit and qualification. New Zealand is unlikely to join an Australian Dominion or Commonwealth, and a qualification of ten-years' membership of the Executive Council of that Colony could long remain unchanged.

The same qualification might extend to the Executive

Council of the Cape, and in British North America to the Executive Council of Newfoundland.

Canada and Newfoundland, the Australian Colonies and New Zealand, and the Cape are the only Colonies in which responsible government is established. Other Colonies, in the official sense of the word "Colonies," could find a sufficient representation in the life peerage of an ex-Governor. There is a Privy Council, however, in Jamaica, and, if it were thought desirable, membership of that body for five years might be made a qualification, as it is a working Council limited to the Executive.

From the Executive it is an easy transition to the Legislature. It is now the custom to create a retired Speaker of the House of Commons a Viscount. But this is a custom, nothing more; nor does it constitute any reason why a five-years' tenure of the same office should not form a legal qualification for a life peerage. This principle might be usefully extended to the Speaker of the Australian House of Representatives, when that body is established.

To allow a ten-years' membership of the Dominion Senate, and of the future Senate of Australia, to qualify for a life peerage, would throw open to the Crown a wide field of selection from among experienced and influential Colonists.

Turning, next, to the representatives of the Empire in foreign parts, it will scarcely be disputed that to have held the office of an Ambassador for two or three years, or of a Minister Plenipotentiary for four or five, should make a diplomatist eligible for a life peerage. Ambassadors and Ministers, the rulers of the Indian Provinces, and the Governors of those Colonies which are without responsible government, with their ripe and various experience of affairs usually conjoin the additional advantage of not being exclusively identified with either of the great historical parties in the United Kingdom.

Proceeding to the Judicature, to have been a Judge of a High Court of Justice in any portion of the British dominions for not less than five years should be a sufficient qualification for a life peerage. And this term might advantageously be shortened in the case of the Lord Chief Justice, Master of the Rolls, President of the Probate, Divorce, and Admiralty Division, Lords Justices of Appeal, and Judges of the High Court of Justice, in England: the Lord Justice General, Lord Justice Clerk, and Lords of Session, or Senators of the College of Justice, in Scotland: the Chief Justice, Master of the Rolls, Chief Baron of the Exchequer, Lords Justices of Appeal, and Judges of the High Court of Justice, in Ireland: and the Chief Justice and Judges of the Court of Appeal, and the Judge of the Exchequer Court for the Dominion, in Canada. In the Colonies, strikingly distinguished in this point from the United States, the Judges are, with rare exceptions, the most respected members of the community, and the most entirely worthy of respect. The acquaintance of Colonial Judges with the practical working of Colonial statutes, especially in relation to land, could not fail to be of service to the House of Lords. Judges, on the other hand, who had served in India, could lift a warning voice with profit and effect against the rash innovations, thoughtlessly and wantonly proposed by English agitators, in the immemorial usages and cherished customs of Hindu and Mohammedan society.

To have filled the office of High Commissioner for Canada, or Agent-General for an Australasian Colony, Newfoundland, or the Cape, for an unbroken term of not less than four years, should form a legal qualification for a life peerage. Of such a provision in a Life Peers Act advantage would, no doubt, be taken in cases where the Agent-General of an important Colony had discharged his duties with more than usual credit and success.

In making the Governorship of Malta, Gibraltar, or Bermuda a qualification for a life peerage, provision has been made for the appearance of distinguished soldiers in a reformed House of Lords. Following the Spanish Senate—a less inapposite example than the American—in spirit, though not in letter, the rank of a Field-Marshal, apart from any length of tenure, should in itself constitute a qualification. A tenure of two years might be demanded from the Adjutant-

General and Quartermaster-General; while, as a matter of form, appointment to the command in chief of the forces should be a qualification equal to promotion to the rank of Field-Marshal. To have held for two years the command of the forces in Ireland; the office of Commander-in-chief in India, or Commander-in-chief in Madras or Bombay—till these separate commands are abolished;—the command of the forces in South Africa, the West Indies, or North America; or the command of the Canadian Militia, should qualify for a life peerage. And so should the command for two years of the defence forces of Australia, when the jealousy and vanity of parochial politicians permit Australia to be united. Officers, qualified by having held command in such different portions of the Empire, could address the whole nation with authority and weight from the Second Chamber of the Imperial Parliament, on the right application of local resources and the common necessities of Imperial defence.

The corresponding rank in the Navy to that of Field-Marshal in the Army is the rank of Admiral of the Fleet. Putting Admirals of the Fleet on the same footing as Field-Marshals, we can find a fair equivalent of the various general officers with extensive local command in the Admirals, Vice-Admirals, and Rear-Admirals commanding a Royal Naval squadron. To have held such a command for two years should qualify in the same way as with the sister branch of the United Service.

The representation of literature, science, and art in a Life Peerage, however attractive in idea, would be a matter of greater difficulty than is commonly imagined. No such body exists in London as the French Academy. In science it is possible to derive some help from the Royal Society, and in art there is the Royal Academy; but in literature there is no official guarantee of excellence. In Canada the Royal Society, suggested doubtless by the French Institute, includes a branch of Letters, with French and English sections; but there is nothing of the kind to be found elsewhere in the British Empire.

With regard to science, it might be laid down that to have

been a Fellow of the Royal Society for ten years, or to have filled the office of President of the Royal Society, President of the Royal Society of Edinburgh, President of the Royal Society of Dublin, or President of the Royal Society of Canada, should qualify for a life peerage. Possibly Astronomers Royal, who had held their position for a certain term of years, might be included.

The annoyance, expressed by many members of the medical profession, that no State recognition of sufficient weight or value has as yet been bestowed on their high and honourable calling, might be removed or mitigated by making the presidency of their corporations a sufficient qualification for a life peerage. To have been President of the Royal College of Surgeons, or the Royal College of Physicians ; of the Royal College of Physicians of Edinburgh, or the Royal College of Surgeons of Edinburgh ; of the King's and Queen's College of Physicians of Ireland, or the Royal College of Surgeons of Ireland, should supply a sufficient test of eminence in the medical profession. To this there might be added the having held for not less than one year the post of Physician or Sergeant Surgeon to the Queen, and the having held for not less than two years the post of Physician or Surgeon Extraordinary to Her Majesty.

In the other departments of applied science it is only possible to particularize the President of the Institute of Civil Engineers.

With regard to art, it is impossible to apply any other test of eminence than that of officially recognized position. To have been a member of the Royal Academy for ten years, or to be or have been President of the Royal Scottish, the Royal Hibernian, or the Royal Canadian, Academy of the Fine Arts should be a qualification. With painting, sculpture, and architecture, as with music, literature, and the drama, all the talent both of the British Isles and British Colonies naturally and inevitably gravitates to the common centre of the capital city of the Empire. Madame Albani and Madame Melba on the stage find their less renowned masculine counterparts in other branches of art, and in literature and science ; and the

Royal Academy and Royal Society of London are not only English, but British and Imperial.

The representation of literature would be a matter of more serious difficulty. No such tests exist as in the case of science and art. It is impossible to assess intellectual eminence, and in the absence of such a tangible and definite test, as is provided in France by the Academy, the Ministers of the Crown would have no lights to steer by. Appointment to the post of Poet Laureate should certainly qualify, and so might appointment to the post of the Queen's Historiographer in Scotland. But beyond this there is nothing definite to go upon, no fixed authority whose decisions command respect, nor indeed any authority at all. Public opinion, being without a guide, is of course chaotic, unreliable, and irresponsible. Even if popular taste were worth consulting, which has never been established, there would be much difficulty in clearly ascertaining its decisions. It would be impossible for a Ministry to have resort to a plebiscite of the readers of the evening papers. A popular vote would probably have installed Robert Montgomery or Martin Tupper as Poet Laureate; it would certainly prefer Mr. Sims to Mr. Swinburne. That the judgment of Ministers may be at fault, we know from the famous instance of the "poet case." And the popular judgment is not more hopelessly wrong than the judgment of experts. All the world has smiled at Byron's critical pyramid, and at the estimate formed by Wordsworth of his contemporaries. In allotting to authors their true place in our literature it takes a long time, a very long time, to get the right perspective. Seldom or never are authors accurately measured in their own lifetime, and that generations afterwards the most competent critics may still stray, from one cause or another, we are reminded by the pronouncements of Mr. Swinburne on Byron, and of Matthew Arnold on Dryden and Pope. The verdicts of one generation are reversed by the next, and a truly great critic is almost as rare a being as a truly great poet. If we adopted the loose Italian qualification, and left the matter to the inscrutable workings of public opinion, we should have people coming forward, like

Mr. Lewis Morris, with certificates of inspiration from popular politicians like the late Mr. Bright, and perhaps from popular divines like the late Mr. Spurgeon. Literature would not be crowned, but the advocacy of some political or religious dogma.

It is not every man of letters who would be in place in the House of Lords. Lord Lytton and Lord Beaconsfield were men of letters, but so were Coleridge and Keats. Even the strange people who invite us to admire Shelley, not only as a great poet, but also as a model of domestic virtue, would scarcely urge his fitness as a politician. Macaulay or Grote or John Stuart Mill would be eminently useful in a Second Chamber, but not Mr. Ruskin or Carlyle. Anthony Trollope unfortunately failed to engulf himself in the House of Commons, but it would have been a national misfortune had Thackeray been elected when he stood for Oxford. In creating men of letters Life Peers the nicest discrimination would be needed, and it would almost certainly be wanting.

But, although literary eminence is a qualification so entirely vague as to be wholly inadmissible, it would be possible to do something for the direct representation of higher education, and thus indirectly for the representation of letters. Nearly all the Universities have for their Chancellors members of the House of Lords, and some of them are represented also in the House of Commons. The Chancellors of the Universities of Oxford, Cambridge, London, St. Andrew's, Glasgow, and Aberdeen, are the Marquis of Salisbury, the Duke of Devonshire, the Earl of Derby, the Duke of Argyll, the Earl of Stair, the Duke of Richmond and Gordon. The Earl of Rosse, an Irish Representative Peer, is the Chancellor of Dublin; and Lord Dufferin is Chancellor of the Royal University of Ireland. Oxford, Cambridge, and Dublin, each return two members to the House of Commons, London returns one member, and the four Scottish Universities return two members between them. But it is more than probable that "University members" will ere long disappear. It is as difficult to justify their presence in the House of Commons on practical grounds as it is to do so in theory. There is nothing, indeed, in the favourite Radical charge that they do not return University Professors. It should be counted unto them for righteousness that they do not. The proper sphere of influence for a University Professor is to be found in his University. But why should the Universities be represented directly in the House of Commons any more than the Army and Navy or the public schools? Why should Oxford be favoured rather than Eton, or Cambridge rather than Woolwich? Why should the Universities possess a special representation more than the Royal Society or any other learned body? The practical effect is at Oxford and Cambridge to give an illusory and ineffectual representation to the Anglican clergy, and in Scotland and Ireland to provide so many cities of refuge for the law officers of the Crown when the Conservatives happen to be in office. University members prejudice the constituencies against the Tory party. They are one of those small and unprofitable abuses which nevertheless rankle in the public mind.

A University should be represented in the House of Lords. It is an aristocratic, not a democratic, constituency, and should be represented in the aristocratic Chamber. University graduates should have a vote for the Upper House of any local Legislature that may be established in England, Scotland, or Ireland. But "University Members," in the Imperial House of Commons, ought to be, and will be, abolished. The right of returning members was originally conferred on Oxford and Cambridge by King James the First and Sixth, but now—

"the London University actually returns a member to the House of Commons, though this institution is nothing but a great machine for conducting examinations." *

If the University of London returns a member, why should not Durham and the Victoria University? And, with Imperial Federation, why not some of the many Universities in the Colonies? But the Colonies would never consent to such a blemish and absurdity, either in the case of their own, or of the Home Universities. "University members" will

* Professor Seeley.

be swept away by the onward march of democracy, and it would be a wise and gracious act on the part of the Universities to petition for their own disfranchisement.

The Universities should be represented in the House of Lords. They are represented in some sort by the Peers whom they elect for their Chancellors, but they should be represented more effectually, and by men in closer touch, and more intimate connection, with University affairs. The Chancellor of a University in the British Isles plays the part of "a Constitutional Sovereign," according to the ultra-Liberal caricature of such a potentate. For the more effectual representation of the Universities, any person who had held the office of Vice-Chancellor for not less than two years should be made eligible for creation as a Life Peer. As a matter of form, the Chancellors should be included, and at Oxford and Cambridge the High Steward, an ornamental functionary who is, however, usually a Peer. At each of the four Scottish Universities, besides the Chancellor and the Vice-Chancellor, there is an officer known as the Lord Rector, who is elected, for two or three years, by the students of the University. Sometimes a prominent politician is chosen, but sometimes a man of science or letters. The inclusion of the Lord Rector would provide a definite qualification for distinguished men of letters. To be Chancellor, then, or to have been for two years Vice-Chancellor, of the University of Oxford, Cambridge, London, St. Andrew's, Aberdeen, Glasgow, Edinburgh, or Dublin; the Victoria University, Manchester; or the Royal University of Ireland: to be High Steward of the University of Oxford or Cambridge: or to have been Lord Rector of a Scottish University, should qualify for a life peerage. The University of Durham has no Chancellor.

In the Colonies, the Chancellor often takes a more active part in the government of the University than in the British Isles. Such Universities as those of Melbourne, Sydney, Adelaide, Toronto, and the Cape might be included by name in a Life Peers Bill. In Australia the University is considered to belong to the State, and is therefore neutral in matters of religion, though colleges for the residence of students in connection with the different denominations are freely permitted and encouraged. This is not the case everywhere in Canada, and the unfortunate influence of the United States has led some of the Provincial Legislators to endow with University powers wretched hole-in-the-corner little institutions under the exclusive control of some religious sect. This observation is not, of course, intended to apply to the great Roman Catholic University of Quebec in the French and Gallican Province of Lower Canada. Some effort has latterly been made to absorb these small sectarian institutions, so detrimental to the interests of culture, into the University of Toronto. If a clause were inserted in a Life Peers Bill, giving the Crown power to qualify the Chancellors and Vice-Chancellors of Universities to which this section of the Act should be extended by Order in Council, and if such power were wisely exercised, the whole higher education of the Empire might be influenced for good.

There are Universities in India, and the presence in the House of Lords of one or two distinguished Orientalists might be of advantage both to politics and Asiatic studies. But, since no means so effectual to scare the Colonies from Imperial Federation could be devised by human ingenuity, as the suggestion that they might be called upon to share their Imperial enfranchisement with East or West Indians, Africans or Asiatics, it would be well to avoid even the appearance of evil. The Indian Universities, moreover, are alien importations, not rooted in the soil, but planted and maintained by ourselves, and it is held by high authority that they have done much harm in giving a wrong direction to the mental activity of a certain class of natives. To include the Indian Universities, but exclude natives of India, would be a gratuitously offensive piece of legislation.

Inadequate and unsatisfactory as it must seem, this system of qualification through office in an University is the only method by which representation could be given to Letters in a Life Peerage.

From literature, science, and art, it is perhaps a descent to finance, and the lofty-souled Americans, quoted by Professor Bryce, would, no doubt, turn up their noses at anything so vulgar as the Bank of England. Nevertheless, since the conduct of this institution has on more than one occasion vitally affected the credit of the community, it might not be amiss for us poor folk who have not the honour to belong to the *haut monde* of Philadelphia, and the Faubourg St. Germain of the Fifth Avenue, to recognize this fact, in our low, plebeian fashion, by making an ex-Governor or ex-Director of the Bank of England eligible for a life peerage.

The revival and extension of municipal self-government in the British Isles has to some extent been attended by its elevation. The chief magistrate of the common capital of the English Kingdom and the British Empire, having fulfilled his year of office, should be eligible for a life peerage; and to the Lord Mayor of London should be joined the Lord Provost of Edinburgh, and the Lord Mayor of Dublin. The great centres of commerce and industry in the United Kingdom might be appropriately honoured by the addition to this list of the Mayors of Liverpool, Manchester, Birmingham, Newcastle, and Belfast, and the Provost of Glasgow. An honourable local pride would be flattered, and a commendable spirit of emulation would be encouraged, by the inclusion of the Mayor of Ottawa, the Mayor of the capital city of each Province of the Dominion of Canada, and the Mayor of Montreal; the Mayor of St. John's, Newfoundland, and the Mayor of Wellington, New Zealand; the chief magistrate of Capetown; and the Mayor of each of the Australian capitals, Sydney, Melbourne, Hobart, Adelaide, Brisbane, and Perth. It might be advisable in a Life Peers Bill to empower the Crown to extend this qualification, by Order in Council, to the Mayor of any city in the Empire with not less than five hundred thousand inhabitants at the previous census.

The inclusion in a Life Peers Bill of the Mayors of Colonial cities; the Chancellors of Colonial Universities; Colonial Judges; the Senators and Privy Councillors of Canada; the

Speaker of the Dominion House of Commons; the Lieutenant-Governors of the Canadian Provinces; the Governors and Executive Councillors of the Australian Colonies, New Zealand, Newfoundland, and the Cape, would give full scope for the introduction into the House of Lords of the Notables of Greater Britain, ere Colonists can be created hereditary Peers in sufficient strength to adequately represent the Colonies, and in anticipation of the Imperial Parliamentary Union of the whole British nation.

The Governors of Colonies without responsible government, the members of the Indian Government, the Lieutenant-Governors and Chief Commissioners of Indian Provinces would represent the Imperial interests of Britain in Africa and Asia. The naval and military officers would express the unity of the Empire in matters of defence, and the diplomatists the balance of her policy and the essential oneness of her interests in every quarter of the globe. The representation of science and art, and, if not of literature itself, at least of literary culture, would give play to an elevating and liberalizing influence as different as possible from the mean and narrow parochialism of a County Council. Art loves to depict the great thoughts and noble ambitions of the founders and champions of Empire, not the sordid and ignoble miscalculations of pedlars whom the irony of Fate may place in power. It is the progress and discoveries of modern science that have alone made the modern Empire possible, and that form the pledge of its perpetual union. In the whole range of English literature there is no such patriot as Shakespeare, nor any Imperialist so fervid and impassioned as, in his own way, was Milton.

The introduction into the House of Lords of Life Peers, of such qualifications as have been briefly outlined, would be a reform altogether different in effect and character from the election of the Second Chamber, in whole or part, by the County Councils of the United Kingdom, or the local Legislatures of the British Empire. Apart from the other evils of the latter system, the election by any local bodies would probably resolve itself in fact into election by the party wirepullers of the British Isles. The scheme which has been considered, on the other hand, would aim, not at the further representation of party, but at finding a more effectual representation than that now afforded, in some measure, by the House of Lords to those great national and Imperial interests, which in the contests of parties are too often overlooked. Instead of deriving its origin from a misunderstanding of the American Senate, it is the logical development and fulfilment of a tendency already existing in the modern Peerage. The propriety and necessity of a class of life peerages is shown by the established practice of bestowing hereditary peerages on men of Senatorial qualification who are without children. That a Senatorial tenure can be substituted for a Baronial, where there exists a Senatorial qualification, without detriment to the Peerage, or disadvantage to the House of Lords, has been shown by the successful experiment in the case of the Lords of Appeal. To follow the example of the Lords of Appeal too exactly, would be to unnecessarily and unwisely limit the discretion of the Crown, and, unless on a scale too minute to be appreciated, would choke up the House of Lords with members sitting *ex officio*. To have all the English Judges, or all the Under Secretaries of State, sitting *ex officio* in the Second Chamber, would be to narrow, not enlarge, the House of Lords. What is needed is a greater variety of representation, a greater degree of elasticity in the Peerage system, not a mere change of limitations. This variety and elasticity is not to be arrived at by pinning a life seat in the House of Lords to a particular office, an Agency-General, or the permanent headship of a department. A rigidity of this kind would be no improvement on the rigidity that now exists: instead of being any better, it would be a great deal worse, for while selection is of the essence of a Senate, heredity is of the essence of a Baronage. An heredity of representation attaching to the office, not the family, is none the less an heredity of representation. It makes a Peerage of succession, though not a Peerage of descent. A new order of the hereditary legislatorship of bureaucrats would meet no want, and would cause just and universal dissatisfaction. The Lords of Appeal now retain their seats after laying down their office. This makes them Life Peers, Peers with a Senatorial qualification and a Senatorial tenure. But before this they were Official Peers, Peers with a Senatorial qualification, but an Official tenure; and, even so, every Lord of Appeal is *ex officio* created a Life Peer. In the case of the Lords of Appeal, members of the appellate tribunal of the House of Lords, this may be right and necessary; but it is not necessary in the other cases which we have considered, and it would prove extremely mischievous. What is wanted, is not Life Peers *ex officio*, but Life Peers qualified by office: not life peerages tied up with this or that office, but life peerages bestowed at the discretion of the Crown on persons qualified by having held such offices. A definite test and fixed qualification is required for Life Peers, so that they may not be perverted into a mere engine of partisan warfare, and a weapon for an arbitrary Minister. This test of fitness is to be secured by attaching it to the tenure of certain offices. Variety and elasticity are to be secured by the number of the offices thus qualifying, the length of tenure required in some cases preventing fraud and trickery; and by making the tenure of such offices to constitute a qualification, but not a title or a claim.

The other needful restraint on the power of creating Life Peers is to be found in affixing a limit to their numbers. It would be necessary to provide that a maximum should not be exceeded, nor more than a certain number created in each year. In the first instance, it might be wise to fix the maximum at fifty, and to ordain that not more than five should be created in one year, including those, if any, created to fill vacancies. Later on, when the system had been in operation for some time, it is possible that the Peers would be willing to consent to an increase of the total to one hundred, and to allow vacancies to be filled as they occurred. But the number of a hundred must be regarded as the extreme and final limit, beyond which it would never be advisable to go.

CHAPTER III.

HEREDITARY PEERS.

THE enlargement of the class of Life Peers, at present limited to the Lords and ex-Lords of Appeal, though on another and less rigid basis, would be a reform of the House of Lords, but it would be a reform of addition, not a reform in the structure of the normal Lords Temporal. A new class of life members would be established, or the existing class would be extended; but the Peers of England and the Union would be unaffected, and so, too, would the Representative Peers of Scotland and Ireland. Yet here again, as we have seen, there is great need for reform. The whole five Peerages of England, Scotland, Great Britain, Ireland, and Great Britain and Ireland, ought to be amalgamated in one Imperial Peerage of the United Kingdom of the British nation. And to some extent this has been taking place. As the tendency towards life peerages may be traced in the peerages of the Lords of Appeal, and the increasing number of normal Union peerages bestowed on men without heirs, so a tendency towards amalgamation has been shown in the increasing number of Union peerages bestowed on Peers of Scotland and Ireland. Two only of the Scottish Peers, the Dukes of Lennox and Buccleuch, have English peerages that were united with their Scottish dignities before the Union; though the Earldom of Loudoun was united with the ancient Barony of Botreaux in 1871, the latter being then called out of abeyance. Eleven Peers of Scotland are entitled to sit in person in the House of Lords in virtue of Great British Peerages dating from 1711 to 1796. But thirty-six Peers of Scotland have, partly by inheritance, but chiefly by creation, been absorbed into the House of Lords from 1808 to 1887. So, of the eighty-seven Irish Peers in the Second Chamber, independently of the Representative Peers system, fifty-eight received the peerages which give them seats during the present century. Still there are eighty-nine Peers of Ireland dependent on representation; and thirty-seven Peers of Scotland, including three Peeresses, in the same predicament. Sir Erskine May, in his "Constitutional History," expresses the opinion, that "at no distant date the Scottish Peerage will probably become absorbed in that of the United Kingdom." But this belief was far too sanguine. Many Scottish peerages, as we saw in the first chapter, come into families through heiresses and pass out of them again in the same manner, while United Kingdom peerages almost invariably pass through males exclusively. A Union peerage is necessarily of much later creation than a Scottish peerage, and there are consequently a far greater number of persons in remainder to the latter than in remainder to the former. Scottish peerages are often for a time united with an English or a Union peerage, and afterwards again disunited. Some examples of this process were given before, and more may be added. Thus the ninth Earl of Dalhousie was created a Baron of the United Kingdom in 1815, and the second Baron was created a Marquis in 1849, but on the death of the latter in 1862, both Barony and Marquisate became extinct. The twelfth Earl of Dalhousie was created Baron Ramsay in the Peerage of the United Kingdom in 1875. The second Duke of Argyll was created Duke of Greenwich in 1719, and before that had been created Earl of Greenwich and Lord Chatham, but these peerages died with him in 1743. The present Duke of Argyll took his seat in the House of Lords as Baron Sundridge of 1766. The second Duke of Athole took his seat in the House of Lords in 1737 in virtue of the English Barony of Strange, but on his death in 1764 this Barony passed to his daughter who had previously married the third Duke of Athole. The fourth Duke was created Earl Strange in 1786, and succeeded to the Barony on the death of his mother in 1805. The only way, in which a Peer of Scotland can be permanently absorbed into the Union Peerage, is by limiting his United Kingdom peerage in exactly the same line of succession as his peerage of Scotland; that is to say, the only way in which the Peerage of Scotland can be permanently absorbed, is by making all Peers of Scotland Peers of the United Kingdom. The only solution is to deal with them as a body, by Legislation; and not individually, by separate creations. Otherwise they would be perpetually cropping up. Besides the actually current peerages of Scotland, there are no less than forty more liable to be revived, though at the present time dormant or attainted, from which, however, three, having already been revived in another form, may be subtracted. In the absence of special legislation, there is no probability that the Peerage of Scotland will "at no distant date become absorbed in that of the United Kingdom." The difference in rights between Peers of Scotland and Peers of England or Great Britain is purely historical in character. It had its origin in a cause which has long since disappeared, and now that the cause has disappeared, the effect ought to follow it.

Nor will the Peerage of Ireland "become absorbed at no distant date in the Peerage of the United Kingdom." The reasoning which applies to the Peerage of Scotland applies with almost as much force to the Peerage of Ireland. And in the latter case, there is another reason for reform, in the fact that Irish peerages may still be lawfully created. It was expressly prescribed at the Union that the number of Irish Peers should be kept up to a hundred, irrespective and exclusive of those also in the Union Peerage; and, although the rule appears to have fallen into desuetude, this alone would make legislation about them necessary.

If the Representative Peers system were taken advantage of to its full extent, there would still be a good many Scottish and Irish Peers left out of Parliament. But it is not so taken advantage of. In the Parliament of July, 1886, the Earl of Strathmore, although created a Baron of the United Kingdom

CHAP. III.]   THE IRISH PEERAGE.   323

in 1887 as Lord Bowes, continued to sit as a Representative Peer of Scotland ; and Viscount Hawarden (Earl de Montalt) and Viscount Powerscourt (Lord Powerscourt), although Peers of the United Kingdom, sat as Representative Peers of Ireland. Thus one Peer of Scotland and two Peers of Ireland were unnecessarily and unjustly hindered from sitting in the House of Lords. A Scottish or Irish Peer who acquires a peerage of England or the Union by creation or inheritance, does not become ineligible to represent the Peers of Scotland or Ireland, nor does he lose his vote for the Representative Peers. In this way those Peers who sit in their own right in the House of Lords, can exclude their less fortunately situated fellows from any true representation. That which was originally intended for the representation of the Scottish and Irish Peerages, has been perverted into a means of nullifying the representation of all Scottish or Irish Peers who are not also Peers of England or the Union. It is manifestly absurd that a Peer who sits in his own person in the House of Lords should elect another Peer to 'represent him over again. He is not in the position of a member of the House of Commons voting for another candidate for that assembly. He is his own constituency, and represents himself. It is absurd that he should be represented twice over. A Peer of England or the Union, who is a Peer both of Scotland and Ireland like the Duke of Abercorn and Lord Verulam, can, if he pleases, be represented three times over in the House of Lords, once by himself, and twice by other people. The differences between one Peer and any other are not so great as to justify such imparities as these. This extravagant species of plural voting would be ridiculous enough if it worked no actual harm, but seeing that the effect is to deprive ordinary Peers of Scotland or Ireland of their representation, and to cancel or neutralize their votes, it cannot be too emphatically condemned. A Peer of Scotland, who is not also a Peer of England or the Union, and who is not chosen as a representative Peer, is excluded from Parliament altogether. It is monstrous that he should be excluded by the votes of Peers who enjoy seats independent of election. The Representative Peers system was expressly devised for the benefit of Peers of Scotland who were not Peers of England or the Union, because they were not Peers of England or the Union. It is a flagrant abuse that Peers of Scotland who have acquired the full rights of Union Peers should continue to exercise the rights of Scottish Peers, and should exercise them to the detriment of their less favoured fellows. And this is equally true, *mutatis mutandis*, of the Peers of Ireland.

At the present day, when no real difference exists between Scottish and Irish Peers and Peers of the Union, when so many of the former have been absorbed, at least for the time, into the latter, the Representative Peers system is an unjust and offensive anachronism. The whole five Peerages should be amalgamated and placed on the same footing. Peers of Scotland and Ireland should sit in the House of Lords under their proper titles, and not assume inferior rank like a crowned head travelling *incognito*. The House of Lords, like the House of Commons, belongs to Scotland and Ireland just as much as to England: and the Peers of any one of the three ancient kingdoms are as much entitled to sit in it as the Peers of any other. To put Scottish and Irish Peers on the same footing as Peers of England, Great Britain, and Great Britain and Ireland should be accepted by Unionists as a measure of Union ; and by Home Rulers as disposing of any claim on their part to form the Second Chamber of a local Legislature.

In an amalgamation of the Peerages, it would not be necessary to destroy the historical distinction between Peers of Ireland and other Peers, though it would be necessary to provide that no more Peers of Ireland should be created, any more than Peers of England, Scotland, or Great Britain. For the future all new Peers would be Peers of Great Britain and Ireland ; but for the union of the Peerages it would be sufficient to enact that any Peer of Scotland or Ireland succeeding to his peerage after a given date should be entitled to receive a writ of summons, in the same way, and on the same conditions, as a Peer of England or the Union. There would be no occasion whatever suddenly to flood the House of Lords with all the Scottish and Irish Peers, who are neither Peers of the Union nor Representatives of their own Peerage. The process of amalgamation would take place gently and gradually, not with any violent disturbance. It would be the logical fulfilment and systematic development of tendencies already actively at work, the tendency towards amalgamation shown by the increased number of Union peerages bestowed on Scottish and Irish Peers, and the same tendency displayed in a slightly different form by the cessation since 1868 of the creation of new Irish peerages. Whatever other reforms may be adopted or rejected, all hereditary Peers should be put on the same footing, and this could be effected easily and quietly by the almost imperceptible operation of such a measure as has here been sketched.

But although the Representative system, as applied to Scottish and Irish Peers, ought to be abolished, in another way it should be applied more widely. Although all hereditary Peers should be placed on the same footing, this is not to say that all, or any, hereditary Peers should be hereditary legislators. That hereditary legislatorship is no necessary incident of an hereditary peerage, we can see from the example of the Scottish and Irish Peers. Since the Radical objection is to hereditary legislators, it might not be unwise to take them at their word, and for hereditary legislators to substitute elected legislators, hereditary Peers elected by the members of their own order. The great complaint of the Radicals against the House of Lords is that it is a House of hereditary legislators. Now this, as we saw, is only partly true; but that is no reason why it should not be made untrue altogether. And there are other and more weighty arguments for loosening the hitherto indissoluble connection between a peerage of England or the Union, and a right to sit in person in the House of Lords. In the first place, there is the fact that the Peerage is becoming Senatorial in character as regards qualifications, and that a Senatorial qualification calls for a Senatorial, instead of a Baronial, tenure.

Now, heredity is of the essence of Baronage, but selection is of the essence of a Senate. If hereditary Peers are to form an element in the Second Chamber, then the hereditary Peerage must for this purpose be subjected to the test of a further selection, either by the Crown, or by itself, or by both. To develop the Senatorial aspect of the House of Lords, there is no need whatever to abolish the hereditary Peerage, or to stop the further creation of hereditary Peers. All that is required is that Peers who have inherited a peerage should be submitted to a test of personal fitness for legislatorship— a test to be supplied, either by qualification through office, and the consequent nomination of the Sovereign, or by election by their fellows. It cannot be pretended that the application of such tests to the Union and English Peers is any derogation to their Peerage, for the latter of these tests has been applied for nearly two centuries to the Peerage of Scotland; and a method of representation, that is good enough for a Scottish Lord with three or four centuries of peerage and five or six of nobility, is good enough and to spare for the grandson of an English cotton-spinner. It is impossible to maintain that a man, whose father was created a Peer twenty or thirty years back, after filling a subordinate post in an Administration that was certainly not "epoch making," has a better title to a seat in the House of Lords, independent of election, than the holders of peerages of such antiquity as the Earldom of Mar and the Earldom of Caithness, of such historic fame as the Earldom of Rothes and the Earldom of Morton, the Earldom of Dundonald, and the Viscounty of Falkland. That a man has done good service, though not great service, to the country in very recent times, may be an excellent reason for his own seat in the House of Lords, may be an excellent reason for the hereditary peerage enjoyed by his descendants; but it is no reason whatever why these latter should be privileged to the disadvantage of those, whose names are identified through centuries with the national life and historic greatness of the country. The Peerage is becoming Senatorial in the character of its qualification, and the tenure of seats in the

House of Lords by hereditary Peers should become Senatorial in character likewise. To reform the House of Lords, while maintaining and fortifying the hereditary Peerage, it is necessary that the hereditary Peers should consent to be represented in the Second Chamber by those members of their order only who possess a Senatorial qualification.

The great multiplication of the Union Peerage in modern times is another reason why all such Peers should not, as a matter of course, be entitled to sit in the Upper House. The Lords Temporal have become too numerous for a Legislative Chamber, while they are still far too few to include even the heads of the nobility. The multiplication of the Peerage proceeds apace, and shows no sign of slackening. The very numbers of the Peers will shortly necessitate a revision of the tenure of their seats. The great and growing number of Peers, entitled to sit in the House of Lords, increases the public scandal of the paucity in number of the Peers who habitually discharge their legislative duties, and the infinity in number of the Peers who, on occasion, exercise their legislative rights to the discomfiture of the Liberal party in Great Britain. This scandal was felt long ago.

"The political weight of the House of Peers," wrote Sir Erskine May, " has been much affected by the passive indifference which it ordinarily displays to the business of legislation. The constitution of that assembly, and the social position of its members, have failed to excite the spirit and activity which mark a representative body. This is constantly made apparent by the small number of Peers who attend its deliberations. Unless great party questions have been under discussion, the House has ordinarily presented the appearance of a select committee. The indifference," he adds, " of the great body of the Peers to public business, and their scanty attendance, by discouraging the efforts of the more able and ambitious among them, further impair the influence of the Upper House." *

These evils, conspicuous when Erskine May published his history, have greatly increased in the thirty years that have since elapsed. A new Peer usually attends the Upper Chamber with some diligence, but his successor, who, having inherited his seat, is therefore an hereditary legislator, is

* " Constitutional History."

not, as a rule, an *habitué* of the House of Lords. The fact that so many Peers entitled to sit in the House appear to regard themselves as possessing a right that entails no corresponding duties, gives wide and just offence, and greatly weakens the influence of the House of Lords upon the nation.

The establishment of a large number of life peerages would provide a means for the more direct representation of the Colonies, but this representation would lose much of its effect if there is no change in the tenure of their seats by the hereditary Peers. Without such change the life Peers would form too small a proportion of the whole. The materials at present existing in the Colonies for an hereditary Peerage are scanty and deficient, but in the course of time and by degrees a number of Peers may be established in the Colonies. Unless the sessions of the Imperial Parliament are very greatly shortened, it will be necessary to allow these Colonist Peers to be represented by a portion of their number. Otherwise they will either remain away from Westminster, in which case the Colonies would lose their representation, or else, by becoming absentees, they will gradually lose all weight in their Colonies.

Not only does the vivid contrast between the number of Peers who show strong party spirit, and the number of Peers who show strong public spirit, undermine the position of the House of Lords in public favour, but the fact that no Peer can divest himself of his seat in the Upper Chamber, nor be divested of it by his fellows, tells against the House of Lords. Every error of taste or judgment, on the part of a person with a handle to his name, is by ignorant or malevolent people in the lower strata of society placed to the account of the House of Lords. The popular mind confounds the House of Lords with the Peerage, and the Peerage with the titled aristocracy. Consequently, every titled person, whose private affairs attract unfavourable public notice, is used by the more unscrupulous Radicals as an argument against a Second Chamber. And Radical writers and speakers of a better kind, who ought to be above all such devices, do not hesitate to take advantage of popular ignorance, and to ask their audience what they think of a House with Lord Blank in it, though Lord Blank may never have been near the House of Lords since the day he took his seat. A Peer who takes no part in politics, and has never taken part in them, is warned off the turf, and promptly the Radicals begin to argue that their measures are thrown out in the Second Chamber by a majority of blacklegs and swindlers. This, no doubt, is a flagrantly and flagitiously dishonest argument, but, unfortunately, it is an argument that tells. If you reply that such a Peer never sits or votes in the House of Lords, the answer is ready that there is nothing to prevent him from doing so. And the answer is true. Peers who have been warned off the turf—if they exist in the plural number—as a fact never do vote; but they are still members of the House of Lords. Now, if all Peers, not otherwise qualified for a seat in the Upper Chamber, were submitted to the test of the Representative Peers system, Peers who had brought discredit on their order would never be elected. "The fierce light that beats upon a throne" beats also on a seat in the House of Lords, and even on a baronetcy. A number of journals have no other reason of existence than to chronicle the deeds and misdeeds of distinguished members of society, and in the daily press many papers are only too ready to minister to a diseased appetite for scandal. Every titled person who becomes unpleasantly conspicuous brings discredit on the House of Lords.

As for the melodramatic rubbish about "the wicked nobleman," and the paradoxical distinctions made by the unwritten code of Society between various moral delinquencies, the latter may be contemptuously disregarded, and to the former it is sufficient to reply that the House of Lords is not the House of God, and does not pretend to be that which it is not. If there are black sheep in the Second Chamber, they have at least the redeeming virtue of abstaining from clothing themselves in the garb of moral reformers. And if Peers are to be disqualified to sit in the House of Lords for breaches of the Seventh Commandment, then, admitting the validity of Lord Rosebery's argument with regard to election by constituencies, Peers so disqualified should be allowed to stand for election to the House of Commons. Immorality, in the more restricted sense in which that word is used by Society in this connection, is no evidence whatever of political incapacity or intellectual weakness, nor does it necessarily imply personal dishonour. Without going so far as the Frenchman who declared that without the defects the qualities would be impossible, it is permissible to point to the great natural law of compensation which forbids either a nation or a man to present a complete uniform type of human excellence. There is no necessary connection between private virtue and public virtue, private vice and public immorality. Some of the best and greatest public men in our history have had liaisons. A proposal to disqualify Wellington or Nelson would commend itself to no sane and healthy mind. The great men who founded the British Empire in the eighteenth century, and maintained it into the nineteenth, were men of splendid virtues and magnificent vices. Unfortunately we are living in a Lilliputian age, when men seek to dwarf everything down to their own level, and there are those who, in the nominal interest of public morality, but really to gratify some personal or private grudge, would rejoice to "condemn Manlius in sight of the Capitol, and Scipio on the anniversary of Zama." It is reported of Lord Bolingbroke that, when some wretched scandalmonger of the period sought to find favour with him by speaking of the avarice of Marlborough, the Tory statesman finely replied, "He was so great a man that I had forgotten that he had that failing." But now the failings of a great man are the only things about him that are noted. Sheridan is remembered only by his duns, Burns by his whiskey, Coleridge by his opium. The spirit is still alive that refused Byron a resting-place in Westminster Abbey—Byron, whose monument is re-arisen Greece, and whose works will continue to delight millions when the Abbey has crumbled into dust, and the last Dean and Chapter have been long buried and forgotten.

It is perhaps not unprofitable to call to mind the famous

saying of Prince Talleyrand, *Les pères de famille sont capables de tout*. Certain it is that domestic virtue is the refuge of those who have nothing else to fall back upon, and that the ascendency of *la morale bourgeoise* has always and everywhere coincided with a decay of public spirit. To allow no Peer to take his seat "except the House be satisfied of his godliness," is a proposal which does not need to be seriously considered. But, although no moral censorship of the Puritan description is admissible, there should be some means by which Peers who have incurred deserved obloquy should be excluded from the House of Lords. Even if peers ought not to lose their seats for immorality, they ought most certainly to lose their seats for conduct which in the Army would forfeit a commission. And this would be insured by a system of election. With such a system, Peers who had compromised the reputation of their order would be quietly unseated at the next election, or would anticipate such an event by previous resignation. A Representative Peers system would in an inoffensive and unostentatious manner serve every good end of a formal moral censorship, without being liable to be abused, as the latter system would be beyond all doubt, for party purposes. The dignity and honour of the House of Lords would be sufficiently safeguarded, without dragging the Peerage through the mire of political divorce suits.

Few but the most rabid partisans can feel any real sympathy with the coarse, unfounded, and malicious accusations which Radical extremists hurl against the House of Lords, forgetting that in befouling and insulting a great national institution they befoul and insult the nation itself. But there is no reasonable human being who sympathizes with incompetence and inefficiency. Oratorical brickbats and rhetorical dead cats arouse a feeling in favour of those at, and against, whom they are directed. But it is impossible to be more Royalist than the King, and the general, who persistently throws away his chances, quickly damps the enthusiasm and eventually destroys the attachment of his followers. The rights of each individual Peer, as they now exist, are a bar and an obstacle to the just measure of influence properly belonging to the Peerage as a whole. If the strength and efficiency of the House of Lords are to be thoroughly maintained or restored, then individual Peers, instead of insisting on their right to sit in person, must be content to be represented by the most competent and capable members of their order. The hereditary legislators in the House of Lords must be improved by a dual process of elimination and selection. Such a reform will in no way affect the Peerage, considered for the moment as an institution apart from the House of Lords. Only in their Senatorial capacity will the Peers be affected, and in this in such a manner as to secure their better and more effective representation. It will be the resuscitation in a modern and reasonable form of voting by proxy. It will enable the Peerage at once to reinforce its strength freely from the various elements of aristocracy existing in the British nation, and to take up in Parliamentary warfare an almost impregnable strategical position.

The whole five Peerages should be amalgamated into one Imperial and Pan-Britannic Peerage, and to this Imperial Peerage a Representative Peers system should be applied. But the new Representative Peers system should not be a dull, mechanical, and unintelligent copy of the Scottish or the Irish Representative Peers system. It should not follow the Irish system in making the Representative Peers life members of the Second Chamber. It should not follow the Scottish system in making Peers not returned as Representatives ineligible for the Lower House. There are a large number of Peers to whom it would not be applied at all. The creation of Scottish Peers ceased with the Anglo-Scottish Union. The creation of Irish Peers was checked by the Great British and Irish Union. But the creation of United Kingdom Peers would continue to flow on unimpeded. Now, an ordinary peerage of the United Kingdom does not make its first possessor an hereditary legislator. If he is without heirs, he is in effect a Life Peer. If he has heirs, he is none the less as fresh to the House of Lords as is a Life Peer. His legislatorship does not become hereditary till it has been inherited. With regard to new Peers, the Radical objection to "hereditary legislators" is altogether out of place. Nor would it be possible to put new Peers on the same footing as Peers who have inherited their peerages without injuring the House of Lords, and unwarrantably encroaching on the prerogative. New Peers are presumably created for their personal fitness; they commonly include the most distinguished public servants of each generation, not belonging to the Peerage by birth. To remove them from the House of Lords, or even to make their seats dependent on election, would largely tend to diminish the attraction of the House of Lords for able and aspiring Commoners. To deprive the House of Lords of the presence of these men, many of whom have passed a lifetime in the House of Commons, would increase the possibility of a violent collision between the two Chambers. It would seriously and objectionably limit the power of the Crown. It would be absurdly inconsistent. For it would place these new Peers, whose services had won for them a peerage capable of descending to their heirs, in a position of less dignity and power than the Life Peers whose services had received a less enduring recognition.

To make new Peers dependent for their seats on election, to put Peers by creation in this respect on a footing with Peers by inheritance, would undo more than half the good effected by general reform. It would work badly in practice, and it is unjustifiable in theory. For the application of the Representative system to Peers by inheritance is to make sure of their Senatorial fitness, to supplement the original selection of their stock by the Crown, and the subsequent selection from among their stock by Nature, by the additional test of a yet further selection by their fellows. But in the case of Peers by creation, no such test is needed. For these have been immediately selected by the Crown, and the fitness of the original founder of the peerage is still present. First Peers, therefore, Peers by creation, should remain unaffected by the change. No further test is needed in their case, and it would be ludicrous that they should hold their seats in a way less free and ample than Life Peers.

The importance of the distinction thus established between

Peers by inheritance and Peers by creation will appear more evident when we remember that in January, 1892, there were, excluding the Prince of Wales, three hundred and eighty Peers by inheritance, and, excluding the Duke of Clarence (and, of course, the Life Peers), eighty-six Peers by creation.

But it is not only Peers by creation who, among normal Peers of the United Kingdom, could, and should, remain exempt from the operation of a Representative Peers system. Every Peer by inheritance who receives a promotion in the Peerage, who from Baron, for example, is advanced to Earl, or from Earl to Marquis, must be considered a second founder of his peerage. From a Peer by inheritance he becomes a Peer by creation. He is advanced in the Peerage for the same reason that a new Peer is created, for personal fitness. If he had not been a Peer already, he would have been created a Peer; and his promotion is equivalent to a new creation. For a Peer by inheritance to be selected by the Crown for a further peerage, is proof positive that in the opinion of the Monarch, or the Monarch's advisers, such a Peer is personally qualified, apart from inheritance, for a personal seat in the Imperial Senate. This is true of those Peers who are promoted in the Peerage, and it is also true of Peers who, like the present Duke of Richmond, receive a second peerage of the same rank as that which they already possess. Such Peers are Peers by inheritance, but they are also Peers by creation. The exemption of such Peers from the operation of the Representative system, their possession of seats independent of election, is required by logic and reason, and it is also required as a means of enabling the Crown to retain some hold on the hereditary Peerage.

Peers by creation, and Peers by inheritance who, in virtue of a new peerage, have become also Peers by creation, will naturally and obviously hold their seats independent of election. But they do not exhaust the list of Peers to whom a Representative system would be inapplicable. There are, and probably there always will be, a large number of Peers who, under the provisions of such a Life Peers Bill as that sketched in the last chapter, would be qualified for a life peerage, that is to say, who possess a sufficient qualification for sitting in person in the House of Lords. In the case of Commoners, such a qualification remains a qualification, and does not mount up into a title or a claim. But in the case of Peers by inheritance, such a qualification would constitute a claim. For the hereditary right of each normal Peer of the United Kingdom to sit in person in the House of Lords would still remain, subject only to the condition of his personal qualification through election by his fellows. But, if the Peer already possessed a qualification sufficient in the case of a Commoner for a life peerage, it would be unnecessary and absurd to insist on the further qualification of election. Election is accepted as a Senatorial qualification, but where a Senatorial qualification already exists it would be superfluous and preposterous to set it aside in favour of election.

Under the provisions of a Life Peers Bill a good many Peers by inheritance would be entitled to sit in person, as possessing a Senatorial qualification, in addition to the Peers by creation, and the Peers by inheritance who had been re-created. But in the case of Peers it would not be necessary to exact the full qualification required in the case of Commoners. Some of the provisions of the Life Peers Bill might here with great advantage be extended. It would be injudicious to enact that to have attained the rank of Rear-Admiral or Major-General should qualify a Commoner for a life peerage; but this would be amply sufficient to qualify a Peer by inheritance to sit in person. It would be unwise to exact less than a four-years' tenure of the office of Under Secretary of State, or Secretary to the Treasury, in the case of a Commoner; but in the case of a Peer the minimum term could without injury be reduced to two years. It would be unnecessary to insert in a Life Peerage Bill the qualification of holding, or having held, the office of Lord Steward of the Household, Lord Chamberlain of the Household, or Master of the Horse; but this should qualify a Peer for sitting in the House of Lords; and so, too, might a few years' tenure of such other Court offices as those of Treasurer, Comptroller, or Vice-Chamberlain, of the Household. To make a seat in the House of Lords in any way resultant from election by a County Council, could not fail to prove prejudicial to the Senatorial character of the Second Chamber of the Imperial Parliament. But, as a concession to the inherent localism of the Liberal party in Great Britain, to have held for not less than five years the office of Lord-Lieutenant of a county might be permitted to qualify a Peer for sitting in person, and the Liberal party might thus gain a representation in the House of Lords to which the personal qualifications, and the number, of its adherents in the hereditary Peerage would not otherwise entitle it.

Deducting these three classes of Peers by creation, Peers by inheritance recreated, and Peers by inheritance of Senatorial qualification, which two last classes intersect each other, there then remain the Peers by inheritance neither re-created nor of personal qualification ; and to these the Representative Peers system should be applied. The election of Representative Peers for life would be open to more than one objection of gravity. In the first place, it would render the composition of the House less fluid and elastic than their election on a Parliamentary dissolution, whereas the latter system would assimilate the representation of the Peers electors to the representation of the Commoners electors in the House of Commons. In the second place, it would preclude the possibility of quietly getting rid of undesirable members of the House of Lords. In the third place, it would be an extremely imperfect method of representation. A Peer once elected would be independent of his constituents for life. No matter how far the electors and elected might respectively change or develop their opinions, relief from an unexpected situation could only be obtained by the voluntary resignation or death of the latter. Such representatives would soon cease to represent their constituents, to whom from the first they would be wholly irresponsible. After the first batch of representatives had been elected vacancies would only occur through death, and since it could not with confidence be hoped, or with reason be expected, that the representatives would be obliging enough to die off by sections, every election

CHAP. III.] MODES OF ELECTION TO THE PEERAGE. 337

would be hotly and fiercely contested, and the whole body of Peers electors would claim, and be allowed, to vote at each vacancy. Under such a system, the representation of minorities would have no existence.

The other alternatives are election for a fixed term of years, a certain proportion of the representatives retiring by rotation, or election for the duration of a Parliament. It is probable that the latter system would be adopted, for the former is open to some of the objections to election for life. Moreover, under the first system another difficulty would arise—namely, that, whereas the number of Peers by inheritance would be constantly augmented by the succession of their heirs to the peerages of Peers by creation, the number of Representative Peers, unless limited for all time, would stand in need of perpetual readjustment. Only election for each Parliament could keep the Peers Representative in living touch with the Peers electors.

To follow the Scottish and Irish precedents, and fix the number of Representative Peers for all time, would be to make no provision for the possible requirements of the future, and would constitute too great an infringement of the existing rights of the Peers to be readily accepted by them. To permanently fix the number of representatives, say at a hundred, would make too great a change in the position of the unqualified Peers by inheritance, having in view the other elements of the House, and would curtail their rights too sweepingly to receive, or indeed to call for, their assent. Far better would it be to lay down the rule that the number of Peers Representative should bear a certain proportion to the number of the Peers electors, which proportion might gradually grow less with the expansion of the Peerage, but should never descend below a certain minimum.

The Peers otherwise entitled to sit in person, whether as Life Peers, as Peers by creation, as Peers by inheritance re-created, or as Peers by inheritance qualified by office, sitting in person would of course possess no vote for the representatives of the Peers whose seat was dependent on election. The Peers electors, the Peers without seats in

Z

their own right, might be empowered to form themselves into electoral colleges, each for the return of one Peer Representative. Such an electoral college might in the first instance consist of three or four Peers, and the number could afterwards be raised by slow degrees. It may be said that such an electoral college would be too small, that the number of four would produce dead-locks, and that the number of three would cause the disfranchisement of one-third of the electors. And this would very likely happen, if the electoral college were composed of the three or four Peers nearest one another in precedence or in chronological order of admission into the peerage. But it would not happen, or it would only happen in very rare and exceptional instances, if the composition of the electoral colleges were left to the individual volition of the Peers. For then Peers of the same way of thinking would naturally range themselves together. The composition of electoral colleges would become the subject of previous extra-Parliamentary arrangement, and ties and difficulties of that kind could be easily avoided by an amicable understanding with the Peers electors of the other party or parties. No better system could be devised for the representation of minorities.

The electoral roll would be in a constant state of change as Peers completed a non-elective qualification for sitting in person, or as such Peers died and were succeeded by unqualified heirs. In the event of a Representative Peer dying during a Parliament, or acquiring a non-elective qualification for sitting in person, or becoming a Peer by creation through advancement in the Peerage, it would be well to leave a vacancy thus caused unfilled till the next general election. For the three or four Peers best entitled to vote, to the exclusion of all the others, could not easily be ascertained, since the members of the electoral college which returned the late representative might all, in one way or another, have ceased to be electors. Nor would it be necessary to fill up such a vacancy, when the total number of Representative Peers was left unfixed, as it would be were there a maximum not to be exceeded.

To carry out this scheme, it would not be necessary to interfere in any way with the Peers now sitting in the House of Lords in their own right, nor even with persons, being of age, who might succeed to a peerage in the immediate future. It would be only requisite to enact that no Peer, born after a certain date, and succeeding to his peerage after the Bill had become law, should be entitled to receive a writ of summons, unless, or until, he possessed one of the qualifications for sitting in person mentioned in the statute, but that every Peer so excluded should have a vote for a representative; that so soon as the number of excluded Peers reached six or eight, as the case might be, they should be permitted to form themselves into electoral colleges electing representatives at each general election; and that each elected representative should receive a writ of summons to the ensuing Parliament. The "certain date" might very well be fixed at ten years previous to the date of the Bill becoming law. Thus all existing rights would be completely protected, and all prospective rights would receive a reasonable measure of protection, while it could not be pretended that future Peers then children under twelve years of age had suffered any real injury. This great reform in the Second Chamber could be carried out without the least hardship or injustice to individuals, and without inflicting on any person whatsoever a merited or unmerited reproof. It would be effected by no violent or sudden change, but by a gentle and gradual transition from the old order of things to the new.

It would be necessary so far to encroach upon the royal prerogative as to deprive the Crown of the power of summoning eldest sons of Peers in their fathers' Baronies, unless they possessed the qualifications required of Peers themselves for sitting in person. But this encroachment would be more apparent than real, for it would still be in the power of the Crown to bring such eldest sons into the House of Lords by bestowing upon them a new peerage. Instead of sitting by an anticipated hereditary right, they would hold their seats as Peers by creation.

Princes of the Blood Royal, and more particularly the

monarch's eldest son, who, unlike his younger brothers, is by birth a Peer and not a Commoner, would be unfit candidates for the suffrages of an electoral college. It would be necessary, therefore, to provide that all persons in the line of succession to the throne should be exempt from the operation of the Representative Peers system, and that their royal descent, whether through males or females, should qualify, and entitle, them to sit in person.

Peers by inheritance not entitled to sit in person, whether by personal qualification, or as the elected representatives of their fellows, or as Peers re-created by advancement in rank or the duplication of their peerage, should be allowed to stand for election to the House of Commons. The fact that they themselves would be represented in the Upper House of the Imperial Parliament is no reason at all why they should not represent other people in the Lower Chamber. And if it be said that there would, on the other hand, be no Commoners sitting in the House of Lords to represent Peers, there is the obvious rejoinder that, without taking count of the Lords Spiritual, there would be the body of Life Peers who, since their peerages would be neither inherited from their ancestors nor transmissible to their descendants, would in effect be Commoners sitting in the House of Lords for life. And it might further be replied that, whereas these would owe their seats to the selection of the Monarch, irrespective of the wishes or opinion of the hereditary Peers, the Peers elected to the House of Commons would be indebted for their seats to the free and deliberate choice of their constituents. It would not be so much an extension of the privileges of the Peers, as an extension of the field of selection open to the Commons; nor could it be consistently opposed by those whose professed desire it is that the two Chambers should work in harmony, and who vigorously and incessantly complain that the House of Lords is out of sympathy with the House of Commons. But the first duty of a Peer after his duty to the Queen and country is to the Peerage, not to himself. Consequently, no Peer qualified to sit in person in the House of Lords, even though by election against his will by other Peers, should be permitted to remain in the House of Commons if a member, nor to abandon the Upper Chamber in favour of the Lower, whether in the supposed interests of his party, or to consult his personal ambition. Whether a Peer who wishes to become a Commoner, should any such exist, might not be permitted to surrender his peerage, is another matter which it would take too long to discuss. Certainly, it may be said in passing, a Peer permitted to surrender his peerage should only be permitted to surrender it in favour of the next heir, and should be required at the same time to surrender any estates settled to go with the peerage ; and it is possible that, having done so, and having succeeded in finding a place in the House of Commons, he might then be aroused by the grins and sneers of his Radical associates to a sense of the fact that, in parting with his rank, he had parted with all that had given him importance, and realize that he had been the dupe of his own vain, paltry, and egotistical ambition. But no Peer, qualified to sit in person in the House of Lords, should be allowed to become, or remain, a member of the House of Commons. For the privileges and public position conferred by a peerage it is a small price for a Peer to pay that he should in return give his best personal support to the prestige of his order and the Second Chamber. As for the injury done, or supposed to be done, to the interests of a party, by the sudden withdrawal of a party leader from the House of Commons to the House of Lords, it is a matter of regret to many patriotic citizens that the party system cannot be once and for ever broken up ; and any injury to any party, or to all parties, must by such be regarded as matter for rejoicing. But if party is to be considered, then it is not at all clear that much or any injury is done. The scene of debate has largely shifted from the House of Parliament to the country at large, and in such public discussions a member of the House of Lords from the comparative leisure of his Chamber is able to take part with greater freedom than a member of the House of Commons. But in any case the rule must be rigid and unvarying. A Peer cannot be permitted to pick and choose. He occupies a great public position, and with its privileges and rights he also assumes its duties and responsibilities.

To sum up, for an effective reform of the House of Lords it is necessary not only, or chiefly, to introduce a considerable number of Life Peers into the House, but also to revise the tenure by which Peers of England and the Union, and Representative Peers of Scotland and Ireland, hold their seats. Following out a tendency already active, the whole five Peerages of England, Scotland, Ireland, Great Britain, and Great Britain and Ireland, should be thrown into one Imperial Peerage, and from the body thus formed all the useless, incompetent, undesirable, or indifferent elements should be excluded. The exclusion of the unfit can be arrived at by a selection of the fittest. First, those Peers are singled out who, owing their seats to the nomination of the Sovereign, have received the express and formal guarantee of the highest official authority of the Empire. To these Peers by creation must be added those Peers by inheritance whose succession to the fitness, not less than the peerage, of their founders has by the same public authority been publicly and solemnly affirmed. Next come those Peers by inheritance, who possess similar qualifications to those demanded of Life Peers, though tested by less severe and rigorous conditions. Finally the bulk of the Peers by inheritance are reached, and to these is committed the task of singling out from among themselves for their representatives the most eminent and able of their fellows.

The suggested reforms would allow of the fuller and freer expansion of the Peerage, and of the not entirely inadequate representation of the Colonies by members of the new class of Life Peers ; and by unfelt and imperceptible gradations the Lords Temporal would pass from that which it is now, in constitution, though not in composition, a mediæval, territorial, and local Baronage, into a modern, national, and Imperial Senate. These reforms would also have the great moral effect of holding up the public service, which is the service of the country, as the standard of merit in the British Empire, instead of wealth, the too engrossing pursuit of which by all classes constitutes a national danger, a menace to society, and a peril to the State. They would do much to restore patriotism and public spirit, and to enable men to realize the unity and grandeur of the nation. By attracting rich men to the public service, and spurring Peers to justify their titles and support their ancestry, they would increase popular respect for the service of the country, and thin the dangerous and useless class of idle and unpatriotic rich. By such reforms as these, the hereditary principle, freed from its rank overgrowth, would acquire fresh force, vigour, and vitality, and, carefully pruned in its expression, would be intensified in strength. The fancied reproach of "hereditary legislators" could find no application to a House, in which every member, not of the Blood Royal, owed his seat to nomination or election; while the hereditary Peerage itself would be unimpaired, and all that is valuable in hereditary legislators would be preserved and perpetuated in a new and less invidious form.

CHAPTER IV.

LORDS SPIRITUAL.

IN the preceding pages, little has been said of the present or future of that other class of members of the House of Lords, the Lords Spiritual, and little is said about them as a rule by Radical critics of the Second Chamber. They are not hereditary legislators in the same sense as Peers of England and the Union who have inherited their peerages; and, forming but a small proportion of the Upper Chamber, they take but little part in current politics and non-ecclesiastical legislation. The case against the Bishops in the House of Lords, if case there be, is a case, not against the House of Lords, but against the Church of England as an Establishment. It rests on the assumption that the State recognition accorded to the Anglican episcopate is a violation of the principle of religious equality.

As we have seen, the presence of the English Bishops in the House of Lords is historically due to the fact that, at the Unions of 1707 and 1801, no new Parliament was called into existence, but two existing Parliaments were blended into one. The Parliament of the United Kingdom is the Parliament of England, changed only by union with the Parliaments of Scotland and Ireland. In Scotland the Presbyterian Establishment had no Bishops to be brought into the House of Lords. In Ireland the Anglo-Irish Church Establishment which existed at the time of the Union was swept away by the Irish Church Act, 1869, and the prelates who had represented the Anglo-Irish Church in the Upper House were by the operation of that measure thenceforth excluded.

The fact that the dominant religion in the English Kingdom is represented by some of its official rulers in the Second Chamber of the Imperial Parliament, while the dominant religion in the Kingdom of Scotland and the dominant religion in the Kingdom of Ireland are not so represented, does not constitute a national grievance of Scotland or Ireland. And by the Liberal party in Great Britain it is not put forward as a national, or Nationalist, grievance, but only as a grievance of the English Nonconformists.

To enter into the general question of English Disestablishment would be irrelevant and tedious. It is enough to say that the presence of the Bishops in the House of Lords, while other religious bodies are not there represented, is due to the peculiar relations existing between the Church of England and the State. Their exclusion from the House would, so far as it went, be a measure of disestablishment, though not of disendowment, and the proposal to exclude them raises the question of disestablishment, and not the question of the reform or abolition of the House of Lords. The objection to the presence of the Bishops is merely a particular form of the much larger and more general objection to the relations existing between the Church of England and the State. So long as those relations continue, it is idle to complain of the Lords Spiritual as a violation of the principle of religious equality. If the Nonconformist bodies stood in the same relation to the State, then they, too, would, if they desired it, be represented by their official rulers in the Second Chamber of the Imperial Parliament. The presence of the Bishops in the House of Lords, if it constitutes a Nonconformist grievance, constitutes a grievance against the Church of England as an Establishment, not a grievance against the House of Lords, and in a review of the position of the House of Lords it scarcely needs to be considered. But just as there are good and sufficient reasons for the reform and expansion of the Lords Temporal, quite apart from the unfounded Radical charges brought against them, so there are good and sufficient reasons for the reform and expansion of the Lords Spiritual, quite apart from this pretended Nonconformist grievance.

In the event of a local Legislature being established in England for purely local English affairs, it is certain that in the Upper House of such a body neither the Peers nor the Bishops would, as such, find place. If, therefore, the official rulers of the Church of England are to have seats in any legislative body they must continue to sit as at present in the House of Lords. Their presence there is a relic of the time when the Imperial Parliament was only the Parliament of England, and has, therefore, a certain seeming inappropriateness to the supreme governing body of the Empire. But, rightly developed, the principle underlying the Lords Spiritual would assist to complete and perfect the Imperial and Senatorial character of a reformed Second Chamber.

As there has been an expansion of the British people, both in the British Colonies and British Isles, so, too, there has been an expansion of British Christianity; and as the English nation of the British people has expanded, both in England and the Colonies, so, too, has the English Church.

There has been an expansion of the Church of England in England. To the nineteenth-century growth of the diocesan episcopate is due the new Parliamentary distinction between London, Durham, and Winchester, and the other suffragan sees of Canterbury and York. There are now seven diocesan Bishops of the Church of England, not including Sodor and Man, without seats in the House of Lords. When the projected division of the sees of Gloucester and Bristol, at present united, has taken place, there will be eight Bishops without seats; and when the projected diocese of Birmingham has been established, there will be nine Bishops without seats. Probably the subdivision of the old dioceses which has resulted in the modern creation of the sees of Manchester, Liverpool, Ripon, Wakefield, Newcastle, Southwell, St. Albans, and Truro will be carried still further, and there will be a continued increase in the number of diocesan Bishops and Bishops without seats. The funds for the endowment of these new sees have been obtained, partly by the private subscriptions of individual Churchmen, and partly by cutting down the income of the Bishop whose see was subdivided. But the establishment of a new diocese is an expensive business, and it has been repeatedly stated on episcopal authority that, great as have been the contributions of private munificence, the need for new bishoprics has not yet been fully supplied.

In addition to the new diocesan Bishops, and partly, as it may be supposed, to make good the lack of a more extended diocesan episcopate, an order of suffragan Bishops has been brought into existence, or rather revived (under an Act of Henry VIII.), who play much the same part in the Church of England as Bishops *in partibus infidelium* in the Church of Rome. Each of these suffragan Bishops is attached to a diocese, and, so to speak, serves on the staff of the diocesan. In January, 1892, there were no less than seventeen of these suffragan Bishops—the Bishop of Dover attached to the archdiocese of Canterbury, the Bishops of Beverley and Hull attached to the archdiocese of York, the Bishops of Marlborough and Bedford (London), the Bishop of Guildford (Winchester), and the Bishops of Barrow (Carlisle), Colchester (St. Albans), Coventry (Worcester), Derby (Southwell), Leicester (Peterborough), Nottingham (Lincoln), Reading (Oxford), Richmond (Ripon), Shrewsbury (Lichfield), Southwark (Rochester), and Swansea (St. David's). Besides these suffragan Bishops, several diocesans were aided in their labours by other Bishops, variously styled "assistant" and "coadjutor."

There has been an expansion of the Anglican episcopate in England, and there has been an expansion of the Anglican episcopate in the British Colonies. The Anglican Church in British North America was represented before the present century by the two Bishops of Nova Scotia and Quebec. But in January, 1892, there were twenty Anglican bishoprics in the Dominion of Canada, besides the diocese of Newfoundland. At the same date there were seven sees in the Anglican Province of the West Indies, and seven sees in the Anglican Province of New Zealand. There were nine dioceses comprised in the Anglican Church of South Africa, of which, however, two, Pretoria and Bloemfontein, were in the Dutch Republics. There were six Anglican bishoprics in New South Wales, two in Victoria, two in Queensland, and one in each of South Australia, Western Australia, and Tasmania. The periodical conference sometimes called "the Pan-Anglican Synod," though embracing also Scottish, Anglo-Irish, Indian, and missionary Bishops, and Bishops of the Anglican Church in the United States, attests the growth and importance of the Anglican Church in the British Colonies.

With an expansion of England there has been an expansion of the Church of England. And with an expansion of Ireland there has been an expansion of the Church of Rome in Ireland. Ireland, and the Church of the Irish, have overflowed into the great cities of Great Britain, and into the Great British and Irish Colonies. Englishmen are apt to speak of the Colonies as Greater Britain, but this is an inadequate description. Just as the United Kingdom is not Great Britain only, but Great Britain and Ireland, so the Colonies are not Greater Britain only, but also Greater Ireland. The Irish alone would constitute a large Roman Catholic element in the Colonies; but, besides the Irish, there are other Roman Catholic subjects of the Queen in the Colonies which we acquired from the Spaniards and the French. Not to speak of Mauritius or Malta, St. Lucia or Trinidad, there is a great fragment of the Gallican Church in Lower Canada. The Roman Catholic element in the British Colonies is proportionately far greater than in the British Isles. In 1891 five Cardinals were British subjects. In 1892 there were within the British Empire twenty-eight archbishoprics, and ninety-seven bishoprics, of the Church of Rome.

And as the Church of England and the Church of Rome have grown out into the British Colonies, with the British people, so also have the Presbyterianism of Scotland and the various forms of English Nonconformity.

It is clear, therefore, that the present representation of ecclesiastical interests in the House of Lords, however suitable to the days when the Imperial Parliament was the

Parliament of England, and the Anglican Church was conterminous and coextensive with the Kingdom of England, is, from an Imperial point of view, altogether out of date, having regard both to Anglican expansion, and to the inclusion of so many other religious bodies of importance in the modern Empire. To take into account Asiatic religions is as entirely out of the question as to take into account Asiatics themselves; but if the ecclesiastical interests of the British nation are to be efficiently represented in the House of Lords, then that assembly should include the representatives, not of the Church of England only, but of the whole Anglican Communion within the Empire, not of the Anglican Communion only, but of all the principal forms of British Christianity. If the representation of the Church of England by her official rulers in the House of Lords is a violation of the principle of "religious equality," then the equality can be restored by bringing the representatives of other religious bodies into the Second Chamber.

The Nonconformists, in their complaints against the presence of the Bishops, appear to forget that, on the other hand, the Anglican priesthood are ineligible to the House of Commons, while their own ministers may without restraint be elected to that body. But if, even so, their presence is regarded as a grievance, then, surely, the remedy is very simple. Let us follow the example of the Hungarian House of Magnates, in which the representatives of Roman and non-Roman Catholicism sit side by side with the representatives of the Lutheran and Calvinist Confessions. Let Presbyterianism, Protestant Dissent, and Roman Catholicism sit side by side with the non-Roman Catholicism of the Anglican Communion. Then these bodies will, as regards representation in the House of Lords, be placed on a footing of perfect equality with the Church of England. Let a class of Life Peers be established, nominally and legally Lords Temporal, but really and in effect Lords Spiritual, and let the members of this class be chosen by the Crown from among the most eminent prelates of the Church of Rome and the most distinguished representatives of Nonconformity.

Prelates of the Church of Rome, being bound to celibacy, can, in effect, be created Life Peers now. Presbyterian and Nonconformist ministers, however, are usually married, and for their inclusion a formal Life Peers Bill would be necessary. The disestablished Church of Ireland is informally represented in the House of Lords in the person of Lord Plunket, who happens to be the Anglo-Irish Lord Archbishop of Dublin; and the present Lord Petre is in holy orders of the Church of Rome. But it is improbable that any "hereditary legislator" would be a Baptist or Wesleyan minister. If the Nonconformists are to be represented in the House of Lords, an Act of Parliament will be needed for that purpose.

The Archdeacon of London, in a liberal and Christian spirit, has suggested that the President of the Wesleyan Conference, and the Chairmen of the Baptist and Congregational Unions, should be made *ex officio* members of a reformed House of Lords.

"The reorganization of the House of Lords," he prophesies, "will come some day, and it will be made more of a Senate. The hereditary element will remain, but other elements will be introduced. The annual presidents of the chief Nonconformist communions would rightly represent the interests of their organizations in such a body, and speak with authority on the questions of peace, war, and public morality and well-being."

The spirit of this suggestion is admirable, but its precise form is open to objection. In his zeal for Christian charity the Archdeacon has failed to dwell on the constitutional aspect of his proposal. He has overlooked a fact which to the lay mind seems most material, namely, that, whereas the diocesan episcopate of the Church of England are in effect appointed by the Crown, the Wesleyan President and so forth are elected by private and voluntary associations for religious purposes. The practical working of the *congé d'élire* system makes the Archbishops and Bishops in the House of Lords as truly Crown nominees as the Lords of Appeal or any of the newly created Peers of the United Kingdom. But the Crown exercises no sort of control over the choice of its Chairman by the Baptist Union. To concede to the

Nonconformist annual conferences the right of electing members of the House of Lords would be a startling and most dangerous invasion of the prerogative and Constitution. The Pope himself never possessed the power of creating Lords Spiritual. "Mitred and parliamentary Abbots," as Bishop Stubbs tells us, "were not identical." The Pope might bestow the mitre as he pleased, but the King alone could grant the right of receiving a summons to Parliament. The proposal of Archdeacon Sinclair, in the precise form in which he has advanced it, is inadmissible for the same reasons, amongst others, as those which forbid the concession of *ex officio* seats in the House of Lords to the Agents-General of the Colonies. But the spirit of the proposal is entirely in accord with the suggestion that life peerages should be created for the representation of Roman Catholic and Nonconformist interests. Agents-General cannot, as such, be admitted into the House of Lords; but to have filled the office of Agent-General should be a qualification for a life peerage. And the President of the Wesleyan Conference cannot, as such, be admitted into the House of Lords; but ex-Presidents of the Wesleyan Conference should be members of the class from which the Crown would be empowered by statute to select suitable persons for creation as Life Peers.

If the Nonconformists believe themselves to have a grievance in the presence of the Bishops in the House of Lords, then the way to remove it is—not to agitate for the expulsion of the Bishops, but to pass a law admitting Nonconformist divines. If the exclusive representation of the Church of England in the Second Chamber of the Imperial Parliament is felt as an injustice, then the remedy lies, not in depriving religion of all express and formal representation, but in extending the representation, now limited to the Church of England, to the Roman Catholic, Presbyterian, and Nonconformist bodies. The Nonconformists may object to the exclusive representation of the English Church; but they would scarcely object to the representation of Theism or Christianity. If they do so object, then the conclusion becomes irresistible that their attachment to Christianity is far surpassed in intensity and fervour by their hatred of Anglicanism. Surely this cannot be true of the Nonconformists as a whole. Surely some, at least, of them must be accessible to measures of conciliation conceived in the amicable spirit of Archdeacon Sinclair. But if this be so, if rather than concede to the Church of England a share in the representation of religious interests in the House of Lords, they would abolish the representation of religious interests altogether, then it may not be amiss to remind them that it is only for the representation of Presbyterianism and Nonconformity that legislation would be necessary. If their objection to the presence of the Bishops is so violent and stubborn that, rather than acquiesce in its continuance, they would refuse such concessions as might be held out to themselves by a Life Peers Bill, then it may be worth while to call their attention to the fact that no Life Peers Bill would be needed for the introduction of Roman Catholic prelates into the Second Chamber. One Peer, by inheritance, is already a clergyman of the Church of Rome. There is nothing to prevent the Crown from making other Roman Catholic clergymen Peers by creation. A Roman Catholic priest bound to celibacy would, in effect, be a Life Peer. But to bring a Nonconformist minister into the House of Lords would, in nineteen cases out of twenty, entail the creation of a perpetual peerage.

If the Protestant Dissenters entertain an opinion that the services of their ministers to the general community are not such as to merit public recognition, it is not for those of us who do not happen to be Protestant Dissenters to vehemently dispute the truth of this contention. But no such obstacle exists to the representation of the Church of Rome, the attitude of whose rulers, when properly approached, is towards the State that of statesmen, and towards society that of men of the world. This great international and cosmopolitan association acts under other influences than those which dominate the being of some hole-in-the-corner English sect. If the Nonconformists feel conscientious scruples as to their own representation by means of a Life Peers Bill, it would be extremely wrong to force representation upon them. But the fact that they were unwilling to consent to their own representation, would be no reason for depriving the Church of England of her representation, nor for withholding representation from those religious bodies whose members are not troubled with the uneasy qualms of the Nonconformist conscience.

The Roman Catholics put forward no objection to the conferring of public honours on the chief rulers of their Church. The *Tablet*, a recognized organ of English Roman Catholic opinion, has publicly lamented that the late Cardinal Manning was never made a member of the House of Lords. The Church of Rome, in the British Empire, has an Imperial importance which is not possessed by English Nonconformity. Outside of Great Britain and India, the Roman Catholic subjects of the Queen are chiefly of French or Irish origin. There has been an expansion of Ireland with an expansion of Great Britain. We have annexed fragments of the French Colonial Empire, and fragments of the French Church. It is a matter of first-rate importance that these French and Irish Roman Catholics should be well affected to the Empire. With the exception of the Dutch element in South Africa, they are the only British subjects of European blood who are not yet thoroughly blended with the remainder of the British nation. To secure their active allegiance to the Empire would be to free it from its most pressing domestic difficulties. Both have it in their power to work the Empire great harm; and the Irish, in Ireland, form its constant distraction. Both have some reason for disaffection—the Irish in the memory of past injustice and oppression, the French in the recollection that their ancestors came into the Empire as a consequence of French defeat. Both are peculiarly sensitive to religious influences, and remarkable among modern peoples for the unbounded trust and confidence which they repose in the hierarchy of their Church. It would seem, therefore, to the interest of the Empire to approach them on the side on which they are most easily accessible, and to confirm their loyalty, or alleviate their disaffection, by securing to itself the vigorous support of their most trusted and venerated guides. The Church of Rome never repels advances from the State not incompatible with her spiritual freedom, and nothing but an undue consideration for a moribund and anti-national fanaticism can hinder a formal arrangement with the Vatican. If the Irish or the French Canadians were Buddhists, we should not hesitate to enlist the services of the Grand Lama. If they were Mohammedans, we should hasten to establish friendly relations with their Imaums and Mollahs. To regard the Latin branch of Christianity, alone among the world's religions, with insurmountable repugnance or incurable suspicion, can serve no better end than to provide, at the expense of the Imperial interests of Britain, a modern point to the old sarcasm on the love of Christians for one another.

In Canada, the Cardinal Archbishop of Quebec is a personage of the highest political importance. Such a Prince of the Roman Church should be recognized as what he is— a magnate of the British Empire. The fact exists, dislike it who may. To turn it to account, there is only required its graceful acknowledgment.

Puritan bigotry may, perhaps, be still too powerful, even now, to permit of a full and formal arrangement with the Papacy, but in the meantime steps may be taken in the right direction. To grant to particular Roman Catholic dioceses an heredity of representation in the House of Lords would be impossible while the Britannic Crown has no direct and constitutional voice in the appointment of their Bishops. But to have held a position of dignity and weight in the Latin hierarchy should be a qualification, and to have held it with advantage to the Empire should be considered to establish a claim, to a seat in the Imperial Senate, whether granted under the provisions of a Life Peers Bill, or conveyed, as it can be at present, through a life peerage in effect.

Those members of the Church of England who, unlike

the Archdeacon of London, would regard the proposed concessions to the Nonconformists and the Latin Christians as uncalled for and extreme, may prudently and usefully reflect that the English Church, as regards the House of Lords, now holds a unique position, not shared even with the Presbyterian Establishment in Scotland, and that this position, however thoroughly justified by history, requires much explanation to be rightly apprehended by the popular mind. The cause, which requires elaborate and lengthy explanation, is with a democracy apt to be condemned unheard. If the Protestant Dissenters welcome a Life Peers Bill, then, with their own representatives in the Second Chamber, it will become impossible for them to complain of the presence of the English Bishops. As the exclusion of the Bishops would, so far as it went, be a measure of disestablishment, so the inclusion of Nonconformist divines would be a measure of establishment. Removing the social raws and resentment of the English Nonconformists, it would, at the same time, render more remote the possibility of the disestablishment and disendowment of the Church of England. If, on the other hand, the Protestant Dissenters opposed a Life Peers Bill, the public would perceive that for their alleged grievance relief had been offered and refused, and that it was by their own deliberate choice that they were not, like the Church of England, represented in the House of Lords. And that this was so, would become still more apparent if, on the rejection of a Life Peers Bill, dignitaries of the Church of Rome were advanced to peerages of the normal type, as they could be with perfect ease and safety.

Some jealousy may no doubt exist in Anglican bosoms as to the Church of Rome, from the uncompromising attitude of Roman advocates in ecclesiastical controversy, and the modern development of the Papal prerogative. But, even if high and severe Anglicans regard the Church of Rome in England as an " Italian schism," which, however technically accurate a sentence, seems scarcely dispassionate or judicial, it is impossible for them to say this of the Church which now recognizes the Pope in Ireland, or of the Church of France in

Quebec. Rather must the Anglican Church in Canada be looked upon as an intruder, on the strict theory of National Churches. The true National Church of Ireland, too, never accepted the Anglican Reformation. The disestablished Church of Ireland was, and is, merely the Church of the English colonists, the Church of the English Pale. And the Irish in England are Roman Catholics by the same right by which the English and their descendants in Ireland adhere to the Anglo-Irish Church. We have, in effect, Churches which are national, but no longer territorial. And it should be remembered that, if some of these Churches disagree with the Anglican in continuing to adhere to the Roman obedience, their episcopate is none the less, according to Anglican doctrine, that of the Universal Church. To dwell with undue emphasis, not to say undue acerbity, on the differences between the Anglican and Latin branches of historic Christianity, is, as we have just seen, not calculated to promote the union of the Empire. And still less can it be described, in the ecclesiastical sphere, as conducive to the re-union of Christendom.

To oppose the admission of Irish, Gallican, and other Latin prelates into the House of Lords, would be neither Christian nor patriotic. It would tell against the union of the Empire. It would tell against the re-union of Christendom. And it would also tell against the union of the Anglican National Churches in the Empire. No action on the part of the State could give a more complete or public disavowal of Erastian theories about the English Church than a development of the Parliamentary recognition, now accorded to the Bishops of the Church of England, into a Parliamentry recognition accorded to the Bishops of the Anglican Communion. It would be a proof that the Imperial Parliament regarded the Church of England, not as an Establishment confined to the territorial limits of the English Kingdom, but as a great spiritual society extending through the world; to adopt Oriental terminology, the Holy Orthodox Church of the British Empire. That all Bishops are not for Parliamentary purposes of equal value is evident from the distinction now established between the Bishop of London, for example, and the Bishop of Hereford or Worcester. And in a true Imperial Parliament, representing the whole British nation, there would be no difficulty in passing a measure to transfer some of the English seats to the Primates of the Colonial Churches, provided, of course, that the Crown received, as it well might, a sufficient voice in the appointment of these latter. But, in the meantime, the Home episcopate should facilitate this and strengthen their own position, by welcoming representatives of the Roman Catholic, Presbyterian, and Nonconformist bodies into the House of Lords. If, in a Life Peers Bill, to be a Bishop of the Church of Rome was made a qualification for a seat in the Imperial Senate, it would be impossible to deny a like qualification to the office of a Bishop in any branch of the Anglican Communion. At present, the only way of rewarding or recognizing the public service of a Colonial Bishop is to translate him to an English see, which may be pleasant enough for the Bishop, but does not always afford an equal degree of satisfaction to the deserted diocese, more especially when a man of judgment, ability, and culture is replaced by one of quite inferior efficiency. To make Colonial Bishops eligible for a life peerage of the kind under discussion, besides providing the Colonies with a fresh method of representation, would emphasize the spiritual aspect of the English Church, promote the solidarity of the Anglican Communion, and beneficially affect the status of the Colonial episcopate and priesthood.

There are good reasons, then, why both the Church of England and the English Nonconformists should welcome such a Life Peers Bill as has been proposed. No hostility to such a measure is to be anticipated from the Church of Rome, and neither the Established Church in Scotland nor the Church, which is called Free, hold such tenets with regard to the supposed unlawfulness of a mutual recognition of the Church and State as have been advanced in modern times by some of the English Nonconformists.

With regard to the Church of Rome, it would be sufficient to enact that any British subject being a Cardinal, Archbishop or Bishop of that Communion should be eligible for a life peerage under the statute.

For the representation of Presbyterianism, it might be provided that any person who had filled the chair of Moderator of the General Assembly of "the Church of Scotland," of the Free Church of Scotland, of the United Presbyterian Church of Scotland, of the Presbyterian Church of England, of the Presbyterian Church of Ireland, of the Presbyterian Church of Canada, of the Presbyterian Church of Australia, or of the Dutch Reformed Church in South Africa, should be eligible in the same manner as a Roman prelate. The above list includes all the Presbyterian Churches in the Empire not too insignificant to be taken into consideration. In Canada and Australia the Presbyterian bodies, Free, Established, or "U.P.," have been united in one Church. To the ex-Moderators thus enumerated there might, perhaps, be added the Dean of the Order of the Thistle, who is always a clergyman of the Scottish Established Church.

The representation of English Nonconformity is a matter of greater difficulty on account of the endless division of its sects. Obviously for the purpose in hand it is necessary to discriminate, and to have regard to probability of permanence. The principal bodies of English Nonconformity are undoubtedly those of the Methodists, the Baptists, and the Congregationalists or Independents. The first of these are by far the most powerful and popular of Dissenting bodies, and among their many subdivisions the most important is that of the Wesleyan Methodists. The Wesleyan Methodists in the British Isles have an annual Conference, and in Australasia a Conference which is triennial. To have presided over these meetings should form a qualification for a life peerage. In Canada all the Methodists are united in an United Methodist Church. The presidency of this body should in like manner constitute a statutory qualification. To include as a qualification the having held the post of Chairman of the Baptist or Congregational Union should complete a sufficiently ample provision for the representation of Nonconformity. It must be remembered that the great majority of Nonconformist bodies agree in everything but some small point, and that the representative of one would on all questions likely to come before the House of Lords represent the wishes and opinions of the others. The numberless divisions of Nonconformity are due rather to a mysterious repugnance to discipline and organization than to any real and substantial difference of intellectual or moral atmosphere. They stand to one another as the Established Church of Scotland to the Free, not as the Free Church of Scotland to the Church of Rome. If the list of Nonconformist qualifications given above appears too small, it should be borne in mind that there are a large number of ministers embraced under each head who, in civic phrase, have "passed the chair." It is impossible to include societies which, like the Salvation Army, are entirely dependent for their life on a contemporaneous personality. It is impossible to include religionists like the Unitarians or Irvingites, who, however deserving of public respect as good citizens and loyal subjects, form an inappreciable fraction of the ecclesiastical world. And in the event of such exclusion causing offence in any quarter, it would be well to recollect that, while the Cardinals and Episcopate of the Church of Rome would be qualified under the Bill, no such direct representation would be offered to the Jesuits, Oratorians, and monastic orders, who play a highly important part in the Roman system. Selection is of the essence of a Senate, and in dealing with popular religion one must draw the line before reaching the Positivists or Madame Blavatsky. The present age is sometimes described as one of the decay of religious belief, but, whether or not religious belief is in its decadence, it is certain that superstitious credulity was never more vigorous and active. Nothing is more remarkable than the spread of low forms of faith, nor does anything convey so grave a reflection on the intelligence and patriotism of the British nation, as the fact that men are found to discard the robust and virile religion of their ancestors for the contemptible and effeminate superstitions of the East.

For the representation of the Anglican Churches outside

England it would be sufficient to provide that a Bishop or Archbishop of any Church, in open and visible communion with the see of Canterbury, should be qualified for creation as a Life Peer. But, as a matter of national and Imperial, rather than ecclesiastical, interest, it might also be provided that the Dean of Westminster should be eligible for a summons to the Imperial Senate. St. Peter's Abbey Church, the scene of the coronation of all British Monarchs and the consecrated memorial of genius, is a shrine of far other than merely local interest, and its guardian, the successor of the former Abbots, has the whole British Empire for his parish.

Were it thought well to develop the representation of religious interests yet further, there might be included, in the Chief Rabbi of the Jewish congregations of the Empire, the principal ecclesiastical officer of the great religion out of which Christianity has sprung.

The representation of English Nonconformity side by side with Scottish Presbyterianism, the Anglican Communion, and the Church of Rome, would, to all minds capable of reasoning, effectually and finally remove whatever grievance the Nonconformists may now believe themselves to suffer from the exclusive representation of the Church of England. It would strengthen the position of the English Church, both as an Estate of the Realm, and as an Imperial society. It would conciliate the rulers and adherents of the Church of Rome. In doing these things it would benefit and fortify the Empire, and it would at least not weaken, or depress, the House of Lords. It would be the fitting crown and appropriate conclusion of the great work of the removal of civil disabilities on account of religion; the sign and symbol of participation by Britons of all cults and creeds, not only in a common liberty, but in a common Empire.

It would be necessary, as in the previous Life Peers Bill, to fix a maximum of Peers to be created, and this practical, though not formal, extension of the Lords Spiritual, a restoration in some sort of the Parliamentary Abbots, would necessarily increase the proportion of ecclesiastics to the House at large. If the Bishops of the Church of England were willing to surrender six of their seats, and content themselves with the presence of fifteen of their number in addition to the two Primates and the three primatial Bishops, the total number of Life Peers might be fixed at twenty, thus making forty ecclesiastical members of the House in all. If it were thought unadvisable to touch the existing Anglican representation, the number of Life Peers might be fixed at twenty-four, thus making a total of fifty ecclesiastical Senators. In either case it would be necessary to specify a maximum limit of yearly creations.

CHAPTER V.

CONCLUSION.

IN previous chapters we have examined the origin, history, constitution, and composition of the House of Lords; the charges advanced against it, and against the Peerage, by the Liberal party in Great Britain; and the incompatibility of the proposed Radical remedies with the maintenance of the Constitution and the Empire. We have since seen, in the immediately foregoing pages, that, although the Radical case breaks down completely on examination, there is nevertheless urgent need for the reform of the House of Lords, for a further expansion of the Peerage, and the accelerated and systematized development of the Second Chamber of the Parliament which meets at Westminster into a true Imperial Senate. Having previously considered and dismissed suggested changes of exotic origin, derived directly or indirectly from a misconception of the Second Chamber of the American Congress, we sought in the present constitution of the House of Lords for the certain indication of the true and safe lines of reform. From the example of the Scottish and Irish Peers we drew the lesson that a seat in the House of Lords, independent of qualification or election, is not of the essence of a peerage that has been inherited; that it is as possible for Peers as it is possible for Commoners to obtain full representation as a constituency. And, from the example of the Lords and ex-Lords of Appeal, we learned that a Senatorial qualification should be attended by a Senatorial tenure. From the one we derived the principle of the representation of heredity by further selection: from the other the principle of qualification through office. As it was found that whatever difference may have once existed between Peers of Scotland or Ireland and Peers of England and the Union had now altogether disappeared, so it was urged that this fact should receive formal recognition by the amalgamation of the whole five Peerages into one, and a cessation of the creation of new Peers of Ireland, in like manner as the creation of Peers of England, Peers of Scotland, and Peers of Great Britain, has already ceased. Reason having been shown why a Baronage cannot by itself discharge the functions of a Senate, although its selected members may well constitute the most useful and important section of an Upper Chamber, it was next argued that the representation of members of the amalgamated Peerage, devoid of any personal qualification for a Senatorial seat, should be collective, as in the case of Scottish and Irish Peers, not individual, as in the case of Peers of England and the Union. Carefully refraining from copying, with Chinese exactness, either the Scottish or Irish Representative Peers system, we proposed that the best points in each should be combined, thus making the Representative Peers responsible to their constituents, and leaving to the rejected candidate for the Upper House the consolation of eligibility to the House of Commons.

Turning to the question of Life Peers we took warning from the Second Houses of Crown life nominees which exist in various portions of the Empire. It was seen clearly both that the number of Life Peers must be securely limited, and that the precise nature of an indispensable qualification cannot with too great exactness be defined. The idea of a Peerage *ex officio*, a lay counterpart of the English Bishops, which has been suggested for the inclusion of the Agents-General, was rejected as altogether inadmissible. Sketching an outline of the qualifications suitable for insertion in a Life Peers Bill, it became obvious that such a measure would provide the means of bringing distinguished Colonists into the House of Lords, in numbers not wholly disproportionate to the importance of the Colonies, before the hereditary Peerage can be recruited from eminent Provincials in sufficient strength to adequately represent the Provinces. The exclusive representation of the National Church of the English Kingdom in the Second Chamber of the Imperial Parliament of the United Kingdom, which is accounted a grievance by the English Nonconformists, was admitted to supply a reason for the introduction of a second and smaller class of Life Peers, Lords Temporal in legal form, but Lords Spiritual in effect, who should be chosen by the Crown from among the leading pastors of all the principal Christian Communions in the Empire.

Glancing at the composition of such a reformed House of Lords we can perceive that from the Life Peers Bill proper would be obtained a body of Senatorial members equally useful and ornamental, influential and respected ; Ministers of the Crown ; Ambassadors ; Indian and Colonial Governors ; Privy Councillors; Generals and Admirals; Judges from every quarter of the Empire ; Indian administrators ; Colonial politicians ; representatives of the great seats of commerce and industry ; the directors of Imperial finance and the chief magistrates of Provincial capitals ; and the spokesmen of science and art, and, if not of letters, at least of literary culture. Coming next to Peers by creation, among normal Peers of the United Kingdom, there would be found in these some of the most eminent Commoners in each generation, fitting recruits of the ancient Baronage of the three Britains, and men not less distinguished for their public services than the most prominent Life Peers. In conjunction with the new Peers of modern eminence, it is permissible to hope, there would be placed from time to time heads of certain of those untitled, but pre-eminently aristocratic, families of the British Isles which have hitherto fortuitously evaded the Peerage, but whose accession to the ranks of the official nobility would at once enrich and fortify its historic character, and in a time of great and sweeping change serve to secure their own perpetuation. In the Peers by inheritance advanced or duplicated in the Peerage, and the Peers by inheritance with personal qualifications, the House of Lords would retain the *élite* of its present members, to whom would be added the elect of the remainder of the hereditary Peerage. The House of Lords could not be said to suffer any loss from the proposed reform, when it retained such Peers as the Dukes of Rutland, Richmond and Gordon, Devonshire, and Westminster, Lords Dufferin, Salisbury, Lansdowne, Lothian, Londonderry, Cadogan, Cowper, Howe, Harrowby, Derby, Jersey, Brownlow, Onslow, Kimberley, Mount-Edgcumbe, Northbrook, Spencer, Zetland, Aberdeen, Kintore, Hopetoun, Rosebery, Reay, Morley, Balfour of Burleigh, Grey, Kenmare, and Lathom, and excluded others whom it were invidious to mention.

The small class of ecclesiastical Life Peers, containing Cardinals and other prelates of the Church of Rome, Colonial Bishops of the Anglican Communion, and the representatives of Presbyterianism and Nonconformity, would bridge over the gulf between the Lords Spiritual and Lords Temporal, and between the English Church and other forms of British Christianity.

Such a reform of the House of Lords as has been placed before the reader differs altogether from the fanciful and impertinent proposals, alike unthinking and undignified, unphilosophic and unpatriotic, for turning the Upper House into something quite other than it is, for framing it anew on the model of the Senate of Liberia or Kamtchatka, for sweeping away this great national institution to make room for the political discoveries of Iceland or Japan. It is difficult to treat with tolerance the worthless gimcrackery of political cheap-jacks who seek to palm off their second-hand wares on a too trusting public, and to do so have the insolent temerity to flout a Constitution which they are without the wit to understand. The British Constitution may not have descended from Mount Sinai amid lightning and thunder, like Moses and the Cobden Club, but at all events it is the Constitution of the British Empire, and it has proved itself compatible with, if not essential to, the creation and the continued maintenance of the greatest and most wonderful political dominion that the world has ever seen. Judged by results, the Constitution of the British Empire will successfully emerge from a comparison with all the Constitutions of the globe, not excepting the Constitution of that former fragment of the British Empire, the United States. Such a Constitution, though with no pretensions to divinity, is surely entitled to respect, and the writer claims that in his suggestions he has respected it. The reforms suggested come from no extraneous source, are borrowed from no alien politics, but consist in faithfully following out to their legitimate conclusion tendencies already existing in the Peerage and principles already imbedded in the structure of the House of Lords. And they have a further recommendation in the fact that they can all be carried out without disturbing the present members of the House of Lords, and by a gentle and gradual transition.

That the reforms in question would nominally increase the power of the Crown over the Second Chamber cannot be disputed, nor even that they would, to a less extent, practically increase the control of the Crown over the Second Chamber. But as to the nominal or theoretical increase in the power of the Crown, it must be remembered that the Crown has at present the nominal or theoretical power of creating every British subject a Peer, not to say of calling up the whole House of Commons to the House of Lords. And as to the practical and real power of the Crown over the Second Chamber, that no doubt would be increased, but at the same time the efficiency of the House of Lords would be promoted in a corresponding degree, and, far from forfeiting its independence, with an increase in efficiency it would gain an increase in power. To bestow upon the Crown a power without limit of creating Life Peers would, with a weak or unscrupulous Monarch, destroy the independence of the House of Lords. But to bestow upon the Crown a power of creating a limited number of Life Peers, possessed of carefully defined qualifications, would strengthen the House of Lords while effectually safeguarding its independence.

To advocate a revision of the tenure of their seats by Peers by inheritance, while at the same time vindicating the hereditary principle, may at first sight appear weak-kneed and inconsistent. But apart from the fact that the philosophy of history is a sealed book to the average Parliamentary elector, the practical considerations of the vast increase in the numbers of the Peerage, and the necessary limit of numbers in an efficient Second Chamber, imperatively demand a change of some sort, and to urge the better representation of the hereditary principle is not to press for its elimination.

The Lords Temporal, as a local and territorial Baronage, have lost their former Parliamentary efficiency. What now remains for them is to fulfil the "manifest destiny" of the House of Lords as an Imperial Senate. The Radical clamour for the destruction of the Constitution must not blind our eyes to the necessity for its extension and completion; and the Constitution of 1801, for the nineteenth century good and indispensable, will for the twentieth century be as antiquated and archaic as the Constitution of 1707 had shown itself to be in 1800. The maintenance of the House of Lords is essential to the maintenance of the Empire, but the House of Lords as the Second Chamber of the Imperial Parliament cannot be maintained for all time in the precise form in which it now actually exists. A day will come when, if the Parliament of the United Kingdom is to remain the supreme governing body of the Empire, both the House of Lords and the House of Commons will have to be reformed. Canada and Australia are growing into nations, and no nation will long content itself with a position of dependence. The alternatives will present themselves, as they did before, in the case of England and Scotland, and afterwards in the case of Ireland and Great Britain, of closer union or separation. If Canada and Australia are to be represented in the Imperial Parliament, that Parliament will have to delegate the local affairs of the British Isles to the care of British Insular local legislatures. This Imperial Parliamentary Union is the only form of what is called Imperial Federation, which does not involve the abdication by the Westminster Parliament of its present Imperial position. For if the care of Imperial policy is to be committed to some new Council or Assembly, the Westminster Parliament will thereby be superseded as the governing body of the Empire. For the effective control of

Imperial policy there is requisite Imperial power, the Sovereignty, that is to say, of the British Empire. Without this the new Council or Assembly would be a board of advice. With this the new Council or Assembly would supersede the Imperial Parliament. If, therefore, the Imperial Parliament is to become, from the Parliament of the British Isles, the Parliament of the British nation in both Isles and Colonies, First Chamber and Second Chamber must be alike reformed. For the House of Commons no less than for the House of Lords, and for the House of Lords no less than for the House of Commons, as Chambers of the supreme Legislature of the Empire, a time will arrive for being "ended" or "mended." The union of England and Scotland necessitated the fusion of the two Parliaments. The union of Ireland and Great Britain wrought changes in both Houses of the Parliament of Westminster. And the Imperial enfranchisement of Australia and Canada will also require changes of addition and changes of omission in the reinforced Imperial Parliament.

An hereditary Peerage does not exist in the Colonies, as it did in each of the three Kingdoms before their union, nor could a sufficient number of Colonists be created Peers of the normal kind for the adequate representation of the Colonies in a House of Lords otherwise unchanged. If the various elements of the Second Chamber are not readjusted, it is possible that, when the Colonies consider their representation in the Imperial Parliament, they will raise objections to the constitution of the Upper House. At present it serves as a protection of their interests, but this would no longer be the case when they were themselves represented in the Lower Chamber. The House of Lords then, if any regard is to be had to the future, should hasten to take measures to fix itself in the public mind as the Senate of the Empire, thus attracting to itself in advance the attachment of the Colonies, while overawing the Liberal party in Great Britain and their local irritation.

In ordinary circumstances, changes in the constitution of the Upper Chamber mooted by the Peers themselves would be popularly regarded with a not unpardonable suspicion and distrust. The Peerage Bill of 1719, as the last experiment of the kind, would justify much meditation as to the true inwardness of the manœuvre. Fortunately, the Radical agitation for the reform or abolition of the House of Lords has prepared the public mind for legislation in the matter. Measures proceeding from the Peers, and having for their object an increase of non-hereditary legislators, and the submission of hereditary legislators to a further test of fitness, could not for very shame's sake be opposed by the Liberal party in the House of Commons. Thus the House of Lords has it in its power either to force the Radicals to accept its own scheme of reform, or to compel them to desist from further agitation. It may fairly be supposed that not all the Radicals are insincere in their professed objections to the constitution of the Second Chamber, and that others, convinced on reflection that the abolition of the House of Lords is practically impossible without a revolution, would be glad to take what they could get.

The feasibility of a reform of the House of Lords is apparent, and its advisability it has been attempted to set forth. Not because "the House of Lords is based on the hereditary principle, and the hereditary principle is absurd and wrong as a basis for a legislative Chamber," for the House of Lords is not based on the hereditary principle, though the hereditary principle has been one of its great elements of strength; not because "the House of Lords oppresses the people," for it protects the people; not because "the Peerage is not aristocratic," for no more genuinely aristocratic body has ever existed; but because the union of Parliamentary peoples must be a Parliamentary Union, and because without such a union the British Isles and the great self-governing British Colonies must inevitably drift apart, the House of Lords must, like the House of Commons, be reformed, developed, and enlarged in its constituency.

The abolition of the House of Lords is just as much and just as little a question of practical politics as the abolition of the House of Commons. Nor can any extreme power compel the reform of the Second Chamber. But though the House of Lords cannot be reformed, save by addition, nor abolished, save by a revolution, without its own consent, it can, by a long continued course of inaction and stagnation, render itself morally impossible as the Second Chamber of a true Imperial Parliament, and it can force the nation to choose between the loss of the Constitution and the loss of the Empire. The threats and menaces of demagogues and agitators are as unavailing as they are out of place, but those who regard the Constitution and the Empire with equal reverence, as they recall the share taken by the Peers in the creation of the modern Empire and the existing Constitution a century ago, so, in order to consolidate the one through the development and readjustment of the other, they will repose all trust and confidence in the hereditary and oft-tried patriotism, the sagacity and the statesmanship of the House of Lords.

APPENDIX A.

PEERS OF IRELAND NOT HEREDITARY LEGISLATORS (JAN., 1892) IN THE ORDER OF THEIR ADMISSION INTO THE PEERAGE.

1. Kingsale, Baron . 1181
2. Dunboyne, Baron 1274
3. Westmeath, Earl of . . . 1621   Delvin, Baron 1286
4. Dunsany, Baron . 1439
5. Louth, Baron . 1541
6. Inchiquin, Baron 1543
7. Mountgarret, Viscount . . 1550
8. Cavan, Earl of . 1647   Cavan, Baron . 1618   1st Baron, Oliver Lambart, Governor of Connaught.
9. Castle - Stewart, Earl of . . 1800   Castle-Stewart, Baron . 1619   1st Baron was the 3rd Scottish Lord Stewart of Ochiltree. The 1st Lord Ochiltree was the 4th Scottish Lord Avondale. The 1st Lord Avondale was Andrew Stuart, Chancellor of Scotland.
10. Charlemont, Viscount . . 1665   Caulfield, Baron 1620
11. Dillon, Viscount . 1622   1st Viscount, Theobald Dillon, Lord President of Connaught.
12. Valentia, Viscount . 1622   1st Viscount, Sir Fras. Annesley, Bt., Privy Councillor of Ireland.
13. Kilmorey, Earl of . . . 1822   Kilmorey, Viscount . . 1625
14. Sherard, Baron . 1627

APPENDIX A.

15. Annesley, Earl	1789	Mountmorris, Baron	1628	
16. Taaffe, Viscount.	1628			
17. Carrick, Earl of	1748	Ikerrin, Viscount	1629	
18. Downe, Viscount	1680			
19. Lisburne, Earl of	1776	Lisburne, Viscount	1695	
20. Lanesborough, Earl of	1756	Newtown-Butler, Baron	1715	1st Baron, George Evans, Privy Councillor of Ireland.
21. Carbery, Baron	1715			
22. Molesworth, Viscount	1716			1st Viscount, Robert Molesworth, Ambassador.
23. Chetwynd, Viscount	1717			1st Viscount, Walter Chetwynd, Ambassador.
24. Southwell, Viscount	1776	Southwell, Baron	1717	
25. Aylmer, Baron	1718			
26. Ashbrook, Viscount	1751	Castle-Durrow, Baron	1733	
27. Desart, Earl of	1793	Desart, Baron	1735	
28. Mexborough, Earl of	1766	Pollington, Baron	1735	
29. Milltown, Earl of	1763	Russborough, Baron	1756	
30. Mountmorres, Viscount	1763	Mountmorres, Baron	1756	
31. Farnham, Baron	1756			
32. Lisle, Baron	1758			
33. Winterton, Earl of	1766	Winterton, Baron	1761	
34. Mountcashell, Earl of	1781	Kilworth, Baron	1764	
35. Kingston, Earl of	1768	Kingston, Baron	1764	
36. Lifford, Viscount	1781	Lifford, Baron	1768	1st Viscount (and Baron) James Hewitt, Lord Chancellor of Ireland.
37. Portarlington, Earl of	1785	Dawson, Baron	1770	
38. Lucan, Earl of	1795	Lucan, Baron	1776	
39. Mayo, Earl of	1785	Naas, Baron	1776	1st Earl (and Baron), John Bourke, Privy Councillor of Ireland.

IRISH PEERAGES. 373

40. Doneraile, Viscount . . 1785	Doneraile, Baron . 1776	
41. Templetown, Viscount . . 1806	Templetown, Baron . 1776	
42. Macdonald,Baron 1776		
43. Massy, Baron . 1776		
44. Newborough, Baron . . 1776		
45. Wicklow, Earl of 1793	Clonmore, Baron . 1778	
46. Bangor, Viscount 1781		
47. Belmore, Earl of 1797	Belmore, Baron 1781	
48. Muskerry, Baron 1781		
49. Harberton, Viscount . . 1791	Harberton, Baron . 1783	
50. Muncaster, Baron 1783		
51. Clonmell, Earl of 1793	Earlsfort, Baron . 1784	1st Earl, John Scott, Chief Justice of the King's Bench, Ireland.
52. Antrim, Earl of . 1785		
53. Kilmaine, Baron 1789		
54. Clonbrock, Baron 1790		
55. Caledon, Earl of 1801	Caledon, Baron 1790	
56. Rosse, Earl of . 1806	Oxmantown, Baron . 1792	
57. Waterpark, Baron . . 1792		1st Baron(ess) Sarah, wife of Sir Henry Cavendish, Bt., Privy Councillor and Receiver-General of Ireland.
58. Bandon, Earl of . 1800	Bandon, Baron 1793	
59. Graves, Baron . 1794		1st Baron, Thomas Graves, Admiral.
60. Avonmore, Viscount . . 1800	Yelverton, Baron . 1795	1st Viscount (and Baron), Barry Yelverton, Chief Baron of the (Irish) Exchequer.
61. Huntingfield, Baron . . 1796		
62. Bantry, Earl of . 1816	Bantry, Baron 1797	
63. Crofton, Baron . 1797		
64. Headley, Baron . 1797		
65. Hotham, Baron . 1797		1st Baron, William Hotham, Admiral.

66. Teignmouth,
    Baron . . 1797   1st Baron, Sir John Shore,
                                                  Bt., Governor-General of
                                                  India.
67. Ffrench, Baron . 1798
68. Norbury, Earl of 1827   Norbury, Baron 1800   1st Earl (and Baron), John
                                                  Toler, Chief Justice of
                                                  the Common Pleas, Ire-
                                                  land.
69. Frankfort, Vis-   Frankfort,
    count . . 1816   Baron . 1800   1st Baron, Lodge Evans
                                                  Morres, Chief Secretary
                                                  to the Lord Lieutenant.
70. Ashtown, Baron . 1800
71. Clanmorris, Baron 1800
72. Clarina, Baron . 1800   1st Baron, Eyre Massey
                                                  General.
73. De Blaquiere,
    Baron . . 1800   1st Baron, John de Bla-
                                                  quiere, Chief Secretary
                                                  to the Lord Lieutenant.
74. Dunalley, Baron 1800
75. Langford, Baron 1800
76. Radstock, Baron 1800   1st Baron, William Walde-
                                                  grave, Admiral.
77. Ventry, Baron . 1880
78. Wallscourt, Baron 1880
79. Rendlesham,
    Baron . . 1800
80. Gort, Viscount . 1816   Kiltarton,
                            Baron . 1810
81. Castlemaine,
    Baron . . 1812
82. Decies, Baron . 1812   1st Baron, William Beres-
                                                  ford, Archbishop of
                                                  Tuam.
83. Garvagh, Baron . 1818
84. Guillamore, Vis-
    count . . 1831   1st Viscount, Standish
                                                  O'Grady, Chief Baron of
                                                  the (Irish) Exchequer.
85. Oranmore, Baron 1836   1st Baron, Dominick
                                                  Browne, Privy Council-
                                                  lor of Ireland.
86. Dunsandle, Baron 1845
87. Bellew, Baron . 1848
88. Fermoy, Baron . 1856
89. Rathdonnell,
    Baron . . 1868

APPENDIX B.

PEERAGES OF THE UNITED KINGDOM, CREATED BETWEEN THE ACCESSION OF QUEEN VICTORIA AND AUGUST, 1886, EXCLUDING THOSE OF LIFE PEERS, PEERESSES (UNLESS TRANSMITTED TO DESCENDANTS), AND THE PRINCE OF WALES.

THE Baronies of Campbell, Eddisbury, Acheson, Herbert of Lea, and Buckhurst, are also excluded (*see* Part II., ch. i.). The new peerages bestowed on Peers of England or the Union promoted in the Union Peerage are not included. The peerages created on the advice of a Ministry are distinguished by prefixing the name of the Premier of the Administration. Under A will be placed Peers of Scotland or Ireland brought into the Union Peerage, with their Scottish or Irish styles in brackets; and under B will be placed Commoners raised to the Peerage.

No peerages are included but those which were in existence on January 1, 1892.

1. VISCOUNT MELBOURNE (April, 1835).

A.

1837.	1.	Innes, Earl (Duke of Roxburghe).
1838.	2.	Rossmore, Baron (Lord Rossmore).
1838.	3.	Kintore, Baron (Earl of Kintore).
1838.	4.	Lismore, Baron (Viscount Lismore).
1838.	5.	Carew, Baron (Lord Carew).
1841.	6.	Oxenfoord, Baron (Earl of Stair).

B.

1837.	1.	Leicester, Earl of.
1838.	2.	De Mauley, Baron.
1838.	3.	Wrottesley, Baron.
1838.	4.	Sudeley, Baron.
1838.	5.	Methuen, Baron.
1839.	6.	Stanley of Alderley, Baron.
1839.	7.	Leigh, Baron.
1839.	8.	Wenlock, Baron.
1839.	9.	Lurgan, Baron.
1839.	10.	Monteagle of Brandon, Baron.
1839.	11.	Seaton, Baron.
1839.	12.	Keane, Baron.
1841.	13.	Congleton, Baron.
1841.	14.	Vivian, Baron.

II. SIR ROBERT PEEL (September, 1841).

B.

1846. 1. Gough, Baron.	1846. 3. Ellesmere, Earl of.
1846. 2. Hardinge, Viscount.	

III. LORD JOHN RUSSELL (July, 1846).

A.	B.
1847. 1. Dartrey, Baron (Lord Cremorne).	1850. 1. Londesborough, Baron.
	1850. 2. Truro, Baron.
1849. 2. Elgin, Baron (Earl of Elgin).	1851. 3. De Freyne, Baron.
1850. 3. Clandeboye, Baron (Lord Dufferin).	

IV. EARL OF DERBY (February, 1852).

B.

1852. 1. St. Leonards, Baron. | 1852. 2. Raglan, Baron.

V. VISCOUNT PALMERSTON (February, 1855).

A.	B.
1856. 1. Kenmare, Baron (Earl of Kenmare).	1856. 1. Aveland, Baron.
	1856. 2. Belper, Baron.
1856. 2. Talbot de Malahide, Baron (Lord Talbot de Malahide).	1857. 3. Ebury, Baron.
	1858. 4. Chesham, Baron.
1857. 3. Skene, Baron (Earl Fife).	

VI. EARL OF DERBY (February, 1858).

B.

1858. 1. Chelmsford, Baron.	1859. 4. Tredegar, Baron.
1858. 2. Churston, Baron.	1859. 5. Egerton of Tatton, Baron.
1859. 3. Leconfield, Baron.	

VII. VISCOUNT PALMERSTON (June, 1859).

A.	B.
1860. 1. Kinnaird, Baron (Lord Kinnaird).	1859. 1. Lyveden, Baron.
	1860. 2. Brougham, Baron.
	1861. 3. Westbury, Baron.
	1861. 4. Russell, Earl.
	1861. 5. Fitzhardinge, Baron.
	1861. 6. Cromartie, Countess of.
	1863. 7. Annaly, Baron.
	1863. 8. Houghton, Baron.

PEERS CREATED DURING PRESENT REIGN. 377

VIII. EARL RUSSELL (November, 1865).

A.

1866. 1. Meredyth, Baron (Lord Athlumney).
1866. 2. Kenry, Baron (Earl of Dunraven).

B.

1866. 1. Romilly, Baron.
1856. 2. Northbrook, Baron.
1866. 3. Halifax, Viscount.
1866. 4. Edinburgh, Duke of.

IX. EARL DERBY (July, 1866).

A.

1866. 1. Monck, Baron (Viscount Monck).
1866. 2. Hartismere, Baron (Lord Henniker).
1866. 3. Brancepeth, Baron (Viscount Boyne).

B.

1866. 1. Lytton, Baron.
1866. 2. Hylton, Baron.
1866. 3. Penrhyn, Baron.

X. MR. DISRAELI (February, 1868).

A.

1868. 1. Bridport, Viscount (Lord Bridport).
1868. 2. Gormanston, Baron (Viscount Gormanston).

B.

1868. 1. Cairns, Baron.
1868. 2. Kesteven, Baron.
1868. 3. Ormathwaite, Baron.
1868. 4. O'Neill, Baron.
1868. 5. Napier of Magdala, Baron.

XI. MR. GLADSTONE (December, 1868).

A.

1869. 1. Dunning, Baron (Lord Rollo).
1869. 2. Balinhard, Baron (Earl of Southesk).
1869. 3. Hare, Baron (Earl of Listowel).
1872. 4. Ettrick, Baron (Lord Napier).
1873. 5. Breadalbane, Baron (Earl of Breadalbane).
1873. 6. Somerton, Baron (Earl of Normanton).

B.

1869. 1. Lawrence, Baron.
1869. 2. Penzance, Baron.
1869. 3. Howard of Glossop, Baron.
1869. 4. Castletown, Baron.
1869. 5. Acton, Baron.
1869. 6. Robartes, Baron.
1869. 7. Wolverton, Baron.
1869. 8. Greville, Baron.
1870. 9. O'Hagan, Baron.
1871. 10. Sandhurst, Baron.
1872. 11. Selborne, Baron.
1873. 12. Aberdare, Baron.
1874. 13. Moncreiff, Baron.
1874. 14. Coleridge, Baron.
1874. 15. Emly, Baron.
1874. 16. Cottesloe, Baron.
1874. 17. Carlingford, Baron.

378   APPENDIX B.

XII. MR. DISRAELI (February, 1874).

A.

1875.	1.	Douglas, Baron (Earl of Home).
1875.	2.	Ramsay, Baron (Earl of Dalhousie).
1876.	3.	Fermanagh, Baron (Earl of Erne).
1880.	4.	Shute, Baron (Viscount Barrington).

B.

1874.	1.	Hampton, Baron.
1874.	2.	Winmarleigh, Baron.
1874.	3.	Connaught, Duke of.
1876.	4.	Harlech, Baron.
1876.	5.	Alington, Baron.
1876.	6.	Tollemache, Baron.
1876.	7.	Gerard, Baron.
1876.	8.	Sackville, Baron.
1878.	9.	Norton, Baron.
1878.	10.	Cranbrook, Viscount.
1880.	11.	Haldon, Baron.
1880.	12.	Wimborne, Baron.
1880.	13.	Ardilaun, Baron.
1880.	14.	Lamington, Baron.
1880.	15.	Donington, Baron.
1880.	16.	Trevor, Baron.
1880.	17.	Rowton, Baron.

XIII. MR. GLADSTONE (April, 1880).

A.

1881.	1.	Tweeddale, Baron (Marquis of Tweeddale).
1881.	2.	Howth, Baron (Earl of Howth).
1881.	3.	Reay, Baron (Lord Reay).
1884.	4.	Strathspey, Baron (Earl of Seafield).
1884.	5.	Sudley, Baron (Earl of Arran).
1884.	6.	De Vesci, Baron (Viscount de Vesci).
1884.	7.	Herries, Baron (Lord Herries).
1885.	8.	Powerscourt, Baron (Viscount Powerscourt).
1885.	9.	Northington, Baron (Lord Henley).

B.

1880.	1.	Sherbrooke, Viscount.
1880.	2.	Brabourne, Baron.
1881.	3.	Ampthill, Baron.
1881.	4.	Albany, Duke of.
1881.	5.	Derwent, Baron.
1881.	6.	Hothfield, Baron.
1881.	7.	Tweedmouth, Baron.
1882.	8.	Bramwell, Baron.
1882.	9.	Alcester, Baron.
1882.	10.	Wolseley, Baron.
1884.	11.	Tennyson, Baron.
1884.	12.	Hampden, Viscount.
1884.	13.	Monk Bretton, Baron.
1884.	14.	Northbourne, Baron.
1885.	15.	Rothschild, Baron.
1885.	16.	Revelstoke, Baron.
1885.	17.	Monkswell, Baron.
1885.	18.	Hobhouse, Baron.
1885.	19.	Lingen, Baron.

XIV. MARQUIS OF SALISBURY (June, 1885).

A.

1885. 1. Elphinstone, Baron (Lord Elphinstone).
1885. 2. Colville of Culross, Baron (Lord Colville of Culross).

B.

1885. 1. Halsbury, Baron.
1885. 2. Iddesleigh, Earl of.
1885. 3. Ashbourne, Baron.
1885. 4. St. Oswald, Baron.
1885. 5. Wantage, Baron.
1885. 6. Esher, Baron.
1885. 7. Deramore, Baron.
1885. 8. Montagu of Beaulieu, Baron.
1886. 9. Hillingdon, Baron.
1886. 10. Hindlip, Baron.
1886. 11. Grimthorpe, Baron.

XV. MR. GLADSTONE (February, 1886).

A.

1886. 1. Kensington, Baron (Lord Kensington).

B.

1886. 1. Herschell, Baron.
1886. 2. Burton, Baron.
1886. 3. Stalbridge, Baron.
1886. 4. Hamilton of Dalzell, Baron.
1886. 5. Brassey, Baron.
1886. 6. Thring, Baron.

APPENDIX C.

COMPOSITION OF THE HOUSE OF LORDS (1892).

IN January, 1892, there were sixty-six Peers of England, Great Britain, or the United Kingdom, who either were, or had been, judges or Chancellors themselves; or could look back to Chancellors or judges as the founders of their peerages; or, in some cases, being Peers of Scotland or Ireland, as the founders of the Scottish or Irish peerages which eventually won for their possessors incorporation in the House of Lords.

There were sixty-six peerages having, in like manner, naval or military commanders for their founders.

There were a hundred and fifteen peerages held by Peers, and two held by Peeresses, which owed their origin to high civil service to the State.

This computation is arrived at in every instance by reference to the first Peer, and the immediate cause of his peerage; and no subsequent services, however eminent, have been considered to affect the origin of a peerage. Peerages have, in many instances, been subsequently illustrated and justified, but no notice has been taken of such cases. On the other hand, it is impossible to apply any other test than that of having filled some public office. Hence, while some peerages may have been excluded whose founders greatly influenced the fortunes of the State, others by the same rule have been included that commemorate services which are possibly of less renown.

In the case of Scottish and Irish Peers absorbed into the Peerage of Great Britain or the United Kingdom, or, by the calling of a Barony out of abeyance, into the Peerage of England, it is a not unfair assumption that where the Peer so absorbed was himself a general or statesman, the absorbing peerage may be placed to his personal account, but that where the Peer absorbed was without such personal qualification, we must look to the original founder of his Scottish or Irish peerage.

Many of the Peers, placed under one head or another, had also inherited large landed property; but in every case they had performed services, or held rank or office, which would have been sufficient to win for a man without such property a seat in the House of Lords.

Where a peerage having become extinct has been revived for a representative of the former Peers, the same rule has commonly been followed

COMPOSITION OF HOUSE OF LORDS. 381

as in the case of Scottish and Irish Peers sitting in their own right in the House of Lords.

Where a Peer has inherited a second peerage of another origin, he is entitled to be considered to sit in virtue of whichever peerage would give him the better moral claim to a seat in the Upper Chamber.

Frequently a Peer, on promotion in the Peerage, changes not only his title but the name of his peerage, and from Lord This becomes the Earl or Viscount That, or from Marquis of one town or county the Duke of another. In the following list of English, Great British, and United Kingdom peerages, the names and style of Scottish and Irish Peers will be found in brackets after the Union peerage, and the name and style of the original founder of the peerage, wherever that differs from the name and style of its present possessor, will also be found placed in brackets, and in every case printed in italics.

The Peers then, at the date given, descended from Chancellors or law Lords, or law Lords themselves, were the Duke of Manchester (*Earl of Manchester*); the Marquis of Camden (*Earl of Camden*); the Earls Bathurst (*Lord Apsley*), Cairns, of Cottenham, of Coventry (*Lord Coventry*), Cowper, *of Cromartie, of Eldon*, of Ellesmere (*Lord Ellesmere*), of Guilford (*Lord Guilford*), *of Hardwicke*, of Harrowby (*Lord Harrowby*), of Lovelace (*Lord King*), *of Macclesfield, of Mansfield, of Nottingham, of Rosslyn, of Selborne, of Shaftesbury*; Viscount Falmouth (*Lord le Despencer*); Lords *Abinger, Ashbourne*, Balinhard (*Earl of Southesk*), Botreaux (*Earl of Loudoun*), Bramwell, Brodrick (*Viscount Middleton*), *Brougham and Vaux, Campbell and Stratheden, Chelmsford*, Clanbrassil (Earl of Roden : *Viscount Jocelyn*), Coleridge, Denman, *Ellenborough, Erskine, Esher, Field, Gifford*, Gormanston (*Viscount Gormanston*), Halsbury, Hay (*Earl of Kinnoull*), Herschell, Hobhouse, Howth (Earl of Howth : *Baron Howth*), Kenyon, Ker (Marquis of Lothian : *Lord Newbottle*), *Manners, Moncreiff, Monkswell, North, O'Hagan*, Oxenfoord, (Earl of Stair : *Viscount Stair*), *Penzance, Plunket, Romilly*, Rosebery (*Earl of Rosebery*), St. *Leonards*, Somers, Strathspey (*Earl of Seafield*), *Tenterden, Thurlow, Truro, Walsingham, Westbury*, Wigan (*Earl of Crawford*), and Wynford.

The peerages whose founders were, or are, naval or military commanders were those of the Dukes of Beaufort (*Earl of Worcester*), *Marlborough*, Newcastle (*Earl of Lincoln*), and *Wellington;* the Earls Amherst (*Lord Amherst*), Cadogan, of Camperdown (*Viscount Duncan*), Cathcart, *of Carlisle, of Chesterfield*, Craven (*Lord Craven*), of Dartmouth (*Lord Dartmouth*), *of Denbigh, of Derby*, of Effingham (*Lord Howard of Effingham*), of Gainsborough (*Lord Barham*), *Grey, Howe,* Lichfield (*Lord Anson*), Lindsey, Nelson (*Viscount Nelson*), *Pembroke,* Poulett (*Lord Poulett*), Powis (*Lord Clive*), *Sandwich, Scarborough, Shrewsbury, Stanhope, Strafford, Suffolk, Vane* (Marquis of Londonderry), Viscounts Bridport (*Lord Bridport*), *Cobham, Combermere, Exmouth, Hardinge, Hill, Hood, Gough, Leinster* (*Duke of Leinster*), *St. Vincent, Torrington,* and *Wolseley;* Lords *Abercromby, Alcester,*

APPENDIX C.

Beaumont, Brancepeth (*Viscount Boyne*), *Byron, de Saumarez, Dorchester, Fitzhardinge, Gardner,* Granard (*Earl of Granard*), *Harris, Hawke, Keane, Minster* (*Marquis of Conyngham*), *Napier of Magdala, Niddry* (Earl of Hopetoun), *Raglan, Ramsay* (Earl of Dalhousie), *Rodney, Sandhurst, Seaton, Southampton,* and *Vivian.*

Those peerages which had or have for their founders Secretaries of State, Lords of the Treasury, Ambassadors, Colonial and Indian Governors, and the like, were those of the Dukes of Bedford (*Earl of Bedford*), Brandon (Duke of Hamilton), Grafton (sitting as *Earl of Arlington*), Leeds, Northumberland (*Earl of Northumberland*), Portland (*Earl of Portland*), *Somerset,* and Sutherland (*Lord Gower*) ; the Marquises of Bath (*Viscount Weymouth*), *Bute, Dufferin and Ava,* Exeter (*Lord Burghley*), Normanby (*Earl of Mulgrave*), Northampton (*Earl of Northampton*), Ripon (*Lord Grantham*), Salisbury (*Earl of Salisbury*), and *Winchester ;* the Earls of Abingdon (*Lord Norreys*), *Albemarle, Aylesford, Berkeley,* Warwick and Brooke (*Lord Brooke*), Brownlow (*Lord Brownlow*), *Buckinghamshire, Clarendon,* Cowley (*Lord Cowley*), Doncaster (Duke of Buccleuch : *Lord Scott, of Buccleuch*), *Durham, Granville, Harrington,* Hillsborough (*Marquis of Downshire*), *Iddesleigh, Ilchester, Jersey,* Lonsdale (*Viscount Lonsdale*), Lytton (*Lord Lytton*), *Malmesbury, Minto,* Mount Edgcumbe (*Lord Edgcumbe*), Onslow (*Lord Onslow*), *Orford, Portsmouth, Russell,* Temple of Stowe (Duke of Buckingham and *Earl Temple*), and Wharncliffe (Baron Wharncliffe) ; Viscounts *Bolingbroke, Canterbury,* Clancarty (Earl of Clancarty), *Cranbrook, Cross, Gordon of Aberdeen* (Earl of Aberdeen), *Halifax, Hampden, Hutchinson* (*Earl of Donoughmore*), *Melville,* Oxenbridge (*Lord Monson*), Portman (*Lord Portman*), *Sherbrooke,* and *Sidmouth ;* Lords *Aberdare, Ampthill, Ashburton, Auckland, Basing, Belper, Boyle* (Earl of Orrery), *Brabourne, Brassey,* Carleton (*Earl of Shannon*), Carlingford, Carysfort (Earl of Carysfort : *Lord Carysfort*), Chaworth (Earl of Meath : *Lord Brabazon*), *Clanwilliam* (Earl of Clanwilliam), *Clifford of Chudleigh, Colchester, Connemara, Cottesloe, Deramore,* Douglas (Earl of Home : *Lord Home*), *Eddisbury* (and Stanley of Adderley), *Elgin* (Earl of Elgin and Kincardine), *Emly, Ettrick* (Lord Napier, of Merchistoun), Fisherwick (Marquis of Donegall : *Lord Chichester*), Foxford (Earl of Limerick : *Lord Glentworth*), *Grantley, Hampton, Hatherton, Heytesbury, Knutsford, Lawrence, Lingen,* Lovel and Holland (*Earl of Egmont*), *Lyveden, Meredyth* (*Lord Athlumney*), *Monck* (Viscount Monck), *Monk Bretton, Monteagle of Brandon,* Northington (*Lord Henley*), *Norton, Oriel* Viscount Massereene and Ferrard), *Petre, Reay* (Lord Reay), *St. Oswald,*
• *Sandys,* Sheffield (*Earl of Sheffield*), *Somerhill* (*Marquis of Clanricarde*), *Stalbridge, Stanley of Preston,* Stuart of Castle Stuart (*Earl of Moray*), *Wantage,* and *Worlingham* (Earl of Gosford).

Besides these, the peerages of two ladies, the Viscountess Hambleden and the Baroness Macdonald of Earnscliffe, commemorated the services of a First Lord of the Treasury and a " Prime " Minister of the Canadian Dominion.

COMPOSITION OF HOUSE OF LORDS. 383

There were six peerages in the House of Lords of royal origin, besides those giving seats to the heir apparent and his eldest son, the Dukedoms of Albany, Connaught, and Edinburgh, held by Princes of Saxe-Coburg-Gotha, the Dukedoms of Cumberland and Cambridge held by Princes of Hanover and Brunswick, and the Dukedom of Norfolk representing the Earldom of Norfolk bestowed in 1312 on Thomas of Brotherton, third son of Edward I.

Of peerages conferred on the representatives of literature, science, and art, as such, there was but one, the Barony of Tennyson held by the Poet Laureate ; for the first Lord Lytton, like the second, was not only a man of literary genius but a statesman.

Thus, putting aside the five Lords and ex-Lords of Appeal (Lords Blackburn, Hannen, Watson, Morris, and Macnaghten), out of four hundred and eighty-eight normal peerages of England, Great Britain, and the United Kingdom, sixty-six had their origin in naval and military, sixty-six in judicial, and one hundred and seventeen in other civil, services to the Empire, eight found their cause and source in the Monarchy, and one owed its existence to poetry.

But if, extending our view beyond the prime origin of a peerage, each subsequent promotion in rank were held to amount to a new creation—and it would be difficult, if not impossible, to rebut such a contention—this enumeration would require to be very greatly extended.

Thus, for example, the fourth Earl of Uxbridge, and first Marquis of Anglesey, was Master-General of the Ordnance, a Field Marshal, and Lord Lieutenant of Ireland. The first Earl and sixteenth Baron Delawarr was Speaker of the House of Lords, a General of Horse, and Captain-General and Governor of New York and New Jersey. The second Lord Conway and first Earl and Marquis of Hertford was Lord Lieutenant of Ireland and an Ambassador. The second Baron and first Earl Waldegrave was an Ambassador. The second Baron Ardrossan and first Earl of Winton in the Peerage of the United Kingdom, thirteenth Scottish Earl of Eglinton, was Lord Lieutenant of Ireland. The second Viscount and first Marquis Townshend was a Field Marshal, Master-General of the Ordnance, Governor of Jersey, and Lord Lieutenant of Ireland. The second Baron Wycombe and first Marquis of Lansdowne, Earl of Shelburne in Ireland, was a General, a Secretary of State, and First Lord of the Treasury. The fourth Earl and first Duke of Devonshire was a Lord Justice of England, and a Commissioner for the Union with Scotland. The second Lord Capel and first Earl of Essex was Lord Lieutenant of Ireland, First Lord of the Treasury, and an Ambassador.

Among the Peers previously enumerated are some who under this scheme of origin might put forward a double claim to a seat in the Upper Chamber.

Thus the Earl of Shrewsbury and Talbot represents not only the Richard Talbot, Constable of Ireland, Marshal of France, Lieutenant of Ireland, Lieutenant-General of Aquitaine, Governor and Lieutenant-General of France and Normandy, from whom he inherits England's premier Earldom, but Charles, Lord Talbot, Lord High Chancellor of Great Britain. The third Lord Talbot of 1733 was created Earl Talbot in 1784, and the fourth Earl Talbot succeeded as eighteenth Earl of Shrewsbury in 1856.

The first Viscount Falmouth was Vice-Treasurer of England for seventeen years, but the present Viscount as Lord le Despencer holds the Barony created for Hugh le Despencer, Justiciar of England, in 1264.

The first Viscount Gordon, fourth Scottish Earl of Aberdeen, was Secretary of State for Foreign Affairs, and a First Lord of the Treasury; and the first Earl of Aberdeen was Lord President of the Court of Session and Lord High Chancellor of Scotland.

Thomas Villiers, the first Earl of Clarendon of the present creation, was a Minister Plenipotentiary, Lord of the Admiralty, Chancellor of the Duchy of Lancaster, and a Lord of Trade and Foreign Plantations. But his wife was a granddaughter of the last Earl of Clarendon of 1661 creation, and the first Earl of 1661 was Edward Hyde, Lord High Chancellor of England.

The first Lord Ettrick, in the Peerage of Scotland Lord Napier of Merchistoun, has been an Ambassador and Governor of Madras, and the first Lord Napier was a Lord of Session.

The Duke of Norfolk, as Earl of Arundel, represents through John Fitzalan, fourth Lord of Clun, and sixth of Oswaldestre, who succeeded to that Earldom in 1243, William de Albiney, Ambassador in 1165 and 1167, and joint commander of the royal army in 1173.

In January, 1892, the House of Lords had four Peers in it who had held the office of Lord Lieutenant of Ireland, the Marquis of Londonderry, Earl Cowper, Earl Spencer, and the Earl of Aberdeen, and one Peer who was then holding it, the Earl of Zetland; four past or present Viceroys of India, the Marquis of Dufferin and Ava, the Marquis of Ripon, the Marquis of Lansdowne, and the Earl of Northbrook; four past or present Governors-General of Canada, Lords Monck, Dufferin, Lansdowne, and Stanley of Preston; five Peers who were holding or had held minor Indian governments, Lords Napier and Ettrick, Reay, Connemara, Harris, and Wenlock; and five who filled or had filled the office of Governor of one of the greater Australasian Colonies, the Earls of Jersey, Onslow, Hopetoun, and Kintore, and Lord Carrington.

The Upper Chamber contained three Peers who had held the post of Secretary of State for Foreign Affairs, Lord Salisbury, Lord Derby, and Lord Rosebery; six Peers who had held the office of Secretary of State for India, Lord Cross, Lord Cranbrook, Lord Kimberley, Lord Derby, Lord Salisbury, and the Duke of Argyll; five Peers who had held the office of Secretary of State for the Colonies, Lord Grey, Lord Derby, Lord Kimberley, Lord Stanley of Preston, and Lord A. Knutsford; four Peers who had been Secretary of State for Home Affairs, Lord Cross, Lord Cranbrook, Lord Sherbrooke, and Lord Aberdare; two Peers who

COMPOSITION OF HOUSE OF LORDS.

had been Secretary for Scotland, the Duke of Richmond and Gordon, and the Marquis of Lothian ; one Peer who had been Secretary of State for War, Lord Stanley of Preston ; two Peers who had been First Lord of the Admiralty, Lord Northbrook and Lord Ripon ; and one Peer who had been Chancellor of the Exchequer, Lord Sherbrooke.

Among the Peers, who sat or had sat in a Conservative or Liberal Cabinet, were the Duke of Rutland, Lord Harrowby, Lord Cadogan, and Lord Carlingford and Clermont.

The House contained one Lord Chancellor of Great Britain, Lord Halsbury, and two ex-Chancellors, Lord Herschell and Lord Selborne ; the Lord Chancellor of Ireland, Lord Ashbourne ; the Lord Chief Justice of England, Lord Coleridge ; the Master of the Rolls, Lord Esher ; and several retired judges.

Of the flag officers on the active list of the Royal Navy the House of Lords contained but two, the Duke of Edinburgh and the Earl of Clanwilliam ; and of general officers on the active list of the Army, in addition to the Prince of Wales and the Commander-in-Chief, Lord Wolseley, Lord Chelmsford, the Duke of Connaught, the Duke of Cumberland, and Lord Methuen. But there were many members of the Upper Chamber serving in the junior ranks of the United Service, and some, as the Duke of Grafton, Lord Howe, Lord Bridport, Lord Clarina. Lord de Ros, Lord Alcester, and Lord Northampton, who had retired with the rank of flag or field officers.

There were two Peers who were or had been Ambassadors, Lord Dufferin and Ava, and Lord Napier and Ettrick ; and two Peers who were or had been Envoys Extraordinary and Ministers Plenipotentiary, Lord Sackville and Lord Vivian.

In addition to the above, there was a long array of those who had held subordinate posts in an Administration, and of Lord Lieutenants of counties ; nor would these exhaust the list of Peers of public official distinction.

APPENDIX D.

LIST OF PEERS, WHOSE ANCIENT TITLES HAVE BEEN MERGED IN THOSE OF HIGHER BUT MORE RECENT CREATION.

THE Duke of Norfolk in 1483 is the Earl of Arundel of 1155.

The Marquis of Lansdowne, in the Peerage of Great Britain, dates from 1784, but as Baron Kerry and Lixnaw in the Peerage of Ireland, he goes back in unbroken male descent to the year 1200.

The Great British Viscount of Leinster dates from 1747, and the Irish Duke of Leinster from 1766, but the Irish Earl of Kildare dates from 1316, and the Irish Baron of Offaly from 1205. The first Viscount and Duke of Leinster was the twentieth Earl of Kildare.

The Gowers, from Marquises of Stafford, became Dukes of Sutherland in 1833, but since 1839 they have held the ancient Earldom of Sutherland, created in 1228, as heirs, through the Gordons, of the first Earl, William, whose father, Hugo de Moravia, had received Sutherland as a lordship from William the Lion.

Viscount Falmouth, in the Peerage of Great Britain, dates from 1720, but as Lord le Despencer in the Peerage of England he goes back to 1264.

The Earldom of Delawarr dates from 1761, but the Barony of Delawarr from 1299. The first Earl was the sixteenth Baron, in unbroken male descent from Reginald, fifth Baron West, who was summoned to Parliament in 1427 as sixth Lord Delawarr.

The Dukedom of Beaufort dates from 1682. But the first of the family in the House of Lords was Charles Somerset, natural son of Henry, third and penultimate Duke (the fourth Duke left neither legitimate nor natural issue) and seventh Earl of Somerset, whose ancestor John Beaufort, first Earl of Somerset (1397), was a legitimated son of " old John of Gaunt, time-honoured Lancaster." Charles Somerset, who was created Lord Herbert of Ragland, Chepstow, and Gower in 1506 and Earl of Worcester in 1514, married Lady Elizabeth Herbert, daughter and heiress of William, second Baron Herbert of 1461, and Earl of Pembroke of 1468, creation, who had been created Earl of Huntingdon in exchange for the latter dignity; and the second Earl of Worcester succeeded his mother

ANCIENT TITLES MERGED IN MODERN CREATIONS. 387

as Lord Herbert of 1461. After the Somersets had passed from Earls into Marquises of Worcester, and from Marquises of Worcester into Dukes of Beaufort, the fourth Duke married Elizabeth Berkeley, sister and sole heiress of Norborne, Lord Botetourt of 1305. Thus the Dukes of Beaufort date in the Peerage, not from 1682, but from 1461, and since the Barony of Botetourt fell to the fifth Duke in 1803, from 1305.

Viscount Hampden, in the Peerage of the United Kingdom, dates from 1884, but Lord Dacre in the Peerage of England from 1321.

The United Kingdom Barony of Ormonde dates from 1821, but the Irish Earldom of Ormonde from 1328. The first Irish Marquis and United Kingdom Baron was the nineteenth Earl.

The Scottish Earl of Loudoun dates from 1633, but the English Barony of Botreaux from 1368.

The Barony of Tyrone, in the Peerage of Great Britain, dates from 1786, but the Irish Marquis of Waterford (1789) is in the Peerage of the same Kingdom Baron de la Poer of 1375.

The Duke of Brandon, in the Union Peerage, dates from 1711, and the Scottish Duke of Hamilton from 1643, but the same Peer is Earl of Angus of 1389.

The Marquisate of Abergavenny dates from 1876, but the first Baron of Abergavenny, in 1392, was William Beauchamp, fourth son of Thomas, eleventh Earl of Warwick ; or, if not, for this has been questioned, then certainly, as the only possible alternative, by a fresh creation in 1450, Edward Neville, a cadet, like the king-maker Warwick, of the Earls of Westmorland, who had married Elizabeth, daughter of the second Baron of 1392. The first Neville Earl of Westmorland (1397) was Ralph, eighth Baron Neville of Raby. The first Earl of Abergavenny was the seventeenth or fifteenth Baron.

The United Kingdom Barony of Wigan dates from 1826, but the Scottish Earldom of Crawford from 1398.

The United Kingdom Barony of Fingall dates from 1831, but the Irish Earldom of Fingall from 1628, and the Irish Barony of Killeen from 1403.

The United Kingdom Lord Meldrum of 1815 is the Scottish Lord Huntly of 1408.

The United Kingdom Barony of Bowes dates from 1887, but the first ancestor of the Earl of Strathmore in the Scottish Peerage was the Lord Glamis of 1445.

The Dukedom of Montrose dates from 1707, and the Dukedom of Argyll from 1701, each being associated with a later Union peerage, but a Lord Graham and a Lord Campbell were in the Scottish Peerage in 1445.

The 1796 Lord Stuart of Castle-Stuart, in the Peerage of Great Britain, is the Scottish Earl of Moray of 1562 and Lord Gray of 1445.

The United Kingdom Earl of Winton of 1859 is the Scottish Earl of Eglinton of 1508 and Lord Montgomerie of 1449.

The United Kingdom Lord Kilmarnock of 1831 is the Scottish Earl of Erroll of 1452, and Lord Hay of Slains of 1450.

APPENDIX D.

The United Kingdom Marquis of Ailsa of 1831 is the Scottish Earl of Cassilis of 1509, and Lord Kennedy of 1452.

The United Kingdom Earldom of Cathcart dates from 1815, but the Scottish Barony of Cathcart from 1460.

Lord Lovat, in the Peerage of the United Kingdom, dates from 1837, but in the Peerage of Scotland from 1470.

The United Kingdom Baron Douglas of 1835 is the Scottish Earl of Home of 1605, and Baron Home of 1475.

Baron Gormanston, in the Peerage of the United Kingdom, dates from 1868, but Viscount Gormanston, in the Peerage of Ireland, from 1478.

The United Kingdom Baron Houth of 1881 is the Irish Earl of Howth of 1767, but the Irish Baron Howth of 1482.

APPENDIX E.

LIST OF PEERS HOLDING BARONETCIES OR TITLES OF OLDER CREATION THAN THEIR PRESENT PEERAGES.

THERE are more than a hundred Peers sitting in the House with baronetcies of older creation than their peerages ; and many of these baronetcies date from the seventeenth century.

The Earldom of Buckinghamshire dates from 1746, and the Barony of Hobart from 1728, but Sir Henry Hobart, Chief Justice of the Common Pleas, was created a baronet at the first institution of the order in 1611. The ancestors of the Viscount St. John of 1716, and the Earl Ferrers of 1711, Sir John St. John and Sir George Shirley, were also among the earliest batch of baronets.

The Barony of Gerard dates from 1876, the Earldom of Kimberley from 1866, and the Viscounty of Oxenbridge from 1886, but Sir Thomas Gerard, Sir Philip Wodehouse, and Sir Thomas Monson, were created baronets in 1611.

The Viscount Cobham of 1718 creation is descended in direct male line from Sir Thomas Lyttelton, Baronet of 1618.

The Duke of Westminster holds the 1622 baronetcy of Sir Richard Grosvenor ; but, writes Bishop Stubbs, "The great suit between Scrope and Grosvenor for the right to bear the 'bend or' on the field azure, is one of the *causes célèbres* of the Middle Ages ; it dragged on its course from 1385 to 1390 ; a vast mass of evidence was brought upon both sides, and the victory of Scrope was one of the first facts that brought before the notice of the Baronage the antiquity claimed for the house of Grosvenor."*

The Marquis Townshend of 1786 represented Sir Roger Townshend, Baronet of 1617 ; the Lord Bagot of 1780, Sir Hervey Bagot, Baronet of 1627.

The Lord Scarsdale of 1761, the Lord Kesteven of 1868, the Earl of Iddesleigh of 1885, the Lord Wenlock of 1839, and the Lord Poltimore of 1831, represented Sir John Curzon, Sir Thomas Trollope, Sir John Northcote, Sir Thomas Lawley, and Sir John Bampfylde, Baronets of 1641.

---

* "Constitutional History," ch. xxi.

The Earl of Ravensworth of 1874 represented Sir Thomas Liddell, Baronet of 1642; the Marquis of Bath of 1789, Sir Henry Thynne, Baronet of 1641.

The Lord Wrottesley of 1838 creation represented Sir Walter Wrottesley, Baronet of 1642; but he also represented Sir Hugh de Wrottesley, one of the original Knights of the Garter.

The Earl Waldegrave of 1729 represented Sir Edward Waldegrave, Baronet of 1643; the Lord Acton of 1869, Sir Edward Acton, Baronet of 1644.

The Earl of Bradford of 1815 represented Lord Keeper Sir Orlando Bridgeman, Baronet of 1660. The 1801 Earl of Onslow, the 1821 Earl of Stradbroke, and the 1839 Lord Stanley of Alderley all hold baronetcies of 1660. The first Lord Stanley of Alderley was descended from the third son of Thomas, Lord Stanley in 1456.

The Earl of Romney of 1831 represented Sir John Marsham, Baronet of 1663.

The 1801 Earl of Rosslyn holds the 1660 baronetcy of Sir Charles Erskine.

The 1711 Lord Middleton, the 1815 Earl Brownlow, the 1826 Viscount Combermere, are Baronets of 1677; the 1826 Lord de Tabley a Baronet of 1671; the 1871 Marquis of Ripon a Baronet of 1689. The 1813 Earl of Minto holds the 1700 baronetcy of Sir Gilbert Elliott, Lord Justice Clerk.

Among Peers of the United Kingdom, not also Peers of Scotland or Ireland, fourteen, the Earls of Zetland, Grey, and Northbrook, Lords Churston, Congleton, Derwent, Exmouth, Haldon, Hill, Halifax, Heytesbury, Mostyn, Northbourne, and Tredegar hold eighteenth century baronetcies. Lord Churston holds the baronetcy of the eminent judge Sir Francis Buller, and Lord Congleton represents Sir John Parnell, Irish Chancellor of the Exchequer in 1787.

Among Peers of Scotland sitting in their own right in the House of Lords, the Earl of Aberdeen holds the 1642 baronetcy of Sir John Gordon; the Marquis of Breadalbane the 1621 baronetcy of Sir Duncan Campbell; the Earl of Seafield the 1625 baronetcy of Sir John Colquhoun; the Earl of Stair the 1644 baronetcy of Sir James Dalrymple; the Earl of Rosebery the 1651 baronetcy of Sir Archibald Primrose, who, as a Lord of Session, bore the title of Lord Carrington. These baronetcies were acquired in every case before accession to the Scottish Peerage.

Among Irish Peers in like case the Earl of Sefton holds the 1611 baronetcy of Sir Richard Molyneux; the Earl of Kenmare the 1622 baronetcy of Sir Valentine Browne; Lord Gage the 1622 baronetcy of Sir John Gage; the Earl of Granard the 1628 baronetcy of Sir Arthur Forbes; the Earl of Gosford the 1628 baronetcy of Sir Archibald Acheson; the Earl of Arran the 1622 baronetcy of Sir Arthur Gore; the Earl of Egmont the 1661 baronetcy of Sir John Perceval; the Earl of Roden the 1665 baronetcy of Sir Robert Jocelyn; the Marquis of Dufferin the 1694 baronetcy of Sir Robert Blackwood; Lord de Vesci the 1698 baronetcy of Sir Thomas Vesey, Bishop of Ossory and Killaloe.

PEERS HOLDING ANCIENT BARONETCIES. 391

Among Irish Peers not also in the Union Peerage, Lord Valentia holds the 1620 baronetcy of Sir Francis Annesley ; Lord Hotham the 1622 baronetcy of Sir John Hotham ; Lord Macdonald the 1625 baronetcy of Sir Donald Macdonald ; Lord Mountmorres the 1631 baronetcy of Sir John Morres ; the Earl of Lucan the 1632 baronetcy of Sir Henry Bingham ; Lord Kilmaine the 1636 baronetcy of Sir John Browne ; Lord Downe the 1642 baronetcy of Sir Christopher Dawnay ; Lord Southwell the 1662 baronetcy of Sir Thomas Southwell ; Lord Aylmer the 1662 baronetcy of Sir Christopher Aylmer ; Lord Muncaster the 1676 baronetcy of Sir William Pennington ; the Earl of Rosse the 1677 baronetcy of Sir Lawrence Parsons ; the Earl of Kingston the 1682 baronetcy of Sir Robert King. Seven hold baronetcies of the eighteenth century.

Many peerages, again, have been founded by cadet branches of peerage families, and as a matter of aristocracy, if royal creation is to be regarded, they must be carried back to the date of the first peerage conferred on the elder branch of their house.

Thus the Barony of Raglan dates from 1852, but the first Lord Raglan was eighth son of the fifth Duke of Beaufort. The first Duke of Beaufort was the third Marquis of Worcester, the first Marquis was the fifth Earl of Worcester, and the first Earl (1514), Charles Somerset, was incorporated in the Peerage as Lord Herbert in 1506.

The first Lord Penrhyn of 1866 was full brother of the eighteenth Earl of Morton of 1458. The Barony of Erskine dates from 1806, but the first Lord Erskine was third son of the tenth Earl of Buchan of 1469.

The first Lord Grey de Ruthyn (1324) was a younger son of the third Lord Grey of Codnor. The first Lord Berners (1445) was fourth son of an Earl of Ewe. The first Lord Home was descended from a second son of the third Earl of Dumbar.

The first Lord Howard of Effingham was seventh son of the second Duke of Norfolk, and the first Lord Howard of Glossop was second son of the thirteenth Duke of Norfolk. The first Earl of Berkshire was second son of the first Earl of Suffolk, and the first Earl of Suffolk was second son of the fourth Duke of Norfolk. The first Earl of Caryle was descended from the third son of the fourth Duke of Norfolk.

The first Lord Ebury is the third son, and the second Earl of Wilton was the second son, of the first Marquis of Westminster, and the first Lord Stalbridge is the second son of the second Marquis.

The first Earl Granville was second son of the first Marquis of Stafford ; the first Earl of Ellesmere was second son of the second Marquis of Stafford, and first Duke of Sutherland, and of the Duchess-Countess of an Earldom dating from 1228 ; and the first Earl of Cromarty of the present creation is third son of the third Duke of Sutherland and his first Duchess.

The first Earl Russell was third son of the fifth Duke of Bedford, and the first Lord Ampthill was brother of the ninth Duke, and grandson of the seventh.

The first Lord Chesham was fourth son of the first Earl of Burlington, and the first Earl of Burlington was third son of the fourth Duke of Devonshire.

The first Earl Spencer was a grandson of the third Earl of Sunderland, and the first Lord Churchill a younger son of the third Duke of Marlborough.

The first Earl of Montgomery was second son of the second Earl of Pembroke; the first Earl of Carnarvon was grandson of the eighth Earl of Pembroke; the first Lord Herbert of Lea was second son of the eleventh Earl of Pembroke.

The first Lord Manners was a grandson, and the first Viscount Canterbury was a great-grandson, of the third Duke of Rutland; the first Duke of Rutland was the ninth Earl, and the first Earl of Rutland (1525) was the thirteenth Lord de Ros.

The first Earl of Abington was sixth son of the second Earl of Lindsey, and the first Earl of Lindsey was tenth Lord Willoughby de Eresby.

The first Earl of Shannon, in the Peerage of Ireland, was grandson of the first Earl of Orrery, and the first Earl of Orrery was third son of the first Earl Cork.

The first Irish Viscount Boyne was descended from a fourth son of the first Scottish Lord Paisley, and the first Lord Paisley was fourth son of the second Earl of Arran, Duke of Chatelherault in France.

The first Earl of Orkney, in the Peerage of Scotland, was fifth son of the fourth Duke of Hamilton; the first Earl of Kintore was third son of the sixth Earl Marischal; the first Earl of Dunmore was second son of the first Marquis of Atholl; the first Earl of Breadalbane was descended from the third son of the first Lord Campbell, ancestor of the Earls and Dukes of Argyll.

The first Lord Montagu of Beaulieu is second son of the fifth Duke of Buccleuch; the first Earl of Mansfield was fourth son of the fifth Viscount Stormont; the first Lord Wharncliffe was grandson of the third Earl of Bute; the first Lord Niddry was second son of the second Earl of Hopetoun; the first Lord Wantage is a great-grandson of the fifth Earl of Balcarres; the first Lord Lamington was descended from a sixth son of the eighth Earl of Dundonald.

The first Lord Cowley was the sixth son, and the first Duke of Wellington the third surviving son, of the first Earl of Mornington; the first Lord de Mauley was third son of the third Earl of Bessborough; the first Lord Londesborough was third son of the first Marquis of Conyngham; the first Lord Templemore was second son of the first Marquis of Donegal; the first Lord Trevor is the third son of the third Marquis of Downshire; the first Lord Stewart and Earl Vane was second son of the first Marquis of Londonderry.

The first Earl of Clarendon, of the present creation, was third son of the second Earl of Jersey. The first Earl of Aylesford, was second son of the first Earl of Nottingham. The first Earl of Salisbury was second son of the first Lord Burghley. The first Earl of Ripon was second son of the second Lord Grantham.

ENNOBLED BRANCHES OF TITLED FAMILIES. 393

The first Earl of Aboyne, in the Peerage of Scotland, was fourth son of the second Marquis of Huntly ; the first Lord Lindsay of Balcarres was grandson of the ninth Earl of Crawford ; the first Lord Maderty, ancestor of Viscount Strathallan, was second son of the third Lord Drummond ; the first Earl of Melfort was second son of the third Earl of Perth ; the first Viscount Dunblane was third son of the first Duke of Leeds.

The first Lord Langford, in the Peerage of Ireland, was fourth son of the fourth Earl of Bective ; the first Lord Decies was third son of the first Beresford Earl of Tyrone ; the first Lord Radstock was second son of the third Earl Waldegrave ; the first Viscount Mountgarret was second son of the eighth Earl of Ormonde.

The first Byng Earl of Strafford was great-grandson of the first Viscount Torrington ; the first Lord Rowton is grandson of the second Earl of Belmore ; the first Lord Apsley was second son of the first Earl Bathurst ; the first Lord Sondes was second son of the first Lord Monson ; the first Lord Stafford was second son of an Earl of Arundel ; the first Lord Alcester is great-grandson of the first Marquis of Hertford ; the first Lord Southampton was grandson of the second Duke of Grafton ; the first Lord Guilford was second son of the fourth Lord North ; the first Lord Sackville is fourth son of the fifth Earl Delawarr ; the first Lord Stanley of Preston is second son of the fourteenth Earl of Derby ; the first Viscount Hampden was second son of the twenty-first Lord Dacre.

Sometimes a cadet branch of a Peerage family, after establishing a Peerage for itself, succeeds to the representation of the parent stem.

Thus, the fourth Earl of Berkshire succeeded as eleventh Earl of Suffolk in 1745. The fourth Earl Talbot was declared eighteenth Earl of Shrewsbury in 1858. The second Lord Vere of Hanworth succeeded as fifth Duke of St. Albans in 1787. The second Earl of Ripon succeeded in 1859 as fourth Lord Grantham and second Earl de Grey. The sixth Earl of Balcarres succeeded in 1808 as twenty-third Earl of Crawford. The second Earl of Nottingham succeeded in 1729 as sixth Earl of Winchilsea. The fourth Earl of Melfort succeeded in 1800 as twelfth Earl of Perth. The second Earl Vane succeeded in 1872 as fifth Marquis of Londonderry and third Lord Stewart.

The first Earl of Shelburne, in the Peerage of Ireland, and Baron Wycombe in that of Great Britain, was second son of the first Earl of Kerry. The second Earl of Shelburne was created Marquis of Lansdowne, and the third Marquis succeeded in 1818 as fourth Earl of Kerry.

The first Earl of Burlington (1831) was Lord George Cavendish, third son of the fourth Duke of Devonshire, and the second Earl succeeded as seventh Duke in 1858.

The first Earl of Beverley (1790) was Algernon Percy, Lord Lovaine, second son of the first Duke of Northumberland. The second Earl succeeded as fifth Duke in 1865.

Other peerages, again, have passed away from certain families (through

APPENDIX E.

females and otherwise) while they have retained subsequently acquired peerages of later date.

The Dukedom of Newcastle dates only from 1754, but the first Clinton, Duke of Newcastle, was ninth Earl of Lincoln, and the first Earl of Lincoln (1572) was ninth Baron Clinton by writ of 1332, which Barony passed out of the family in 1692 on the death of the fifth Earl.

The Barony of Braybrooke dates from 1788, but the first Baron was fourth Lord Howard de Walden of 1597.

The Earldom of Lindsey dates from 1626, but the first Earl was tenth Lord Willoughby de Eresby of 1313.

The Earldom of Coventry dates from 1697, but the first Earl was fifth Baron Coventry of 1628. The Barony became extinct in 1719 on the death of the fourth Earl.

The Marquisate of Northampton dates from 1812, and the Earldom of Northampton from 1618, but the first Earl was second Baron Compton of 1572. The Barony passed out in 1754 on the death of the fifth Earl. The Earldom of Berkeley dates from 1679, but the Berkeleys were Barons by tenure before 1170 and by writ from 1295 to 1417. In 1421 James Berkeley, son and heir of James, brother of the last Lord Berkeley of 1295, received a fresh Barony by writ, and the nineteenth Baron of this creation was the Earl of 1679. The Barony has since passed out. The first Earl of Shrewsbury of 1442 was sixth Baron Talbot by writ of 1331. The Barony fell into abeyance on the death of the seventh Earl in 1616. The Earldom of Huntingdon dates from 1529, but the first Earl was third Baron Hastings of 1461. On the death of Francis, Earl of Huntingdon, in 1789, the Barony of Hastings, together with those of Hungerford, Botreaux, and Molines, passed out of the family with his sister Elizabeth, wife of John Rawdon, Earl of Moira, whose son was created Marquis of Hastings in 1817. All four of these old Baronies are now united with the Scottish Earldom of Loudoun.

The Earldom of Ferrers dates only from 1711, but the first Earl was the thirteenth Lord Ferrers of Chartley, and the first Baron of Chartley (1299) was son and heir of Robert Ferrers, seventh and last Earl of Derby (of a line created by Stephen in 1138), who was deprived of that Earldom in 1265. The Earldom of Ferrers on the death of the first Earl went to the second son, the eldest son having predeceased his father and died without male issue. The Barony went out of the family through the daughters of the eldest son, and after passing into the possession of the Townshend family has since gone into abeyance.

The Clintons date in the Peerage not from 1754, nor from 1572, but from 1332 ; the Talbots from 1331 as Barons by writ, and long before as Barons by tenure ; the Berkeleys from before 1170.

It is clear, therefore, that the date of the creation of a Peerage gives no true measure of the nobility or antiquity of the family which holds it.

The Irish Earldom of Castle-Stewart dates only from 1800, but the Irish Barony of Castle-Stewart dates from 1619. The first Irish Baron Castle-

Stewart was in unbroken male descent third Scottish Baron Ochiltree, which Barony he had transferred to a cousin. The first Lord Ochiltree was fourth Baron Avondale in the Peerage of Scotland, getting the name of his Barony changed by Act of Parliament in 1543. The first Lord Avondale (1459) was Andrew Stuart, Chancellor of Scotland, and both he and his younger brother Walter, father of Alexander, second Lord Avondale, were sons of Walter Stuart, eldest son of Murdoch, second Duke of Albany. Murdoch was forfeited by the Poet King James the First in 1425. And the first Duke of Albany (1398), and father of Murdoch, was Robert Stuart, Regent of Scotland, and younger son of Robert the Second.

The Great British Barony of Stuart of Castle-Stuart dates from 1796, but the Scottish Earldom of Moray to which it gives a seat in the Upper Chamber dates from 1562. The first Earl of Moray was James Stuart, Regent of Scotland from 1567 to 1570, natural son of James the Fifth but the present Earls are descended in the male line from James Stuart, second Lord Doune, who married Elizabeth, Countess of Moray, daughter of the Regent. The first Lord Doune (1581) was paternally a grandson of the third Lord Avondale, and the first Lord Avondale was paternally a grandson of Murdoch Stuart second Duke of Albany, a Prince of the Blood Royal of Scotland. Thus the present Earls of Moray belong by unbroken male descent to the Royal House of Stuart.

The Duke, Marquis, and Earl of Abercorn dates in the Peerage of Ireland from 1616 as Lord Strabane, in the Peerage of Great Britain from 1786 as Viscount Hamilton, and in the Peerage of Scotland from 1591 as Lord Paisley. But the first Lord Paisley, Lord Claud Hamilton, was fourth son of the second Earl of Arran, Duke of Chatelherault in France, and the Duke of Abercorn is the heir male of the Lords Hamilton, Earls of Arran, and Dukes of Chatelherault, though the Earldom of Arran and other honours of the senior branch of the family passed by marriage to the Douglases, Dukes of Hamilton and Brandon, who since 1761 have been the heads of their own house as Marquises of Douglas and Earls of Angus.

The Irish Earldom of Antrim dates only from 1785, but the first Earl of this line was the sixth Earl of a line dating from 1620. And the first Earl of 1620, Sir Randal Macdonell, created Viscount Dunluce in 1616, was a member of the Clan Donald branch of the great House of the Isles founded by Somerled, Lord or Regulus of Argyll in the twelfth century.

The Scottish Earldom of Airlie dates from 1639, and the Barony of Ogilvy from 1491, but the Earls of Airlie are descended from Gaelic magnates who held a Celtic earldom centuries earlier. "The family of de Ogilvie," writes Robertson,* "sprang from a junior branch of the Earls of Angus whose representative at present in the male line is the Earl of Airlie."

---

* "Scotland under her Early Kings," vol. ii., appendix R.

The United Kingdom Marquisate of Ailsa (1831) conceals from view a Scottish Earldom of Cassilis (1509) and Barony of Kennedy (1451), but long before this Barony the Kennedys had been members of the Baronage. "When the Earldom of Carrick passed by the Countess Marjory to the family of Bruce, her father, Earl Nigel, confirmed the right of the heir male, Roland of Carrick, the ancestor of the Kennedys, to the headship of the family under the earls." * And the Earl of Carrick represented " a Gaelic line of princes which had ruled over Galloway from time immemorial."

In the same way, the Macfarlanes or Clan Pharlane " are undoubted descendants of the old earls of Lennox. The Clan takes its name from Parlane or Bartholomew, a great-grandson of Gilchrist, third son of Alain, Earl of Lennox, and the steps of the pedigree rest upon charter evidence."† The Robertsons or Clan Donnochie " are the male representatives of the old Earls of Athole. Their descent from Duncan, son of Andrew de Atholia, rests upon charter evidence." ‡

The Barony of Strathspey, in the Peerage of the United Kingdom, dates from 1884, but the first Baron was ninth Earl of Seafield in the Peerage of Scotland. The first Earl of Seafield, James Ogilvy, Chancellor of Scotland in 1705, was fourth Earl of Findlater, which latter Earldom has lain dormant since 1811. The titles of Seafield and Strathspey are held by the chief of the Clan Grant, but the Grants were chiefs, and as such noble, for centuries before they inherited a Colquhoun baronetcy or an Ogilvy earldom.

The Earldom of Caithness, in the Peerage of Scotland, dates from 1455, but the first Earl of this creation was third Earl of Orkney, which Earldom he surrendered to the Crown. The first Sinclair Earl of Orkney obtained the Earldom as the son of Sir William St. Clair by his marriage with Isabel, daughter of Malise, Earl of Stratherne, Orkney, and Caithness in 1334; and Earl Malise was the senior co-heir of Thorfinn, Earl of Orkney in 1050 under the Kings of Norway, and Niormaer of Caithness under the Kings of Scotland at the same period.§

The Barony of Stafford dates from 1640, but the first Lord Stafford, William Howard, second son of an Earl of Arundel, was husband of Mary Stafford (created a Baroness in 1640), daughter and heiress of Edward, twentieth Baron Stafford, of a family which held an Earldom of Stafford in the fourteenth century, and a Dukedom of Buckingham in the fifteenth.

The present Earldom of Devon dates from 1553; but for attainders, however, the first Earl of 1553 would have been the fourteenth Earl of 1335 creation. And the first Earl of 1335 was the fifth Baron Courtenay. The present Earls of Devon are descended in direct male line from Philip Courtenay, fourth son of Hugh, the second Earl of the 1335 creation. Thomas the sixth Earl of the original creation was beheaded in 1462,

---

* Robertson.   † Skene, " Celtic Scotland," book iii. ch. 8.
‡ Ibid.   § Ibid., book iii., appendix V.

REVIVED OR RESTORED PEERAGES. 397

and subsequently attainted as a Lancastrian. The seventh Earl was restored in 1471, but also attainted after death as an adherent of the Red Rose. With him became extinct the line of the third Earl, Edward, eldest son of Edward Courtenay, third son of the second Earl. The next line of Earls were descended from Hugh, second son of the same Edward Courtenay. Of these Edward Courtenay was re-created Earl of Devon in 1485 by Henry VII. and William Courtenay in 1511 by Henry VIII. The first Earl of the 1553 creation was a son of Edward, second Earl of the 1485 creation, who had been created Marquis of Exeter in 1525, but was beheaded in 1539, and afterwards attainted.

If English Earldoms descended now as many of them descended in the Middle Ages, the Duke of St. Albans, Lord Vere of Hanworth of 1750 creation, would hold the Earldom of Oxford bestowed on Aubrey de Vere in 1155 in exchange for an earlier Earldom of Cambridge, just as the Duke of Norfolk holds the Earldom of Arundel; and as the King-Maker, a cadet of the Nevilles, Earls of Westmorland, held the Beauchamp Earldom of Warwick and the Montacute Earldom of Salisbury. The first Duke of St. Albans married Lady Diana Vere, eldest daughter and co-heiress of Aubrey, twentieth and last Earl of Oxford, who died in 1703.

Lastly, it must be noticed that many new peerages are merely revivals or restorations of old ones, some of which would at an earlier date have passed without a fresh creation.

The Dukedom of Norfolk, dating from 1483, represents the Mowbray Dukedom of Norfolk created in 1397, and the Earldom of Norfolk bestowed on Thomas of Brotherton in 1312.

The present Dukedom of Northumberland dates only from 1766, but it represents through the seventh Duke of Somerset, created Baron Percy and Earl of Northumberland, the Earldom of Northumberland created in 1397 for Henry, thirteenth Lord Percy, and eighth Baron by writ. The sixth Duke of Somerset, who died in 1748, had married Lady Elizabeth Percy, only daughter and heiress of Joscelyne, eleventh Earl of Northumberland. Sir Hugh Smithson, Baronet of 1660, married in 1740 Lady Elizabeth Seymour, daughter and heiress of Algernon Seymour, seventh Duke of Somerset and first Earl of Northumberland of the new creation, and on the death of his father-in-law, in 1750, succeeded him in the latter Peerage.

The Earldom de Grey, held by the Lord Grantham of 1761 and the Marquis of Ripon of 1871, dates only from 1816, but the first holder of the Earldom, Amabel Campbell, was the daughter and co-heiress of Jemima, Marchioness de Grey, and the Marchioness was the granddaughter of Henry de Grey, eleventh Earl of Kent, who was created Duke of Kent in 1710, and Marquis de Grey in 1740, and died in the latter year. The first Earl of Kent (1465) was Edmund, fourth Lord Grey de Ruthyn, and the Barony of Ruthyn had passed out of the family on the death of the seventh Earl in 1639.

The Earldom of Powis dates from 1804, but the first Earl, son of the ever illustrious Robert Lord Clive of Plassey, and his successor in that Irish peerage, and himself the first Lord Clive in the Peerage of Great Britain, had married in 1784 Lady Henrietta Herbert, sister and heiress of George Edward, second and last Earl of Powis of 1748 creation, who died in 1801. The first Earl of Powis of 1748 was Lord Herbert of Cherbury who had married Barbara Herbert, neice and heiress of William, third and last Marquis and Earl of Powis, who died in 1748. The first Earl (1674) and Marquis (1679) of this line was third Baron Powis; and the first Lord Powis, so created in 1629, was a grandson of William Herbert, first Earl of Pembroke.

The Scottish Dukedom of Athole dates from 1703, and the Earldom of Athole from 1629, but the first Earl, William Murray, second Earl of Tullibardine, was the husband of Lady Dorothea Stewart, eldest daughter of John, fifth Earl of Athole; and the first of this earlier line was John Stewart, created Earl of Athole in 1457.

The first Baron (1806) and Earl (1815) Beauchamp was "lineally descended from William Lygon and his wife Anne Beauchamp, daughter and co-heiress of Richard, second and last Lord Beauchamp of Powyk," which Barony was created in 1447.*

The first Earl of Wilton (1801) and Viscount Grey de Wilton, Sir Thomas Egerton, was "lineally descended from Sir Rowland Egerton, Baronet, and his wife Bridget, sister and co-heiress of Thomas, fifteenth Lord Grey de Wilton by writ of 1295, who was attainted in 1604."

The Earldom of Cromarty dates from 1861, but the Countess in whose favour it was created, Anne, first wife of the third Duke of Sutherland, represented George Mackenzie, third Earl of Cromarty in the Peerage of Scotland of 1703 creation, who was attainted by the Whigs in 1746 for his share in the unsuccessful Royalist rising of the previous year.

The Barony of Kilmarnock dates from 1831, but it represents the Scottish Earldom of Kilmarnock of 1661, and a Barony of Boyd existing before 1459, which were attainted in 1746. The Peer who holds it is Earl of Erroll in the Peerage of Scotland of 1452, and Lord Hay of Slains of 1450, and the first Earl of Erroll was sixth Hereditary Lord High Constable of Scotland by grant to Sir Gilbert Hay in 1315.

The Earldom of Winton, in the Peerage of the United Kingdom, dates from 1859, but the first Earl was the thirteenth Earl of Eglinton, and the heir to the Scottish Earldom of Winton created in 1600, and attainted in 1716. Alexander Seton, third son of the first Earl of Winton, became sixth Earl of Eglinton under a special patent, and assumed the name of Montgomerie. And the first Earl of Winton in the Peerage of Scotland was sixth Lord Seton as holding a Barony created in 1448.

The Earldom of Clarendon, created in 1776, represents, as was seen in an earlier chapter, the Earldom of Clarendon created in 1661.

The Earldom of Manvers dates from 1806, but the first Earl, Charles Medows, who assumed the name of Pierrepont, was nephew and heir of

---

* Sir Harris Nicolas, "Historic Peerage."   † Ibid.

REVIVED AND RESTORED PEERAGES. 399

Evelyn, last Duke of Kingston, who died in 1773. The Dukedom of Kingston was created in 1715, and the first Earl of Kingston, created in 1628, was Robert Pierrepont, Lieutenant-General for the King in 1643.

The Marquisate of Ailesbury dates from 1821, and the Earldom of Ailesbury from 1776, but the first Earl, Thomas Brudenell, was nephew of Charles Bruce, fourth Earl of Elgin in Scotland, and third Earl of Ailesbury (1664) and fourth Lord Bruce of Whorlton (1641) in England, who died in 1747, when his Scottish Earldom devolved on the Earl of Kincardine, while the Barony of Bruce of Tottenham which he had received in 1746 descended to his nephew, a cadet of the Earls of Cardigan, under a special remainder, and his other English honours became extinct.

The Barony of Alington dates from 1876, but the first Lord Alington represented Catharine Alington, sister and co-heiress of George, third and penultimate Baron Alington (1642) in the Peerage of Ireland, and last Baron Alington (1682) in the Peerage of England. The fourth and last Irish Lord Alington died without issue in 1722.

The United Kingdom Barony of Clanbrassil (1821) held by the Irish Earl of Roden, and the Irish Barony of Clandeboye (1800) held by the United Kingdom Marquis of Dufferin and Ava, represent the Hamilton Earldom of Clanbrassil (1647) and Viscounty of Clandeboye (1622), in the Peerage of Ireland, which became extinct in 1675.

The Dukedom of Gordon, in the Peerage of the United Kingdom, dates from 1876, but it represents the Scottish Dukedom of Gordon, created in 1684, which became extinct with the fifth Duke in 1836. Charles, fourth Duke of Richmond, Lennox, and Aubigny married in 1789 Charlotte, eldest daughter of the fourth, and ultimately co-heiress of the fifth, Duke of Gordon.

The Earldom of Bradford dates from 1815, but the first Lord Bradford (1794), Sir Henry Bridgeman, Baronet of 1660, descended in the male line from a Lord Keeper of the Great Seal, was the son and heir of Anne Newport, sister and eventually sole heiress of Thomas, fifth and last Earl of Bradford, who died in 1762. The first Newport Earl of Bradford (1694) and Viscount Newport (1675) was Francis, second Baron Newport of 1642.

The Earldom of Gainsborough dates from 1841, but it represents the Earldom of Gainsborough created for Henry Noel in 1682, and the Viscounty of Campden bestowed in 1628 on Baptist Hicks, both of which became extinct in 1798.

The Earldom of Ellesmere dates from 1846, but the first Earl was second son of the first Duke of Sutherland, and represented on behalf of the senior branch of the Gower family, the Barony of Ellesmere bestowed in 1603 on Thomas Egerton, Lord High Chancellor of England, and the Earldom of Bridgewater to which the second Lord Ellesmere was advanced in 1617.

. The Viscounty of Bolingbroke, created in 1712 for the Tory statesman, recalls the Earldom of Bolingbroke created in 1628 for Oliver, fourth Lord St. John of Bletso, a Parliamentarian, which had become extinct with the third Earl in 1711.

The Earldom of Effingham was created in 1837 for the eleventh Lord Howard of Effingham, but before that the seventh Baron had been created Earl of Effingham in 1731, which Peerage became extinct with the fourth Earl in 1816, and before that the second Baron had been created Earl of Nottingham in 1596, which title became extinct with the third Earl in 1681.

The First Earl of Danby (1674), Thomas Osborne, afterwards first Duke of Leeds, was the son and heir of Sir Edward Osborne, Baronet, by Anne, daughter of Thomas Walmisley, by Eleanor Danvers, sister of Henry, first and last Lord Danvers (1603) and Earl of Danby (1626), who died in 1644.

The Barony of Conway, created in 1703 for the ancestor of the Marquis of Hertford, represents a 1624 Barony, 1627 Viscounty, and 1679 Earldom of Conway, all extinct in 1683.

The Barony of Leigh, created in 1839, is held by the elder branch of the family of the Lords Leigh (1643-1786), to whose estates they succeeded in the present century.

The United Kingdom Barony of Powerscourt (1885) and the Irish Viscounty of Powerscourt (1743) are held by the same family as the Viscounts Powerscourt of from 1665 to 1717 and Richard Wingfield, Viscount Powerscourt, from 1623 to 1634.

The Barony of Tyrone, in the Peerage of Great Britain, dates from 1786, but the first Lord Tyrone was Baron de la Poer of 1375, and second Earl of Tyrone of 1746, in the Peerage of Ireland. And the first Earl of Tyrone, Marcus Beresford, was the husband of Lady Catherine Power, daughter of James, third and last Earl of Tyrone of 1672.

The first Irish Earl of Darnley (1725), John Bligh, was the husband of Theodosia Hyde, Baroness Clifton in the Peerage of England (1608). The Baroness Clifton was the only daughter and heiress of the third Earl of Clarendon by Catharine O'Brien, only daughter and heiress of Henry, Lord of Ibrackan, by Catharine Stewart. And Catharine Stewart was the sister and heiress of Charles, Earl of Darnley and sixth Duke of Lennox in Scotland, and third Duke of Richmond in England, and the granddaughter of Esme Stewart, third Duke of Lennox, by Catharine, only daughter and heiress of Gervase, Lord Clifton.

The Earldom of Tankerville dates from 1714, but the first Earl, Charles Bennet, second Baron Ossulston, was the husband of Lady Mary Grey, only daughter and heiress of Ford, third Lord Grey of Wark, first and last Earl of Tankerville (1695), who died in 1701.

The Earldom of Lonsdale dates from 1807, but a Lowther was Earl of Lonsdale in 1784, though the Earldom became extinct in 1802, and another member of the same family was Viscount Lonsdale in 1696.

The Paget Earldom of Uxbridge, created in 1784 for the nineteenth Baron Paget, and now merged in the Marquisate of Anglesey, represents a former Earldom of Uxbridge held by an elder line of the Lords Paget from 1714 to 1769.

The Earldom of Temple of Stowe dates from 1822, but the first Earl Temple of Stowe was the third Earl Temple of a creation in 1749.

The Earldom of Leicester dates from 1837, but the first Earl was a grand-nephew of Thomas Coke, Earl of Leicester, in 1744.

The Duncombe Earldom of Feversham dates from 1868, and the Barony of Feversham from 1826, but Anthony Duncombe was created Baron Feversham in 1747.

The Walpole Earldom of Orford, created in 1806, represents the Walpole Earldom of Orford created in 1742, which became extinct on the death of the fourth Earl in 1797.

The Earldom of Ravensworth dates from 1874, and the Barony from 1821, but the first Lord Ravensworth, Thomas Henry Liddell, was a nephew of Henry Liddell created Baron Ravensworth in 1747, which peerage became extinct in 1784.

The present Earldom of Cadogan dates from 1800, but the first Earl of this creation, and third Lord Cadogan of Oakley of 1718, was a nephew of the first Lord Cadogan of Oakley, who had been created Lord Cadogan of Reading in 1716, and was created Earl Cadogan in 1718.

The Earldom of Lichfield dates from 1831, and the Viscounty of Anson from 1806, but the first Viscount was the great-nephew of the famous Admiral Lord Anson, Commander-in-Chief of the Fleet, whose Barony of 1747 expired with him in 1762. "His patent of Viscount was being prepared when he died."*

The Earldom of Dudley, created in 1860 for the eleventh Baron Ward, revives the Earldom of Dudley created in 1827 for the fourth Viscount Dudley and Ward. The first Viscount Dudley (1763) was the sixth Baron Ward. Both Viscounty and Earldom expired in 1833.

The first Earl Granville (1815) was a younger son of the first Marquis of Stafford, and great-grandson of Sir William Gower, Baronet, by Jane Granville, aunt and co-heiress of William Henry, third Baron and Viscount Granville and Earl of Bath, and sister of Grace created Countess Granville in 1715, which Earldom expired with its third holder and second Earl in 1776.

The Earldom of Howe dates from 1821, but the first Earl was a grandson of the famous admiral created Earl Howe in 1788, and through his mother inherited from him the Barony of Howe created in the same year.

The Irish Viscounty of Doneraile (1786) and Barony of Doneraile (1776) were created for St. Leger Aldworth, nephew of Hayes St. Leger, fourth and last Viscount Doneraile, who died in 1767. The first Viscount Doneraile of the earlier creation (1703) was the heir male of Sir Anthony St. Leger, K.G., Lord Deputy of Ireland in 1540.

The Barony of Foley, created in 1776, is held by the same family as the Lords Foley of from 1712 to 1766.

---

* Doyle, "Official Baronage."

The United Kingdom Barony of O'Neill, created in 1868, revived for the heirs general of the O'Neills the Barony of O'Neill, which existed from 1793 to 1855, and at various times was united with the higher grades of Viscount and Earl.

The United Kingdom Barony of Loftus dates from 1801, but the first Baron, Charles Tottenham (first Baron 1785 and Viscount 1789 Loftus, and Earl 1794 and Marquis 1800 of Ely, in the Peerage of Ireland), was nephew of Henry, Earl of Ely, and fourth and last Viscount Loftus. And the first Baron (1751) and Viscount (1756) Loftus was Nicholas, heir male of Adam Loftus, Archbishop of Armagh, and Lord Chancellor of Ireland from 1568 to 1575.

The Barony of Sandys, created in 1802 for Maria, Marchioness of Downshire, represents a Barony of Sandys founded in 1743 by a Chancellor of the Exchequer, which became extinct in 1801.

The Barony of Somers dates from 1784, but the first Baron, Charles Cocks, represented his great-uncle, the celebrated Whig Chancellor and statesman, John Somers, whose 1697 Barony of Somers expired with him in 1716.

The Barony of Northington, in the Peerage of the United Kingdom, dates from 1885, but it recalls the Earldom of Northington, created in 1764 for Robert, Lord Henley of 1760, Lord High Chancellor of Great Britain, and extinct in 1786 with the second Earl. The first Lord Henley, in the Peerage of Ireland (1799), had married a daughter of the first Earl who eventually became a co-heiress of her brother, the second Earl.

APPENDIX F.

LIST OF PEERS WHOSE ANCESTORS HAVE DISTINGUISHED THEMSELVES IN THE PUBLIC SERVICE.

THE first Duke of Devonshire, fourth Earl, was a Lord Justice of England and a Commissioner for the Union with Scotland. The second Duke was Lord President of the Council. The third Duke was Lord Privy Seal, and, from 1737 to 1745, Lord Lieutenant of Ireland. The fourth Duke was Lord Lieutenant of Ireland, a Lord Justice of Great Britain, and a First Lord of the Treasury. The fifth Duke was Lord High Treasurer of Ireland from 1766 to 1793.*

The second Earl of Manchester was the Parliamentarian general. The fourth Earl and first Duke was an Ambassador and Secretary of State. The fourth Duke was an Ambassador. The fifth Duke was Governor of Jamaica from 1808 to 1827.*

The second Earl of Sunderland was an Ambassador, Secretary of State, and Lord President of the Council. The third Earl was Secretary of State, Lord Privy Seal, Lord President of the Council, Lord Lieutenant of Ireland, and First Lord of the Treasury. The third Duke of Marlborough was a General, Lord Privy Seal, and Lord Steward. The sixth Duke was Viceroy of Ireland and Lord President of the Council.*

The first Duke of Northumberland was Lord Lieutenant of Ireland. The second Duke, a General, served as Earl Percy in the American rebellion. The fourth Duke was an Admiral. The sixth Duke was a Lord of the Admiralty, President of the Board of Trade, and Lord Privy Seal.*

The first Earl of Northampton, second Baron Compton, was President of the Council of Wales from 1617 to 1630. The second Earl, a Royalist commander, fell fighting for the King in 1643. The third Earl, also a Cavalier officer in the Rebellion, became a Lord of Trade and Foreign Plantations, and Constable of the Tower of London. The fourth Earl was also Constable of the Tower. The seventh Earl was an Ambassador. The second Marquis, and eleventh Earl, was President of the Royal Society from 1838 to 1849.*

---

* Doyle, " Official Baronage."

APPENDIX F.

The second Earl of Pembroke was Lord President of the Council of Wales. The third Earl was Lord Chamberlain. The eighth Earl was a Lord Justice of England, Lord Privy Seal, Lord President of the Council, First Lord of the Admiralty, and Lord High Admiral of Great Britain and Ireland. The ninth Earl was a Lieutenant-General, a Lord Justice, and Groom of the Stole to George II. The tenth Earl was a General and Governor of Portsmouth. The eleventh Earl was a General, an Ambassador, and Governor of Guernsey.*

The second Earl and first Duke of Portland was Governor of Jamaica. The third Duke was Lord President of the Council and First Lord of the Treasury. The fourth Duke was Lord President of the Council and Lord Privy Seal.*

The second Duke of Richmond was a Lieutenant-General, Master of the Horse, and a Lord Justice of Great Britain. The third Duke was a Field Marshal, and for twelve years Master-General of the Ordnance. The fourth Duke was a General, Lord Lieutenant of Ireland, and Governor-General of Canada. The fifth Duke served at Waterloo, retiring from the army as Lieutenant-Colonel, and from 1830 to 1834 was Postmaster-General. The sixth Duke was Lord President of the Council from 1874 to 1880.*

The second Earl of Rutland was Lord President of the North, and "Captain-General of an Army and Admiral of a Fleet against France." The sixth Earl was Admiral of a Fleet. The second Duke, tenth Earl, was a Commissioner for the Union with Scotland. The third Duke was Chancellor of the Duchy of Lancaster for nine years. The fourth Duke was Lord Privy Seal and Lord Lieutenant of Ireland.*

The second Duke of Somerset (restored in 1660) was the Cavalier Marquis of Hertford, and the Lord Beauchamp who in 1610 had married Lady Arabella Stuart. The sixth Duke was Master of the Horse, Lord President of the Council, Speaker of the House of Lords, and a Commissioner for the Union with Scotland. The seventh Duke was a General and Governor of Guernsey. The twelfth Duke was First Lord of the Admiralty.*

The fourth Earl of Shrewsbury was Joint-Ambassador to the Pope, " General of an Army against the Scots," and Lord Steward of the Household. The fifth Earl was Lieutenant-General of the North and Lord President of the Council of the North. The sixth Earl was Earl Marshal of England. The seventh Earl was an Ambassador to France. The twelfth Earl, and first and last Duke, of Shrewsbury was Lord Chamberlain, Secretary of State, Ambassador, Lord High Treasurer, Lord Lieutenant of Ireland, a Lord Justice of England, and a Lord Justice of Great Britain. The third Earl Talbot was Lord Lieutenant of Ireland.*

The second Earl Spencer was Lord Privy Seal, an Ambassador, a Secretary of State, and from 1794 to 1801 First Lord of the Admiralty. The third Earl, as Lord Althorp, was Chancellor of the Exchequer.

---

* Doyle, " Official Baronage."

PEERS WITH DISTINGUISHED ANCESTORS. 405

The fifth Earl has been Lord President of the Council and Lord Lieutenant of Ireland.*

The second Viscount Townshend was a Commissioner for the Union with Scotland, an Ambassador, Lord President of the Council, Lord Lieutenant of Ireland, and from 1714 to 1716 and 1721 to 1730 a Secretary of State. The fourth Viscount and first Marquis was a Field Marshal, Master-General of the Ordnance, Governor of Jersey, and Lord Lieutenant of Ireland. The second Marquis was a Lord of Trade and Foreign Plantations.*

The sixth Fane, Earl of Westmorland, was President of the Board of Trade and Foreign Plantations from 1719 to 1735. The ninth Earl was a General. The tenth Earl was Lord Lieutenant of Ireland from 1789 to 1795, and Lord Privy Seal from 1798 to 1806, and from 1807 to 1827. The eleventh Earl was an Envoy and a General.*

The second Earl of Winchilsea was an Ambassador. The third Earl was an Ambassador and President of the Board of Trade and Foreign Plantations. The seventh Earl was a First Lord of the Admiralty and Lord President of the Council.*

The second Earl of Albemarle was a Lieutenant-General, Privy Councillor, and Ambassador, Commander-in-Chief in Scotland, and a Lord Justice of Great Britain. The third Earl was a General, Governor of Jersey, and in 1762 Commander-in-Chief against the Havannah.*

The second Earl of Buckinghamshire was an Ambassador and Lord Lieutenant of Ireland. The fourth Earl, as Lord Hobart, was Governor of Madras and Secretary of State, and, after succeeding to the peerage, was for four years President of the Board of Control for India.*

The third Earl of Carlisle was a First Lord of the Treasury and a Commissioner for the Union with Scotland. The fourth and sixth Earls were Lords Lieutenant of Ireland, and the fifth Earl was Lord Privy Seal.*

The second Earl of Suffolk was Governor of Jersey. The sixth Earl was President of the Board of Trade and Foreign Plantations. The twelfth Earl was Lord Privy Seal and Secretary of State.*

The second Viscount Torrington was Vice-Treasurer of Ireland for eleven years. The fourth Viscount was a Minister Plenipotentiary for ten years. The sixth Viscount was Vice-Admiral of the Blue. The seventh Viscount was Governor of Ceylon.*

The second Earl of Scarborough was a Lieutenant-General, and for seven years a Cabinet Minister. The third Earl was Envoy Extraordinary for four years. The fourth Earl was a Vice-Treasurer of Ireland.*

The second Earl of Sandwich was Ambassador Extraordinary to Lisbon. The fourth Earl was a General, Ambassador, and Secretary of State, and for thirteen years First Lord of the Admiralty.*

The second Lord Grantham was President of the Board of Trade and

---

* Doyle, " Official Baronage."

Foreign Plantations, a Secretary of State, and from 1771 to 1779 Ambassador at Madrid. The third Lord Grantham, who inherited the Earldom de Grey in 1833, was First Lord of the Admiralty and Lord Lieutenant of Ireland.*

The second Lord Edgcumbe was a Lord of the Admiralty and a Lord of Trade and Foreign Plantations. The third Lord Edgcumbe, and first Earl of Mount Edgcumbe, was an Admiral, and Commander-in-Chief at Plymouth and in the Mediterranean.*

The second Duke of Grafton was Lord Lieutenant of Ireland and a Lord Justice of Great Britain. The third Duke was a Secretary of State, Lord Privy Seal, and a First Lord of the Treasury.*

The second Earl Grey was Secretary of State for Foreign Affairs and First Lord of the Treasury. The third Earl has been Secretary of State for the Colonies.

The third Earl of Hardwicke was Lord Lieutenant of Ireland, and the fourth Earl was Lord Privy Seal.*

The second Lord Wycombe and first Marquis of Lansdowne, in the Union Peerage, was a General, Secretary of State, and First Lord of the Treasury. The third Marquis was a Secretary of State, and from 1830 to 1834, 1835 to 1841, and 1846 to 1852 Lord President of the Council.*

The second Lord Guilford was President of the Board of Trade and Foreign Plantations. The fourth Baron and second Earl was First Lord of the Treasury from 1770 to 1782. The fifth Earl was Governor of Ceylon.*

The first Lord Dalhousie in the United Kingdom Peerage, ninth Earl of Dalhousie in that of Scotland, after serving in the Peninsular War became a General, Governor-General of Canada, and Commander-in-Chief in India. The tenth Earl, second Baron, and first and last Marquis (1849-60) was Governor-General of India from 1847 to 1856.*

The second Earl Bathurst was Lord High Chancellor of Great Britain. The third Earl was a Lord of the Admiralty from 1793 to 1802, Secretary of State from 1812 to 1827, and Lord President of the Council from 1828 to 1830.*

The second Baron and first Earl of Dartmouth was a Lord of Trade and Foreign Plantations, a Lord Justice of Great Britain, Lord Privy Seal, and for seven years a Secretary of State. The second Earl was Lord President of the Board of Trade and Plantations, Lord Privy Seal, and for seven years a Secretary of State. The third Earl was President of the Board of Control for the Affairs of India.*

The tenth and twelfth Earls of Derby were Chancellors of the Duchy of Lancaster. The fourteenth Earl held the chief place in three Administrations. The fifteenth Earl has been Secretary of State for the Colonies and Secretary of State for Foreign Affairs.*

The second Lord Capel and first Earl of Essex was Lord Lieutenant of Ireland, First Lord of the Treasury, and an Ambassador. The second

---

* Doyle, "Official Baronage."

Earl was a Lieutenant-General. The third Earl was Ambassador at Turin from 1732 to 1735.*

The second Baron and first Earl of Harrowby was Chancellor of the Duchy of Lancaster, an Ambassador, President of the Board of Control for India, Secretary of State for Foreign Affairs, and for fifteen years Lord President of the Council. The second Earl was Chancellor of the Duchy and Lord Privy Seal. The third Earl was Vice-President of the Council from 1874 to 1878, and President of the Board of Trade from 1878 to 1880.*

The fifth Marquis of Winchester was the Cavalier who held Basing House for the King from 1643 to October, 1645. The sixth Marquis, a Privy Councillor, was created Duke of Bolton. The second Duke of Bolton was a Commissioner for the Union with Scotland, Lord Lieutenant of Ireland, and a Lord Justice of Great Britain. The third Duke was a Lieutenant-General and a Lord Justice of Great Britain. The fourth Duke was a Lord of the Admiralty from 1733 to 1742. The fifth Duke was Admiral of the White.*

The third Earl of Worcester was an Ambassador. The fourth Earl was an Ambassador, a Commissioner of the Treasury, and Lord Privy Seal. The fifth Earl and first Marquis was Governor and Commander-in-Chief of Raglan Castle in the Great Rebellion. The second Marquis was the famous Cavalier known in history as Glamorgan. The third Marquis of Worcester, and first Duke of Beaufort, was Lord President of the Council of Wales and the Marches and Lord Lieutenant of North and South Wales and the Marches.*

The third Lord Weymouth and first Marquis of Bath was a Secretary of State.*

The second Baron and first Earl of Northbrook has been Viceroy of India and a First Lord of the Admiralty.*

The third Irish Lord Mulgrave, and first Baron and Earl of Mulgrave in the Peerages of Great Britain and the United Kingdom, was a General, Master-General of the Ordnance, Chancellor of the Duchy of Lancaster, First Lord of the Admiralty, and Secretary of State for Foreign Affairs. The second Earl of Mulgrave and first Marquis of Normanby was Governor of Jamaica, Lord Lieutenant of Ireland, Ambassador, Secretary of State, and Lord Privy Seal. The second Marquis was Governor of Queensland, New Zealand, and Victoria.*

The second Irish Lord Clive and first Earl of Powis was Governor of Madras from 1797 to 1803.*

The fourth Baron and first Earl Poulett was a First Lord of the Treasury and a Commissioner for the Union with Scotland.*

The fourth Baron and first Earl Onslow was a Lord of the Treasury, and the present Earl has been Governor of New Zealand.*

The second Earl of Mansfield was an Ambassador for fifteen years, a Secretary of State, and Lord President of the Council. The second

---

* Doyle, " Official Baronage."

APPENDIX F.

Viscount Melville was Chief Secretary to the Lord Lieutenant of Ireland, President of the Board of Control for India, and for seventeen years First Lord of the Admiralty. The second Earl of Minto was an Ambassador, Lord Privy Seal, and First Lord of the Admiralty. The second Earl of Rosslyn was a General, Lord Privy Seal, and Lord President of the Council.*

The third Earl of Malmesbury was Lord Privy Seal and Secretary of State for Foreign Affairs. The second Earl Granville was a Secretary of State for Foreign Affairs and for the Colonies, and Lord President of the Council. The second Lord Cowley was an Ambassador. The fourth Earl of Carnarvon was Secretary of State for the Colonies and Lord Lieutenant of Ireland. The fourth Earl of Clarendon was an Ambassador Extraordinary, Secretary of State, and Lord Lieutenant of Ireland.

The second Earl of Berkeley was an Envoy Extraordinary and Minister Plenipotentiary. The third Earl was Vice-Admiral of Great Britain and for ten years a First Lord of the Admiralty.*

The second Earl of Bristol was an Ambassador and Lord Lieutenant of Ireland. The third Earl was a Lord of the Admiralty, Commander-in-Chief in the Mediterranean, and Vice-Admiral of the Blue.*

The second Earl of Salisbury, who succeeded to that peerage in 1612, took part with the Parliament, and sat in the House of Commons as member for King's Lynn in 1649, and for the county of Hertford in 1654 and 1656, the House of Lords having been "abolished" by a vote of the Lower Chamber in 1649. Under the Monarchy he had been a Privy Councillor, and under the Commonwealth he was a member of the Council of State. The seventh Earl and first Marquis was Lord Chamberlain from 1783 to 1804. The second Marquis was Lord President of the Council and Lord Privy Seal. The third Marquis is the living statesman.*

The second Baron and first Earl Gower was Lord Privy Seal and a Lord Justice of Great Britain. The second Earl Gower and first Marquis of Stafford was Lord Privy Seal and for twelve years Lord President of the Council. The second Marquis of Stafford was Ambassador at Paris.*

---

* Doyle, "Official Baronage."

INDEX.

A

Abbots and Priors, 27, 28, 37
Abolition of the House of Lords, 191, 209, 263, 369; consequences of, 213; difficulties and means of, 219-221
Agents-General, 246
Amalgamation of the Peerages, 324
American Colonies, loss of the, 130
American Senate, the, 243, 249, 254; function of, 258; effect on the British Empire of an, 259
Analogies, continental, 230
Appellate Jurisdiction Act, 31
Archdeacon of London and the House of Lords, 350
Aristocracy and oligarchy, 55; and plutocracy, 84; the Anglo-Irish, 172; Colonial, 290
Australian Senates, the, 227
Austrian Herrenhaus, the, 226

B

Bacon on honours, 111
Baron defined, 25
Baronage, the Peers a, 20, *et passim*
Baronets, 22, 291
Baronies by writ, descent of, 33; by tenure, 33; English, 36
Barons by tenure, 25; by writ of summons, 25; by patent, 25

Beaconsfield, Lord, on the first Reform Bill, 50; on the House of Lords, 65; on honours, 96
Belgian Senate, the, 225
Berwick, Duke of, 83
Bicameral system, 202
Birth and wealth, 87
Bishops in the House of Lords, 63, 186, 346. *Vide* Lords Spiritual
Bluntschli, Professor, on aristocracy, 94; on the British Peerage, 95; on German sovereignty, 127, 128
Bryce, Professor, on the Peace of Westphalia, 49; on hereditary titles, 83, 87; criticisms of, examined, 97, *seqq.*; on the Germanic Empire, 117; on the position of President, U.S.A., 118; on the United States Senate, 224, 243, 249; on the United States government, 254-260
Burke as a *family*-founder, 110

C

Carolinas and the Whigs, the, 292
Charles II. and the Dukes, 81
Christianity, expansion of British, 346; of Anglican, 348; of Non-conforming, 348; of Presbyterian, 348; of Roman Catholic, 348
Church, the, deserts the Monarchy, and the result, 51; Irish, 29, 169; Holy Roman, elective, 119;

of England, position of, 163 ; of Scotland, 164 ; expansion of, 169
Classification of the House of Lords, 45
Colonial view of the House of Lords, 195
Colonies, England and her, 115, 143, 290 ; the Liberal party and the, 146 ; concessions to the, 148 ; interests of the, 150 ; the, and Parliament, 288 ; and titles, 291, *seqq*.
Colonization, British, 194
Colonnas and Dorias, 104, 107
Commoners, 21
Commons, House of, and House of Lords, 179-183 ; as a local Assembly, 247 ; Peers in the, 340
Constitutional safeguards, 204
Continental analogies, 230
Counts Palatine, 26

D

Denmark Landsthing, the, 224
Derby, Peers created by Lord, 60, 376, 377
Descent, legitimate and not, 82
Dicey, Professor, on the Constitution, 205 ; on the United States, 250
Dilke, Sir Charles, on Parliament and the Church of England, 159 ; on abolition of the House of Lords, 192 ; and the Colonies, 199
Disabilities of Nonconformists, 159 ; of Roman Catholics, 166
Disraeli, Peers created by, 60, 377, 378. *Vide* Beaconsfield
Douglas, influence of the, 49
Doyle, James B., on the Lichfield title, 401 ; on some Peers and their ancestors, 403-408

Duke, the first, 27
Dukes and Charles II., the, 81

E

Earl and Earldom, 26 ; by tenure, 23 ; in Scotland, 34
Election and the House of Lords, 288, 332, 364
Elective Second Chambers, 222
Emancipation, Roman Catholic, 168
England and her Colonies, 115, 143, 290
Equality of men, 115
Erskine May, Sir T., on the Peerage Bill of 1719. 8 ; on the Lords Spiritual, 28 ; on Whig and Tory House of Lords, 59 ; on the Scottish Peerage, 321 ; on the attendance in the House of Lords, 327

F

Families, noble, 75 ; rise of, 77
Feudal system in Scotland, 34
Feudalism and Protestantism, 46-51
Florence and its democracy, 218
Foreign affairs, English and American, 260
Fox and the French Revolution, 138
France, the unity of, 128
Freeman, Professor, on the Peerage Bill of 1719, 8 ; on the meaning of "nobility," 20 ; on ennobling, 21 ; on the Witenagemôt, 24 ; on prelates and Earls, 26 ; on the Judges and the House of Lords, 30 ; on the Wensleydale decision, 31 ; on aristocracy, 55 ; on the rise of new men, 88 ; on the growth of the Peerage, 94 ; on the Roman Plebs, 120 ; on the optimates of Venice and

INDEX.

Rome, 126; on separation from Rome, 154; on political disfranchisement, 218; on the Peerage, 236
French Senate, the, 225, 238

G

Gentry, the, 20, 22
George I. and II. and Peerages, 83
—— III., work of, 53-56; and the Lords, 59
German Senate, the, 224, 241
Germanic Empire, the, 117
Gladstone, English Church defence, 160; Peers created by, 60, 377-379
Guernsey, the States in, 250

H

Hallam on high birth, 218
Hayward, Mr. Abraham, on the Bar, 76; on continental aristocracies, 79; on "lines of life," 86
Henry VIII. and secularisation, 8, 28, 29, 154; and the bishops, 29; and James V., 49
Hereditary legislators, 39 *seqq.*, 121, 183, *et passim.*
Home Rule, in Ireland, 131, 174-177; insular, 265
Honours, Bacon on, 111; real value of, 111
Huguenots, the, 130
Hungarian Magnates, the, 226

I

Inderwick, Q.C., Mr., on the Lords States General, 209; on one Chamber, 210
Ireland, Parliament of, 16; Peers of, before the Union, 17; at, 17; Church of, 29, 169. *Vide* Union

Italy, under the Popes, 119; Senate of, 226-232

J

James I. and Union, 5; and the Baronets, 291
—— II. and the Church, 51
—— V. and secularisation, 49
Jenks, Mr., on the Victorian Government, 227
Jersey, the States in, 250
Jews and the Lords Spiritual, 360

K

Kitchin, Dean, on the French nobles, 47
Knights, 22
Knox and the Regent, 49

L

Landed property, duties of, 122
Laws, old English and Irish, 88
Lecky on Peerages, 13
Legislators, hereditary and not, 43-46, 92, *et passim*
Life Peers, 30, 276, 278, 300, 366
Lists and enumerations of Peers, 12-16, 18, 36, 41-45, 50, 68, 70, 78, 93, 97-99, 100, 266, 321, 365, 371-408
Lords, House of: members, 3; non-identity, 3, *et passim;* its two estates, 3; not the Peers, 16, 19-21; not the nobility, 20, 21; a representative, 23; origin of, 24, *seqq.;* its changes, 36-38, 278; composition of, 39-56; in January, 1892, 41-46, 59, 113, 380; and George III., 54; and Victoria, 59; and House of Commons, 179-183; as hereditary legislators, 183, 287, *et passim;* importance of, 184; how it

oppresses, 185 ; abolition of, 191, 209, 263, 369 ; Colonial view of, 196 ; consequences thereon, 213 ; difficulties and means thereof, 219-221 ; in 1649, 209 ; and the Peerage, 216 ; and analogues, 230, *seqq.*; by election, 244, 288, 332 ; conversion of, 262 ; present position of, 266 ; and the Liberal party, 268 ; and its reform, 274, 289, 296, 339, 342, 362 ; becoming senatorial, 279-286, 295 ; and heredity, 284 ; a just grievance against, 286, 298 ; and landed property, 287

Lords Lieutenant, 123

Lords Spiritual, 3, 19, 346-361 ; summoned as Bishops, 27 ; and Henry VIII., 28 ; and the Puritans, 29 ; and the Irish Union, 29 ; present status of, 29 ; and one reform, 278 ; objections to the, 344 ; and suggestive reforms, 349-364. *Vide* Bishops

Lords Temporal, 3 ; as a nobility, 99, 104 ; and one reform, 278 ; at present, 367. *Vide* House of Lords ; Peers

Luther's revolt, 48

M

Macaulay, on the Peerage Bill of 1719, 8 ; on the reign of William III., 52 ; on Sir Edward Seymour, 77

Maine, Sir Henry, on ennobling, 21 ; on birth and wealth, 87 ; on the Brehon tracts, 88 ; on Second Chambers, 203, 204 ; on the House of Lords, 236

Manchester school, the, 144

Marquis, the first, 27

Melbourne, Viscount, Peers created by, 60, 375

Merle d'Aubigné and the Reformation, 47

Monarchies, elective, 117, *seqq.*

Monarchy, the, and the Whig party, 46, 50-56 ; the Church and, 51 ; and a single Chamber, 211 ; changes in, 277

Moray, Regent, and secularisation, 49

Mormaers, the Celtic, 35

N

Names, on family, 104

Napoleonic nobility, 101-104

Nelson and his peerage, 110, 111

Netherlands' Upper Chamber, 224

Nicolas, Sir Harris, on the Wensleydale decision, 31 ; on remainders, 32 ; on descent of Baronies, 33 ; on the Beauchamp title, 398

Nobility, the, 3, 20 ; members of, 20-23 ; basis of, 21 ; indestructibility of, 23 ; Napoleonic, 101 ; and social opinion, 107 ; in foreign states, 126 ; continental, 236

Nonconformists, disabilities of, 159; conscience of, 162 ; and the Lords Spiritual, 349-358

O

Oligarchy and aristocracy, 55

Origin of the House of Lords, 24, *seqq.*

P

Palmerston, Viscount, Peers created by, 60, 376

Parliamentary Union, two kinds of, 5 ; with Scotland, 5 ; with Ireland, 16

Pedigrees, ancient, 72

Peel, Sir Robert, Peers, created by, 60, 376

Peers, status of, 4, 32, 216, 340 ;

INDEX. 413

and poverty, 10; English and
Scotch, 7-9, 283, 320; Scotch
after the Union, 9-16, 215, 283;
Irish, 16-19, 215, 283, 322; by
peculiar tenure, 42; and the
Great Rebellion, 50; creations
since 1837, 59; as statesmen,
134; and reform, 136, 152, 177,
298; and religious disabilities,
153, 164, 177, 296; and Roman
Catholic Emancipation, 168, 177;
Colonial, 292; hereditary, 320-
343; representative, 322, *seqq*.
Vide Life Peers; Lists; United
Kingdom

Peerage, Bill of 1719, 8, 46; what
it is, 23, 92, 108; various grades
of, 27; and plutocracy, 94; expansion of the, 283; a Pan-Britannic, 332

Peerages, dormant in Scotland, 15;
descent of, 15, 32, 35; life, 30,
276, 278, 300-319, 335, 366;
amalgamation of the, 3, 324, 332

Pitt and the Peerage, 97; and the
Tory party, 140; and the Irish
Peers, 160

Plantagenet kings and France, the,
129

Policy of the pseudo-Liberals, 268

Pope, Alexander, on nobility, 74;
on "lines of life," 86

Portugal, the Camara dos Pares of,
226

Poverty and Peerage, 10

Presbyterians and the Lords
Spiritual, 358

Presidents of the United States,
118

Primogeniture, 85, 121

Prince, title of, 27

Priors, Abbots and, 27, 28, 37

Protestantism and Feudalism, 46-51

Prussia, the Herrenhaus of, 224

Puritan tyranny, the, 156

Puritanism and vulgarity, 90

R

Radical case *v*. the House of Lords,
the, 58, *seqq*. A. as a nobility, 59;
as to its constitution, 62, 63; on
the hereditary principle, 64, 114,
298; as oppressing the people, 64,
125, 133, 135, 185; as to rank and
seat, 75; as to its non-aristocracy,
80; as landlords, 298. B. as a
Second Chamber, 113, *seqq*.; on
a just grievance, 286, 298

Radical remedies: ...., 189-
221; conversion, 222-270

Rebellion and the Peers, the Great,
50

Reform of the House of Lords,
need for, 273-299; and the Tory
party, 274

Reformation, the, 47

Representation, Colonial schemes
of, 244; American system of,
256; of Colonies in Parliament,
288; of Literature, 310

Representative system, defects of
the, 180; senatorial, 326

Richelieu and the nobles, 48

Robertson on the De Ogilvies,
395; on the Earldom of Carrick,
396

Rogers, Professor Thorold, on the
Puritan movement, 47; on the
first and second Revolution, 50;
on William I. and the Church,
154

Roman Catholics, loyalty of, 167;
emancipation of, 168; and the
Lords Spiritual, 353-358

Roumania, the Senate of, 225

Royal Family Peerages, 43

Russell, Lord John, Peers created
by, 60, 376, 377

S

Safeguards, constitutional, 204

St. Albans, Lord, on nobility, 11

Salisbury, the Marquis of, Peers created by, 61, 379
Scotland, Peers of, before, at, and after the Union, 11-13; and the Reformation, 49. *Vide* Union
Second Chamber, duties of a, 178; Chambers, 222, *seqq.*
Senate, a United States, 222; the United States, 223; the, in foreign countries, 224; in British Colonies, 226-230; analogues to House of Lords, 230-237; the French, 238
Skelton on the Church patrimony in Scotland, 49
Skene, W. F., on the Celtic Earls, 35.; on the Norman in Scotland, 71; on the Arbuthnots, 78; on the Macfarlanes, Robertsons, and Sinclairs, 396
Southey on Nelson, 110, 111
Spanish Senate, the, 225, 233
"Statesman's Year-Book" on Senates, 224-226
Stubbs, Bishop, on right of Peerage, 20; on the title of Baron, 25; on the Lords Spiritual, 27; on Life Peerage, 31; on husbands of heiresses, 34; on the country Knight, 76; on Knight to Baron, 85; on the Scrope and Grosvenor suit, 389
Summaries, 23, 36, 59, 113, 183, 274, 310, 342, 362
Superfine morality, 330
Sweden, Upper Chamber of, 225
Swift and "Gulliver's Travels," 52
Switzerland, Ständerath of, 225

T

Territorial influence, decay of, 280
Titles, ancient, English, 68-70; Irish, 70; Scotch, 70; and names, 104; Irish chiefs and, 109; submerged in higher, list of, 386-388
Tory party, the old, 274
Toryism, true spirit of, 274
Tynwald of the Isle of Man, the, 250

U

Union, Parliamentary, 5
—— with Scotland, 5; a corporate, 5, 6; with federal privileges, 6; and effect on Scottish Peers, 11, *et passim;* and Scottish law, 166; and its Church, 170
—— with Ireland, 16; effect on its Peers, 17; Pitt and the, 101; and its Church Establishment, 168
United Kingdom and local Legislatures, the, 250
United Kingdom Peers, 4, 13-16, 18, 40 *seqq.*, 60, 92, 375-379
United States Senate, the, 223, 243, 248
Universities and the Lords, 312

V

Venice and its optimates, 126, 130
Veto, use of the Royal, 183
Victoria, Senate of, 226
Viscount, the first, 27

W

Warwick, fall of, 46
Wellington, Duke of, and Reform, 142, 148, 151; on Alsace-Lorraine, 150
Wensleydale case, the, 31
Westphalia, Peace of, 150
Whig Peers, the, 8, 9, 46, 292; and the Monarchy, 51-56; policy of, in eighteenth century, 132
William III. and the Whigs, 52
Witenagemôt, the, 24

LONDON:
PRINTED BY WILLIAM CLOWES AND SONS, LIMITED,
STAMFORD STREET AND CHARING CROSS.

www.ingramcontent.com/pod-product-compliance
Lightning Source LLC
Chambersburg PA
CBHW020100020526
44112CB00032B/592